After Man, Towards the Human:
Critical Essays on Sylvia Wynter

Caribbean Reasonings

Caribbean Reasonings
After Man, Towards the Human: Critical Essays on Sylvia Wynter

edited by
Anthony Bogues

Ian Randle Publishers
Kingston • Miami

First published in Jamaica, 2006 by
Ian Randle Publishers
11 Cunningham Avenue
Box 686
Kingston 6
www.ianrandlepublishers.com

Preface, copyright selection and editorial material
© 2006 Centre for Caribbean Thought, University of the West Indies, Mona

While copyright in the selection, introduction and editorial material is vested in the Centre for Caribbean Thought, University of the West Indies, Mona, copyright in individual chapters belongs to their respective authors and no chapter may be reproduced wholly or in part without the express permission in writing of both author and publisher.

National Library of Jamaica Cataloguing in Publication Data

After man, towards the human : critical essays on Sylvia Wynter / Anthony Bogues, editor

    p. ; cm. – (Caribbean Reasonings)

  Collection of some of the papers presented at the Seminar 'After Man – the thought of Sylvia Wynter'. – Includes index

ISBN 976-637-224-1 (pbk)

1. Caribbean literature — Women authors – History and criticism
2. Women in literature — History and criticism 3. Caribbean literature — 20th century – History and criticism 4. Caribbean Area – Intellectual life
5. Critical Theory

I. Bogues, Anthony II. Series

809.89278 dc 21

Cover photo by Francine B. Price
Cover and Book design by Allison Brown
Printed in the United States of America

Series Editors
**Anthony Bogues
Rupert Lewis
Brian Meeks**

For Sylvia Wynter's students in the
Caribbean and the United States

Table of Contents

Preface xiii

1. Modernity and the 'Work of History' 1
   Demetrius L. Eudell

2. Perceiving Reality in a New Way:
   Rethinking the Black/White Duality of Our Time 25
   Joyce E. King

3. Otherness and the Impossible in the Wake of
   Wynter's Notion of the 'After Man' 57
   Clevis Headley

4. The 'S' Word:
   Sex, Empire and Black Radical Tradition 76
   Greg Thomas

5. After Man, Womens: The Third Sex or Ain't i a Eunuch...... 100
   Patricia D. Fox

6. Reading Said and Wynter on Liberation 131
   Aaron K. Kamugisha

7. Sylvia Wynter's Hedgehogs: The Challenge
   for Intellectuals to Create New
   'Forms of Life' in Pursuit of Freedom 157
   Neil Roberts

8. Notes on the Current Status of Liminal Categories and
   the Search for a New Humanism 190
   Nelson Maldonado-Torres

9. *Biocentrism*, Neo-Ptolemaicism, and
E. O. Wilson's *Consilience*:
A Contemporary Example of 'Saving the Phenomenon'
of *Man*, in the Name of the Human 209
Jason L.R. Ambroise

10. Is the Human a Teleological Suspension of Man?
Phenomenological Exploration of Sylvia Wynter's Fanonian
and Biodicean Reflections 237
Lewis R. Gordon

11. Wynter and the Transcendental Spaces of Carribbean
Thought 258
Paget Henry

12. Legitimizing Africa in Jamaica 290
Nicosia Shakes

13. The Human, Knowledge and the Word:
Reflecting on Sylvia Wynter 315
Anthony Bogues

Contributors 339
Index 342

Preface

This edited volume is a collection of some of the papers presented at the seminar, 'After Man, Towards The Human: The Thought of Sylvia Wynter', held in June 2002 and hosted by the Africana Studies Department, Brown University and the Centre for Caribbean Thought, University of the West Indies, Mona. The seminar marked the continuing collaboration between these two institutions and opened up a series of activities, which are fast becoming a central part of Caribbean intellectual life. It also brought together a wide cross section of scholars, graduate students and the Jamaican public for the first time to engage in a series of exchanges about Wynter's rich oeuvre.

This edited volume is the first in the book series *Caribbean Reasonings* and it is our hope that we will be able to produce a series of edited volumes, which will serve as critical guides to the Caribbean intellectual tradition and resources both for students and the general reader. Each volume will be edited by one of the series editors, Brian Meeks, Rupert Lewis or Anthony Bogues. It is perhaps fitting that we should begin the series with essays on the thought of Sylvia Wynter.

Sylvia Wynter, Professor Emerita of Spanish, Portuguese, African and Afro-American Studies, Stanford University, is one of the Caribbean's most distinguished intellectuals. From her major essay published in *Jamaica Journal* in 1968, 'We Must Learn to Sit Down Together and Talk About a Little Culture: Reflections On West Indian Writing and Criticism' to her most recently published essay, 'Africa, The West and the Analogy of Culture: The Cinematic Text After Man', Wynter has staked out a ground for herself as one of the region's premier cultural and social theorists. Professor Wynter's work is characterized by a sophisticated theoretical acumen which is not only distinctively Caribbean in the ways it deals with the practice of writing and cultural criticism as forms of social practice, but by the very questions with which she grapples. From exciting and rigorous interventions on the nature of Caribbean culture, creative writing, 'folk culture' and its profound meaning for the symbolic universe of Caribbean reality, to her present genealogical critique of Western humanism, Wynter's work locates her not just as a major Caribbean figure, but as a world class intellectual. Her work will, in future decades, be a rich source of investigation of some of the compelling questions that currently face humanity.

Sylvia Wynter's work can be divided roughly into three periods, which although distinct, are interconnected and inform each other, establishing a unique discursive practice. The first period involves the major essays published between 1968–72. These essays include 'Novel and History: Plot and Plantation', the seminal and polemical 'Jonkonnu in Jamaica', 'Creole Criticism: A Critique' and 'One Love: Rhetoric or Reality –Aspects of Afro-Jamaicanism'. During the 1970s Kamau Brathwaite called Wynter's work an 'indigenist critical practice'. In a profound sense, Wynter's work forms part of that group of Caribbean intellectuals, including, notably, Roger Mais, George Lamming, Rex Nettleford and Kamau Brathwaite, who wrestled mightily to decipher the past and fashion a future in a language which was distinctively Caribbean. This group of intellectuals and writers laid the foundations for conceptualizations about the region that were *internal* while elaborating on an inventory of the region's experience in its own language and categories. Like many other thinkers during this period, Wynter also functioned as a public intellectual, writing the framing document for Jamaica's National Heroes and working with the *Jamaica Journal*. During this phase her major novel, *Hills of Hebron,* was published, she wrote plays for the Jamaican stage and was a contributing writer to the seminal *New World Quarterly.*

The second period of her work is centred in the USA in the field of Black Studies. Here, Wynter brought her considerable talents to bear on the question of race and modernity in the West. She also brought to this venture two distinctive things: the first was her Caribbean experience and the second was her training in Spanish Literature. This period was also marked by her essay on Caribbean women writers, 'Beyond Miranda Meanings: Un/silencing the "Demonic Ground" of Caliban's Woman', and a pioneering essay in *Jamaica Journal,* entitled 'New Seville and the Conversion Experience of Bartholomé de Las Casas'. This essay along with two other essays 'A Different Kind of Creature: Caribbean Literature, the Cyclops factor and the Second Poetics of the Propter Nos' and the path breaking '1492: A New World View' were significant because they made clear that Wynter was now exploring a new ground — that of Western humanism and the nature of *man*. In this project, she expanded the ground previously cleared in the 1950s and early 1960s by two extraordinary world figures who emerged from the Caribbean intellectual tradition – Aimé Césaire and Frantz Fanon.

In her present and third stage, in which she remains highly productive, Wynter is now confronting the entire intellectual architecture of the West, arguing in a genealogical fashion about the nature of the concept of *man*. Her work in this period is extraordinarily rich, drawing from the latest developments in French philosophy, the new biology, theories about the philosophy of science, concepts of symbolic order and the Cambridge school of political thought amongst others. What is unique, one might argue, perhaps reflective of her genius, is her method of putting all of this together: it can be described as one of bricolage, profoundly shaped by her central question, in the tradition of Césaire and Fanon: 'What is the human'?

Such an intellectual figure is one that will in the end provoke and hopefully help us to rethink many of our conventional notions. Wynter's work troubles settled waters. But that has been one of the major features of the radical Caribbean intellectual tradition.

The essays presented here stand on their own and we would not recommend any particular order to the reader nor will we present the usual summaries. We will only point to the interdisciplinary nature of the volume as it seeks to cover the range of Wynter's thought. It is left to the reader to make his/her own way, to interpret the essays from whatever standpoint.

And now some acknowledgements are necessary. Paget Henry worked hard on the conceptualization of the seminar and the work on Sylvia Wynter in his book *Caliban's Reason* was the first to bring Wynter's work to a larger audience. The editors wish to acknowledge this. Ms Sheila Grant and Ms Adlyn Smith worked both efficiently and effectively on the seminar. The then Dean of the Faculty of Social Sciences, Professor Barry Chevannes, the Principal of the Mona Campus, Professor Kenneth Hall and the then Vice Chancellor, Professor Rex Nettleford gave tremendous support for which we thank them. So too did Professor Lewis Gordon who was then Chair of Africana Studies at Brown University. In terms of editorial work, this volume would not have been possible without the editorial assistance of Matthew Serrin and Christopher Shortsleeve as well as the organizing skills of Ms Sheila Grant. A grant from the former Dean of the Faculty at Brown University, Mary Fennell, made it possible for Matthew Serrin and Christopher Shortsleeve to work on this project.

Finally we would like to thank Ian Randle and Christine Randle, who agreed to the series and saw its importance. We would also like to thank La-Raine Carpenter for solid and effective editorial work and to Geri Augusto for careful proofreading.

In the end I take all responsibility for errors.

Anthony Bogues
Providence, Rhode Island and Kingston, Jamaica.

1 | Modernity and the 'Work of History'

Demetrius L. Eudell

This obliteration of man from his own origins and his replacement by supernatural beings which are duplicate selves, and behind which real man disappears, **is the work of myths** *which explain the origin of cultural possessions: the origin of fire, hunting weapons, cultivated plants, domesticated animals, and so forth.... Humans invented nothing. They were given everything. Now it is up to them to preserve what they received.*[1]
—Maurice Godelier

There are two great intellectual forces in the modern world, science and history, and while they often seem mutually antagonistic they are in fact fundamentally complementary. Modern science determines the causal laws that govern the motions of matter but, in contradistinction to ancient science, eschews teleology and thus any determination of human ends. While it may thus present humanity with supreme knowledge of the mechanism of nature and open up the possibility for the technological conquest of the natural world and indeed of human nature itself, it does not and in principle cannot tell us what we ought to do or how we ought to live. It is this question that history answers. **History of course is not modernity's only answer to this question.**[2]
—Michael Gillespie

The nationalist leaders know that international opinion is formed solely by the Western press. Now, when a journalist from the West asks questions, it is seldom in order to help us. In the Algerian war, for example, even the most liberal of the French reporters never ceased to use ambiguous terms in describing our struggle. When we reproached them for this, they replied **in all good faith** *that they were being objective. For the native, objectivity is always directed against him.*[3]
—Frantz Fanon

MODERNITY AND THE 'WORK OF HISTORY'

'In the beginning was the Word'. Taken from Genesis in the Bible, Sylvia Wynter has argued that this statement is more scientific than our present system of knowledge, as it recognizes the central importance of the Word, that is, of narrative, of discourse, in instituting, stabilizing, and the reproduction of human cultural systems. If Wynter's assertion can be verified, then the epistemological implications would be significant; in that, it raises not only issues of what we know, but how we know, what we in fact do, or think that we do, know.

Such a question has been interrogated in the discipline of history for some time. Using somewhat new terminology, some recent intellectual trends have called into question 'the ground of history' on the basis of methodology, interpretive framework, and political orientation. As Linda Gordon has noted, although phrased differently, these are not new questions: 'My quarrel with deconstructionist advocates is about the claims for the novelty of what they are doing, not about the value of questioning our access to "reality"'.[4] Some time ago, in a now classic text, E.H. Carr posed the question: What is history? He responded that it was 'a continuous process of interaction between the historian and his facts, an unending dialogue between the present and the past'. Although sounding somewhat archaic, Carr's discussion of the question remains insightful even though it varies from popular discourses and the perspectives of contemporary academics (be it Nietzschean, liberal, or postmodern).

As an example, Carr insisted on the selective and interpretive nature of the facts utilized in making historical representations, noting that while reconstituting 'the past in the historian's mind is dependent of empirical evidence ... it is not in itself an empirical process'. However, we are left to wonder what kind of process it is, as he does not give us an explicit answer to this question. One could surmise, after the writings of Frantz Fanon and Sylvia Wynter, that it is a cognitive process related to the instituting of human consciousness. In the end, Carr's answer to the question 'what is history?' reaffirmed the unexamined assumptions on which the modern disciplinary conception of history is based. In the terms of Maurice Godelier, he obliterated the historian from his/her own origins.[5]

Before Carr, the intellectual history scholar Carl Becker alluded to this relation, one in which although historians employ empirical evidence, it is only within an interpretive frame. In an often referenced essay, 'Everyman His Own Historian', Becker contended that historians were only the most recent example in a long line of storytellers, whose role was to maintain a formulation of a general order of existence for their respective societies: 'We are thus of that ancient and honourable company of wise men of the tribe, of bards and storytellers and minstrels, of soothsayers and priests, to whom in successive ages has been entrusted the keeping of the useful myths'. Becker stated that he was using the term myth, not in a strictly pejorative sense, but rather as a 'once valid version but now discarded version of the human story, as our now valid versions will in due course be relegated to the category of discarded myths'. This phenomenon existed, according to Becker, because history is 'a convenient blend of truth and fancy' that does not depend on facts speaking for themselves, for 'left to themselves, the facts do not speak; left to themselves they do not exist, not really, since for all practical purposes there is no fact until some one affirms it'.

Although Becker assumed an unending progression of the creation of myths for history as well as later in the essay naturalized the origins of the writing of history ('we do not impose our version of the human story on Mr. Everyman; in the end it is rather Mr. Everyman who imposes his version on us'), he nonetheless pointed in the direction of understanding history as being the intellectual production of historians as much as it was anything else.[6]

The insights and tensions of Becker and Carr remain at the centre of the issues presently confronted by the field of historical studies, as they broach questions of its intellectual foundations. Hayden White has argued that to write a history of a discipline or of a science, 'one must be prepared to ask questions *about* it of a sort that do not have to be asked in the *practice* of it'. Such was the enormous task set forth by Peter Novick in his most impressive *That Noble Dream: The 'Objectivity Question' and the American Historical Profession.* As one reviewer pointed out, Novick 'has written a history of the theoretical discourse of a community of non-theorists'. Indeed, 'the disciplinary rule against self-reflection' has caused most historians 'to avoid questions about the meaning of their own work'.[7] Yet, what Novick has accomplished is to ask a question about the nature of writing history as he is writing history. Central to such an investigation, Novick averred, has been the question of objectivity, which has constituted the founding creed of the discipline of history.

According to Novick, adhering to the methodology and perspective of the discipline, the historian must be neutral and disinterested, never degenerating into advocacy. In fact, '[o]bjectivity is held to be at grave risk when history is written for utilitarian purposes' as the historian should adopt a balanced and evenhanded position. The assumption here is that historical facts are a priori to and independent of interpretation. Therefore, 'truth is one, not perspectival. Whatever patterns exist in history are "found," not made'. The basis for this has been archival, that is, written documents. The historian makes a commitment to 'the reality of the past, and to truth as correspondence to that reality'. In this respect, history is distinguished from fiction as it was believed that, unlike the writing of literature, a separation existed between the knower and the known, between fact and value.[8]

Novick's text demonstrates the trajectory that the idea of objectivity has travelled. Its establishment corresponded with the founding of the historical profession in the United States in the 1880s. Central to the professionalization of the writing of history was a specifically American interpretation of German historical scholarship; in particular the work of Leopold von Ranke, whose famous statement on writing history, *wie es eigentlich gewesen,* would be reductively translated as 'as it actually was'. According to Novick, such an understanding naturalized Ranke's idealist epistemology, transforming it into an empiricist one. In order to write history 'as it really was', historical investigation had to be carried out according to the 'scientific method', which was based on the analogy of the physical sciences. In this context, he argued, there was another occurrence of the vulgarization of the views of an important thinker — the ideas of Francis Bacon.

Science was represented as being 'rigidly factual and empirical, shunning hypothesis', and being 'scrupulously neutral on larger questions of end and meaning'. If this methodology was systematically pursued, scholars would be able to write a 'scientific history', the definitive account of the human past.[9]

Novick illustrated that the idea of historical objectivity did not go unchallenged. During, the period between the two World Wars, a small heterodox cadre within the profession, including Charles Beard and Carl Becker, countered the hegemony of the discourse of objectivity with the idea of objectivists identified as historical relativism. According to Crane Brinton, while Ranke's formulation of history 'as it really happened' could in some ways be useful, historians could disabuse themselves of its metaphysical overtones. Rather than facts waiting to be discovered, Brinton insisted that:

> We can now admit that the past in this sense is forever lost to us; that the historian must relate his facts to a pattern, a conceptual scheme of which he can require only that it prove useful; that like the physicist's conceptual scheme for the electron, it proves a convenient way of accounting for known facts and for leading to the discovery of hitherto unknown facts. The historian can get rid of the *incubus of absolutism* implied in "as it really happened" and accept all the advantages of a frankly relativist position. (emphasis added)

Related to the new approach of 'historical relativism' was the then emergent position of the pragmatist school of thought. Like the relativist sensibility, pragmatism launched 'a crusade against the worship of facts' remaining unwilling 'to accept a hard-and-fast fact-value distinction' as well as emphasizing 'change and flux' and 'the human and social elements in knowledge'.[10]

Although not representative of a majority viewpoint, these ideas lodged a sufficiently substantial critique that after the Second World War, some of the insights would be incorporated into mainstream historiography. The implication remained that 'a certain amount of ... relativism could be tolerated without abandoning a larger commitment to objectivity'.[11] Yet, it would be with the social and political movements of the sixites that this paradigm of objectivity received its most blistering critique. During the era of social upheaval, it was not only within the professional university context that the idea of objectivity was under siege. Vietnam, urban riots, and student protests had led many to question the objectivity of the government as well as the media for obscuring the 'truth', one that maintained the status quo. This questioning directly led to the formation of new fields of inquiry in academia such as Black Studies and Women's Studies as well as to the increase in the profession of the group presence of Blacks, White women, and other previously marginalized sectors of United States society.

These new groups reasserted concerns over the nature of an objective practice in the writing of history, insisting that many of their social realities and histories were systematically excluded, and often when included, represented in largely negative terms. This critique helped to solidify then emergent theoretical discourses that attempted to grapple with the necessarily discursive nature of the writing of history. Hayden White has become identified with this 'important shift in the theory and philosophy of history', referred to as the 'linguistic turn'.

According to White, historical narratives are verbal fictions whose contents are invented as much as they are found; hence, the use of the idea of history being a 'fiction-making operation'. The explanatory power of histories lies in 'their success in making stories out of *mere* chronicles'. In this context, the historian employs the 'types of configurations of events that can be recognized as stories by the audience for which he/she is writing'. The historian shares with the audience 'general notions of the forms that significant human situation must take'. In other words, history becomes more than a set of events (facts) that are ordered chronologically, but also something that requires description and characterization that provides an explanation of why the events occurred, what White terms narrativity. Here, one could invoke Becker's statement that facts do not become facts until they have been affirmed. Historians do not discover the past, White argued, but rather construct the past, doing so with narrative strategies not unlike those found in the writing of literature. It is the same manner of making sense, he insists, as both history and fiction endow 'what initially appears problematic or mysterious with the aspect of a recognizable because familiar form'. Therefore, within this context, the distinction between history and fiction collapses, for in the end the former conforms to the generic plot structures associated with the latter: romance, tragedy, comedy, satire, or epic. History, White maintains, is the translation of fact into fiction.[12]

Nancy Partner has provided additional insight along the lines of this analysis. Responding to the age-old question of what is history, she describes it as 'meaning imposed on time by means of language: history imposes syntax on time'. Although an historian uses techniques 'that differ only a little from those of a novelist', there is a notable difference: 'histories are relentlessly overplotted ... even outrageously so for one claiming a higher degree of verisimilitude than fiction'. From choosing where to begin and where to end a story, everything included in a work of modern history must be relevant to its major themes 'since intelligible coherence was the principle selection which determined what would be presented in the book'. Partner remained firmly convinced that 'no amount of pontificating about facts and evidence, research, archives, or scientific methods can get around the central fictionality of history'.[13]

History and Narrative

Redefining history as narrative discourse has significant implications, one of which is an increasing understanding of its structuring role. 'Far from being a neutral medium for the representation of historical events and processes', White proposed, narrative discourse

> is the very stuff of a mythical view of reality, a conceptual or pseudoconceptual "content" which, when used to represent real events, endows them with an illusory coherence and charges them with the kinds of meanings more characteristic of oneiric than of waking thought.

Within this understanding, narrative becomes 'a particularly effective system of discursive meaning production by which individuals can be taught to live a distinctly "imaginary relation to their real conditions of existence",' that is to say, an unreal but meaningful relation to the social formations in which they are indentured to live out their lives and realize their destinies as social subjects. Such a dynamic led White to argue (though a bit mechanically) that for this reason, dominant social groups have a particular interest 'in controlling what will pass for the authoritative myths of a given cultural formation but also in assuring the belief that social reality itself can be both lived and realistically comprehended as a story'. If belief in the adequacy of 'stories to the representation of the reality whose meaning they purport to reveal' ever diminishes, then 'the entire cultural edifice of a society enters into crisis, because not only is a specific system of beliefs undermined but the very condition of possibility of socially significant belief is eroded'.[14]

It is understandable that as a result of such critiques, the idea of objectivity has been under siege. Some historians, however, insist that few believe in such a naïve formulation that they are writing histories that correspond directly to the actual reality of the past. Thomas Haskell, agreeing with Novick, has argued that the idea of objectivity is currently 'viewed with considerable skepticism' and does not sway contemporary historians 'as powerfully as it did the founding generation of the 1880s'. This is especially the case, according to Haskell, with scholars who have been influenced by the recent developments in literary criticism. Partner goes even further: 'All historians know that history is no longer the discipline busily fulfilling its positivistic promise to tell it all as it really happened'.[15]

Nonetheless, while most historians may agree that the facts do not speak for themselves, their attempts to address the implications of the idea and ideals of objectivity have still been able to conserve its ontological basis, or in the words of Owen Barfield, to 'save the appearances'.[16] Robert Berkhofer has suggested that, despite significant intellectual changes, the conceptual foundation of history remains the same:

> Although denaturalization [of race, class, and gender], demystification [of the Other], and dehierarchization [of elite versus popular cultures] have broadened who and what are to be included as part of history and the self-consciousness of the social production of history, they have hardly transformed the basic assumptions about how history is to be written.[17]

A most telling case in point occurred with the publication of *Telling the Truth About History*, a text which attempted to engage many of the new questions posed in the wake of the linguistic turn and of postmodernism, only to draw them back into the unquestioned disciplinary pieties of the established paradigm of the field.[18]

In fact, some historians have proposed that there is really no need to give up the ideal of objectivity, admitting that the full story can never be recounted. As a result, the old formulation of 'passionless, indifference, and neutrality' should be replaced with a relatively more self-conscious understanding of objectivity. Here again, one could invoke Carr, who stated that 'the facts of history cannot be purely objective, since they become facts of history only in virtue of the significance attached to them by the historian'. As a consequence, he insisted that 'objectivity in history ... cannot be objectivity of fact, but of relation, of the relation between fact and interpretation, between past, present, and future'. Who or what conception determines this relation seem to be questions that remain outside the purview of Carr's analysis, although not outside of that of some contemporary historians. Haskell has suggested that maintaining respect for the virtues of self-overcoming, detachment, honesty, and fairness constitutes a sufficient basis for a redefinition of objectivity.[19]

In the judgment of James T. Kloppenberg, Novick opposed a vague notion of relativism as the alternative to the idea of objectivity, and by doing so refused 'to examine in detail the more sophisticated versions of historicism'. According to Kloppenberg, within the objectivity-relative polarity, there exists a more fruitful intermediate position in pragmatic hermeneutics:

> Hypotheses — such as historical interpretations — can be checked against all the available evidence and subjected to the most rigorous critical tests the community of historians can devise. If they are verified provisionally, they stand. If they are disproved, new interpretations must be advanced and subjected to similar testing.

Admitting that this approach may not be perfect, Kloppenberg insisted that it reduces random interpretations, yielding tentative, but not worthless, results.[20]

Allan Megill strongly disagrees with the 'community of the competent' argument: 'But this will not do. There is a disciplinary blindness that prevails within the modernist academy, and not only among historians'.[21] Another way of phrasing the situation may be in epistemological and political terms: What constitutes Kloppenberg's community of historians? And what constitutes evidence? On the latter question, Partner has insightfully described the underlying assumptions embedded in such a notion. Regarding evidence as a sign-system at the heart of the semiotic structure of history, she has asserted that the category of evidence 'is a metaphor based on visual perception'. Taken from the Latinate, meaning in plain sight, that which is represented as evidence is 'evident, present and visible, simply by virtue of its existence, but it is not thereby "evidence".' It is only through its metaphorical transformation into the present pieces of a whole past, the partial *visibilia* of an entire visible world, that it becomes 'evidence'. In other words, 'all historical evidence is a major trope, a figure of speech and thought which organizes and extends the visible present world to induce the invisible past into intelligible form'.[22]

Despite disagreements within the professional writing of history, many have come to terms with some understanding of what could be termed relativism. For instance, much of the new intellectual history remains aware of the relation between experience and meaning, and increasingly has been recognizing how the former is mediated by the latter (as well as how the latter can orient the former). Central to this relation is the role of language, which is understood not only as shaping experience, but also, as constituting it.[23] The result is that the field of history, intellectual or otherwise, becomes 'as much the object of analytic attention as it is a method of analysis'.[24] This understanding has generated several responses, one of which comes in the form of the post-structuralism and deconstruction's insistence upon the undecidability and indeterminancy within texts and contexts, 'unveiling the proliferation of meanings without end in the repetitive, constantly displaced struggle to impose univocal meaning or cultural closure'. Some argue that the philosopher Richard Rorty has adopted an extreme relativist position by suggesting 'the impossibility of reconstructing knowledge and value on historicist foundations'.[25]

However, all of these assertions continue to privilege the question of the meaning of history. Perhaps one could reformulate Carr's question and rather than asking what history is, inquire as to 'what is the function of history?'[26] To respond to this question, it is important to rely upon history, that is, to historicize the discipline, as for example Novick does so excellently with respect to the question of objectivity and the concomitant professionalization of the field in the United States. It may also be useful in this context to culturalize the idea of objectivity. In other words, to illustrate how the discourse of objectivity is one that remains specific to the epistemological field of Western culture. Dorothy Ross has pointed out that modern conception of history was a recent (in historical terms) development:

> It was not until the early nineteenth century that this understanding of history as a continuous procession of qualitative changes came fully into view and that many European thinkers began to interpret the

whole of reality, including what had earlier been conceived as absolute and unchanging, in contextual historical terms.

The aftermath of the French Revolution 'is generally regarded as instrumental in moving European thinkers toward historicism'. The idea would come to the United States about a century later.[27]

In *Hegel, Heidegger, and the Ground of History*, Michael Gillespie has developed this thesis by adumbrating concepts of the past that differ from the modern concept of history in which the discourse of objectivity became central. History, for the Greeks, was related to poetry and philosophy, and aimed at revealing the eternal in the present. This concept was one that was generated from the ground of the Greek conception of being human. For the Greeks, their gods embodied immortality and perfection, existing in a realm beyond change and death, unlike human life, which existed in a transient realm governed by chance. The function of history in such a context was to put human affairs into words in order to provide the ground for realizing human immortality. Thus, in addition to facilitating the revelation of the eternal in the actual, the function of history aimed to preserve the polis, where noble actions could be best performed to sacralize human immortality.[28]

Christianity and History

The Christian concept of history rose as that of the ancient Greek and Roman world gradually dissipated. Christian history synthesized theology with the accounts of classical antiquity, adapting aspects from the former, such as the notion witness, while at the same time reformulating the idea. Gillespie has noted that whereas the Greek conception of history rested upon seeing or contemplation, that is, 'the immediate experience and apprehension of the eternal', for the Christian understanding, it is 'no longer the knowledge of what is seen but the knowledge of God through the witness of the Apostles'. Therefore, it would be 'the witness to the hidden truth or meaning of events as a whole, which comes to light and hence visibility in and through the Word, i.e. in and through Christ' that would become the measure of all things. Once it was no longer the 'experience of the eternal in the actual but the revelation of the eternal in Scripture' that became the standard, then the human viewpoint was utterly subordinated to that which had a direct line of communication with God, thereby legitimating the feudal hierarchy of the clergy over the laity. It would take the Renaissance's *studia humanitatis* to revalorize the socio-human level of existence on the basis, as J.G.A. Pocock has shown, of the transfer of the redemptive process from the church to the state, enabled by the reinvention of the discourse of civic humanism and republicanism, an intellectual revolution that itself became an important move toward the later rise of historicism.[29]

The concept of history that emerged with modernity broke with the Greek and Christian concepts in some significant ways, although in other ways, as Gillespie intimates, it completed the Christian project (such as man as the agent of the absolute or eternal in the actual). Our contemporary understanding of history, he pointed out, revolves around 'two different but related meanings: it is on one hand the totality of events, the *res gestae*, that constitute the unfolding of human civilization, and on the other the account or report of these events, the *historia rerum gestarum*'. Since the Enlightenment, history has been represented as being isomorphic with human actuality, 'which historians merely describe or reconstruct'. It is only on the basis of such an understanding of the human past, one enabled by intellectuals like Hegel, who argued that the development of consciousness he elaborated was identical with the concrete history of the human, that the idea of objectivity could become the foundation of the writing of history. Logically, within the terms of this perspective, other modes of history became deficient; for instance, the Greek approach of revealing the eternal in human affairs did not yield a historical science, it lacked a scientific methodology as well as functioned under the grip of myth. This assessment of Greek history can only be true, in Wynter's terms, within our genre-specific understanding of our social reality, which must necessarily overlook the central point that it was not so much that 'the Greeks were unable to develop a historical science', but rather they were not interested in developing one, as they organized history about completely different purposes than recounting the human past in 'objective' terms. 'Objectivity' was not called for within the logic of the genre-specific understanding of the social reality of Greek society.

This new concept of history remained inseparable from the intellectual mutation at the end of the eighteenth century described by Michel Foucault in *The Order of Things*. Foucault argued that the intellectual categories that underlay the Classical *episteme* would be swept aside by a new order of knowledge, one that would later serve as the foundation of our contemporary disciplinary organization of knowledge in the university system. As a result, the social reality was no longer understood through the taxonomic system of knowledge produced by the fields of natural history, analysis of wealth, and analysis of grammar; but rather, a 'modern manner of knowing empiricities' emerged whereby the 'quasi-transcendentals of life, labour, and language', which were embodied by the new disciplines of biology, political economy, and philology became dominant. Central to this new conceptual framework and organization of reality would be the representation of the human as a purely natural organism, one in relation of direct continuity with organic forms of life, which Foucault termed *man*.[30] It would be precisely on the basis of this new concept of what it means to be human — that is, to be a biological organism that labours and speaks — that coupled with natural scientific breakthroughs would lead to the global hegemony of Western culture. Therefore, the reconceptualization of the discourse of history that occurred at this time provided a narrative of legitimation for this cultural model. History, therefore became in Wynter's terms, the Word of *man*.

This new history, while using terms such as scientific and objective to describe itself, nonetheless served the same function as the earlier formulations of 'history' had in the context of the cultural worlds of the Greeks and the Christians: that is, to reproduce its respective social order. In this sense then, one can argue that history is always objective, as it is, to borrow a fine phrase of Foucault, the order's 'condition of possibility'. Just as Greek history produced Greek subjects, and Christian history produced Christian subjects, so has the history of the ethno-class concept of *man* produced a specific mode of the subject. In other words, as cited by Gillespie at the beginning (and implied by Becker), history is the modern response to the age-old question of how we ought to live. In other ancient societies and civilizations, this was in part the 'work of myth'. Such in our 'modern' context becomes the 'work of history'.

In this respect, the challenge of Black historians such as W.E.B. Du Bois and Carter G. Woodson against the representations of Black history in the United States have wider epistemological implications. Writing during the same period as Novick's 'relativists' Carl Becker and Charles Beard (indeed Du Bois remained critical of the latter's 'mechanistic interpretation'), *Black Reconstruction in America* sought to counter the dominant representation of the era of Reconstruction. In response to the Dunning school of historiography, which argued that Blacks were responsible for the corrupt governments and failures of Reconstruction, Du Bois concluded that 'the best of American universities' were teaching 'lies agreed upon' and then calling it science and truth: 'This is education in the Nineteen Hundred and Thirty-fifth year of the Christ: this is modern and exact social science; this is the university course in "History 12" set down by the Senatus academicus'. One reason, according to Du Bois, accounted for this understanding: 'One fact and one alone explains the attitude of most recent writers toward Reconstruction; they cannot conceive Negroes as men'.[31] The Dunning school of historiography, and the discipline of history in general, therefore served to produce a specific concept of being human – *man*.

This point was also forcefully made by Carter G. Woodson in his now classic, *The Miseducation of the Negro*. Woodson insisted that a correlation existed between the representations of Blacks in the dominant history and their subordinate roles in the society. Whilst the White children were induced to believe that their ancestors had done everything in the past, the representations of Blacks induced Black children to think that their ancestors had done nothing in the past. Woodson clearly understood that without deciphering the narrative strategies and function of the representation in history, the social and political situation of Blacks would not change. Woodson notes:

> No systematic effort toward change has been possible for taught the same history, philosophy, and economics which have established the present code of morals. The Negro's mind has been brought under control of his oppressor. The problem of holding the Negro down is therefore easily solved. When you control a man's thinking, you do not have to worry about his actions. You do not have to tell him to go to the back door. He will go without being told. In fact, if there is not back door, he will cut one for his special benefit. His education makes it necessary.

In other words, if a specific history produced *man*, then this same history produced its ontological lack — the figure of the Black. The function of a counter history then would be, in the terms of Lévi-Strauss, to 'dissolve Man', that is, the de-production of this concept of being human.[32] Such has been the project of not only a 'Black' history, but of all the other 'counter' histories which aimed to challenge the necessarily specific (race, class, gender, sexuality, religion, culture) location of the mainstream writing of history.

Recent Debates

This systemic function of history can be easily seen in a more recent debate, that surrounding the publication of Martin Bernal's *Black Athena: The Afroasiatic Roots of Classical Civilization*. Using archaeological, linguistic, and literary sources, Bernal has challenged the representation of the origins of Ancient Greece as being purely Eurocentric, what he termed the Aryan model that emerged at the end of the eighteenth century. This model, he argued, displaced its predecessor, the Ancient model, in which the cultural debts of Egypt and Phoenicia (resulting from colonization around 1500 BCE) were readily acknowledged by the Greeks, although these societies were not unequivocally revered. In this context, West Semitic and Near Eastern influences on Greek society should also be emphasized. According to Bernal, the displacement of the Ancient Model occurred as a result of the conjunction of the discourses of progress, romanticism, and racism. It is interesting to note how this shift occurred at roughly the same time as Foucault's epistemic shift: 'In general the 18th century was a period of Classicism and one with desire for order and stability, and so Rome was usually preferred to Greece'. Other empires such as Egypt and China would also be devalorized before this shift occurred from the state to the nation, from the aristocracy to the bourgeoisie, as well as from the discourse of monarchy to that of democracy. This new belief in the immaculate concept of Greece would be enshrined in the discipline of Classics, 'in which contemplation of all aspects of Greek and Roman life was supposed to have a beneficial educational and moral effect on the boys who were to be the rulers of Britain and the Empire'.[33]

The criticism generated from the publication of *Black Athena* can be usefully employed to examine questions related to the production of history, an issue of which Bernal has certainly remained cognizant in all his texts. Bernal admitted that he was surprised to discover that a small number of experts were sympathetic to his project, and that even a larger portion, while disagreeing with many of his ideas, nevertheless felt the issues were significant and should be debated. However, a small, but vocal sector, which includes both academia and the mainstream media, has represented his work as being purely a polemic, often using the term Afrocentric as an epithet to discredit his findings. Jacques Berlinerblau estimated that 'negative scholarly reviews of *Black Athena* have outweighed positive or moderate ones by a margin of approximately seven to three'. Mary Lefkowitz's *Not Out of Africa: How Afrocentrism Became an Excuse to Teach Myth as History* has been emblematic of the less than judicious criticism lodged against Bernal. From the title alone, one could easily surmise that the author insists on making a distinction between myth and history. According to Lefkowitz, the unhistorical Afrocentric notions of antiquity (in which Bernal's work is included) 'seem plausible to many intelligent people' because there exists 'a current tendency, at least among academics, to regard history as a form of fiction that can and should be written differently by each nation or ethnic group'. *Not Out of Africa* seems to be premised on the very rudimentary notion of history that defined the practice in the nineteenth century terms of objectivity and science.[34]

But, as it has been argued, can such a sharp line of demarcation between myth and history be drawn? In his incisive essay, 'The History That Literature Makes', Richard Waswo has suggested:

> We see what we look for; our stories tell us what to look for; we find it (whether it's there or not) and then we can act out the stories .... As the languages we speak determine how we know the world, so the stories those languages tell determine how we act in it.

In a collection edited by Lefkowitz and Guy Rogers, some of the contributors remain aware of the necessarily narrative nature of history. Edith Hall phrased it best with three questions that conclude her essay. 'Who on earth did the Greeks *think* they were? Why did they think it? And what is it about the late twentieth century which renders the issue so important to *us*?' This is related to an excellent question posed by Guy Rogers. Rogers, agreeing with others who describe Bernal's project as Eurocentric (ironic coming from classicists), noted that the cultures under study were only relevant to the extent that they help to lay the foundation for Western civilization. For Rogers this undermines Bernal's political objectives, and thus readers should be asking themselves the question: 'Will a four-volume enterprise dedicated to showing how two cultures of the ancient Near East influenced early Greek civilization make Europe less or more culturally arrogant?'[35]

At this point, it may be worth stressing the issue of the function of history. If it is not simply to recover the past, then what purpose does it serve? Is it a moral issue? Does studying the past make one a better person, the way in which according to Bernal, it was thought in the late nineteenth century that studying the Classics did? Why does it matter to us? It could be argued that it matters to us because the 'work of history' is, in the words of Gillespie, to tell us how we ought to live. Thus, more than mere academic questions seem to be at issue.[36] If these issues raised by Bernal were really so unimportant, then why so much scholarly exertion to argue against them? One reason can be related to the centrality of Greek 'civilization' to the modern Western self-conception.

Waswo has gone to lengths to demonstrate that 'from Virgil to Vietnam' the founding myth of Western civilization, one that supplies its cultural identity, has been the legend of descent from Troy. Geoffrey of Monmmouth's twelfth-century *History of the Kings of Britain* made Brut/Brutus, the founder of Brittany and Britain, the most famous of the lineal descendents of Trojan princes. England was joined by a chorus of cities such as Alsace, Toulouse, Mainz, and Venice as well as countries like France, Italy, North Germany, Holland, and Belgium which traced their heritage to Troy. This story 'was popularly regarded as actual history from the earliest Roman historians in the third century B.C. until the eighteenth century of our era', when it would be challenged by historicist claims. Known in the Middle Ages as the *translatio imperii et studii* or the transmission of empire and learning, the story presented civilization as coming from elsewhere, traveling from east to west, a representation that led the philosopher Bishop George Berkeley to maintain that America embodied the apex of the *translatio studii*, which always followed the *imperii*. Gradually, as the myth was discredited, the identification shifted 'from characters in the legend to identification with its authors, the ancient Romans, now seen as the actual source of western civilization'. However, given that this founding belief has such a structuring role, it did not die easily, and preserved its importance by enacting the story in other forms of discourse. While the legend 'had long been poetry', in the seventeenth and eighteenth centuries, the narrative structure, its images and arguments, would be absorbed within historiography, philosophy, law, social theory, and science.[37]

The central motif of an exile searching for a permanent though predestined home structures the fictional plot of Virgil's *Aeneid*. In fleeing the destroyed city of Troy, the escapees founded an empire and brought 'civilization' to the indigenous peoples. While doing so, the issue of not only who possesses 'civilization' and 'culture' emerges, but in fact, the very definition of such terms are put in place. Being represented as coming from outside, the term civilization (*civitas, civilitas* — citizenship, courtesy) that is, belonging to a city, became a defining one: 'Cities are literally what qualified us as civilized, and they required a particular organization of food'. Therefore, related to this notion, was the idea of culture, derived from agriculture, 'to cultivate', which therefore linked culture in all its forms to the working of the soil. This representation necessarily devalorized other ecosystemic worldviews as Waswo notes:

> This definition is created by and for a settled agricultural community that sows, harvests, and builds cities; it qualifies as "savage" (Lati. *silvestris*— "of the woods") all other relations that human beings may have with the earth, such as hunting, gathering, and nomadic pastoralism.

Moreover, the implication here remains such that, when William H. McNeill defined civilization (in *The Rise of the West*) as 'the production of a large agricultural surplus of cereal grains, which permits the congregation of people in cities and their division into specialized occupations', it can be seen that the basis of the Scottish Enlightenment's notion of progress (to which the ideas of objectivity and science are not unrelated) is but a transumptive retelling of the journey Aeneas.[38]

The further implication would also be that Bernal's interjection of the possible Afroasian influence at the origin of Greek society cannot simply be changed as a result of the discovery of new evidence, given that this belief has served a foundational, order-instituting role in

Western culture (and throughout its multiple transformations). Along with the story of Genesis, it is the bedrock of our present narrative of origin by means of which we have come to know ourselves as the specific model of being human that we are, that is, as *man*. Though the terms may be uniquely Western, the process is not. Basing herself on Fanon, Wynter has argued that one only becomes human within the terms of a specific cultural model, and therefore as humans we must come to know our social reality in adaptive terms, terms that enable the realization of the culture-specific model of being human and the reproduction of the social order. If humans are *bios* and *logos* — genes and Words — what Fanon defined as hybridly phylogenic and ontogenic on the one hand, and sociogenic on the other, then culturally-instituted narratives serve such an integrating function to regulate those behaviours in humans which are not genetically pre-programmed. In other words, the 'work of history' becomes the production and reproduction of our present mode of sociogeny, or in the terms of Wynter's amplification of Fanon, sociogenic code.[39]

Conclusion

The question of objectivity can now be seen as one being posed in the terms of a specific culture or mode of sociogeny. One of the recurring criticisms of the *Black Athena* project has been that it has encouraged an Afrocentric interpretation of the past. Afrocentric scholars, just as earlier Black scholars such as Du Bois and Woodson, had incisively perceived the relation between representations in history and the ordering of society. As a result, some may have fabricated an ancient Egypt in order to replace what Bernal has identified as the fabrication of ancient Greece. But, there is a question that remains, that of the 'why' of the fabrications in the first place. And this is a question that the paradigm of objectivity, as presently conceptualized, cannot answer. Yet, given the current situation of the world — and the competing conceptions of the nature of our present global reality — it is one that needs a response.

To do so, it becomes imperative to understand the relativity of modes of being human, including our own present hegemonic, Western one. Essentially, we only know the history of the world (and therefore of the human) in the terms of a Western perspective, which is history through modes of production, beginning with the hunter-gathers and then culminating in the figure of *homo œconomicus*, or *man*. This narrative of origin sees earlier modes of food production and social organization such as hunter-gatherer, nomadic, semi-nomadic, pastoral, feudal-peasant as representing the lack of our present industrial (or post-industrial) technological mode; thus, not as alternative ways that humans have come to know their culture-systemic reality. As Waswo noted, 'there is no regress, for the simple reason that there has been no progress'. Or as Hans Blumenberg has pointed out, the classic formula that the course of things proceeded 'from mythos to logos' is a 'dangerous misconstruction' that 'does not permit one to recognize in myth itself one of the modes of accomplishment of logos'. The assumption was that,

> somewhere in the distant past the irreversible "spring forward" [*Fort*sprung] took place that determined that something had been put far behind us and that from then on only "steps forward" [*Fort*schritte "progresses"] had to be executed.

Blumenberg interrogated this supposition:

> But was the spring really between the "myth" that had said that the earth rests on the ocean or rises out of it and the "logos" that had translated this into the so much paler universal formula that everything comes out of water and accordingly is composed of it?

When comparing these two formulations, it can be argued that 'it was a question of the same interest, only of fundamentally different means by which to pursue it'. According to Blumenberg, the function of myth has been to confront what he identified as the 'absolutism of reality', where humans 'came close to not having control of the conditions of existence' and in fact, believe that we lack control of them. This phenomenon emerged as a result of a lack of a clearly defined biological niche for the species, an interpretation that correlates with current theories of human origins in which humans adopted an upright, bipedal posture as a result of discovering that while going from the shelter of forests to the openness of the savanna, biological instincts were unable to deal with this new reality. It was in this context that humans created 'culture' — our culture's term for what Wynter has identified as 'auto-instituting technologies' by means of which each order ensures its institution and stable replication as a form of life.[40]

Moreover, once created, each mode of being human (that is, culture) assumes that its understanding of the world is the only, if not the optimal, mode. However, such an understanding of the relativity of being should not be confused with the epistemological resignation implied in a position of cultural relativism that assumes the impossibility of knowing other modes. The reason here is quite simply that there have been unconscionable costs that resulted from a lack of a self-correcting paradigm. In other words, the idea of objectivity cannot simply be abandoned, for it could, as Habermas has noted, have horrifying consequences:

> It was possible for fascism to give birth to the freak of a national physics and Stalinism to that of a Soviet Marxists genetics (which deserves to be taken more seriously than the former) only because the illusion of objectivism was lacking. It would have been able to provide immunity against the more dangerous bewitchments of misguided reflection.[41]

At the same time, as the citation at the beginning from Fanon intimates, the elaboration of a paradigm of objectivity in the humanities and social sciences has not been able to free the subordinated groups from their intellectual and political domination.

Whereas today there is almost a consensus on the relation between the Dunning school of historiography and the socio-political situation of Blacks in the United States during the era of Reconstruction, no such understanding exists today between the situation of the world, with respect to issues such as poverty and the global maldistribution of wealth and resources, and our present system of knowledge. As Mark Poster has argued, 'very little discussion is taking place, both within the academy and outside it, about the methods and topics of historical analysis in relation to a changing world' with work that 'resonates less and less with general social and cultural concerns'. Yet, if Patrick Geary's assertion that 'we historians are necessarily to blame for the creation of enduring myths about peoples, myths that are both tenacious and dangerous' can be acknowledged, then the implication would be that such a relation, though usually unstated, does exist. Count Gobineau, described by Michael Biddis as 'the father of racist ideology', promoted an understanding of race as the defining element in his formulation of the evolution (especially the decline) of civilizations throughout history. As well, D.W. Griffith insisted that it was history, specifically Woodrow Wilson's *A History of the American People* that authenticated his film 'Birth of a Nation'.[42]

It would seem necessary that historical inquiry, and knowledge in general, turn their attention to their systematic elaboration of the effects of such a relation, what Habermas has defined as 'knowledge and human interests'. In the context of history, it would mean, as Lévi-Strauss argued, that history is 'never history, but history-for'. In other words, as F.R. Ankersmit has described the situation, that given the overproduction of works in all fields of history, the time may very well have come 'that we should *think* about the past rather than *investigate* it'. This means that, for historians, emphasizing 'meaning is more important than reconstruction and genesis'. Once history has been redefined and redirected toward specifically defined purposes, then debates over objectivity and relativity, truth and falsity, can no longer have their present centrality, as they are understood to be functioning in the terms of a culture-specific paradigm, one that has social effects. This would also mean that the study of the past would have to be related, in the vein of Fanon and Wynter, to the study of consciousness. As David Chalmers argues, laws fundamental to understanding conscious experience 'centrally involve the concept of information'. History could no longer be simply the transmission of information (though to be fair, it is certainly more self-reflective in the contemporary context). It would nonetheless have to mean that the investigation of the 'work of history' would become as important as has, for our present biocentric disciplinary paradigm, that of the history of work.[43]

Notes

1. Maurice Godelier, *The Enigma of the Gift*, trans. Nora Scott (Chicago: University of Chicago Press, 1999), 179. Emphasis added.
2. Michael Allen Gillespie, *Hegel, Heidegger and the Ground of History* (Chicago: University of Chicago Press, 1984), ix.
3. Frantz Fanon, *The Wretched of the Earth* (New York: Grove Press, 1967), 60-61.
4. Linda Gordon, 'Comments on *That Noble Dream*', *American Historical Review* 96 (June 1991): 685. Hereafter abbreviated as *AHR*.
5. E.H. Carr, *What is History?* (New York: Alfred A. Knopf, 1964), 24, 35.

6. Carl Becker, 'Everyman His Own Historian', *AHR* 37 (January 1932): 221-236.
7. Hayden White, 'The Historical Text as Literary Artifact', in *History and Theory: Contemporary Readings*, eds. Brian Fay, Philip Pomper, and Richard T. Vann (Oxford: Blackwell Publishers, 1998), 7; David A Hollinger, 'Postmodernist Theory and *Wissenschaftliche* Practice', *AHR* 96 (June 1991): 688; and Mark Poster, *Cultural History and Postmodernity: Disciplinary Readings and Challenges* (New York: Columbia University Press, 1997), 48-49.
8. Peter Novick, *That Noble Dream: The 'Objectivity Question' and the American Historical Profession* (Cambridge: Cambridge University Press, 1988), 1-2.
9. Ibid., 21-40. Novick noted that 'in the nineteenth century, the term *eigentlich* had an ambiguity it no longer has: it also meant "essentially" ... reflecting a widespread romantic desire to open oneself to the flow of intuitive perception'.
10. Ibid., 134-154. Emphasis added.
11. Ibid., 415.
12. White, 'The Historical Text as Literary Artifact', 15-33.
13. Nancy F. Partner, 'Making Up Lost Time: Writing on the Writing of History', *Speculum* 6 (January 1986): 90-117.
14. Hayden White, *The Content of Form: Narrative Discourse and Historical Representation* (Baltimore: Johns Hopkins University Press, 1987), ix-x.
15. Partner, 'Making Up Lost Time', 117.
16. See Owen Barfield, *Saving the Appearances: A Study in Idolatry* (Middletown, CT: Wesleyan University Press, 1988), 47-49.
17. Robert F. Berkhofer, Jr., *Beyond the Great Story: History as Text and Discourse.* (Cambridge, MA: Belknap Press of Harvard University Press, 1995), 8.
18. Joyce Appleby, Lynn Hunt, and Margaret Jacob, *Telling the Truth About History* (New York: Norton, 1994).
19. Thomas Haskell, '"Objectivity is Not Neutrality": Rhetoric versus Practice in Peter Novick's *That Noble Dream* in *History and Theory: Contemporary Readings*, 306; Carr, *What is History?*, 159.
20. James T. Kloppenberg, 'Objectivity and Historicism: A Century of American Historical Writing', *AHR* 94 (October 1989): 1018.
21. Allan Megill, 'Fragmentation and the Future of Historiography', *AHR* 96 (June 1991): 695.
22. Partner, 'Making Up Lost Time', 105.
23. John E. Toews, 'Intellectual History after the Linguistic Turn: The Autonomy of Meaning and the Irreducibility of Experience', *AHR* 92 (October 1987): 882.
24. Joan Wallach Scott, *Gender and the Politics of History* (New York: Columbia University Press, 1999), 3.
25. Toews, 'Intellectual History after the Linguistic Turn', 902, 905.
26. This approach is generously borrowed from Sylvia Wynter's where she has posed the question that instead of asking what aesthetics mean, we may begin to ask what aesthetics do? See 'Rethinking "Aesthetics": Notes Toward a Deciphering Practice' in *Ex-Iles: Essays on Caribbean Cinema*, Ed. Mbye Cham (Trenton, NJ: Africa World Press, 1992), 237-279.
27. Dorothy Ross, *The Origins of American Social Science* (New York: Cambridge University Press, 1991), 4; and Dorothy Ross, 'Historical Consciousness in Nineteenth Century America', *AHR* 89 (October 1984), 911.
28. Gillespie, *Hegel, Heidegger and the Ground of History*, xii, 3-6.
29. Ibid., 7; J.G.A. Pocock, *The Machiavellian Moment: Florentine Political Thought and the Atlantic Republican Tradition* (Princeton: Princeton University Press, 1975); J.G.A. Pocock, 'Languages and Their Implications' in *Politics, Language and Time: Essays on Political Thought and History* (Chicago: University of Chicago

Press, 1989), 3-41; Ross, 'Historical Consciousness in Nineteenth Century America', 911.
30. Michel Foucualt, *The Order of Things: An Archaeology of the Human Sciences* (New York: Vintage, 1973). See especially chapter 8 entitled 'Life, Labor, and Language'.
31. See the final chapter 'The Propaganda of History' in W.E.B. Du Bois, *Black Reconstruction in America 1860-1880* (New York: Atheneum, 1983), 711-729.
32. Claude Lévi-Strauss, 'History and Dialectic' in *The Savage Mind* (Chicago: University of Chicago Press, 1966), 245-269.
33. Martin Bernal, *Black Athena: The Afroasiatic Roots of Classical Civilization, Volume 1: The Fabrication of Ancient Greece 1785-1985* (New Brunswick, NJ: Rutgers University Press, 1987), 22-38, 317; and Martin Bernal, *Black Athena Writes Back: Martin Bernal Responds to His Critics*, ed. David Chioni Moore (Durham, NC: Duke University Press, 2001), 2-11.
34. Bernal, *Black Athena Writes Back*, 11; Jacques Berlinerblau, *Heresy in the University: The Black Athena Controversy and the Responsibilities of American Intellectuals* (New Brunswick, NJ: Rutgers University Press, 1999) 6; and Mary Lefkowitz, *Not Out of Africa: How Afrocentrism Became an Excuse to Teach Myth as History* (New York: Basic Books, 1996), xiii-xiv.
35. Richard Waswo, 'The History That Literature Makes', *New Literary History* 19 (Spring 1988): 541-560; Edith Hall, 'When is a Myth Not a Myth? Bernal's "Ancient Model"' in *Black Athena Revisited*, eds. Mary R. Lefkowitz and Guy MacLean Rogers (Chapel Hill: University of North Carolina Press, 1996), 347; and Guy Maclean Rogers, 'Multiculturalism and the Foundations of Western Civilization' in *Black Athena Revisited*, 443.
36. Berlinerblau argued that central to Bernal's position was the political responsibility of intellectuals.
37. Waswo, "The History That Literature Makes", 544; and Richard Waswo, *The Founding Legend of Western Civlization: From Virgil to Vietnam* (Hanover, NH: Wesleyan University Press/University Press of New England, 1997), xi-xii, 1-6, 194.
38. Waswo, 'The History That Literature Makes', 546-48; and Waswo, *The Founding Legend of Western Civlization*, 186-195.
39. See Sylvia Wynter, 'Towards the Sociogenic Principle: Fanon, Identity, the Puzzle of Consicous Experience, and What It Is Like to Be "Black"', in *National Identities and Sociopolitical Changes in Latin America*, eds. Mercedes F. Durán-Cogan and Antonio Gómez Moriana (New York: Routledge, 2001), 30-66.
40. Hans Blumenberg, *Work on Myth*, trans. Robert M. Wallace (Cambridge, MA: The MIT Press, 1985), 3-33.
41. Jürgen Habermas, *Knowledge and Human Interests*, trans. Jeremy J. Shapiro (Boston: Beacon Press, 1968), 315.
42. Poster, *Cultural History and Modernity*, 38; Patrick J. Geary, *The Myth of Nations: The Medieval Origins of Europe* (Princeton: Princeton University Press, 2002), 157; Michael D. Biddis, *Father of Racist Ideology: The Social and Political Thought of Count Gobineau* (New York: Weybright and Talley, 1970); Lee D. Baker, *From Savage to Negro: Anthropology and the Construction of Race, 1896-1954* (Berkeley: University of California Press, 1998), 132.
43. Lévi-Strauss, 'History and Dialectic', 245-269; F. R. Ankersmit, 'Historiography and Postmodernism', *History and Theory* 28 (May 1989): 137, 152. Emphasis in original. David Chalmers cited in Wynter, 'Towards the Sociogenic Principle', 31.

2 | *Perceiving Reality in a New Way: Rethinking the Black/White Duality of Our Time* [1]

Joyce E. King

Racialization is an ideological process, an historically specific one. Racial ideology is constructed from pre-existing conceptual (or, if one prefers, 'discursive') elements and emerges from the struggles of competing political projects and ideas seeking to articulate similar elements differently. **An account of racialization processes that avoids the pitfalls of US ethnic history remains to be written.**[2]

—Michael Omi and Howard Winant

[T]he phenomenon of "Race," unlike the related issues of "gender" and "class," has remained hitherto untheorized.[3]

— Hypothesis 10

[T]o conflate blackness into "multiculturalism" alongside miscellaneous other forms of identity is to obfuscate an understanding taught to us through long, bitter experience. In America, race matters, but blackness matters in more detailed ways.[4]

—David Lionel Smith

Come on, children, and think.[5]

—James Brown, The Godfather of Soul

Introduction: Epistemological Panics and the Normative Espisteme

It is commonly understood that education is not neutral, that knowledge is a social construction of reality, and that both 'reality' and 'knowledge' pertain to specific cultural contexts. Nevertheless, knowledge (and knowledge production) as well as education that is centred within the cultural and social reality of a specific group, say,

African-Americans, are regarded as inherently vested in narrow group self-interest and is, therefore, an undemocratic, even divisive way of knowing.

This accusation was frequently levied against Black scholars, for example, during the heyday of the epistemological panics — or cultural wars — that raged in the academy and the media around curriculum knowledge in the 1990s. This term is a corollary to the notion of 'moral panic', originated by Cohen and Hall, Critcher, Jefferson, Clarke, and Roberts, who use it in the British context. Elsewhere I have written that moral panic refers to 'the emergence of a perceived threat to the values and interests of a society in its mass media'.[6] 'Epistemological panic' is used here to suggest a corollary perceived threat to certain values and interests in the academic disciplines and in curriculum knowledge-in-use in schools and school textbooks.[7]

Diane Ravitch has argued that separatism is the inevitable result of 'particularistic' multiculturalism (for example, Afrocentrism), which she claims involves nothing more than 'ethnic cheerleading' or encouraging students to 'identify with dead civilizations on foreign continents'. What Ravitch characterizes as 'particularistic' knowledge, from her ideological perspective, is not education at all but 'filiopietism', that is, the 'excessive (and ergo, "disuniting") veneration of one's ancestors'.[8] Maxine Greene, on the other hand, concedes that as a result of 'our metanarrative' and the effects of persistent racism, African-American youth, for example, may have 'difficulty' feeling proud of their heritage. That is, certain groups may need specific knowledge that is invested in restoring a 'personal history' in order to recuperate a hidden heritage of heretofore excluded 'contributions'. The truth, however, is actually much more complex.[9]

As other observers of the way society's metanarrative functions mythologically in the service of a false American identity have recognized, the 'hidden heritage' argument paradoxically obfuscates the long history of white appropriation of African-American culture. Ralph Ellison has observed, for instance, that 'most Americans are "culturally part Negro"' whether they realize it or not.[10] This chapter poses fundamental questions about just what constitutes 'our' metanarrative, that Ravitch seemed to embrace (and defend) for the sake of societal cohesion, and that Greene seemed more willing to expand, for the same apparent reason. If indeed the metanarrative needs to be more 'inclusive', what is wrong with the knowledge that it embodies? Is this story merely incomplete or is it a social construction of reality that is cognitively, conceptually, and morally flawed? What are the implications of the conceptual (or discursive elements) of this metanarrative? What is really at stake in debates about multicultural education and curriculum change? For example, is there any relationship between the way Ravitch characterizes the African-centred challenge to mainstream curriculum knowledge and the 'high stakes' testing regime that has all but made this challenge irrelevant?[11] More specifically, this chapter asks: What are the implications of this metanarrative for teacher education, for Black liberation, and ultimately, for human freedom?

In order to demonstrate the necessity and the possibility of perceiving reality in a new way these questions are posed from a Black Studies alterity perspective. As the corpus of Sylvia Wynter's work demonstrates, this way of knowing is *altercentric* with respect to the metanarrative of our times, that is to say, the discourse of *race*.[12] Grounded in the sociocultural and historical experience of the liminality of African-descent people, the Black Studies theoretical perspective, as critique, is not merely *another way* of seeing,[13] that is, an alternative way of 'constructing' reality, but entails deciphering our contemporary social reality. This perspective of alterity is not due to an inherent biological/racial/cultural difference but is the result of a 'historically specific process':[14] the dialectic of socially constructed *otherness* that prescribes the liminal status of African-descent people (and indigenous American Indian) as beyond the boundary of the normative (Eurocentric) concept of *self/other*. Most importantly, this alterity perspective is centred in the historic encounter of the Red, Black, and White people during the founding of the 'Americas' and the colonial domination of Africa. As will be shown, it transcends a vindicationist perspective that seeks to relativize or rectify the chauvinism of Eurocentric knowledge claims and delusions of superiority.[15]

The chapter will contrast the Black Studies theoretical perspective of alterity with: (a) recent debates about multicultural education, Afrocentricity, and curriculum change and (b) the way teacher education students I have taught over the years have (mis)perceived aspects of the US social reality, including the process of racial formation. Wynter's theoretical analysis/practice of alterity, which is grounded in the Black Studies intellectual tradition, demonstrates how a deciphering practice — which is consistent with the critical intentions of African-centred curriculum approaches — can illuminate categories of *dominating* and *liberating* modes of thought in educational discourse and practice.

Ann Weider compares capitalist, democratic, and liberationist 'Afrocentrisms'. Molefi Asante, the leading Afrocentric theorist, has argued that 'Afrocentricity' is not a black *version* of 'Eurocentricity'.[16] However, if an Afrocentric paradigm is represented as one more centrism (likewise for feminism, for that matter) among various 'multicultural' *alternatives* to Eurocentrism, its concept of reality is likely to remain *within* the Eurocentric paradigm's binary structure of value-opposition (that is, 'our' metanarrative). Conversely, a perspective of alterity actually seeks not only to decipher this metanarrative or concept of reality but to *transmute* it. I have discussed elsewhere the limitations of this alternative, which I describe as 'Expanding Knowledge'.[17] There exists a more profound alternative of critique and possibility, which I have called 'Deciphering Knowledge', within the Black Studies intellectual tradition that transcends this contradiction. Wynter articulates this alterity perspective in terms similar to Nietzsche's concept of the 'transvaluation of value' and finds support for it in the work of Eritrean anthropologist, Asmarom Legesse. According to Wynter, Legesse 'notes that the liminal groups of *any* order are the ones most able to "free us"' from the 'ordering' normative 'categories and prescriptions' of our epistemic orders.[18] W.E.B. Du Bois, Frantz Fanon, Ida Wells Barnett, and Cheikh Anta Diop represent other examples of this intellectual tradition at the same time that Afrocentric scholars may appeal to their work for culture-centric authority but without transcending the normative episteme.

The Wynterian Black Studies Alterity Perspective

> Whites continue to wonder . . . whether "blacks are capable of real intellectual achievement" . . . at the heart of the matter is a belief once freely voiced, but no longer openly aired, that African genes do not provide a capacity for complicated tasks.[19]

Following Sylvia Wynter, I will argue that because a Black Studies alterity perspective seeks not just to refute but to *explain* the social role of the Black/White duality that is enacted and normatively proscribed within the culture-systemic ideology of race, this deciphering practice offers a new way of perceiving reality that transcends the personal knowledge or 'personal history' of individuals or a specific group. This alterity perspective shares with Marxism the expectation that a goal of knowledge is not just to describe reality but to change it. Instead of positing the primacy of the dialectical relation between labour and capital and the mode of economic production, Wynter's Black Studies alterity perspective analyses the cultural mode of production of the human subject, of consciousness itself. Its terms are the 'governing narratively' instituted discourse or prescriptive rules or 'codes' that Wynter has identified — codes that regulate human behaviour, including the systems of economic and social relations that constitute labour as a category or that of gender. It also shares with the Marxist theoretic the notion that certain 'forms of life' (including material existence) enable, influence, distort, or foreclose certain forms of thought, consciousness, and cognitive autonomy.

Wynter explains the idealized 'West' of the Eurocentric imagination in terms of a cultural model framework. She analyses this metanarrative or episteme as part of the Judeo-Christian cultural model that was 'based on a binary opposition between the *Fallen Flesh* and *Redeemed Spirit*',[20] that is, between the laity and the clergy of Europe's feudal period. The hegemonic scholastic order of knowledge that prevailed normatively defined the laity outside the bounds of redemptive value. Within our present cultural model, Wynter suggests, blackness is to whiteness as the feudal laity was to the clergy. Like the laity (men and women excluded from 'grace' by virtue of their enslavement to Original Sin), 'we are not saved', by ameliorative reforms aimed at including 'us' in this new world order.[21] This is because 'the specific value terms of the opposition' (between 'blackness' and 'whiteness') must also be transformed. This is what had to happen when the fifteenth and sixteenth- century 'lay humanists' broke with their hegemonic order of knowledge. To find freedom the lay humanists had to transform the premises of their episteme that 'narratively instituted' their status in the social order. In so doing, they brought in a new *secularized* order of knowledge that made the natural sciences and humanities possible.

This is the knowledge that is embodied in our academic disciplines today and which bolsters the metanarrative of our times.

However, this revolution of humanism, which permitted *man* to be perceived in biological not theological terms, also made it possible to perceive humans as *naturally* inferior or superior according to their putative genetic traits. As Cose observes in *The Rage of a Privileged Class*, and as Andrew Hacker also emphasizes in his review of this publication, the persistence and significance of this belief cannot be ignored. Hacker writes:

> The ascription of *inbred* incapacity is the ultimate expression of racism, the one hardest to eradicate, not least because most people will deny they hold this view. It is a shackle that Americans of African origin have had to bear since they were first brought here as slaves. Could there have been something, whites wondered that rendered the black race suitable for bondage? This suspicion has by no means disappeared, even among those who wish they could rid themselves of it.[22]

Wynter draws an analogy between the role that a Black Studies alterity perspective must play in abolishing such beliefs and the overthrow of the metanarrative of the feudal scholastic order by the laity. Instead of *ontogeny*, as Wynter explains, there is sociogeny. Instead of *man* perceived 'as a natural organism', that is, as genetically (biologically) inferior or superior, human freedom requires a new perception/concept of the human as an 'always already' socialized subject. Otherwise blackness will remain as the *conceptual other*, or alter ego, to the category of whiteness.

Nihilated Identity: The Untheorized Black/White Duality of Our Times

> *Everybody talking 'bout heaven ain't goin' there.*
> Traditional African-American Spiritual

'Heaven', in the folk thought, proverbial wisdom, and sacred music of our enslaved ancestors, 'represented an expanded universe and vision of equitableness that was also a moral and spiritual critique of the existing order'.[23] That is, 'our ancestors confronted the slave system that denied their humanity' with the autochthonous knowledge and spiritual authority that what the master was 'talking 'bout' did not represent reality (truthfully or accurately) but instead represented the interests of the social category to which the master belonged.[24] In the last decades of the twentieth-century debates within the academy among literary theorists and educators, as well as in the public media — about multiculturalism and representations of race and identity in education, school texts, and the literary 'canon'— have provided an opening to clarify and distinguish among various theoretical perspectives and positions in Black Studies. This includes Afrocentric scholarship, Afro-American literary theory and criticism, and other new/postcolonial, postmodern studies. These debates were engaged from a variety of ethnic, Black/feminist, and multicultural perspectives.

In contrast to the theoretical position of some liberal, (Black and White) postmodernist, feminist, multicultural, and progressive theorists/educators, I want to suggest that a Black Studies alterity perspective that centralizes race does not inherently reify the mode of thought that it intends to critique. Thus, I take a position that differs from scholars like Henry Louis Gates who disparage what he calls 'the paranoid dream of cultural autarky',[25] represented more recently in the 'postblack' confusion. My position finds support in Legesse's concept of 'liminality' that Wynter uses to articulate the perspective advantage of alterity that a 'nihilated (*neantisé*) identity' and the status of 'Abject Otherness' can afford African-descent people.[26] Wynter's analysis of nihilated identity stands in interesting contrast with Cornel West's interpretation of and emphasis on the 'nihilism' of the Black community. West emphasizes the 'nihilistic threat' posed by 'battered identities rampant in black America'. According to West: 'the major enemy of black survival in America has not been and is neither oppression nor exploitation but the nihilistic threat — that is, loss of hope and absence of meaning'.[27]

The perspective presented here is not only that 'race matters' but more importantly that blackness matters.[28] Yet, as will be demonstrated, this perspective does not inevitably 'essentialize' race/difference as a matter of reductive, fixed biological 'essence'. Neither does it focus on 'narrow notions' of racial identity simply in order to (re)tell a counterdiscourse of celebratory African origin-stories, extol compensatory African-American contribution-stories, or relate explanatory how-we-got-'ovah'-our-oppression-poverty-and-exclusion stories. Rather the emphasis is on a critique of knowledge in order to make rethinking reality and rewriting knowledge possible, and this includes rethinking the historically constructed Black/White duality of our time. Prager describes this duality this way:

> It is not the mere fact that blacks hold a dual identity in this country which has constrained achievement, to one degree or another, every ethnic group and racial group has faced a similar challenge. The black experience in America is distinguished by the fact that the qualities attributed to blackness are in opposition to the qualities rewarded in society. The specific features of blackness as cultural imagery are almost by definition those which the dominant society has attempted to deny in itself, and it is this difference between blackness and whiteness that defines, in many respects, American cultural self-understanding. For blacks, then, the effort to reconcile into one personality images which are diametrically opposed poses an extraordinarily difficult challenge.[29]

To analyse the ideological premises of this value-opposition between 'blackness' as the *conceptual other* to normative 'whiteness' is not to exclude difference that is pertinent to other groups but seeks to describe the classifying logic in which 'non-blacks' who are 'non-whites' are constructed as 'in-between categories' within this cultural model, for example, as 'honorary whites'. (Interestingly, some blacks can also be perceived as 'white-blacks', that is, as 'different', as not 'really' black).[30] Thus, this duality is a fundamental feature of our socioexistential reality. Its significance and mode of functioning are misconstrued however in contemporary debates about culture, identity, race, multiculturalism, curriculum transformation, and social change. Unfortunately, neo-conservative, neo-liberal, and progressive scholars/educators evade the culture-systemic premises of the metanarrative of race upon which the social framework and our present order of knowledge are founded. One reason is because the ideological interests with respect to these premises in various theoretical approaches remain unexplicated, unexamined, and, therefore, untheorized.[31]

New Frontiers of Being and Knowing: From Ontogeny to Sociogeny

It is this imperative shift from ontogeny to sociogeny, from *l'etre* to *l'étant*, and the new frontiers of being and knowing that such a shift opens, that is to be, I believe, the gift of the New World to the Old, the gift of that Other America.[32]

According to Omi and Winant 'race' or the 'black/white color line' (that Du Bois so aptly identified) is a 'pre-eminently *socio-historical* concept' that has been 'rigidly defined and enforced'.[33] Further, 'racialization', their term for the 'extension of racial meaning to a previously unclassified relationship, social practice or group', is an 'ideological process' that is 'historically specific'.[34] The following selected examples are presented to illuminate aspects of the ideological hegemony that need to be theorized if we are really to know our times profoundly, not just in terms of the way that we (mis)construe social reality, given its representation in our textbooks and scholarly disciplines and our personal experiences in situations like the encounters described below:

(1) Rushing to catch a plane, I found a seat on a crowded San Francisco airport parking lot bus, and as I sat down and caught my breath, I looked straight ahead at the illustration on the t-shirt a young white guy standing just in front of me was wearing. In jagged black letters the word '*SUBHUMANZ*' was spread above a drawing depicting a procession of bedraggled, half-naked, bushy-haired, primitive-looking Black people who were bent over, carrying and dragging huge stones single-file up the crumbling steps of some kind of temple. There were pyramids in the distant background. The pillars were cracked and leaning over: the place was either falling down or being built up; I couldn't tell which.

(2) In my graduate school educational psychology seminar in 1969, an eminent Stanford professor, and author of one of the standard textbooks in the course, explained that Black children are not successful in school because 'they have no culture. . . . They don't appreciate Bach and Beethoven'. The professor supported his point by presenting research

that 'shows that their mothers don't communicate with them effectively'. The Black T.A. avoided my gaze. I asked the professor: 'Do you know who James Brown is?'

(3) In 1983 after attending the funeral of a Tongan student in California, a veteran Black teacher described the elaborate rituals she participated in and observed. Her conclusion: 'Their [Tongan] culture is really strong. Too bad we [Black people] have lost all ours'. I wondered if this teacher's graduate study included the educational psychology professor's textbook that I had encountered in the 1960s.

(4) To orient a new student teacher to her classroom a White teacher in an 'exemplary' suburban school described the Black children in her class this way: 'Now, there are two groups of Black children here: The "white-Blacks," who will benefit from your teaching, because they have white values and the "black-Blacks," who will not. They are less capable intellectually and will be behavior problems, because they have black values'.[35]

(5) At a Sociology of Education conference in 1987, a prominent educational researcher was asked if his findings regarding the success 'minority' students achieve through cooperative learning strategies also applied to 'model minority' Asians. He explained that his research focus was on Black students. But he added quickly with a hearty laugh: 'Maybe we should give all the Black kids Japanese mothers!' The raucous laughter that erupted nearly drowned out another researcher's equally mirthful rejoinder: 'No, no! Let's give 'em Jewish mothers!'[36]

If these examples reflect the knowledge our metanarrative incarnates, does such knowledge distort the perception and cognition of teachers and researchers and shape empirical research? Does the multicultural 'joke' above have deeper, cultural roots that signify concepts of being human (for example, socialized) that are beyond the awareness of the jokesters? Are the prevailing explanations of the variability of academic success for students of different social/cultural backgrounds adequate? When I told a colleague about the latter incident, she snapped: 'Well, they better make sure they give those Black kids Black grandmothers if they want them to survive *this* system'.³⁷ The culture-systemic framework reflected in these incidents is global, as the following examples illustrate:

(6) On the Berkeley, California public radio station (KPFA) Carmen de Monte Flores, a Puerto Rican psychologist speaking on a panel about racism said: 'In Puerto Rico there is a phrase which is often used: "Y tu abuela? Donde esta?" The English translation is: "Where's your grandmother?". . . . In a well-known Afro-Puerto Rican poem that I heard as a child growing up, this refrain is repeated over and over again . . . that phrase [means] that you were hiding your grandmother because she was black. The phrase was a challenge to come out. It was a challenge to deal with the shame of racism. My great-grandmother was black. Nobody ever talked about her. My great-grandfather and father were Spanish. . . . It was only necessary to say that we were Spanish to make us feel better than others or at least whiter'.

(7) Most of the population of Mexican origin in the U.S. are (sic) indigenous/mestizo and, while they may not acknowledge it, also have African blood stemming from the colonial period. The same racial characteristics generally hold true for the growing US population of Central Americans and many South Americans. Puerto Ricans, Cubans, Dominicans and other people from the Caribbean are generally of African, Spanish or Indian ancestry or a mix of all three . . . . The practice of bunching Latinos into the white category (of the census) is tantamount to giving them 'honorary white' status.³⁸

(8) The scene is a beauty parlor in Mexico City. A recently arrived Guatemalan (Mayan?) Indian man sits in a salon chair with pink curlers in his hair. As he leaves the shop, with less straight, almost curly hair and melts into the crowd, the voice-over says: 'He leaves the beauty parlor, hopefully looking a little less Indian and hoping this will help him land a job'.³⁹

The teacher education students I have taught were not very likely to understand much of what is going on in the incidents just described. The systemic nature of the metanarrative of 'race' escapes their conscious awareness. Typically, my students claimed to be and wanted to remain 'colour-blind'. In 12 years at Santa Clara University I had two Black teacher education students from 1983 to 1994. My students believed that *seeing* difference is tantamount to *creating* difference where none really exists. When confronted with the realities of racism in schools and social inequity, students tended to attribute these systemic indicators to the faulty character of individuals (that is, whites who are prejudiced or Blacks who do not try hard enough to 'make it'), that is, to the inevitable fallibility of 'human nature'. Some of the students I taught at Santa Clara University were also uncomfortable with standard textbook definitions of racism, because they believed, as Haberman[40] has observed, that systemic concepts are 'overgeneralizations'. In fact, I can recall no student teacher who entered our credential programme with a developed theoretical understanding of racial formation or of their own racial identity development. Likewise, my students also failed to grasp that what they *know* and have learned about the history of the US and experiences of diverse peoples is not neutral nor objective. Because what is involved here seemed to be more than 'resisting racial awareness', I coined the term 'dysconscious' to more accurately describe their ways of being and knowing and to reflect the way these students typically (mis)perceived social reality.[41]

School Textbooks and the Ideology of Race

A letter to a Palo Alto newspaper in 1994 stated:

Ethnic studies should be carried on under the auspices of each ethnic group and not paid for by public school funds.... Schools are supposed to bind the community together and promote community problem-solving.[42]

The incidents like those cited above exemplify the ontological lack that blackness represents within the racial ideology or the 'Black/White' duality of our times. In these antinomies blackness epitomizes the negation of what is socially valued. The teachers and education students I have worked with in the last 20 years are not aware of nor do they understand why this phenomenon occurs within the local US culture and that it has global ramifications as well. Therefore, they cannot begin to develop a pedagogical response to the 'racial problem' in the schools. Nor have they learned that this apparent binary value-opposition constitutes a continuum of valences such that at different times and in different locations a Red/White duality (that is, indigenous Indian-ness), like blackness, is the self-aversive negation to be negated. ('Y tu abuela? Donde esta?') Other categories associated with 'varying degrees of Africanness'[43] or blackness, non-blackness, and non-whiteness (for example, Mulattoes, Mestizos, Mexicans, Asians) may be degraded[44] or regarded as 'honorary whites'. Thus, this hierarchy of racial ideology rationalizes and legitimates the social framework and it remains in tact. And so far as my teacher education students are concerned, I continue to ask: 'What is wrong with their education?'[45] The following examples from the controversial 1992 California history textbook adoption are illustrative:

(1) The California State Board of Education adopted History Social Science textbooks that included an illustration of a 'civilized' white Cro-Magnon man living in a cave in France (who wears clothes, has tools and fire, and shaves) juxtaposed (in the narrative) with 'naked, dark-skinned' proto-humans living 'on the plains of eastern Africa millions of years ago'; they speak a 'strange language'; they offer the imaginary (6th grade) reader a 'bloody' bone to eat. They pound the bone on the ground with a rock, to eat the red marrow 'oozing' from the bone.[46] The Teacher's Edition of the text says: 'Cro-Magnons not only looked like modern people, they also had a similar lifestyle; Cro-Magnons looked like us'.[47] On another page a small map identifies Cro-Magnon sites around the world. However, the full-page illustration of Cro-Magnon man locates him in a cave in France.

As a member of the California Curriculum Commission, I complained about the implications of this pseudo-comparison between the image of the European cave-dweller and the description of the almost human Africans. A fellow commissioner deflected my concerns by declaring that she 'showed this picture to an anthropologist at the University of California, (Berkeley) who said the depiction of Cro-Magnon man is accurate and (laughs) that, "At least the guy's not blond".'

(2) During textbook evaluation week (during the California Curriculum Commission's 1992 History/Social Studies adoption), the lone Mexican American teacher on the sixth grade textbook review panel sent me an urgent message. She was waiting for me outside the evaluation room. When I arrived, through tears, she said: 'They're discussing a book that deals with ancient Mexico — the Aztec civilization — and it's all about human sacrifice. I don't know how to answer this. These professors know more than I do. What can I say? What can I do? How can I give this book to my Chicano students back in Fresno?'

She reached out to me because I had previously presented the training session on the inclusion of diversity and the evaluation criteria the panels of teachers and university professors would use in their review and assessment of the books under consideration.[48] During this textbook evaluation process — after these reviews were completed — and I saw the 'handwriting on the wall', I publicly opposed their adoption because these texts contained numerous forms of bias and distortions. In my judgment these books and the California curriculum framework that guided the review and adoption process were *conceptually flawed.*[49]

Later, I showed three illustrations in the California textbooks to a group of Black parents and educators whom I also interviewed. We discussed my critique of these representations and Sylvia Wynter's Black Studies analysis of the conceptual flaws in these books, including the illustrations that represented: (1) Cro-Magnon man versus the bone-crushing darker-skinned proto-humans; (2) the Kongo king, who, in a chapter on the origins of slavery in Africa, gets involved in the trade in 'slaves' as he develops a taste for fancy European trade goods like the leather boots he is shown wearing; (3) and a runaway enslaved African American, whose empty stomach, tired feet, and sharp eyes that enable him 'to see at night' are delineated in the captions.[50] Specifically, we considered the way these textbook representations '*mis-equate* the slave trade with the European immigrants' Ellis Island experience' by insisting that the US is a nation of immigrants. With great prescience, considering the epidemic of school shootings at Columbine High School and other communities across the nation that have involved *white* students, one of the parents said: 'This shows that they are not ready to deal with a total change in the culture. And here are all these kids riding around with guns — and it's the White kids, too'.[51]

Acting Black: A Dialectic of Cultural Hijacking and Denial/Love and Theft

> Fascism's 'round the corner
> and every human's a gorner
> unless we lay to rest
> the nation state's interest
>
> You know fascism equals ideology
> when poor white trash are
> replaced with technology
> Fascism's invading mental collectivity
> by hiding behind invented ethnicity.[52]
>
> —The Metaphysical Rappers of Institute NHI

There has been little research or discussion in the debates or controversy about multicultural curriculum change (in schools or higher education) that addresses theory and methods of teaching and learning about the culture-systemic process of racial formation. We depend upon a liberal education — within a college curriculum that continues to require supplementary ethnic/women's studies courses— to deepen teachers' understanding of our diverse society. This is because the academic disciplines are often less than culturally inclusive with respect to the knowledge that is imparted and the way students are taught. A fundamental paradox of liberal learning (and teacher development) is that participating fully in 'cultivating' our *common* humanity requires affirming knowledge of one's own cultural background and perspectives. Moreover, even as philosopher Martha C. Nussbaum notes that 'we need academic instruction to steer us',[53] for the most part, academia is not prepared for this responsibility. This is because 'much racial theory', as Omi and Winant observe, 'treats race as a manifestation or epiphenomenon of other supposedly more fundamental categories of sociopolitical identity', that is, 'ethnicity, class and nation'.[54] Moreover, simply multiculturalizing the curriculum without 'an account of racialization processes', that is linked to the larger struggle for social change and that 'avoids the pitfalls of US ethnic history'[55] is inadequate to the urgent task we are facing. Academic scholarship and textbooks that purport to offer a 'history of multicultural America' (like Takaki's *In a Different Mirror*) bear close scrutiny, because the strategy of 'ethnicizing' the experience of all groups does not address fundamentally the problem of *race*. That is to say, the premises of the value-opposition in inferior/superior human/nonhuman; and inclusion/exclusion remain.

Scholars who offer competing analyses risk being labelled, vilified, and baited as self-interested, racist, separatist, essentialist by the careerist 'multiculturalized professional managerial class',[56] as well as by the media. It has been my experience that university faculty often lack the knowledge needed to decipher the obfuscation in both academic writing and the media. 'Critical "race" theorizing' and 'critical white studies' represent possible exceptions that confirm the rule. Too many students continue to graduate from teaching credential programmes as uninformed about their own group's experiences as they are about the intersections of the experiences of various groups, particularly relationships between the Euro-American immigrant experience and the Black Experience. (This observation applies to students preparing for other careers as well, including medicine, business, and so on.)[57]

In the academic disciplines and textbooks that scholars produce, erasure, invisibilization, monoculturalism, and marginalizing inclusion of the history and contributions of diverse peoples to the society have contributed to the problem. For example, in *The Black Jacobins* C.L.R. James pointed out that knowledge of 'the contribution of the slaves to the making of America as a civilization' is an omission from 'the whole sphere of historiography'.[58] Holt's elaboration upon the continuing importance of this point is worth quoting at length:

> Economically, the modern world as we know it grew out of European exploration and geographic expansion and was consolidated with the expansion of capitalist social relations in the late eighteenth and nineteenth centuries. Scholars like W.E.B. Du Bois, C.L.R. James, and Eric Williams have shown from various angles that the histories of European capitalist expansion, which are so crucial to the development

of the modern world and modernity, cannot be fully understood without acknowledgment of the central role of Africans, and specifically of Africans in the Americas. . . . C.L.R. James was among the first to suggest that . . . even the very idea of freedom itself [was] bound up with slavery in the Americas and . . . sometimes even . . . with the slaves' revolutionary initiatives.[59]

The 'contributions' of other groups have been excluded as well. Because black culture has permeated and transformed US culture so thoroughly, it is, however, simultaneously unseen and ubiquitous, misrepresented and misconstrued. Prospective teachers do not see the hegemonic interests at work in past and present absorption — cultural hijacking — and inclusion of Black cultural forms in this society (and globally). Following is a student-teacher's journal entry that exemplifies the limited perception regarding who has contributed what to this society's development:

> As far as voting goes, I believe that people should vote if they are employed because there are so many people who are not employed and living off the tax dollars of those who are employed. So many people have the system all figured out with living on welfare and receiving more money with the more children they have. These people are allowed to vote! Do they do anything to help our country become a better place to live? No. So why, should these people who contribute nothing and actually milk the system for everything it's worth be allowed to vote? . . . . (Jill [not her real name], is a 22-year-old white woman).[60]

This viewpoint mirrors the cultural ignorance, monocultural arrogance, and 'counter-egalitarian' sentiments of people in the general population who oppose 'minority' demands for 'group rights' to redress historical wrongs.[61] An Op-Ed page of the *San Francisco Chronicle* addressing the possibility of reparations (written about the same time in 1994) further illustrates this point:

> Yet another attempt by underachieving, separatist blacks to obtain by legal fiat, what they are incapable of achieving through honest hard work, persistent personal effort and willful assimilation . . . . Still

another attempt to arrogate unto themselves the respect and benefits the rest of us have had to work generations for. HR 40 is nothing but societal extortion . . . . Now they want a cash payoff? How much tax money has been dumped down the rat-hole of social programs since LBJ's signing of the civil rights bill? . . . Someone had better explain to them that when the internal parasite becomes too greedy, it kills its host and thereby commits suicide . . . . When in God's name, is enough, finally enough?[62]

Contemporaneously with this belief structure (of willful and dysconscious denial), the white establishment's commercialization and exploitation of blackness continues the contradictory historical pattern of 'love and theft', a dialectic of absorption, (mis)appropriation and denial that hijacks black cultural style. The 'Be like Mike' commercials featuring megastar basketball player Michael Jordan that appeared a few years ago, and Eminem's recent ascendancy as the pre-eminent (white) rapper, are just two exemplars of the historical pattern of white cultural appropriation or 'acting Black' that increasingly defines American popular culture, performing arts and expressive style. The national fascination with black culture and style,[63] like the minstrel 'delineators' and black music imitators of previous eras, coexists with a deeply embedded national fear of the cultural originators themselves, in this instance, young Black males, who are emulated, impersonated, envied but also criminalized, jailed, killed, and abhorred (as if 'no humans are involved').

Enabling student teachers (and other educators) to recognize the premises of the Black/White duality and to perceive reality in a new way requires deciphering such contemporary contradictions in popular culture and the academic disciplines. This can begin with rereading and rewriting history. However, there is little in the research literature in teacher education (and certainly no funding for such research) that addresses this kind of learning and development: reading history critically, rethinking one's own identity in the process, and deconstructing one's dysconsciousness and miseducation. Sleeter has examined the ways that experienced white teachers resist multicultural education and racial awareness.[64] However, Haberman suggests that college-level education is 'wasted' on young people who have not developed sufficient cognitive flexibility and intellectual maturity.

Additional examples from the journals of two student teachers illustrate different intellectual and emotional responses to the challenge of greater *self*-knowledge that is involved.

> The thought of questioning the importance of the great Christopher Columbus never entered my mind — until after the readings in class (Zinn). I took it for granted ... that Christopher Columbus was the man who discovered the new world and from textbooks I learned that he "enlightened and taught" the Indians .... Why have I *never* heard that unless the Indians brought Columbus a certain amount of gold, he would cut off their hands causing them to bleed to death? Because our historians chose not to "value" this perspective.
> (Judy [not real name], a 22 year-old white woman, after reading Howard Zinn's *A People's History of the United States* and Sylvia Wynter's *Do Not Call Us 'Negros'*).[65]

Jill, on the other hand, commented that 'history cannot be changed, so why not live for tomorrow instead of hanging on yesterday?' Jill also 'finds it interesting' that:

> when studying the slave trade from Africa there are parts which are rarely discussed. Black African men were selling other black African men to white people to bring to the United States. People of their own color were selling one another into slavery. The finger is often pointed at the white man but it is the black man who was at the starting point of the trade. The black man as well as the white man made money off of the slave trade.

This journal entry calls attention to one of the most powerful orthodoxies regarding *race* and societal inequity in mainstream thought, history, and popular (dys)consciousness. This perception of African-American enslavement contrasts sharply with the reality that 'every people, every race, has passed through a stage of slavery'.[66] This ideological representation merits further deciphering, and critical discussion.

Do Not Call Us *'Negros'*: Call us *Black*

> Have the students imagine they live in a Kongo village in the year 1577...and debate whether to sell slaves to the Portuguese (and discuss political, economic and moral aspects of the issue). *Across the Centuries.*[67] [Teacher's Edition]

The journal entry above illustrates a common but not accidental (mis)understanding of the origins of the transatlantic slave trade. This account conforms to a popular and scholarly ideology that became a focal point in the controversial adoption of the ('multicultural') history, social science seventh-grade textbook *A Message of Ancient Days* in California in 1992. Wynter wrote the monograph *Do Not Call Us 'Negros': How Multicultural Textbooks Perpetuate Racism* (originally as a letter/essay to the California State Board of Education) in order to decipher this and other orthodoxies of the founding metanarrative of the US that includes the enslavement of Africans and indigenous peoples in the Americas. Wynter's deciphering analysis from a Black Studies alterity perspective is consistent with the conclusions of scholars like Basil Davidson, Carter G. Woodson, W.E.B. Du Bois, and C.L.R. James. In this monograph Wynter explains how the 'misrepresentation of the indigenous peoples is essential to the representation' of 'American history'[68] in other grade level texts.

Just as earlier rationalizations of slavery that were advanced in the scholarship of the 'neo-plantation school' historians such as Ulrich B. Phillips had to be displaced by more truthful accounts — Wynter's cultural model analysis of the founding narratives of our order of knowledge explicates more of the social totality and illuminates the cognitive distortions of orthodox historiography. This orthodoxy is actually acultural because its own cultural premises, assumptions, and beliefs remain unexamined. For instance, at the height of the controversy over the California history textbook adoption, Stanford University historian Carl Degler was recruited to give the orthodox account of the origins of the transatlantic trade when he and Sylvia Wynter appeared on 'The MacNeil-Lehrer Newshour'. Degler's remarks were predictably consistent with the student teacher's journal entry. He states:

If you talk about the slave trade, for example, you have to point out that the slaves came over to the New World *primarily* because Africans enslaved them first or captured them in war and sold them to the Europeans.[69]

Wynter's point that, 'there were no "Africans" then', illuminates the conceptual distortion in Degler's orthodox historical narrative. The *existential reality* and sociocultural identity of the Congolese included neither a continental (African) nor a *racial* self-conception of being 'African'. Moreover, the Congolese people 'used the term "negro" to denote *lineageless* men or women'.[70] This understanding contrasts with the way the Portuguese eventually came to see all 'Africans' as 'Negroes' and as potential slaves. The institutionalization and ideological justification of *racial* slavery involved a process of *racial formation* that included the social construction of conceptual categories that conflated negro/African (slave) and white/European (free). Thus, as Wynter's original scholarship has documented, the Congolese King warned the king of Portugal, whom he addressed as 'his royal brother': 'Do not call us *Negros*. Call us Black (*Preto*)'.[71]

Historian Basil Davidson has suggested that greater inquiry 'into the mind of the European and the conditions in Africa'[72] is needed. Teachers in particular need such in-depth study to critique textbook representations and to develop more truthful curricula. African language study offers an undeveloped possibility for teachers' intellectual growth and professional development. For instance, deciphering the meaning of the word *slave* in the Songhay-Senni (Songhay language) of Mali reveals a significant insight into the culture and values of the diverse people who built the Songhay Empire, West Africa's last and greatest classical civilization. Hassimi Maiga has taught Songhay-Senni in the US in classes for middle school and college students, teachers, and parents. Maiga's ongoing pedagogical research reveals that learning the meaning of the word 'slave' in Songhay-Senni can have a liberating effect on the consciousness of African-Americans studying this language and their African heritage. In Songhay-Senni, *slave (barK´ya)* literally means 'one who does not *even* have a mother'. This single word/concept affirms the significance of lineage in the 'mind' of Songhay people.

Another conceptual flaw in American historiography of slavery relates to the lack of emphasis given to the cultural belief system of the Europeans which enabled those *buying* the 'slaves' to see their actions as 'legitimate' and 'morally just'. [73] This recognition requires consideration of the Christian concepts, 'just title' and 'just war', through which the Catholic Church *officially* sanctioned the capturing and selling of both indigenous Indians and African 'slaves'. Thus, *racial* slavery was rationalized *within the terms* of the ethical and moral criteria of the church. These criteria legitimated the 'military expeditions' that various European nations ultimately engaged in to get slaves — in the context of 'just wars' that exacerbated the inter-African warfare to which the trade in enslaved peoples of Africa contributed. This cultural belief system and the economy of slave *production* that is rationalized also justified the prior enslavement of the Indians on the basis of their practices of *physical sacrifice*, which supposedly signalled a (genetic) 'Lack of Natural Reason'.[74] Africans were substituted for Indians after the Spanish priest Las Casas successfully argued that the religious practices of the indigenous Indian peoples constituted an *error* not the *absence* of reason.

The encounter of three different cultural belief systems, of the Red, Black and White peoples, signals the 'more detailed' ways in which blackness (as signifier of human 'genetic defectivity') mattered then and still matters now. Like Woodson before her, Wynter stresses that a continuing consequence of our cultural model (or mode of reasoning) and our founding narratives of origin is a system of education that systematically demotivates Black, Latino, and American Indian youth. Wynter concludes, as did Woodson, that the disciplines of the West's cultural heritage, canonized in the curriculum, are deeply implicated in the construction and maintenance of the 'two reservations' for Black and Indian peoples. That is why Wynter insists that knowledge itself must be 'rewritten' not just multiculturalized.

Likewise Toni Morrison suggests, in *Playing in the Dark*, that a rereading of US national fiction is also necessary to decipher the ways that race, in the form of invented 'Africansm', functions dialectically in literature and in the social imagination of White writers and readers. She examines the 'problem that race causes'[75] in the nation's literature by demonstrating how the 'sycophancy of white identity' functions hegemonically in representations of 'the Black' that are encoded in 'racial hierarchy, racial exclusion, and racial vulnerability and availability in fiction'.[76] These analyses by Wynter and Morrison produce new knowledge which by deciphering the discursive instantiation of racial ideology, enables new ways to perceive reality. Their approaches represent a form of *deciphering knowledge* that offers greater potential for achieving cognitive autonomy (from our debilitating and dangerous metanarrative) — and therefore also offers more possibilities to produce and to use knowledge to change the social reality.

Knowledge for the Twenty-First Century

We begin this segment with comments from Clyde Woods. He states:

It has not occurred to the members of the neo-plantation school of social science that working-class Blacks have their own epistemology, their own theory of social change, and their own theories of class and ethnic depravity.... In order to construct societies based on social and economic justice, a new form of consciousness must emerge.[77]

Swedish scholar Gunnar Myrdal concluded that 'Negro thinking is almost completely determined by white opinion — negatively and positively'.[78] In contrast, Black youth in and out of school are perceiving reality and their own education in new ways. Progressive rap groups like Public Enemy, whose leader, Chuck D, helped to create an organization called Human Education Against Lies (HEAL), have expressed their awareness of the ways education is implicated in the miseducation that Carter G. Woodson described in 1933.[79] Whether or not the object of their analysis is the metanarrative as such, they are engaged in an emergent alternative discourse. Much of this discourse critiques precisely what Ravitch defends uncritically and what Greene welcomes as 'pluralism'. In the early 1990s a collective of Sylvia Wynter's students at Stanford University organized themselves as the 'Institute NHI'.[80] They distributed a counter-hegemonic 'reader' that described the 'mis-diagnosis' of the 'global-systemic crisis' and 'the mis-education of the human'. Entitled *What is Wrong With Our Education? Knowledge for the 21st Century* and composed of news clippings, quotations, and commentary, the NHI reader called for 'an analysis of the limits of our present body of knowledge and a call for the rewriting of knowledge'.[81] The NHI Reader:

> put forth the [Wynterian] hypothesis that just as there are laws of nature that govern the physical universe there are laws of culture that govern our human social reality.[82]

The Institute NHI disseminated and popularized the alterity theoretic of their mentor, Sylvia Wynter, and the tradition of Black Studies scholarship that her work extends. Their intellectual activism was also inspired by a specific challenge that Harold Cruse laid down to Black students in his keynote address on May 19, 1993 during Malcolm X Week at Stanford University. The Institute NHI also presented their views regarding a planned curriculum change at Stanford University to a group of conservative alumni and challenged the right-wing *Stanford Review*. A press release that announced the organization stated: 'Institute N.H.I. offers a *new vision* to ameliorate the systemic pathologies of racism, poverty, joblessness, and environmental degradation that plague us while also threatening the viability of the human species as well'. The reader further explains their understanding of the problem that needs to be addressed. It states:

> Given the contemporary global crises which confronts the human species as a whole, the question that we pose is, "what is the connection between these crises and our system of education?" For, unlike present-day discourse on education which focuses on the type of education that our present world-system needs—i.e., a "multicultural" education for a "multicultural" world, or the "back-to-basics" approach to prepare a workforce to compete in the technological age—the question that we pose is not "what type of education our world needs," but more profoundly, what type of world does our education (including the 'multicultural' and 'back-to-basics' approach) *create?*[83]

Members of the Institute NHI published a journal, developed alternative instructional materials for schools, made presentations on other campuses, and created multimedia products (like 'metaphysical raps') to disseminate their ideas and to *organize students elsewhere*.

This activism is in the scholar/activist tradition of Black intellectuals like Frantz Fanon, W.E.B. Du Bois, and more recently, Harold Cruse, Sylvia Wynter, Angela Davis, and Manning Marable, particularly with respect to the role of the Black intellectual in the struggle for social change. Wynter urges intellectuals to 'marry their thought' to the jobless, 'the global new poor' — Fanon's *les damnés de la terre* (the wretched of the earth), the 'populations of the U.S. inner cities and the Third World Shantytown archipelagoes'.[84] In 'an open letter' to academics Wynter wrote:

> The starving 'fellah', (or the jobless inner city N. H. I., the global new poor, or les damnés) Fanon pointed out, does not have to inquire into the truth. They *are* the truth. It is we who institute this 'truth'. We must now undo their narratively condemned status.[85]

The Institute NHI students worked with Sylvia Wynter to organize a symposium that addressed the *colour line*, the plight of the inner-city populations and global poor. The symposium, entitled 'The Two Reservations: Western Thought, The Colour Line and *The Crisis of the Negro Intellectual*, Revisited', challenged participants to consider 'our hitherto inability, as the intelligentsia of the Black, the Red, the Latino and the "native" peoples of the world to':

> elaborate a *native radical theory* of social transformation based on the singularity of our *peculiar racial development in the Western world, and therefore of a new conception of human freedom*[86] (Crisis) (Symposium: Major Themes/Questions for Discussion).

During the symposium scholars of various theoretical persuasions addressed questions the NHI students posed concerning Wynter's interdisciplinary Black Studies culture-systemic theoretic and Harold Cruse's call for a 'Cultural Revolution', that is, for the 'Negro' to 'develop and use a new set of ideas . . . [and] cast them in a theoretic frame'.

The symposium participants included students, faculty, and even two parents of Stanford students. After two days of panels, multimedia presentations, and a public forum, the invited scholars and student organizers worked collaboratively to produce the symposium's concluding statement, 'No Humans Involved: Hypotheses Towards a New Theoretical Synthesis'. This Manifesto consists of 12 hypotheses, such as the following:

> "White establishment figures" can be understood in two ways: as "white" people affiliated with the "establishment" or as people whose allegiance is to the "white establishment," regardless of their race and reference group-orientation. Thus, it is not the "race" of these establishment figures that matters, but their political paradigms and modes of thought. [87]

The point here is that neo-conservatives have appropriated the *language* of racial equality to avoid racial collectivity. Neo-liberals still expect the mythical 'melting pot' ethnic paradigm of social amalgamation to resolve 'the Negro problem'. Liberals and progressives point to cross-group alliances and other forms of social 'integration' (such as interracial marriage) as signs that black culturalist or nationalist 'separation' and 'racial-thinking' are outmoded. The radical postmodernist paradigm rejects such 'essences' in favour of multiple identities and so-called 'hybrid' subjectivities. Or as Woodford noted in *The Black Scholar* theme issue on 'the multicultural debate':

> We are witnessing a strong attempt by white establishment figures on both the left and the right to eradicate the distinction between Black group-consciousness, or nationalism and Black separatism.[88]

Or as Semmes also observes:

> the label 'segregation' is incorrectly applied to any group-focused effort by African Americans ... to rectify the past and current effects of White supremacist oppression and structured inequality.[89]

The late Harold Cruse continued a tradition of autonomous 'group-affirming' Black thought, a tradition established earlier by radical Black scholars. Cruse asserted that achieving not just racial but cultural democracy is not a dualistic (either/or) choice between integration versus separation but requires overcoming 'blocked cultural pluralism'.

I want to affirm that parallels exist between the lynching by rope of African-Americans and the continued lynching in the classroom (that Woodson identified) through conceptual/historical distortions in the academic disciplines and textbooks; between the abduction of bodies for the slave economy and the hijacking of consciousness for the globalized market economy. These are reflections of the black/white duality of our time that have been produced in an Age of Reason and Enlightenment that has coexisted with and made possible the West's exploration and domination of the peoples who became 'non-white'. What remains and what needs to be abolished is a cultural mode of rationality that juxtaposes blackness not only with varying criteria of conceptual whiteness, goodness, that is to say, with humanness. Nowadays, as has also been the case in the past, other groups can be assimilated into that category, but people of African descent always remain on the bottom.

Conclusion

This chapter has presented a brief account of Wynter's analysis of racism in California textbooks and the academic disciplines and the work of other scholar activists, including the Institute NHI students whose intellectual commitments reflect the power of the Wynterian theoretic. Wynter's Black Studies alterity perspective calls for a new theoretical synthesis in order to rewrite the knowledge in the academic disciplines. The aim is to replace the status organizing principle of 'The Gene', that is manifested in our narratively instituted biologistic concept of the human (which permits us to talk about 'mixed' people and 'African blood') with a recuperation of the 'The Word'. With Melba Joyce Boyd I want to insist that 'we need intellectuals committed to the elevation of the collective consciousness of the planet, carrying the codes of revolution into the [new] millennium'.[90]

Notes

1. In an analysis of the 'new discourse of the Antilles' represented by the work of Caribbean writer, Edouard Glissant, Wynter (1990) adapts the phrase, 'to perceive reality in a new way', from Glissant to signal a conceptual movement 'from a loss of trust in physical nature to a loss of trust in our modes of subjectivity'.

2. Michael Omi and Howard Winant, *Racial Formation in the United States* (New York: Routledge, 1986), 64. Emphasis added.
3. The Two Reservations: Western Thought, The Color Line, and *The Crisis of the Negro Intellectual, Revisited*. Concluding Symposium Statement. 'No Humans Involved', Hypothesis 10. (Stanford University, March 1994).
4. David Lionel Smith, 'Let My People Go', *The Black Scholar* 23, no. 3/4 (1993): 75-76.
5. From the recording, 'Think': 'Think about the good things; think about the bad things; think about all the things that I've tried to do'. The late Mel Watkins's (1971) brilliant analysis of James Brown as 'artist and entertainer', as the 'personification of blackness', and 'the embodiment of a black life style' is essential reading for 'anti-essentialists'.
6. Joyce E. King, 'Culture-centred Knowledge: Black Studies, Curriculum Transformation and Social Action' in *Handbook for Research on Multicultural Education*, J.A. Banks and C.A. McGee Banks ed. (New York: Macmillan, 1995), 265-90. See also Hazel V. Carby, *Reconstructing Womanhood: The Emergence of the African American Women Novelist* (New York: Oxford University Press, 1987), 190.
7. Arthur Schlesinger, *The Disuniting of America: Reflections on a Multicultural Society* (Washington, DC: President's Committee on the Arts and the Humanities, 1991).
8. Diane Ravitch, 'Diversity and Democracy', *American Educator* 14 (Spring 1990): 16-20.
9. Maxine Greene, 'The Passions of Pluralism: Multiculturalism and the Expanding Community', *Educational Researcher*, 22, no. 1 (1993): 13-18.
10. Ralph Ellison, 'What America Would Be Like Without Blacks' in *Going to the Territory* (New York: Random House, 1986), 104-112.
11. Joyce E. King, 'Black Education: A Transformative Research and Action Agenda for the New Century (Mahwah, NJ: Lawrence Erlbaum Publishers, 2005).
12. The term *altercentric* is Sylvia Wynter's. Personal communication, March 18, 1994. It is used in a *dialectical* and *paradoxical* manner to refer to the liminal perspective of 'alterity' that Black people (in the US) have access to as a result of the alter-ego status of conceptual 'blackness' in relation to 'conceptual whiteness'.
13. Cynthia Hamilton, 'A Way of Seeing: Culture as Political Expression in the Works of C.L.R. James', *Journal of Black Studies* 22, no. 3 (1992): 429–43.
14. Michael Omi and Howard Winant, *Racial Formation in the United States: From the 1960s to the 1980s* (New York: Routledge, 1989).
15. Drake (1987) notes that one of the stated objectives of the American Negro Academy, founded in 1897 by Du Bois and others, was 'The Defense of the Negro Against Vicious Assaults'. He notes that: 'during the previous two centuries' this 'vindicationist' tradition or 'defense' was carried on by educated Black men and women who 'had spoken and written' against apologist justifications of slavery based on the supposed inferior 'animal-like' nature of African-descent people (xvii). That there is a continuing need for the relativization and rectification of the ideology of Eurocentric chauvinism, however, can be seen in Neusner's (1989) articulation of a more 'enlightened' version of this cultural ignorance and 'racial' arrogance:

> A critical question that demands our study of other cultures is why it is that the West has created what the rest of the world now wants. Why did capitalism not begin in India, for example? . . . . Why is

there no science in Africa? Why has democracy only been grafted onto the political structures in Asia? And conversely, why are all of them to be found indigenously in the West? To answer such questions, we must begin where science, economics, politics, and technology began and from whence they were diffused. They uniquely flourished in the West, and to begin with, in Western Europe.

16. Molefi K. Asante 'African American Studies: The Future of the Discipline', *The Black Scholar* 22, no. 3 (1992): 22; Ann Weider, 'Afrocentricisms: Capitalist, Democratic and Liberationist Portraits', *Educational Foundations* 6, no. 2 (Spring 1992): 33-43
17. See Joyce E. King, 'Culture-Centered Knowledge: Black Studies, Curriculum Transformation and Social Action' in *Handbook for Research on Multicultural Education*, eds. J.A. Banks and C.A. McGee Banks (New York: MacMillan, 1995), 265-90.
18. Sylvia Wynter, 'The Ceremony Must Be Found: After Humanism', *Boundary 2*, no. 11 (1984):3 & no.12 (1984):1, 38.
19. Andrew Hacker, 'The Delusion of Equality', *The Nation* 258, no. 13 (1994): 457-59.
20. Sylvia Wynter, 'Rethinking "Aesthetics"': Notes Towards a Deciphering Practice in *Ex-iles: Essays on Caribbean Cinema*, ed. M. Cham (Trenton, NJ: Africa World Press,1992), 237-279).
21. Derrick Bell, *And We Are Not Saved: The Elusive Quest for Racial Justice* (New York: Basic Books, 1987).
22. Andrew Hacker, 459.
23. This phrase is taken from the African-American Spiritual that includes this refrain:
'When I get to heaven, Gonna put on my shoes And walk over God's heaven'. See Sterling Stuckey's 'Through the Prism of Folklore: The Black Ethos in Slavery', *The Massachusetts Review* 9, no. 3 (Summer 1968) and his *Going through the Storm: The Influence of African American Art in History* (New York: Oxford University Press, 1994) for the source and fuller elaboration of this insight.
24. Clarence Munford, *Race and Civilization: Rebirth of Black Centrality* (Trenton, NJ: Africa World Press, 2001).
25. Henry Louis Gates, *Loose Canons: Notes on the Culture Wars* (New York: Oxford University Press, 1993), 131-151.
26. Sylvia Wynter, 'Beyond the Word of Man: Glissant and the New Discourse of the Antilles', *World Literature Today* (May 1990): 640, 643.
27. Cornel West, *Race Matters* (Boston: Beacon Press, 1993),15.
28. David Lionel Smith, 'Let My People Go', *The Black Scholar* 23, no. 3/4 (1993): 74-76.
29. Jeffrey Prager, 'American Racial Ideology as Collective Representation', *Ethnic and Racial Studies* 5 (1982): 99-119.
30. N'gai Croal (1994), a Black student at Stanford University, describes this paradox: 'As we watch basketball on television one of you wishes he were black. But do you mean black like Emmitt Till or Usef Hawkins? Probably not. It's more likely that you mean black like Michael Jordan or Shaquille O'Neal. Yes. They're different, they're not really black, they're more than black — tortured logic plays in your mind like a drum'.
31. Sylvia Wynter's explanation of these culture-systemic premises was an important point of departure for the work of the American Educational Research Association's Commission on Research in Black Education (1999–2001).

32. Sylvia Wynter, 'Beyond the Word of Man: Glissant and the New Discourse of the Antilles', *World Literature Today* (May 1990): 646.
33. Michael Omi and Howard Winant, *Racial Formation in the United States* (New York: Routledge, 1986), 60.
34. Ibid., 64.
35. Joyce E. King, 'Introduction: In Search of African Liberation Pedagogy', *Journal of Education* 172, no.2 1990): 3-4. This situation only came to light because the student teacher, let's call her Cindy, decided to tell me about it. She confessed that she could no longer remain quiet about what she was seeing in her student teaching assignment; and she chided her peers, saying that all teachers need not only this kind of class but even more preparation to resist such injustice in the schools.
36. Ibid., 20.
37. Personal communication, Gloria Ladson-Billings, March 1987.
38. Roberto Rodriguez and Patricia Gonzales, 'Black, White, and Other', *San Francisco Chronicle* March 14, 1994, A-21. See, also, the comments of Juan Garcia Salazar, a Black Ecuadorian historian and folklorist in M. Fleming, '*African Legacy Hispanic Magazine* (January/February1994): 86-92. Garcia Salazar prefers to 'identify continentally with other blacks rather than linguistically with other Spanish-speakers' (92).
39. Transcribed from KQED documentary, n.d.
40. Martin Haberman, 'The Rationale for Training Adults as Teachers' in *Empowerment through Multicultural Education*, ed. C.E. Sleeter (Albany, NJ: Suny, 1991), 275-86.
41. Joyce E. King, 'Dysconscious Racism: Ideology, Identity and the Miseducation of Teachers', *Journal of Negro Education* 60, no. 2 (1991): 1-14.
42. Letter to the Editor: C. S., *The Palo Alto Weekly* (March 9, 1994):17.
43. Mali Michelle Fleming, 'African Legacy', *Hispanic Magazine* (January–February, 1994): 86-92.
44. For instance, in an analysis of anti-imperialism in US fiction Walter B. Michaels (1992) refers to the fact that in 1900 'Mrs. Jefferson Davis described Filipinos as "fresh millions of negroes," [who are] even "more ignorant and degraded" than those at home' (656, note 2).
45. Environmentalist educator David Orr (1991, 1992) poses this question with respect to the well-educated people who are making decisions that contribute to the destruction of the environment.
46. Sylvia Wynter, *Do Not Call Us Negroes: How Multicultural Textbooks Perpetuate Racism* (San Francisco: Aspire Books), 1992. The italicized words were omitted during subsequent revisions that followed community protests.
47. Ibid., 116.
48. This criterion, 'Inclusion of Cultural Diversity', states: 'Whether treating the past or present, textbooks and other instructional materials portray the experiences of men and women, children and youth, as well as the experiences and perspectives of different racial, religious, and ethnic groups. Both in United States history and in world history, the interaction of groups receives special attention. Whether they are in conflict, cooperation, or live in relative isolation, diverse cultural groups are accurately depicted'. Criterion no. 8. Curriculum Development and Supplemental Materials Commission (History-Social Science Instructional Materials Evaluation, 1990), 5. [Total rating points possible: 25 of 1,050.]
49. Joyce E. King, 'Diaspora, Literacy and Consciousness in the Struggle Against Miseduaction in the Black Community', *Journal of Negro Education* 61, no. 3 (1992): 317-40.

50. An illustration of a 'free Black abolitionist printer' replaced the 'run-away slave' in a more recent edition, Professor Kennell Jackson, a Stanford University historian, remarked, 'Not likely', when told about the replacement illustration. His point is that such a person would have been rare. According to Jackson, white people would have done such printing (Interview, March 1994, San Francisco, California).
51. Joyce E. King, 'Diaspora Literacy and Consciousness in the Struggle Against Miseducation in the Black Community', *Journal of Negro Education* 61, no. 3 (1992): 317-40.
52. Personal Communication, Thomasyne Lightfoot Wilson, March 15, 2005.
53. Martha C. Nussbaum, *Cultivating Humanity: A Classical Defense of Reform in Liberal Education* (Cambridge: Harvard University Press, 1997), 117.
54. Michael Omi and Howard Winant, *Racial Formation in the United States*, 66.
55. Ibid., 64.
56. R.W. Gilmore, 'Public Enemies and Private Intellectuals: Apartheid USA', *Race & Class* 35, no.1 (1993): 72.
57. It is also worth noting that at this critical time when 'race', or the colour line, continues to define the twenty-first century, Black Studies programmes described recently as 'past their prime' are struggling to survive in the academy. See R. Wilson, 'Past Their Prime?' *The Chronicle of Higher Education* (April 22, 2005): A9-11.
58. C.L.R. James, *The Black Jacobins* (New York: Vintage Books, 1963), 149.
59. T.C. Holt, *The Problem of Race in the 21st Century* (Cambridge: Harvard University Press, 2002), 10-11.
60. This student lived for a year and went to high school in South America; she graduated from UCLA with a BA degree in History, including three courses in West African history.
61. Michael Omi and Howard Winant, *Racial Formation in the United States*, 127.
62. The letter writer uses this analogy to explain her strong objection to HR 40, proposed legislation in California that called for an examination of the continuing effects of slavery and suggests remedies for redress that could include reparations (February 24, 1994), A-18.
63. Joyce E. King, 'Race and Education: In What Ways Does Race Affect the Educational Process? A Response' in *Thirteen Questions: Reframing Education's Conversation*, eds. J. L. Kincheloe and S. R. Steinberg (New York: Peter Lang, 1995), 159-79.
64. Christine E. Sleeter, 'Resisting Racial Awareness: How Teachers Understand the Social Order from their Racial Gender and Social Class Locations', *Educational Foundations* 6, no. 2 (Spring 1992): 7-32. See also Christine E. Sleeter, 'How White Teachers Construct Race' in *Race, Identity and Representation in Education*, eds. C. McCarthy and W. Crichlow (New York: Routledge, 1993), 157-71.
65. This International Studies major lived in West Africa for a year in college after completing a high school study-abroad experience in Northeastern Brazil. She speaks French and Portuguese as well as English.
66. C.L.R. James, 'The Atlantic Slave Trade and Slavery: Some Interpretations of their Significance in the Development of the United States and the Western World' in *Amistad* 1, eds. J.A. Williams and C.F. Harris. (New York: Vintage Books, 1970), 119.
67. B. Armento and G. Nash et al., *A Message of Ancient Days* (Boston: Houghton Mifflin, 1991),152.
68. Sylvia Wynter, *Do Not Call Us Negroes*, 39.

69. Joyce E. King, 'Diaspora Literacy and Consciousness in the Struggle Against Miseducation in the Black Community', *Journal of Negro Education* 61, no. 3 (1992): 317. Degler is noted for advancing the proposition that people with darker skins (that is, Africans) have been universally 'looked down upon'. Also, see Ann C. Bailey, *African Voices of the Atlantic Slave Trade: Beyond the Silence and the Shame* (New York: Beacon Press, 2005) for a discussion of trans-Atlantic African enslavement from the perspectives of indigenous West African people.
70. Sylvia Wynter, *Do Not Call Us Negroes*, 87.
71. Ibid., 88. Emphasis added.
72. Basil Davidson, *Black Mother* (Boston: Little Brown, 1961), 6. See also Joyce E. King, 'Diaspora, Literacy and Consciousness Against Miseducation in the Black Community', *The Journal of Negro Education* 61, no. 3 (1992): 329.
73. Sylvia Wynter, *Do Not Call Us Negroes*, 82-3.
74. Ibid., 87.
75. Toni Morrison, *Playing in the Dark: Whiteness in the Literary Imagination* (Cambridge: Harvard University Press, 1993), 14.
76. Ibid., 14.
77. Clyde Woods, *Development Arrested: The Blues and Plantation Power in the Mississippi Delta* (London: Verso, 1998).
78. Gunnar Myrdal, *An American Dilemma: The Negro Problem and Modern Democracy* (New York: Pantheon, 1972), 474.
79. Joyce E. King, 'Nationalizing the Curriculum or Downsizing the Citizenship?' in *The Hidden Consequences of a National Curriculum*, ed. E. Eisner. AERA Presidential Public Service Monograph (Washington, DC: American Educational Research Association, 1995), 119-44.
80. This explanation of the group's name is included in the Symposium's concluding statement: ' "No Humans Involved" or "NHI" is a phrase or acronym used by judicial officials of Los Angeles in referring to cases of intra-homicide among young Black males of the inner cities. From our perspective the acronym is more than an acronym. It is everything'. (See also Sylvia Wynter, 'No Humans Involved: An Open Letter to My Colleagues', *Voices of the Diaspora: The CAAS Research Review* 8, no. 2 (1992): 18.
81. Institute NHI, 'What is Wrong with our Education?' (unpublished manuscript, 1994).
82. Ibid., 1
83. Ibid.
84. Sylvia Wynter, 'Rethinking "Aesthetics": Notes Towards a Deciphering Practice', in *Ex-iles: Essays on Caribbean Cinema,* ed. M. Cham (Trenton, NJ: Africa World Press, 1992), 241.
85. Sylvia Wynter, 'No Humans Involved: An Open Letter to My Colleagues', *Voices of the Diaspora: The CAAS Research Review* 8, no. 2 (1992): 18.
86. Institute NHI, 'What is Wrong with our Education?'
87. Ibid.
88. John Woodford, 'The Malcolmized Moment: En-gendering and Re-politicizing the X Man', *The Black Scholar* 23, nos. 3/4 (1993): 38.
89. Clovis E. Semmes, *Cultural Hegemony and African American Development* (Westport, CT: Praeger, 1992), 105.
90. Melba Joyce Boyd, 'Time War: A Historical Perspective on Two Novels by Frances Ellen Watkins Harper', *The Black Scholar* 23 nos. 3/4 (1993): 9.

3 | Otherness and the Impossible in the Wake of Wynter's Notion of the 'After Man'

Clevis Headley

Wilson Harris claims that a certain deprivation haunts contemporary society. This deprivation emerges from the alienation between our current society and past traditions; in short, we have simply lost traditions. Since this loss deprives us of the capacity to understand certain matters, Harris concludes that this deprivation mutates into a certain 'kind of uniform function, the sort of uniform narrative which we tend to read'.[1] So, according to Harris, the deprivation of having lost contact with certain traditions has resulted in an imaginative incapacity. Indeed, he observes that we presently suffer from the illiteracy of the imagination. Here Harris is not talking about the mechanics of reading and writing but rather the activity of how we interpret and make sense of the world. According to Harris, 'We tend to read the world in a uniform kind of way, a uniform kind of narrative, a uniform kind of frame'.[2] This tendency to read the world in terms of a uniform narrative inevitably results in a block function, namely, uniform functions of reading create a situation where there is 'a total refusal, a total difficulty to read the world in any other way, to make any other kind of adjustment'.[3] Certainly Harris champions the literacy of the imagination, the ability to read the world in imaginative and creative ways instead of being locked into block function.

My reasons for beginning with Harris's idea of the illiteracy of the imagination requires no justification, for clearly Sylvia Wynter serves as a paradigmatic case of the literacy of the imagination. Wynter brilliantly demonstrates the art of reading the world creatively and imaginatively. My focus in this brief essay will centre on her imaginative reading of the modern conception of the human/*man* and the importance of thinking the human, other than within the origin narrative of the modern West.

Celebrating Otherness

Michael Theunissen captures the recent Western philosophical infatuation with the *other*. He writes:

> Few issues have expressed as powerful a hold over the thought of this century as that of "The Other". It is difficult to think of a second theme, even one that might be of more substantial significance, that has provoked as widespread an interest as this one; it is difficult to think of a second theme that so sharply marks off the present ... from its historical roots in the tradition. To be sure the problem of the other has at times been accorded a prominent place in ethics and anthropology, in legal and political philosophy. But the problem of the other has certainly never penetrated as deeply as today into the foundations of philosophical thought — the question of the other cannot be separated from the most primordial questions raised by modern thought.[4]

But despite the current commotion over *otherness*, a nagging and irritating dissatisfaction casts a dark cloud over this feverish concern. This dissatisfaction emerges partly from the fact that discourse about *otherness* has itself been seemingly homogenized into a totality, a sameness, a one dimensional perspective blind to alternative mediations of otherness. The dominant take on *otherness* focuses on singularity, the particular other, with the result of being unable to successfully counter the challenge of connecting singularity with collectivity. Furthermore, even attempts to think of *otherness* as collectivity are not beyond repudiation. When we frame *otherness* as collectivity, we end up with the current craze over identity politics. But the problem here is that otherness becomes configured as a radical difference such that many who are politically motivated to pursue various agendas compete to determine whose cause is the most urgent, which ultimately metamorphoses into competition over the badge of victimhood;

otherness becomes a victimology. And the critics of identity politics parade to the charge that identity politics regressively undermine the universal goals and values of the Enlightenment. Finally, *otherness* as identity politics leads to a rethinking of subjectivity in terms of recognition, so that we are told that current identity politics consists of struggles by marginalized groups for recognition. Hence the notions of politics of recognition and of identity politics. Here otherness becomes implicated in the dialectics of recognition for if, indeed, identity politics is nothing more than a pathetic demand by the oppressed to be recognized, then there is no movement beyond the pathology of recognition. Social recognition comes only from the oppressor. Hence the obvious paradox: Subjectivity as recognition depends upon the very sources of oppression for recognition.

What is the 'After Man'?

It is my contention that Syvia Wynter is of major significance precisely because she offers us both a different viewpoint as well as a new focal point from which to theorize otherness. The very idea of 'after man' would certainly seduce gullible and unsophisticated readers to immediately interpret the 'after' in 'after man' teleologically, that is, as moving toward some goal or endpoint. Such a reading would mistakenly interpret the 'after' in 'after man' as the diachronic surpassing of man, or what has come to be known as the death of the 'subject'. Similarly, the 'after' in 'after man' should not be taken as signaling some utopian androgynous society, a world beyond gender, some anatomical liberation. Some thinkers would even read 'after' in 'after man' literally as the advent of woman. It is not that these possible readings fail to disclose certain emancipatory goals but, rather, they are blind to the true significance of Wynter's radical rethinking of otherness outside the cultural-specific order of consciousness of *man*.

Wynter changes our focal point by approaching otherness structurally rather than temporally, that is, by framing otherness in terms of differences in cultural-specific orders of consciousness or modes of mind. Put differently, she has the courage to think the possibility of otherness beyond the transcendental horizon of the code of *man*. This is a significant step beyond understanding *otherness* as reciprocally achieved intersubjectivity and as singularity, the unique individual. With regard to her new point of view on otherness, Wynter frames *otherness* in terms of what is the *other* of *man*, namely the African and other non-European peoples. Wynter writes:

> "Man" is not the human, although it represents itself as if it were. It is a specific, local-cultural conception of the human, that of the Judaeo-Christian West, in its now purely secularized form. Its *"Other"* is therefore not *woman*, as I hope to show. Rather because *Man* conceives of itself, through its Origin narrative or "official creation story" of Evolution, as having been bio-evolutionarily selected, its *"Other"* and *"Others"* are necessarily those categories of humans who are projected, in the terms of the same Origin narrative, as having been bio-evolutionary dysslected— i.e. all *native* peoples, and most extremely, to the ultimately zerodegree, all peoples of African descent, wholly or partly (i.e. *negroes*), who are negatively marked as *defective humans* within the terms of Man's self-conception, and its related understanding of what it is to *be* human.⁵

We must be careful not to read Wynter as advocating a racial thesis such that the African can be made the equal of the European simply by the miraculous act of a formal, symmetrical extension of the category of human to include Africans. Wynter's point is radically different. She is not chasing after procedural moral parity simply by extending the scope of Enlightenment categories inscribed in the formalist rhetoric of premature universality and "phantom objectivity". Wynter's point is more radical in that she is assaulting the transcendental grounds of a particular historical configuration of the human or *man*. On my reading of Wynter, I identify two senses of otherness in her thinking. There is not only the idea of the African as *other*, but also the idea of the *other* understood as that which is to come. For in calling into question the Eurocentric historically contingent *truth-for* concept of *man*, Wynter also wants us to think beyond these concepts and boundaries. Perhaps it would not be an exaggeration to say that she favours draining these concepts of their signification. This thinking that is situated in the context of the discursive space of the 'after man', invites us to think what is impossible, given the current conditions of possibility of the European concept of the human. The current totality, the current system of sameness, which is the cultural code of Europe gives rise to the concept of the human as bio-evolutionarily selected and does not allow for African subjectivity. African subjectivity is impossible or rather there is the impossibility of African subjectivity precisely because the current conditions of the possibilities of the human do not facilitate African subjectivity. The categories of the current concept of *man* appear to function as a solvent with regard to African subjectivity. Hence, in deconstructing the Western episteme of the human, Wynter challenges us not only to rethink *otherness* within the cultural-specific order of *man* but also to think of *otherness* as welcoming the what is to come, what is beyond the confines of our current episteme, namely, what is exterior to the order of *man*. According to her,

> [t]he Idea behind the phrase ... "after man" is to suggest that the function of the [Africana philosophical text] for the twenty-first century will be to move outside this field, this concept, in order to redefine what it is to *be* human.[6]

In another context, Wynter writes:

> The central thrust of the 'after man' ... is ... to propose, given the role of *defective Otherness* analogically imposed upon the peoples and countries of Africa and the black diaspora by the representational apparatus of our Western world system ... that the challenge to be met by the black African, and indeed the black diaspora, [philosophical text] of the twenty-first century will be that of deconstructing the present conception of the human, *Man*, together with its corollary definition as *homo oeconomicus*; to deconstruct with both, the order of consciousness ... to which this conception leads and through which we normally think, feel and behave.[7]

We have *otherness* both as African and that which is not present but that which is to come. Clearly, if African subjectivity requires a space 'after man', this possibility further requires moving beyond the Western cultural mode. We should add that Wynter also gestures toward the possibility of a new history of the human freed from the current Man's history-for which puts itself forward 'as if it were transcreedal, supercultural, universal'.[8]

The Fusion of Liminality and Opacity

We also find in Wynter's thinking a connection between both the possibility of an African subjectivity beyond the Western concept of the human and the need of moving beyond the current opacity of thought to summon what is not yet possible, not yet actual. Here, opacity and liminality merge. First, the African becomes a liminal person to the extent that the categories of *man* do not apply to him, and yet it is this very impossibility that facilitates the possibility of a Western concept of the human premised upon these same categories. Legesse writes that,

> [t]he liminal person is not irrelevant to the structured community surrounding him. On the contrary, he is its conceptual antithesis and therefore very relevant to its continued existence. It is by reference to him that the structured community defines and understands itself.[9]

The structural exclusion of the African from the cultural-specific order of consciousness of the human is a precondition for the possibility of a definition of the human as European. The African person is seen as the *other* to man, made to experience himself 'as the deviant Other to being human within the terms of *Man*, within the terms of the memory, and order of consciousness therefore to which [the African person] is submitted'.[10] In another context, Wynter writes about 'all peoples of African descent wholly or partly ... lawlikely inscribed as the ultimate boundary marker of non-evolved, dysselected, and therefore barely human, being'.[11]

The opacity of the categories of *man* must necessarily be addressed to the extent that in 'making opaque of our own agency and authorship' to ourselves these categories are made to seem as natural and as discovered and arguably not the products of human actions and decisions. The realization of the contingency of cultural-specific order of consciousness underscores that no system of categories is immune to cognitive unsettling. Here we should note that Wynter's insight is contrary to Godelier's contention. Godelier asserts that

> The sacred is a certain relationship with the origin of things in which imaginary replicas step in and take the place of real humans. The

sacred is a *certain type of relationship that humans entertain with the origin of things*, such that, in this relationship, the real humans disappear and in their stead appear duplicate of themselves, imaginary humans. The sacred can appear only if something of human beings disappears.[12]

Furthermore '*the sacred conceals something from* the collective and individual consciousness, *something contained* in social relations, something essential to society, and in so doing the sacred distorts the social, makes it *opaque* to itself'.[13] Wynter underscores the fact that the opacity of the agency and authorship of the cultural-specific order of consciousness of *man* is not grounded in the supernatural, gods, God or ancestors but rather in a desupernaturalization of agency, a certain 'naturalistic/biologized' mode of agency. Here we have a naturalization of opacity.

On Transcending Epistemes: Root Metaphors of Thought

But it is not easy to speculate about the possibility of moving beyond a cultural-specific order of consciousness and actually succeed in achieving this task. In other words, if we assume that all thinking emerges from certain transcendental categories, then the question is precisely how it is possible to transcend the categories which are the conditions of the possibility of current styles of thinking. Put differently, we may be caught in a weak double bind: while, on the one hand, there is a desire to reject a certain style of thinking about *man*, there is also, on the other hand, the realization that thinking beyond the cultural-specific order of consciousness of *man* is still influenced by the conceptual code of *man*. We recall Wynter's claim that the

> *episteme* is always the expression of the way in which we know ourselves adaptively in the terms that we inscript ourselves and are reciprocally inscripted to be. The *episteme*... functions to enact a specific genre of being human, to elaborate its governing code or sociogenic principle.[14]

It is my contention that Wynter in her various writings challenges intellectuals of African descent to venture to new horizons, to sail on oceans never tamed before by human efforts, to experience the splendid art of ways of world making, that erotic vocation of charting new ways of being. She writes about the possibility of effecting

> the deconstruction of the mechanisms by means of which we continue to make opaque to ourselves, attributing the origin of our societies to imaginary beings, whether the ancestors, the gods, God or evolution, and natural selection, the reality of our own agency with respect to the programming and reprogramming of our desires, our behaviours, our minds, ourselves, the I and the we.[15]

I construe this ethical challenge, this obligation to welcome the new, to welcome the impossible as a matter of abandoning dead metaphors. Hence, I maintain that conceptual boundaries are transgressed not in the sense of merely inverting them but, rather, by displacing such concepts through the introduction of new metaphors; revolutionary thinking is thinking commensurate with the creation of a new metaphoricity. Stephen Pepper asserts that root metaphors structure thought. Again, Wynter reminds us that the current concept of the human was made possible by various root metaphors characteristic of Western culture. Accordingly, it is obvious that a redefinition of the human is contingent upon a new metaphoricity. Pepper describes the phenomenon of root metaphor as follows:

> A man desiring to understand the world looks about for a clue to its comprehension. He pitches upon some area of commonsense fact and tries if he cannot understand other areas in terms of this one. This original area becomes then his basic analogy or root metaphor.[16]

If it is true that thinking proceeds by means of root metaphors, then obviously Wynter's deconstruction of the Western concept of the human, her notion of 'after man' summons the need for a new style of thinking, a thinking which requires new root metaphors. Indeed, I would suggest that the Africana philosopher must abandon the Platonic and the Cartesian model of the thinker as a transcendental self-contained subject totally detached from history, culture, language and the body.

Before proceeding, it is imperative that we acknowledge few inescapable questions. Which tradition(s) should the Africana philosopher turn to for inspiration? Is the Africana philosopher fated to remain within the Western prison house of consciousness? Whose root metaphors will structure and shape the thought of the Africana philosopher?

Africana Philosophy as Ogun Practice

The following is an example of how a change in root metaphors will take place. Instead of a hyperrational model of intellectual activity or of the seductive opposite of the intellectual as burdened by rigid demands of ideological purity, the Africana philosopher must see himself or herself as an 'ogun' philosopher. Ogun is one of many deities populating West African pantheons. Ogun is popularly known as the god of hunting, iron, and warfare. However, Ogun's presence in the minds of his followers takes two common images. As Sandra Barnes writes:

> Ogun conventionally presents two images. The one is a terrifying specter: a violent warrior, fully armed and laden with frightening charms and medicines to kill his foes. The other is society's ideal male: a leader ... who nurtures, protects, and relentlessly pursues truth, equity, and justice. Clearly, this African figure fits the destroyer/creator archetype.[17]

Africana philosophers cannot only model themselves on Ogun in the sense of engaging in deconstructive, as well as constructive, enterprises but also see themselves as engaged in an Ogun hermeneutic, an Africana interpretative enterprise devoted to the task of critique but also to a suspicion of all totalities. In so doing, Africana philosophers welcome the impossible; they create space for what is not yet here but is to come. Such an hermeneutic will offer the Africana philosopher the opportunity to participate in the 'infinite interpretability of reality'. Furthermore, this hermeneutic can shatter the 'gallery of mirrors' which distort and deform the African reality and yet serve as a rule-governed representation of this reality. The Africana philosopher can also become the embodied fusion of the Ogun warrior, as well as of the liminal person. Hence, the Africana philosopher will

> remind us that we need not forever remain prisoners of [the Western *truth-for*] prescriptions. He [will generate] conscious change by

exposing all the injustices inherent in structure, by creating a real contradiction between structure and anti-structure, social order and man-made anarchy.[18]

The Africana philosopher will also take the lessons of opacity seriously. To this end, he/she 'must no longer accept concepts as a gift, nor merely purify and polish them, but first make and create them, present them and make them convincing'.[19] The Africana philosopher must withhold trust from those concepts that they have not created.

The Ogun archetype can also serve as an ontology of life or, rather, of existence. The implications of an Africana philosophy of existence informed by Ogun themes can certainly follow Wynter's lead in deconstructing the Western notion of *man*. Commenting on Soyinka's appropriation of Ogun, Barnes writes:

> For [Soyinka], Ogun is a tragic figure because he presides over human's struggle to master themselves. The Ogun artist either labors to create explanation where there is none, or dooms himself to live in an unbearable void. The predicament is posed as an existential battle between being and nothingness. Balance is achieved through willpower. For Soyinka, *Will* triumphs when the individual is reconciled with the paradoxical truth of destructiveness and creativeness in [the individual].[20]

The Africana philosopher as warrior, as the Ogun artist, will use words as swords to raid the reigning categories, to achieve Being against the assigned structural nothingness of the code of *man*.

I want to make it clear that my use of Ogun is not an attempt to exclude the use of other African gods or archetypes as metaphors of life for Caribbean peoples. Nor should my appeal to Ogun be taken as a literal call for physical destructiveness. Rather, I appropriate Ogun to serve as a metaphorical means for conceiving Africana intellectual activities. In this regard, I am urging a different concept of what black intellectual activity should be. My sentiments here are identical to those described by Patrick Taylor in his analysis of the difference between mythical narrative and liberating narrative. If the Anancy tale is associated with a mythical narrative, I think that it would be correct to associate Ogun with a liberating narrative. Essentially the Anancy tale offers us a world where struggles for freedom are captive to a predetermined bondage where the oppressed can never claim freedom, for the logic of the situation is such that to win is to lose. At the risk of trying the reader's patience, I will quote at length from Taylor:

> The Anancy tale is an example of mythical narrative. The core of mythical narrative is the basic plot or generic unity of the work, its *mythos*, or mythical center. Such core myths draw on the archetypal patterns of cultural tradition in order to render meaningful new, contradictory, lived experiences. Myth provides a cultural order to reality and informs human activity. At the same time, this cultural order is transformed as human activity opens up new realms of experience that its mythical structure must encompass.
>
> In the colonial and neocolonial situations, mythical narrative enhances the self-image both of the community and of the individual and unifies the colonized in opposition to the colonizer. However, it depicts sociopolitical life in terms of an endless struggle in which the colonized are trapped, even when they win. In addition, mythical narrative is vulnerable to ideological appropriation wherein myth functions to legitimate the status and power of particular classes or groups in society. Lacking any intrinsic critical base, it may be used either to defend an oppressive status quo or to justify a rival group destined itself to become the agent of domination.[21]

I find the tendency of mythical narrative to view the human situation as severely limited by an impossibility of freedom to be counter productive to genuine human agency. If the slave can passively trick the master, human agency is rendered pathological. It is not too much of an exaggeration to hold that mythical narrative presupposes a concept of subjectivity of recognition. The subjectivity of a subordinate party is dependent upon recognition from a dominant party. This pathology of recognition flourishes in a situation where the master always maintains his status as the only source of legitimacy.

A liberating narrative sanctions the radical alteration of the world for the purpose of realizing freedom. Here, there is no sense of being imprisoned in a pathological battle for recognition; rather there is the desire to transform the world such that human agency can flourish. I have identified Ogun with liberating narrative precisely because of the positive energy associated with Ogun. The Ogun figure conjures images of affirmative worldmaking; it conjures up images of the infinite expression of creative agency in the service of freedom. Taylor writes of liberating narrative:

> In contrast to the trickster tale ... liberating narrative ... orders the irrational Caribbean world in terms of a meaningful structure, but this ordering presupposes the reality of human freedom and sociopolitical participation. In other words, the world is not a fixed, pre-given entity; it is possibility. Liberating narrative, like mythical narrative, renders new experiences of reality meaningful in terms of a cultural tradition. Liberating narrative, however, makes a decisive break with mythical narrative when it goes radically beyond the latter to assert the necessity of freedom. It attacks mythical and ideological categories for sustaining oppressive situations that restrict and hide human freedom. Liberating narrative grounds itself in the story of lived freedom, the story of individuals and groups pushing up from below ... to reveal the ambiguity and multilayeredness of reality.[22]

I have appropriated Taylor's distinction between mythical and liberating narrative to illustrate the idea of the Africana intellectual as an Ogun figure. The intent here is not to advocate mindless destructiveness but, rather, to underscore the point that the struggle for freedom is partly a struggle against modes of consciousness that are not consistent with the desire of the oppressed to obtain freedom through acts of human creative agency. Before turning to the conclusion of this essay, I want to briefly address one possible objection to Wynter's view of the African as the *other* of Europe.

How to Think About the *Other*

It is certainly the case that Wynter's critics will fault her for imposing certain unnecessary burdens upon African peoples to the extent that they are seen as that *other* of Europe and must exist in a world totally dominated by the Western conception of the human. I will entertain a number of possible objections to Wynter's position and use some insights from Richard Bernstein to offer Wynter a great degree of philosophical support for her claim that the African is the *other* of Europe.

One possible objection to Wynter's position is that in making the African the *other* of Europe, the African is seen as beyond the bound of intelligibility. If it is true that we can only make sense of the *other* relative to the category of the *same*, then to view the African as the radical *other* of Europe means that, to the extent that thought is structured on the basis of Eurocentric categories and concepts, there is no way of making African intelligible within the current episteme. Bernstein warns us of this notion of the impossibility of understanding the *other.* Understanding the *other* is possible so long as we are willing to cultivate the requisite degree of imagination required for escaping the limitations of a reigning system of thought. Bernstein states the issue in the following manner*:*

> Acknowledging the radical alterity of "the Other" does not mean that there is *no* way of understanding the Other, or comparing the I with its Other. Even an asymmetrical "the Other" as an "absolute Other," where this is taken to mean that there is *no* way whatsoever for relating the I to "the Other," is unintelligible and incoherent. We must cultivate the type of imagination where we are at once sensitive to the sameness of "the Other" with ourselves *and* the radical alterity that defies and resists reduction of "the Other" to "the Same."[23]

There is also the possible criticism that, even if efforts are made to understand the radical *otherness* of Africans, there is no guarantee that such efforts will be successful. The threat of miscommunication is also connected to the possibility that even the attempt to do justice to the other is vulnerable to failure. Indeed, failure has greater likelihood of occurring than success in doing justice to the other. Again, even efforts to do justice to the African appear to be impossible to the extent that the African is seen as the real *other* of Europe.

It is possible to meet the challenge posed by this objection by insisting on the importance of ethics. The appeal to ethics ensures vigilance with regard to the imperative to grant justice to the *other.* The difficulty of this effort cannot serve as an excuse for abandoning this obligation. Here we should also be cognizant of the fact that, when referring to ethics, we are not implying adherence to an a priori set of principles but, rather, we understand ethics in the sense of being absolutely concerned and focused on the other.

Wynter certainly would urge that we avoid the dangers mentioned above. The imperative to do justice to the other cannot, and should not, be abandoned for fear of failure. Again, Bernstein insightfully addresses the complexity of granting justice to the other:

> We can never escape the real practical possibility that we will fail to do justice to the alterity of "the Other".
>
> But the response to the threat to this practical failure should be an ethical one — to assume the responsibility to acknowledge, appreciate and not to violate the alterity of "the Other". Without such acknowledgment and recognition no ethics is possible. We must resist the dual temptation of *either* facilely assimilating the alterity of "the Other" to what is "the Same" ... *or* simply dismissing ... the alterity of "the Other" as being of no significance — "merely" contingent. We must also resist the double danger of imperialistic colonization and inauthentic exoticism when encountering "the Other."[24]

Finally, the thesis that Africans are the *other* of Europe might give rise to the idea that the condition of African people can be remedied once they escape being seen as the *other*. *Otherness* is seen as frustrating efforts to promote an inclusive conception of the human; *otherness* compromises the goal of *sameness*, the effort to unify all human beings within a global mode of consciousness. This way of thinking presupposes the contingency of *otherness*, namely viewing *otherness* as not an integral part of the structure of human existence but an unfortunate element that does more harm than good in furthering a global collectivity. There is nothing in Wynter's position that necessarily commits her to the idea of *otherness* as a contingent obstacle to global inclusive collectivity. Rather, for Wynter, *otherness* exists as a structural feature of human self-instituting activities and other epistemic endeavours. Bernstein similarly underscores the structural permanence of *otherness* in the context of human encounters. He writes:

> Learning to live with the instability of alterity; learning to accept and to encounter radical plurality which fully acknowledges *singularity* —

is always fragile and precarious. It makes no sense to even speak of a "final solution" to this problem — *the* problem of human living. No one can ever fully anticipate the ruptures and new sites of the upsurgence of alterity. This is a lesson that we must learn again and again. And it has been painfully experienced in our time whenever those individuals or groups who have been colonized, repressed, or silenced rise up and assert the legitimacy and demand for full recognition of their own non-reducible alterity. The search for commonalities and precise points of difference is always a task and an obligation.[25]

Conclusion: Fragments as Redemption

I want to conclude by attempting to face head-on Wynter's challenge to move beyond the Western mode of mind of man, but more generally to move beyond cultural representations that are cognitively defunct and the grand narratives that masquerade as transcendental 'planes of transcendence'.

I suggest that Africana philosophers can, among other things, embrace the metaphor of fragments to describe the condition of Africana thinkers in the wake of Wynter's theorizing of the 'after man'. Following David Tracey, I share the view that 'Fragments are our spiritual situation…. [F]ragments [are] a sign of hope, perhaps the only sign of hope for redemption'.[26] But I want to be clear. By embracing the metaphor of fragments, I am not understanding fragments as meaning a broken whole or totality; fragments are not the opposites of totality for, this view would imply that there remains a desire for a reconstitutive system or totality. Here I reject a teleological understanding of things which presuppose a whole by which fragments are seen as disordered pieces of a whole. The intended meaning of fragments here is messianic in the sense 'of the hint of redemption'.[27] Roughly speaking there are at least three takes on fragments. First,

> the radical conservatives, see 'fragments' with regret and nostalgia as all that is left of what was once a unified culture; the second, the postmodernists, see 'fragments' as part of their love of extremes and as thereby emancipatory toward and transformative of the deadening hand of the reigning totality system, the rationality of modern onto-

theology; the third group ... sees fragments theologically as saturated and auratic bearers of infinity and sacred hope, fragmentary of genuine hope in some redemption, however undefined.[28]

With this later group we must resist 'the drive to systematize, to render a totality system'.[29] Rather, we should retain the fragment, the image pregnant with transgressive potentialities, in the name of some conceptual architectonic of which the fragment is a secondary feature.

The metaphor of fragments can aid in rethinking representations of African/Afro-Caribbean existence while thinking in fertile space of the 'after man'. Kamau Brathwaite has used the notion of fragment as an analytical tool to interpret the Caribbean situation. Unlike the tendency to view the Caribbean situation as problematic due to the less than harmonious encounters of cultures in the Caribbean, Brathwaite's views configure this interaction in a language of asymmetry, catastrophe, and flux and not as the crippling absence of unity and sameness. He declares:

> so what I'm going to talk about this labourer in my context. and this context is one of culture and by culture i mean the texture and lifestyles of peoples ... culture seen as dialectic of motion ... history as achievement/failure, flux & equilibrium; as catastrophe; or rather, as equilibrium *and* catastrophe.[30]

Indeed, Brathwaite thinks that catastrophe is not antithetical to epistemology. The rhythm of catastrophe, the kaleidoscope of fragments, yields original possibilities of things. Brathwaite finds evidence of the significance of fragments to Caribbean consciousness in the literature of Wilson Harris. He writes:

> On the whole, our literature has so far — with certain exceptions — failed to see itself — *to act itself out* — as omens of catastrophe ... one exception to this is the work of wilson harris: e.g. *the palace of the peacock* (1960), *the whole armour* (1962), *the waiting room* (1967), *tutatumari* (1968) ... the very style which harris uses, especially in these novels — the implosions that literally take place within the books — so that the world of the novel reflects a physio-cultural explosion — are re/enactments of catastrophe. and the result is that you have *fragments* —

indeed some of the words in harris's (later) work are actually blown away out of the novel.[31]

Ultimately Brathwaite claims that the main concern of Caribbean literature has been fragments. This concentration is, to a large extent, the natural consequence of the historical predicament of the area. Denied the chance of realistically arguing for the hegemony of a local tradition or the prior purity of a local tradition shared by its various constituents, the embrace of fragments is a creative and a free act, rather than a sign of disorder. Brathwaite writes:

> but in general Caribbean literature has been concerned with fragments rather than with wholes and certainly with fragments rather than with broken wholes ... its main concern has been with the peasant and with the autobiographical development of the artist — his or her own faustian personality.[32]

It also bears noting that the theme of fragments has been underscored more recently by Antonio Benítez Rojo. While calling attention to the flux, dynamism, and instability of the Caribbean, he utilizes the metaphor of fragments to structure the Caribbean mode of being. He writes:

> Where does this instability come from? It is the product of the plantation (the big bang of the Caribbean universe), whose slow explosion throughout modern history threw out billions and billions of cultural fragments in all directions — fragments of diverse kinds that, in their endless voyage, come together in an instant to form a dance step, a linguistic trope, the line of a poem, and afterwards repel each other to form and pull apart once more, and so on.[33]

Often, there is the tendency to attribute an amnesiac consciousness to Afro-Caribbean peoples, viewing them as a people with a blank slate memory who survive in islands floating on the remnants of former cultural totalities. The redemptive hope of fragments would render suspect the tendency to theorize Afro-Caribbean society in terms of metaphors of hybridity, mixture, fusion, creolization, mongrelization. Although the biography of the use of these concepts reveals efforts to reach some kind of existential equilibrium, there is the hidden assumption of a lost purity or lost totality. Consequently, we are invited to fuse various fragments of prior totalities. But, in coming to understand our situation as one best described by the metaphor of fragments, in the sense of redemptive hope, it then becomes possible to use certain images to undermine modes of consciousness that make African peoples always the other of *man*.

Notes

1. Wilson Harris, 'Literacy and the Imagination' in *Wilson Harris: The Unfinished Genesis of the Imagination* (London: Routledge, 1999), 77.
2. Ibid., 77.
3. Ibid., 79.
4. Michael Theunissen, *The Other*, trans. Christopher MaCann (Cambridge: The MIT Press, 1984), 1.
5. Sylvia Wynter, '"Africa, The West and the Analogy of Culture": The Cinematic Text After Man' in *Symbolic Narratives/African Cinema: Audience, Theory and the Moving Image*, ed. June Givanni (London: BFI Publishing, 2000), 25.
6. Ibid., 25.
7. Ibid., 26.
8. Sylvia Wynter, 'The Re-Enchantment of Humanism: An Interview with David Scott', *Small Axe 8* (2000): 198.
9. Asmarom Legesse, *Gada: Three Approaches to the Study of African Society* (New York: The Free Press, 1973), 115.
10. Sylvia Wynter, '"Africa, The West and the Analogy of Culture": The Cinematic Text After Man' in *Symbolic Narratives/African Cinema: Audience, Theory and the Moving Image*, ed. June Givanni (London: BFI Publishing, 2000), 33.
11. Ibid., 36.
12. Maurice Godelier, *The Enigma of the Gift* (Chicago: University of Chicago Press, 1999), 171.
13. Ibid., 173.
14. Sylvia Wynter, 'The Re-Enchantment of Humanism: An Interview with David Scott', *Small Axe 8* 2000), 199.
15. Ibid., 194.
16. Stephen Pepper, *World Hypothesis: Prolegomena to Systemic Philosophy and a Complete Survey of Metaphysics* (Berkeley: University of California Press, 1970), 91.
17. Sandra Barnes, 'The Many Faces of Ogun' in *Africa's Ogun: Old World and New* (Indianapolis: Indiana University Press, 1977), 2.
18. Asmarom Legesse, *Gada: Three Approaches to the Study of African Society* (New York: The Free Press, 1973), 271.
19. Friedrich Nietzsche, *The Will to Power*, trans. Walter Kaufman and R. Hollingdale (New York: Vintage, 1968), 409.
20. Sandra Barnes, 'The Many Faces of Ogun' in *Africa's Ogun: Old World and New* (Indianapolis: Indiana University Press, 1977), 18.
21. Patrick Taylor, *Narratives of Liberation: Perspectives on Afro-Caribbean Literature, Popular Culture, and Politics* (Ithaca: Cornell University Press, 1989), 2.
22. Ibid., 3.

23. Richard Bernstein, *The New Constellation: The Ethical-Political Horizons of Modernity/Postmodernity* (Cambridge: The MIT Press, 1991), 74.
24. Ibid., 74.
25. Ibid., 75.
26. David Tracey, 'Fragments: The Spiritual Situation of Our Times' in *God, Gift, and Postmodernity*, eds. John Caputo and Michael Scanlon (Bloomington: Indiana University Press, 1999), 173.
27. Ibid., 182.
28. Ibid., 173.
29. Ibid., 178.
30. Kamau Brathwaite, 'Metaphors of Underdevelopment: A Poem For Herman Cortez', in *The Art of Kamau Brathwaite*, ed. Stewart Brown (Chester Springs PA: Dufour, 1998), 232.
31. Ibid., 235.
32. Ibid., 236.
33. Antonio Benítez Rojo, 'Three Words toward Creolization' in *Caribbean Creolization: Reflections on the Cultural Dynamics of Language, Literature, and Identity*, eds. Kathleen M. Balutansky and Marie-Agnés Soutieau (Gainesville: University Press of Florida, 1998), 55.

4 | *The 'S' Word: Sex, Empire and Black Radical Tradition (After Sylvia)*

Greg Thomas

> Aaaaayeee babo.
> I spit on the ground
> I spit language on the dust
> I spit memory on the water
> I spit hope on this seminary
> I spit teeth on the wonder of women, holy volcanic women
> Recapturing the memory of our most sacred sounds.
>
> Come
> where the drum speaks
> come tongued by fire and water and bone
> come praise God and
> Ogun and Shango and
> Olukun and Oya and
> Jesus
> Come praise our innocence
> our decision to be human.[1]
>
> —Sonia Sanchez

An Opening

Mapping Intersections: African Literature and Africa's Development (Volume II of Annual ALA Selected Papers) begins with Sylvia, or her 'absence'. Editors Anne V. Adams and Janis A. Mayes will be compelled to note:

> Unfortunately, Sylvia Wynter's brilliant contribution ... does not appear in this collection. The only extant hard copy of her text was destroyed in a home fire; and, as fate would have it, the machine used to record the roundtable proceedings mangled Wynter's voice almost beyond

recuperation. However, we did succeed in recovering and transcribing some of [her] intervention.[2]

We are told that Wynter proposed in 'What Is the Role of Literature in Africa's Development?' that we move 'entirely beyond' current academic discipline, 'whether we call it literary theory, cultural studies, deconstruction, structuralism [or] post-structuralism'. She proposes that we 'go beyond' and 'break through', which is to say *break free*, in the interests of radical transformation.

In a previous essay on Wynter 'Sex/Sexuality & Sylvia Wynter's Beyond' I focused on Wynter's essay titles. We have read, for example: 'On Disenchanting Discourse: "Minority" Literary Discourse and Beyond', 'Beyond the Word of Man', 'Beyond Miranda's Meanings' and 'Beyond the Categories of the Master Conception'. Another, unpublished paper was presented as 'Beyond Liberal and Marxist-Leninist Feminisms'. This intellectual resolve has seriously impressed me. A 'Here-*After*' may replace or transmute 'Beyond' in Wynter's most recent writings (as in '*After* Man, Towards the Human'), but her concerns remain very much the same.

'The Word of Man' refers to Europe's 'inhumane humanism', that colonial *Nommo* in which a specific discourse or language generates a specific order of consciousness, mode of being, model of subjectivity, a concept of 'humanity' that structures society or social behaviour for Western bourgeois dominance. This 'ethno-class' *Man* is indeed what we need to get *Beyond*, as a kind of mental and physical maroonage. My own essay title thus invokes one central aspect of *man*'s word: The 'S' Word stands for *sex*— The Words of Man *and* Woman diagrammed so studiously by Sylvia Wynter's Word. This Man/Woman complex creates a supposedly 'natural' erotic/sex/gender to be assumed by the 'civilized', if not the colonized, in a 'history of sexuality' that is a 'history of *empire*' and vice versa.

Toward Sexual De-Colonization/Erotic Self-Determination

When Wynter states in the *Small Axe* interview that she does 'presuppositional' thought, against the grain of British empire, empiricism, she puts her project in the most striking terms. She speaks of '*ontological* sovereignty', saying we know nothing of it.[3] She contrasts this concept with 'political sovereignty', whose focus has been 'the state', and 'economic sovereignty' whose focus has been 'the market'.[4] So which bodies of 'knowledge' give us 'the real' (or 'the human') as it pertains to 'sex' I ask. Where is our sovereignty on this score? What in the world is more presupposed than sexual ontology in our current and historic relations of subjection? Not to mention our struggles against subordination. Can't we speak of erotic self-determination, therefore, sexual de-colonization, and embody anti-empire: that is, sex/gender independence in Black/African worlds?

Nowadays, one often hears in Europe and Anglo-North America that sex or sexuality is not in fact 'natural' but 'socially constructed'. Typically, such talk will invoke the names of Michel Foucault or Judith Butler, in due course, with no reference to sexual thought which is not centrally Western or Occidentalist. Foucault's three-volume *History of Sexuality* shows how concepts of heterosexuality and homosexuality first emerge in 'modern [nineteenth century] Europe'. Yet he cannot be said to 'denaturalize' erotic identity in truth. He makes historicity in sexuality synonymous with Europe's *history*, as 'the rise of the West'. Butler mobilizes this Foucault in her more Western-philosophical than historical reflections on gender. She interestingly says she started writing *Gender Trouble* 'as an interrogation of the deep heterosexism of most feminist theory'.[5] Both that text and *Bodies That Matter* argue that gender is so deep-rooted metaphysically that it has become co-extensive with 'humanity', that no 'human being' will be recognized as a 'human being' unless its sexual identity is made decidedly clear. However, Butler did not consider that this construct of humanity was itself racialized in white, Western bourgeois terms. This must be why Sylvia Wynter has said that *Gender Trouble* would be much more radical had it been about *Genre* Trouble.[6]

Thus, despite European appropriations of the subject, we can reconstruct an African/Diasporic tradition of thought that not only denaturalizes dominant sexual ontologies *for real*, but does so furthermore in *anti-imperialist* fashion. It would treat sex categories as explicit categories of empire. It would do more than criticize 'sexism' or 'homophobia' and leave it at that, while leaving their conceptual foundations intact. It would take *core* concepts (of 'The Core') like 'manhood' and 'womanhood', 'heterosexuality' and 'homosexuality', and demonstrate their *historical contingency*; their *cultural specificity*, as well as their *socio-political undesirability*. Significantly, such a tradition, dynamic by definition, could almost begin and end with Sylvia Wynter. So what follows is a critical schematic survey which it should be our pleasure to expand and extend again and again.

Sylvia Wynter, Then Man, The Father, Or 'Family's' Matrix

In the review article, 'One Love — Rhetoric or Reality: Aspects of Afro-Jamaicanism', Wynter counters quasi-*fascist* middle-class sociological ideas about 'sexual immorality' among the masses. This exploited majority is maligned for having 'temporary' as opposed to 'responsible' family relations. It is maligned for having 'litters' as opposed to 'moderate' numbers of children in monadic nuclear units.[7] Wynter begins by specifying traditional Western notions of 'motherhood', 'marriage' and even 'concubinage',[8] before reshifting all the 'blame' and 'shame' shuttled onto scapegoats. She shows how those 'temporary' bonds decried by sociologists and middle classes are dictates of a world-historic system. For the 'material base' of the 'economic status quo', its extreme 'flux' and 'instability' precludes 'fathering' and 'mothering' in a colonial mode outside the privileged. African orientations are, moreover, undoubtedly in effect. Nevertheless, 'temporary responsibility' for offspring is imposed upon this one class of males as 'total responsibility' is demanded of females.[9] The familial reality is in large part a reflection or refraction of the material reality, so much so that Wynter's 'One Love' assails *The Irresponsibility of the Social/Economic System* that stigmatizes its Black majority as incapable of 'sexual responsibility' (or 'sexually immoral').[10]

The central conceits of bourgeois propaganda are confronted here, not simply assumed. They are seen to be products of cultural systems and economic relations. Wynter remarks on one hand that 'high society' upholds domestic ideals which require a range of resources it refuses non-elites. The 'have nots', thanks to their exploitation, financially support those 'have gots' and their socio-sexual arrangements.[11] On the other hand, Wynter remarks that 'heavy paternalism' is 'exaggerated' amongst middling classes even as they feel lack of 'fathering' (and 'mothering' or 'family responsibility') is the province of 'lower' classes.[12] This last observation ties 'One Love' to 'Sambos and Minstrels', a slightly later essay where Wynter argues that blackness is 'the symbolic negation' of 'manhood' as much as whiteness.[13] The 'ideology of paternalism' was examined vis-à-vis the 'Southern Paterfamilias' of US slavery. 'Sambo' was characterized as an invented 'non-norm', one who is the object of a 'constant cultural and emotional terrorism'.[14] This terror is executed by 'Sambo's paternal father', so this white 'father' can experience himself as a 'master/father'.[15] The link between 'Sambos and Minstrels' and 'One Love', between Dixie plantation and Caribbean neo-colony, is telling. The generic pretensions of *man* and his 'family' are globally refused by Wynter.

Toni Cade Bambara: *Blackhood* versus 'Masculine/Feminine' Madness

These metaphysics of sex could hardly be attacked more bluntly than by Toni Cade Bambara, 'short story writer' turned 'video activist' and well-known visionary. Her polemic 'On the Issue of Roles' was published in *The Black Woman*, an anthology put together in part to 'set the record straight on the matriarch and the evil Black bitch'.[16] Just months before its appearance, Bambara reviewed another collection of writings by an unknown white woman, on 'The Southern Negro Woman Today', for The *Liberator* magazine. 'Don't bother to read this book',[17] Bambara wrote, as she reflects on 'humanity' under white-supremacist rule: 'Why do we continually hold out for the hope that whites are actually human but just need wakin' up to that fact? There's a topic for Black Studies. Might shed some light on the colonization era(s). Why do we go for it? My grandmother says it's cause we so human we cannot perceive of folks being otherwise. Meanwhile, Grandma is dead and it wasn't natural causes'.[18] We are told to wait for *The Black Woman* and we were not disappointed.

'On the Issue of Roles' issues a summary review of white disciplinary dogma in anthropology, history, psychiatry and biological science before rejecting the 'madness of masculinity and femininity'[19] by and large, and for Black people especially. Bambara describes the 'usual notions of sexual differentiation' as an 'obstacle to political consciousness' and a 'hindrance to full development', not to mention a bunch of 'merchandising non-sense'. The standard mythology of 'male superiority' or 'female inferiority', and its strict 'separation and antagonism between the sexes',[20] cannot conceal the reality that 'human nature is a pretty malleable quality;[21] that ideas of 'what a girl's supposed to be like' and 'what boys supposed to be like'[22] are, at bottom, relative and arbitrary. This complete renunciation of the social framework of gender was written as part of Black Power/Black Consciousness in North America.

Bambara's concern is with revolutionary sovereignty, for sure. She writes: 'we need to let go of all notions of manhood and femininity and concentrate on Blackhood'. She is not at all 'squeamish' about being labelled 'neuter'.[23] This prioritization of 'Blackhood' is twice repeated, significant as it is. It realizes that no notion of sexual identity exists outside specific contexts of history and culture, not to mention race and class. It understands that sex and gender paradigms are not 'universal' in scope. Certain cultural historical contexts colonize others with colonial erotics in tow. Bambara's call for a focus on 'Blackhood' would combat sexual universalism under empire and keep sexual self-determination in mind. This is why she cites *A Dying Colonialism* by Frantz Fanon, his 'African Revolution' in Algeria. This is why she proposes a 'study of the corruptive and destructive white presence',[24] since most discussions of gender are dependent on 'Western models', that is, 'white models or white interpretations of non-white models' of inquiry. Notably, Bambara holds out the possibility that there are 'no [perfect] models', the fear that we could have to create 'from scratch'.[25] In any case, the subject of sex is to be thought in terms of 'Struggle'. We see her inscribe this same revolutionism in fiction when we read 'A Tender Man', for example, a fine tale from her Pan-African/Bandung collection *The Seabirds Are Still Alive*.

Merle Hodge: The Whip-Hand of 'Male-Female' Geo-Politics

Novelist and political activist Merle Hodge also brings sex, geo-politics and storytelling together in several essays. If she does not reject gender division as such, she does reject its normative naturalization for white world hegemony. In 'Challenges of the Struggle for Sovereignty: Changing the World versus Writing Stories', Hodge casts fiction as a 'prime weapon of political conservatism'.[26] She says she began writing texts like *Crick Crack, Monkey* 'in protest' against her colonial education and its storybook norms. That schooling was 'the enterprise of negating our world and offering us somebody else's world as salvation'.[27] When

Hodge writes on 'cultural penetrations' of neo-colonialism, noting that 'invasion and occupation under the guise of entertainment'[28] is as serious as the counter-revolution in Grenada, and that US television came to Trinidad as soon as the British flag came down, she looks at three 'fundamental areas' of life: 'language, family, and religion'.[29] On family, Hodge confirms Wynter's 'One Love' remarks:

> these arrangements do not fit the storybook prescription: in our family systems the head of the family can be female or male; legal marriage is not mandatory; the family spills beyond one household to include cousins, aunts and uncles, grandparents, and even godparents as functional members.[30]

It is Caribbean women of stigmatized class and family domains who fill Hodge's anti-colonial fiction in her search for 'everyday models of sovereignty'.[31]

This desire for self-determination drove a much earlier paper, 'The Shadow of the Whip: A Comment on Male-Female Relations in the Caribbean', where Hodge thinks such relations in terms of 'disruption' or the 'violence of history'.[32] Physical violence is recognized. Narrow concepts of violence are expanded and connected to 'aesthetics'. Hodge insists that the idealization of 'white womanhood' is at the root of current Black male disrespect for Black females. She even dubs such disrespectors 'victims of mesmerism',[33] the white mesmerism of gender. Ultimately, Hodge maintains that 'when the black man no longer evaluates his women by the standards of a man who once held the whip hand over him', it will be 'one stage of his liberation from the whip hand'.[34] This would be sexual de-colonization, *proper*, or perhaps in part. A certain 'manhood and womanhood' are exploded, decoded as neither natural nor universal, even if compulsory sex categorization is not.

Hodge saw gender politics in geo-politics again in her 'introduction' to Erna Brodber's report, *Perceptions of Caribbean Women: Towards a Documentation of Stereotypes*. Adding analysis of novels to Brodber's analysis of church and press, the writer of *For the Life of Laetitia* as well as *Crick Crack, Monkey* maps a 'discrepancy' between 'ideal women' and 'real women' onto the 'tension' between 'official' and 'real' culture.[35] This is the 'distance' between 'metropolitan bourgeois culture' and 'indigenous peasant culture' in the Caribbean.[36] Hodge condemns the 'crippling mystique of femininity' while remaining conscious that power in socio-sexual politics is scarcely local. There are 'parent companies' of 'consumer products' as well as advertising or mass media marketing (which import canons of gender targeting 'women'); there are 'manufacturers' of global capitalism who, like local 'policy makers',[37] are more than content with today's order of things. Geopolitics *is* sex politics always, it seems, at present.

Ifi Amadiume: African 'Matriarchy' and 'Neuter Constructs'

And they take on new meaning with Ifi Amadiume, academic, activist and author of *Male Daughters, Female Husbands: Gender and Sex in an African Society*, a stunning study named one of 'Africa's 100 Best Books of the 20th Century' by Zimbabwe's International Book Fair.[38] One of only ten scholastic works to be so honoured, this text gets little honour or recognition in the West. It is after all a hardcore response to anthropological imperialism, both masculinist ('patriarchal') and feminist versions.

Amadiume examines gender in socio-cultural systems of Nnobi across three periods, pre-colonial, colonial and 'neo-colonial', to correct the 'erroneous and ethnocentric' view that presumes 'a universal subordination of all women at all times in history and in all cultures'.[39] The analysis is actually two-fold, at least. There is a reconsideration of the term concept 'matriarchy', which gets expanded treatment later in *Re-Inventing Africa: Matriarchy, Religion and Culture*. Then, there is what that work calls 'a neuter construct'.[40] Amadiume makes a general distinction between 'biological sex' and 'ideological gender' which stresses how 'flexible' gender is in traditional Igbo society. She also remarks a linguistic structure with few sex divisions, its word for 'humankind', *mmadu*, being genderless like its subject pronouns;[41] and she affirms social roles can be conceived apart from sex in such a language.[42] The title *Male Daughters, Female Husbands* refers to Nnobi 'females' who assume positions of 'sons', on the one hand, and 'females' who practise 'woman-to-woman marriage' on the other. We often read that 'daughters' are socially 'male' with respect to 'wives' in patrilineage. We also read that 'female husbands' married to 'men' may themselves overshadow their 'male husbands' so totally that these 'males' are no longer known by their own names.[43] Amadiume concludes that while there was a 'dual sex' principle operative in Nnobi or Igbo society, as in many African societies, where 'men' and 'women' play juxtaposed social roles, there was no necessary correspondence between 'sex' and 'gender'.[44] 'Sex barriers' are 'broken down' by 'flexible genders'.[45]

The author's interests extend beyond flexibility, however, or 'malleability' as Bambara had put it. She adamantly notes that these 'women' (that is, 'male daughters') are never required to assume 'masculine' garb or manners when they access resources and positions of authority in spaces between 'gender' and 'sex'. They are not 'Margaret Thatcher's' of 'single-sex' patriarchy in Europe. There are various sexual ideologies and political traditions that empower them as a specific 'female' group. This empowerment was the primary focus of Amadiume's *African Matriarchal Foundations: The Case of Igbo Societies*, along with *Male Daughters, Female Husbands* which was published in the same year.

Concepts of 'patriarchy' and 'matriarchy' are revisited through the work of Cheikh Anta Diop. He wrote in *The Cultural Unity of Black Africa* that both categories are *assumed* by Western social thought in a sorely problematic way. Matriarchy is framed as a 'universal' stage of human development defined by 'savagery' or 'barbarism' and 'sexual promiscuity'. Patriarchy is a supposedly superior stage of history characterized by 'rationality' and 'monogamous marriage'. Of course, patriarchy proves to be uniquely Western in this Aryanist scheme; slated to embody its 'primitive' matriarchy are Africans as well as 'Indians' of North America.

After Diop, Amadiume rejects Europe's 'evolution' conceit and redefines African 'matriarchal heritage' as traditions or ideologies of female empowerment. She asks, since patriarchal rule is nowhere absolute, why should absolute dominance be required of matriarchy?[46] Its elements centrally include: (a) spiritual 'religions' of 'Goddess Worship'; (b) 'Women's Councils', or autonomous rather than auxiliary political organizations; (c) primary economic agency in production; and (d) whole worldviews based on 'Mother-Focus'. This compound of female militance would be attacked, along with 'flexible gender', by the 'new sexual politics' of colonialism.[47] The attack continues with neo-colonialism, of course. For both promote a monopoly of power by 'males', for 'men' (or in Wynter's terms, *Man*).

Nkiru Nzegwu: 'Dual-Sex' Equity Minus 'Gender'

Though Amadiume's *Re-Inventing Africa* and *Male Daughters, Female Husbands* define 'African women' in categorical opposition to 'European womanhood', by means of neuter constructs as well as matriarchy, Nkiru Nzegwu believes these books do not go far enough beyond Western gender. Her 'Questions of Identity and Inheritance: A Critical Review of Kwame Anthony Appiah's *In My Father's House*' ably exposed Appiah's biologization of 'fatherhood' on white patriarchal terms. In 'Chasing Shadows', this academic philosopher, artist and art historian will concede Amadiume's 'boldness of purpose' and 'flashes of brilliance';[48] but, at the same time, and in an admittedly 'pedantic tone',[49] Nzegwu critiques her hard for retaining gender as an 'ontological' concept. Indigenous Igbo data is sharply reinterpreted by Nzegwu who claims this whole idea of 'matriarchy' is misleading and that colonialism brings 'male-privileging traditions' to Igboland.[50]

In any case, the point of matriarchy's reinvention by Amadiume must not be missed. She never defines it as sheer 'dominance'.[51] She sees patriarchy and matriarchy as counter-posed tendencies in specific historical contexts rather than real instances of complete and total domination. Nor does she restrict matriarchy to sex/gender nullifications like 'male daughters' or 'female husbands'. It is also not confined to *continental* Africa, as it were: 'We know that this aspect of African matriarchal heritage is still evident among Black families in the Caribbean and the United States, as social scientists have written a lot about mother-focus in Black families'.[52] This 'mother-focus' is synonymous with matriarchy in Amadiume, not to mention other aspects of 'language and culture',[53] or structures of solidarity and such, already outlined above.

Hodge invoked 'matriarchy' herself as African heritage for hemispheric America. So did Claudia Jones. Carole Boyce Davies shows as much with allusion to *Re-Inventing Africa* itself. These writings go well beyond more seminal responses to matriarchy's stigma by Angela Y. Davis ('Reflections on the Black Woman's Role in the Community of Slaves') and Lucille Mathurin ('The Reluctant Matriarch'). Indeed, Amadiume may amaze most on this score in 'Grassroots Revolution', a powerhouse poem found in *Ecstasy*, one of her two collections of poetry.

Still, she does presuppose 'manhood' and 'womanhood', with respect to Nzegwu, though not in any simple monological fashion. It would be more accurate to say that manhood*s* and womanhood*s* are presupposed, productively presupposed even and, often if not always, *decomposed.* Nzegwu prefers 'dual-sex' systems to rhetorics of 'gender'[54] since 'gender' in general assumes 'sex-differentiation' must necessarily result in 'sex-discrimination',[55] as is certainly the case in the West. Their dispute over notions of 'Igbo patriarchy' notwithstanding, Nzegwu and Amadiume agree that indigenous cultural traditions provide powerful resources for 'modern [neo-colonized] women'.[56] They also believe the distinction between 'biological sex' and 'ideological gender', so to speak, is unproblematic, as if the latter is not actually part and parcel of the former. Is this why Ama Ata Aidoo could avow, correctly or incorrectly, while many African societies would 'doubt gender and biology as bases for judging'[57] people ('women'), they would all make body-type judgments in the end?

Oyeronke Oyewumi: Anatomy of 'Sex' in 'Gender's' Empire?

Oyeronke Oyewumi, self-described 'gender scholar', aims to dispute biological determinism in *The Invention of Women: Making an African Sense of Western Gender Discourses.* This 'history of gender', however, written as an analogue of sorts to Foucault's 'history of sexuality',[58] somehow severs sexuality from gender and inscribes a biologism of both at various levels. Oyewumi argues provocatively that the category 'woman' did not exist in Yorubaland 'prior to its sustained contact with the West'.[59] But this argument, nowhere near as ambitious as it appears, would be more radical were 'gender' not defined in such a seriously restrictive way.

It is not defined analytically as *any* sexual articulation of *human* bodies. It is defined instead as those articulations which are hierarchical and oppositional. So serious sexual articulation can obtain or remain and be defined as something other than 'gender'. The Yoruba are said to give primacy to 'age' or 'seniority' rather than 'gender' as a general principle of social organization;[60] and here Oyewumi slides into 'anatomical sex' as she argues against female subordination. She offers 'new' concepts like 'anamale', 'anafemale' and 'anasex'[61] to explain how Yoruba can make sexual distinctions that matter 'only' in reproductive processes. Unfortunately, old anatomy remains 'destiny' inasmuch as roles in reproduction are social roles with normative relevance in *The Invention of Women*. Though she faults Western feminists for failing to grasp how 'physical bodies are *always* social bodies'[62] in the West, for failing to separate sex and gender critically, Oyewumi collapses them herself 'outside' the West among the Yoruba, in their name. She writes that sex differentiation was 'superficial',[63] without 'social difference' and without any 'underlying assumptions',[64] while also writing that 'reproduction, obviously, is the basis of human existence';[65] that 'certain differences are more fundamental than others';[66] and that 'all distinctions between men and women [sic]' are *not* 'fabrications'. Sex is much more than 'superficial' after all. Oyewumi 'obviously' identifies 'intercourse' with 'procreation'. She loads all physical desire into this 'physiology' of 'reproduction', reductively and as if it were already and exclusively there. It is not just reproductive *capacity* which is seen as 'essential biological fact'.[67] Reproductive 'roles' are assigned to reproductive capacities, with reproductive capacity simply assumed. Those who are 'sexed' in a particular way, as it were, but who cannot or do not or would not 'procreate', in a particular fashion, would thus be discounted, as *genitalist* norms get ascribed to biology's 'nature'.[68]

Paradoxically, while Westerners invent 'gender discourse' in Oyewumi, they somehow do not invent discourses of anatomy, physiology and biology, *disciplines* which she uses to give social significance and sanction to 'sex' in the alleged absence of 'gender'. There may as well be 'women' in Yorubaland. For this invention is anchored by a universalist naturalization of heterosexuality, a strange 'heterosexuality' indeed without 'women', despite Oyewumi's use of *Foucault*; and despite her ironic referential reliance on a host of white *lesbian* feminists. She embraces Western 'science' or *scientism*, its culturally specific and historically contingent sex and sexuality, even though this 'science' would not classify Africans as 'human', as 'men' or 'women', 'heterosexual' or 'homosexual' in point of fact.

Interestingly, in a footnote, Oyewumi faults *Male Daughters, Female Husbands* for not interrogating gender further as a foundational category of analysis.[69] She takes the same position as Nzegwu, on the surface. Still, Amadiume's working concept of gender is not nearly as anaemic as *The Invention of Women*'s. Oyewumi radically reinscribes *ontological sex* far more radically than Amadiume or Nzegwu ever would. 'Biocentrism' remains, to quote Wynter, despite Oyewumi's 'bio-logic' critique. Before *Re-Inventing Africa* — and *Daughters of the Goddess, Daughters of Imperialism: African Women Struggle for Culture, Power & Democracy*, where Amadiume contrasts opposing classes of 'female' empowerment in Africa after colonialism — *Male Daughters* did fend off lesbian categorical imperialism without a correspondingly explicit rejection of heterosexual imperialism.[70] Its central distinction between sex and gender is in addition not completely consistent. The title, for instance, is not '*Female Sons*, Female Husbands'. Nor should it be, necessarily. This irregularity was purposeful. Its provocation reflects some much-needed attention to the social ideology of sex itself, beyond the ideology of gender, per se. In other words, Amadiume's 'neuter constructs' point us well beyond 'anatomy is destiny' or strict heterosexualism as naturalized by Oyewumi, even as they point us beyond her own provisional distinction between 'biological sex' and 'ideological gender', too.

Cheryl Clarke: Militant 'Sex' Literacy in Black Power Revolt

Poet and essayist Cheryl Clarke's work is extremely important here, especially *Home Girl*'s 'The Failure to Transform: Homophobia in Black Communities'. Many regard her statement a 'classic', and with good reason if 'classic' can mean 'cutting-edge' as opposed to 'old guard'. Its thoughts remain far from conventional still. The poet's polemic does not restate but significantly disrupts how typical takes on 'homophobia' demonize Black *revolution* in Western academe.

Clarke knows 'homophobia' in Black life is 'reflective' of 'homophobia in America',[71] a place where we make great sacrifices to live. A conference on 'self-determination' is her point of departure. She attacks US Puritanism, its 'ruling class' homophobes, their state and society, their sin-obsessed Christianity and their 'insular privatized nuclear' family units. The 'conservative black bourgeoisie' and its 'reformist civil rights' camp are scorned, by extension, in favour of 'progressive' Black Power.[72] When Clarke critiques Black Power, or rather its Black Arts, she remains crucially class-militant. Her review of 'intellectuals and politicos' LeRoi Jones, Ed Bullins and Calvin Hernton on the one hand, and Michelle Wallace, Mary Helen Washington and bell hooks on the other, pinpoints the petty-bourgeois character of their 'homophobic postures'.[73]

Her position is confirmed by Charles I. Nero's *Brother to Brother* commentary on novels by Toni Morrison: 'Morrison's homophobia, as that of so many other black intellectuals, is perhaps more closely related to Judeo-Christian beliefs than to the beliefs of her ancestors .... [T]hese intellectuals contribute to upholding an oppressive Eurocentric view of reality'.[74] For it is 'the *Western* institution of heterosexuality'[75] which Clarke criticizes, super-conscious of its cultural specificity. She goes on to criticize 'gays and lesbians', black and white, who condemn Black people as a whole based on comprador statements spread by white capitalist media. A tradition of 'tolerance' that both 'accepts' and 'exoticizes' is finally upheld in 'poor and working-class' Black communities which have historically been 'receptacles' for white social 'outcasts', white *sexual* outcasts, despite contemporary condemnations.[76] Tolerance is not enough though, for revolutionaries in particular; and Clarke is consistent in her insistence that 'revolution' is what Black people 'desperately need'.[77]

These ideas are several times extended in a way that is iconoclastic with regard to categories. More recently in 'Transferences and Confluences', Clarke reads Black Arts poetics as a 'militant literacy'[78] whose 'rejection' of Occidentalism and 'embrace' of revolutionism would make possible later poetries of Black lesbian feminism. This is true despite widespread espousal of 'compulsory manhood and heterosexuality'.[79] Black Arts literati reified 'heterosexuality' and 'nation', according to Clarke, like Black lesbian feminists would reify 'lesbian sexuality' and 'lesbian "ways of knowing"'.[80] But these 'Africans in North America' cleared 'two hundred years worth' of *word space*, ideally combing 'revolutionary literacy' with a 'literacy of sexuality'.[81] In 'A House of Difference', a critical tribute to Audre Lorde, Clarke speaks of Lorde's 'diasporic identity, her Black Atlantic heritage, her pan-Africanist consciousness'[82] as well as her 'sexual legacy'; then there's 'our own contamination by the systems we seek to overthrow'.[83] 'Living the Texts *Out*' returns again to Black Power's orature and literature of rebellion, as Clarke lays bare her own poetic mission:

> to imagine an historical Black woman-to-woman eroticism and living—overt, discrete, coded, or latent as it might be. To imagine Black

women's sexuality as a polymorphous erotic that does not exclude desire for men but also does not privilege it. To imagine, without apology, voluptuous Black women's sexualities.[84]

Lorde's rearticulation of *Zami* resounds. So does 'The Failure to Transform'. Clarke's 'classic' essay did not just entrench 'gay and lesbian' categories of identity. Taking gender categories for granted, it promoted 'the boundless potential of human sexuality',[85] beyond 'heterosexual/homosexual' division, and pictured revolutionary transformation as a 'mental restructuring'[86] in 'the liberation of the total being'.[87] This has hardly been the agenda of institutionalized sexual politics in later years.

Black Panther Elaine Brown: Resisting 'The Bourgeois Cancer'

Though Elaine Brown boasts her Black Panther Party (BPP) was the first Black political organization to put 'gay and lesbian' liberation on the agenda, as a *Black* issue no less,[88] Clarke does not consider such praxis in her focus on Black Arts. When Brown writes her autobiography, *A Taste of Power: A Black Woman's Story*, we get more than your average 'movement memoir' about life as a Panther. She tells the tale of her promotion to their 'Central Committee', how this promotion coincides with their recognition, as anti-colonial internationalists, of 'China's correct recognition of the proper status of women as equal to that of men',[89] and her eventual rise to BPP 'Chairman' and de facto 'Minister of Defense' during Huey P. Newton's three-year exile in Cuba. Though her personal relationship with Newton has preoccupied many, Brown's profound opposition to sexual convention as a Panther is somehow perversely ignored.

Newton barely enters Brown's narrative before her story is half-told. She twice states she loved him because he was, in his own words, 'not a man ... not a woman ... just a plain-born child'.[90] Love is in no way reduced to 'romance'. Its entanglement with romance is nonetheless exposed and subject to passionate critique. 'Becoming Huey's Queen' titles a chapter in which Brown confronts an ideology of erotic ownership, the idea of being 'someone's man' or 'someone's woman', and confirms her party's ideological rejection of gender. The desire to 'belong' to someone in sociosexual terms is called 'the bourgeois cancer',[91] a sickness that infects Black bodies thanks to white culture's bourgeois socialization. *A Taste of Power* documents an individual yet collective struggle against this cancer, therefore, a cancer that would have a female Panther renounce her 'instincts to be a free being ... all over a band of gold'.[92] While others may continue to identify as 'women', or 'men', Brown maintains: 'I, on the other hand, was a politico, a partner, a comrade, notably with "pussy", which was sometimes relevant'.[93] Even this distinction is not noted for 'reproduction' but *pleasure* (*pace* Oyewumi), a pleasure had among politicos/partners/comrades who resist ruling-class sex ontologies. Gender can be used strategically, against itself, as 'another weapon ... of the revolution',[94] but it cannot be naturalized with its basic race-and-class norms. Brown narrates her real struggle to see with 'new eyes' newly liberated 'eyes' in Malcolm X/El-Hajj Malik El-Shabazz mode, and never loses sight of this fact.

A Taste of Power began by reflecting on 'the madness ... just inherited'[95] as Brown assumes BPP leadership with Panthers under attack by the Federal Bureau of Investigation (FBI). It also closes with reflections on madness, which Bambara saw at the core of 'masculinity' and 'femininity' in 'On the Issue of Roles'. For Brown, there was 'love.... inside the madness'[96] she inherited. This was a 'temporary'[97] madness which revolution would certainly cure. So *Seize the Time!* titles one of Brown's two recorded albums of song. Tragically, though, she must concede in the end: 'The Black Panther Party had given me a definition. . . . Now the barricades the party had erected against oppression seemed to be eroding'.[98] When the party ceases to be revolutionary, or revolutionist, under relentless pressure of racist state persecution, its anti-sexist/anti-gender ideals seem to crumble. The 'madness of masculinity and femininity' can take over, after tough efforts to put theory into permanent practice. The words 'Panther' and 'comrade' take on 'gender connotations' previously denounced,[99] despite Newton's post-exile statements promoting sexual equality in party leadership. Black revolution is scarcely the culprit, of course, as academic critics regularly assume. Counter-revolution is in the form of the FBI's COINTELPRO which finally subverts, among other things, BPP resistance to conventional sex schemes.

Brown's riff on this colonial class cancer is based in Oakland's 'national headquarters', not to mention southern California. It does not entail guerilla offshoot accounts, for example, where Assata Shakur could reign as Black Liberation Army's 'Soul', 'High Priestess', 'Sister Love' and even 'St Joanne' (*à la* Joan of Arc) in white media imaginations.[100] Still, when Brown critiques certain Black Power brokers for 'sexist masculinity' *and* middle-class opportunism, her critique is made in the name of revolution; when she insists that her 'party was so far to the left of the civil rights and black nationalist men, nothing in their philosophies was dreamt of in ours',[101] latter-day liberals and social democrats are no less indicted; and when she laments politico capitulation to non-revolutionary postures, she worries 'history might come to define the party for its worst, not its best'.[102]

This has certainly come to pass for some, or many. Brown would later counter an anti-BPP book review written by Alice Walker, who selectively mined *A Taste of Power* to generalize Panther 'sexism' and 'homophobia', with a brilliant exposé of homophobia and gender-conservatism in Walker's own *New York Times* Op-Ed. Kathleen Cleaver could have this same mentality in mind when she balks at constant questions about 'women's role in the Black Panther Party': 'The assumption held that being part of a revolutionary movement was in conflict with what the questioner had been socialized to believe was appropriate conduct for woman'.[103] Brown, whose working-class profile is rare among such 'radical female icons', challenges bourgeois 'sex cancers' which current critics, 'masculinist' and 'feminist', uncritically embrace. She and her Panther partners 'glorify [their] best' and 'criticize [their] worst', to be sure, 'even knowing all the whys and wherefores', toward an *anti*-colonial future. Indeed, Brown asks of comrades and *slaves*:

> Can we not unite in revolutionary love? Can we come to understanding and embrace before we are no more? We Africans lost in America, still trying to decide on our name when we still don't have a place to be.

Sylvia Wynter, Now: *After* Euro-Class 'Sex/Gender/Sexuality'

The subjects of 'bourgeoisism'[104] and Black Power/Consciousness bring us right back to Sylvia Wynter. '[*Euro*]-class' *Man*, or colonial 'being', is 'bio-economic' by nineteenth-century Christian time. This is tellingly the time of 'heterosexuality' and 'homosexuality's' conceptual 'birth'. When Wynter tracks *His* Word in 'Africa, the West and the Analogy of Culture', she insists that *Man* is not 'The Human'. She further insists that 'Woman' is not his 'Other' or antithesis.[105] Man *and* Woman appropriate 'humanity' for the white West, as a couplet. 'The Rest of Us' are neither 'men' nor 'women'. We are instead deemed 'Sub-Human', 'Defective Humanity', 'Non-Human', 'Human Others'. We get a genealogy of these sex concepts in the *Small Axe* interview where Wynter, harking back to sixteenth-century 'Native/Nigger' formulations, states:

> So now we see these categories emerging that had never existed before—whites who see themselves as "true" men, "true" women, while their Others, the "untrue" men/women, were now labeled as *indio/ indias* (Indians) and as *negros/negras* [Negroes].... You see, I am suggesting that from the very origin of the modern world, of the Western world system, there were never simply "men" and "women".[106]

Nor have there ever been simply 'males' and 'females', as 'Venus Hottentot' histories and 'comparative anatomy' reveal. Indeed, Wynter's essay '1492: A New World View' maintains that from

> this ultimate mode of otherness based on "race", other subtypes of otherness are then generated — the lower classes as the lack of the normal class, that is, the *middle class*; all other cultures as the lack of the normal culture, that is, *Western culture*; the nonheterosexual as the lack of *heterosexuality*, represented as a biologically selected mode of erotic preference; women as the lack of the normal sex, *the male*.[107]

Man's 'invention' of sex/gender/sexuality is as a 'modern' preserve of white middle-class Europe, and Europe's white 'America' of course. There is no retreat to be found in 'anatomy' or 'physiology' or 'biology', all sciences of 'biocentric' empire. They propagandize *True Manhood* and *True Womanhood*, through 'male/female' dimorphism, with *True Heterosexuality* and *True Homosexuality*, all in fundamentally racist fashion. Wynter's anti-imperialist denaturalization of sex, her demystification of gender and sexuality, is amazingly complete. *Sexual* 'ontological sovereignty' can be had. Erotic self-determination is possible — *desirable* with sexual decolonization.

Closing

Finally, I return to Sonia Sanchez's '*decision* to be human' in 'Aaaayeee Babo', as an epigraph. To decide on 'human being' means not to presuppose it, even beyond *Man*'s specific 'humanism', as a sacrosanct point of departure. We could decide to throw it away in favour of some other articulation. Decisively, Sanchez remembers and honours Toni Cade Bambara in *Like the Singing Coming off the Drums*, a collection of 'Love Poems', like so:

> Amiri Baraka wrote that Jimmy Baldwin was God's black revolutionary mouth. So were you Toni…
>
> This is how I lay down my Praise…
>
> This is how I lay down my Love:
>
> We are not Robert Oppenheimer quoting
> Indian literature: I have become death.
> We are. Must be. Must quote,
> i have become life
> and oppose all killings, murderings,
> rapings, invasions, executions,
> imperialist actions.
> i have become life
> and I burn silver, red,
> black with life for our children
> for the universe for the sake
> of being human.
>
> What we know today is that this
> earth cannot support murderers,
> imperialists, rapists, racists, sexists
> homophobes. This earth cannot
> support those who would invent
> just for the sake of inventing
> and become death.

> We must all say i have
> become life, look at me
> i have become life.[108]

Dancer, actress, playwright, novelist and intellectual critic, Sylvia often says that when she writes she would like to sound *in theory* like Aretha Franklin 'Queen of Soul', baptizing African Gods *in song*.[109] We get another Black revolutionary mouth for sure, sounding truly divine in her 'secular' transcendence. Sanchez, 'shaking loose our skin' in poetry, resounds Sylvia marvelously. She who proclaims:

> all our present struggles with respect to race, class, gender, sexual orientation, ethnicity, struggles over the environment, global warming, severe climate change, the sharply unequal distribution of the earth's resources ... are different facets of the central ethno-class *Man/Human* struggle.[110]

Occidentalism will tell us again and again what 'gender and sexuality' thought looks like, as in its race, class, age or generation, geographical location and so on. This basic prototype fits not one soul in our 'Black Radical Tradition', a *Triangular* Tradition as I reconstruct it. These writings are all too rarely read, even more rarely read together, and call for something other than evasion and isolation. Some may be stronger on certain points than others, points we could commence to list: (1) Continental cultural-historical consciousness; (2) Pan-African and Diasporic scope of vision; (3) concrete political application in the present, for a future of grass-roots militancy; (4) opposition to compulsory categorization or corporeal dichotomization; and (5) ideological anti-heterosexualism. . . . None, it seems, get at the root like Sylvia Wynter. We cannot get at the root without her conceptual *root-work*. The Sex Word and its related categories of existence — white Western bourgeois existence — may crumble in her wake.

Notes

1. Sonia Sanchez, 'Aaaayeee Babo (Praise God)' in *Shake Loose My Skin: New and Selected Poems* (Boston: Beacon Press, 1999).
2. Anne V. Adams, and Janis A. Mayes, eds. *Mapping Intersections: African Literature & Africa's Development* (Trenton, NJ: Africa World Press, 1998), 10.
3. George Lamming writes somewhat similarly on 'Cultural Sovereignty' in his American Library Association keynote address collected by Adams and Mayes (1988, 255-63).
4. Sylvia Wynter, 'The Re-Enchantment of Humanism: An Interview with David Scott', *Small Axe* 8 (2000): 136.
5. Judith P. Butler, *Gender Trouble: Feminism and the Subversion of Identity* (New York: Routledge, 1990), 83.
6. Personal Conversation (Palo Alto, CA, Spring 2001).
7. Sylvia Wynter, 'One Love — Rhetoric or Reality? — Aspects of Afro-Jamaicanism', *Caribbean Studies* 12, no. 3 (1972): 84.
8. Ibid., 84.
9. Ibid., 86.
10. Ibid., 85.
11. Ibid., 68.
12. Ibid., 85.
13. Sylvia Wynter, 'Sambos and Minstrels', *Social Text* 1 (Winter 1979): 150.
14. Ibid., 152.
15. Ibid., 151.
16. Toni Cade Bambara, *The Black Woman: An Anthology* (New York: Mentor Books, 1970), 11.
17. Toni Cade Bambara, 'Book Review: Silent Voices: The Southern Negro Woman Today', The *Liberator* (November 1970): 23.
18. Ibid., 18.
19. Toni Cade Bambara, *The Black Woman: An Anthology*, 102.
20. Ibid., 101.
21. Ibid., 103.
22. Ibid., 107.
23. Ibid., 109.
24. Ibid., 104.
25. Ibid., 109.
26. Merle Hodge, *Crick Crack, Monkey* (London: André Deutsch, 1970), 202.
27. Ibid., 202.
28. Ibid., 203.
29. Ibid., 205.
30. Ibid., 205.
31. Ibid., 208.
32. Merle Hodge, 'The Shadow of the Whip: A Comment on Male-Female Relations in the Caribbean' in *Is Massa Day Dead?: Black Moods in the Caribbean*, ed. Orde Coombs (New York: Anchor Press, 1974), 111.
33. Ibid., 118.
34. Ibid., 118.
35. Merle Hodge, 'Introduction' in Erna Brodber's *Perceptions of Caribbean Women: Towards a Documentation of Stereotypes* (Cave Hill, Barbados: Institute of Social and Economic Research [Eastern Caribbean], University of the West Indies, 1982), viii.
36. Ibid., ix.

37. Ibid., xiii.
38. Check out Africa Book Centre at www.africabookcentre.com.
39. Ifi Amadiume, *Male Daughters, Female Husbands: Gender and Sex in an African Society* (London: Zed Books Ltd, 1987), 189.
40. Ifi Amadiume, *Re-Inventing Africa: Matriarchy, Religion, & Culture* (London and New York: Zed Books Ltd, 1997), 151.
41. Ifi Amadiume, *Male Daughters, Female Husbands: Gender and Sex in an African Society*, 89.
42. Ibid., 90.
43. Ibid., 48.
44. Ibid., 51, 67.
45. Ibid., 28, 89.
46. Ibid., 187.
47. Ibid., 140.
48. Nkiru Nzegwu, 'Chasing Shadows: The Misplaced Search for Matriarchy', *West Africa Review* 2, no.1 (2000): 2.
49. Ibid., 3.
50. Ibid., 7.
51. Ibid., 18.
52. Ifi Amadiume, *African Matriarchal Foundations: The Case of Igbo Societies* (London: Karnak House, 1987), 82.
53. Ibid., 82.
54. Nkiru Nzegwu, 'Gender Equality in a Dual-Sex System: The Case of Onitsha', *Jenda* 1, no.1 (2001): 1.
55. Ibid., 7.
56. Ibid., 1.
57. Ama Ata Aidoo, 'The African Woman Today', *Dissent* (Summer 1992): 323.
58. Oyèrónké Oyewùmí, *The Invention of Women: Making an African Sense of Gender Discourses* (Minneapolis: Minnesota University Press, 1997), xi.
59. Ibid., xi.
60. Ibid., 31.
61. Ibid., 34.
62. Ibid., xxi.
63. Ibid., 33.
64. Ibid., 36.
65. Ibid., 34.
66. Ibid., 35.
67. Ibid., 36.
68. We'd definitely do well to return here to *Ngambika*'s scrupulous 'Introduction' by Carole Boyce Davies (1986), particularly her comments on *compulsory* motherhood and constructions of 'barrenness'.
69. Ifi Amadiume, *Male Daughters, Female Husbands: Gender and Sex in an African Society*, 184.
70. Ibid., 7.
71. Cheryl Clarke, 'The Failure to Transform: Homophobia in the Black Community' in *Home Girls: A Black Feminist Anthology*, ed. Barbara Smith (New York: Kitchen Table, Women of Color Press, 1982), 197.
72. Ibid., 198.
73. Ibid., 201-5.
74. Charles I. Nero, 'Towards a Black Gay Aesthetic: Signifying in Contemporary Black Gay Literature' in *Brother to Brother: New Writings by Black Gay Men*, ed. Essex Hemphill (Boston: Alyson Publications, Inc., 1991), 235.

75. Cheryl Clarke, 'The Failure to Transform: Homophobia in the Black Community' in *Home Girls: A Black Feminist Anthology*, ed. Barbara Smith (New York: Kitchen Table, Women of Color Press, 1982), 201.
76. Ibid., 206.
77. Ibid., 200.
78. Cheryl Clarke, 'Transferences and Confluences: Black Poetries, the Black Arts Movement, and Black Lesbian Feminism' in *Dangerous Liasons: Blacks, Gays, and the Struggle for Equality*, ed. Eric Brandt (New York: The New Press, 1999), 192.
79. Ibid., 196.
80. Ibid., 206.
81. Ibid., 210-11.
82. Cheryl Clarke, 'A House of Difference: Audre Lorde's Legacy to Lesbian and Gay Writers' in *Má-Ka: Diasporic Juks: Contemporary Writing by Queers of African Descent*, eds. Debbie Douglas, Courtney McFarlane, Makeeda Silvera and Douglas Stewart (Toronto, Ontario: Sister Vision, 1997), 195.
83. Ibid., 193.
84. Cheryl Clarke, 'Living the Texts Out: Lesbians and the Uses of Black Women's Traditions' in *Theorizing Black Feminisms: The Visionary Pragmatism of Black Women* (London and New York: Routledge, 1993), 224.
85. Audre Lorde, *Zami: A New Spelling of My Name* (Freedom, CA: The Crossing Press, 1982), 200.
86. Ibid., 200.
87. Ibid., 208.
88. Elaine Brown, 'Empowering All Women' (keynote speech for UNC-Chapel Hill's Women's Week: March 27, 2001). See *The Huey P. Newton Reader* (Newton 2002), for BPP documentation.
89. Elaine Brown, *A Taste of Power: A Black Woman's Story* (New York: Anchor Books, 1992), 304.
90. Ibid., 243.
91. Ibid., 260.
92. Ibid., 377.
93. Ibid., 381.
94. Ibid., 137.
95. Ibid., 15.
96. Ibid., 355.
97. Ibid., 437.
98. Ibid., 443.
99. Ibid., 441.
100. See Evelyn Williams (Chicago, Lawrence Hill, 1993) in addition to Assata Shakur (Chicago: Lawrence Hill, 1987).
101. Ibid., 363.
102. Ibid., 443.
103. Kathleen Neal Cleaver, 'Women, Power, and Revolution' in *Liberation, Imagination, and the Black Panther Party: A New Look at the Panthers and Their Legacy*, eds. Kathleen Neal Cleaver and George Katsiaficas (New York: Routledge, 2000), 124.
104. Wynter coined this term for us during the annual Coloniality Working Group conference at SUNY-Binghamton (April 27–29, 2000). Characteristically, she asked us to carry it on.
105. Sylvia Wynter, 'Africa, the West, and the Analogy of Culture: The Cinematic Text after Man' in *Symbolic Narratives/African Cinema: Audiences, Theory, and the Moving Image*, ed. June Givanni (London: British Film Institute, 2000), 25.

106. Ibid., 174.
107. Sylvia Wynter, '1492: A New World View' in *Race, Discourse, and the Origin of the Americas: A New World View*, eds. Vera Lawrence Hyatt and Rex Nettleford (Washington and London: Smithsonian Institution Press, 1995), 42.
108. Sonia Sanchez, *Like the Singing Coming Off the Drums: Love Poems* (Boston: Beacon Press, 1988), 126-8.
109. Personal Conversation (Binghamton, NY, Spring 2000).
110. Sylvia Wynter, 'Un-Settling the Coloniality of Being/Power/Truth/Freedom: Toward the Human, After *Man*, Its Over-Representation', *CR: The New Centennial Review* 3, no.3 (Fall 2003): 4.

5 | *After Man, Womens: The Third Sex or Ain't i a Eunuch*

Patricia D. Fox

> [T]he projection of a new mode of extra-human agency represented as directly authoring our present ethno-class or descriptive statement of the human, Man, not only enables Man's over-representation as if it were the human itself, but also the over-representation of our present hegemonic imperative of securing the well being, security and overall interests of Man, as if it were that of securing the well being, security and overall interests of the human species itself.... [This projection] leads to the following conclusion. This is that there can be no alternative to the capitalist mode of economic production as the only mode of economic production able to provide the material conditions of existence both for our present mode of the human (which over-represents itself as if it were the human itself), and for the stable production and reproduction of our present Western-bourgeois social order or "nature-culture collective," in whose now globally extended interrelationship field, Man can alone realize itself as an economically defined mode of being. As a mode of being whose optimal referent nation-state worlds are logically those of the G7 rich, and so-called "developed countries," as contrasted with the poor and so-called "underdeveloped" countries; at the same time as its optimal referent subjects are the now increasingly incorporated global middle classes, to which as academics we all belong.[1]
>
> —Sylvia Wynter

In order to get to 'after man', of the small 'm' variety, one must get to 'after womens', those females who fall outside the categories of man and woman, in their falsely universalist — and bourgeois — guises. Hence, this meditation queries the type of 'human/human order' overtly proposed or implicitly produced in texts focused on African or African-descended female characters in the Spanish-speaking world. While the *negra* and *mulata* — in flesh and in fiction — may no longer exist below the radar of Hispanic discourse, her inclusion or agency is often predicated on the demonizing or the erasure/death of her male counterparts. However as Sylvia Wynter suggests 'rather than only voicing the "native" woman's hitherto silenced voice' as endpoint, the challenge lies in 'calling into question our "native", and most ultimately, niggah women's role as the embodiment to varying degrees of an ostensible "primal" human nature'.[2] That call urges those who produce and critique these texts to 'ask: What is the systemic function of her silencing? ... Of what mode of speech is that absence of speech both as women (masculinist discourse) and a "native" women (feminist discourse) an imperative function?'[3] In order to adopt that inquisitive posture, this essay follows, on the one hand, Addison Gayle's urging in 'Blueprint for Black Criticism' to propose definitions, alternatives, paradigms, images, symbols, metaphors, and values 'in continual revolt against [attempts] to dehumanize man'.[4] On the other, following the advice in the earlier 'Blueprint for Negro Writing' by Richard Wright, this project takes its clues from 'negro folklore' which 'rose out of a sense of a common life and a common fate', predicting that 'at the moment this process starts, at the moment when a people begin to realize a meaning in their suffering, the civilization that engenders that suffering is doomed'.[5]

After Womens

Accordingly, this paper wonders if the standard categories of Blacks and women, in the language of equal opportunity, are mutually exclusive and if, as a result, declaring oneself a Black woman, the third sex, represents the height of oxymoron. Now, oxymoron suggests the unholy linking of two words which each logically fight against, subvert or cancel out the meaning of the other, something along the lines of 'friendly fire' where a chummy bullet leaves one just as dead as does hostile ammunition. In terms of the present discussion, the mix of Blackness and Femaleness does not automatically insure a share in womanly perks, a contradiction that Sojourner Truth recognized when she asked 'Ain't i a woman?'[6] Typically, in Hispanic literature and discourse, the mix of gender and race only insures that *mulatas* get to be tragic, while *negras* must settle for playing pitiful whether morosely atwitter on the plantation (*Cumboto: cuento de siete leguas*, Ramón Díaz, 1960; *Maria,* Jorge Isaacs, 1867); running the revolution

(*La negra Angustias,* Francisco Rojas González, 1944); as the power behind the inept titan of capitalism (*El amor en los tiempos de cólera,* Gabriel García Márquez, 1985); or, as mammy-in-waiting to their lighter Latino sisters (*Eva Luna,* Isabel Allende, 1987).

This paper also wonders if the proper identifying term for the non-melanin challenged female might be woman Black, rather than Black woman, so that what appears substantive and what seems adjectival or ancillary might more easily and quickly be discerned. In that spirit, Sojourner Truth's remarks at the Second National Woman's Suffrage Convention in Akron, Ohio in 1852 rebut what 'that little man in black there say' about women occupying 'sacred spaces', carriages into which they are helped, and the 'best places everywhere' to which they are privileged. Her rejoinder makes clear that 'nobody ever' imagined her as a woman Black holding unchallenged right to those same spaces. Truth ignores her exclusion from that discourse and instead, in response to the little man's snide insinuation of universal female frailty, she boasts 'no man could head me' and 'I could work as much and eat as much as a man when I could get it'.[7] Her belligerence ironically confirms that, within the binarily opposed logic of the cultural terms of the day and within the juxtaposed situational frames of reference proposed by feminist and africana/womanist interventions — absent from one, central to the other —she is not a 'real' woman precisely because of her mannishness, especially because of her blackness. In consequence, her plea and her point reach deaf ears because they call into question womanly universality and belligerently foment a challenge to the reigning system of meaning.

In the After/Word to *Out of Kumbla: Caribbean Women and Literature,* Sylvia Wynter pinpoints 'the contradiction inserted into the consolidated field of meanings of the ostensibly "universal" theory of feminism by the variable "race"',[8] a contradiction implicitly anticipated in the query posed by Sojourner Truth. Significantly, at the Equal Rights Convention in 1867, no longer indentured to slavery nor suffrage, Sojourner Truth will announce, 'I come from another field — the country of the slave'.[9] Accordingly, these juxtaposed assertions reveal a preoccupation that the celebration of women of African descent finding their voices often overshadows a more profound challenge to the system of meaning of the West, within which ideals of change, evolution and progress represent integral parts of the fabric of a collective 'you've come a long way, baby' worldview. In consequence, on the threshold of a new millennium, the westerly desire to picture ourselves, our discourses and the solution to our problems as in movement, marching towards sure (teleological) resolution and closure becomes ever more hypnotic, in this case, forgetting that the field of the slave and the consolidated field of meanings signal not the hybridity of the woman Black, but rather her liminality and the demonzied 'vantage point outside the space-time orientation'[10] from which she negotiates a terraced reality.

Consequently, mouthy woman Blacks like Sojourner Truth represent the breakout contradiction, the 'invisible heart which compels exploration'[11] and accordingly deserve more esteem as such theorizing Achilles' heel. In that context, the woman Black's liminality represents the state of being in limbo 'neither here nor there ... betwixt and between',[12] a state in which 'license and taboo simultaneously go into force, and most normal roles are neutralized'.[13] Within the normal order of things, such ambiguity elevates a figure who 'straddles secular categories'[14] to the realm of the supernatural. That is to say, those beings judged anomalous 'are lifted out of the social system'[15] and into the realm of the symbolic. From that vantage point, the illiterate and mouthy Sojourner Truth recognized the positive prospects of oxymoronic self-cancellation, observing that 'man is in a tight place, the poor slave is on him, woman is coming on him, and he is surely between a hawk and a buzzard'.[16] With hawk eye and buzzard patience, the woman Black incarnates 'the breakdown of dominant systems as a result of their immanent rigorism' described by Hans Blumenberg which leads 'with fateful inevitability' to the 'self-uncovering of the marginal inconsistencies from which doubt and opposition break into the consolidated field'.[17] Thus the woman Black's fundamentally transgressive potentiality to the claims of discourse should not be ignored, cannot be underestimated. As Legesse notes:

> The liminal person is not irrelevant to the structured community surrounding him. On the contrary, he is its conceptual antithesis and therefore very relevant to its continued existence. It is by reference to him that the structured community defines and understands itself.[18]

Hence, despite a literary and cinematic history of bit parts, the African-descended character nevertheless enjoys a purloined centrality as catalyst. The narrative cannot proceed without her; the protagonist— whether African-descended male, European-descended male or female — cannot get along without her input and presence. She makes herself indispensable — stepping in to raise orphaned children, to organize the household, often the business, and sometimes the nation, as faithful helpmeet/servant, hidden lover or flamboyant mistress. Staged as a comedic or cautionary foil, she is the driving force for the success of insecure male protagonists and needy female counterparts in the face of their self-serving abuse, cowardice, duplicity, or ambition.

Having now attained centre stage, what seemingly makes the *negra* or *mulata* so attractive, discursively at least, resides in her conceptualization as portal-bridge —projected as a porous and amenable fusion of differences which supposedly confirms all that talk about *mestizaje* and hybridity — something that the truculent *negro* avoids or from which he is always already barred.[19] Two texts provide examples. The movie *Flores de otro mundo* [Flowers from another world], a Spanish-Dominican co-production sympathetically presents the main *mulata* character, Patricia, as a hard-working, Dominican single mother looking to contract a marriage of convenience with a tongue-tied farmer in rural Spain. Her less domesticated Cuban party-girl confidante Milady — a *negra* — serves as foil to Patricia's sacrificial goodness. Fran, the black ex-husband, receives harsher treatment, predictably demonized even though his situation as impoverished immigrant in a globalized world (niggah, jobless, criminalized) presumably results from the self-same factors that contributed to his former spouse's search for stability and legality.[20] In, María Nsue Angüe's novel *Ekomo* (1985), the first to appear from a Guinean woman writer, the first person narrator, through prefiguration and flashback in epic, pastoral and coming of age/coming to consciousness tonalities, offers a metaphor for Africa's present day plight.[21] The heretofore unheard and inquisitive subaltern narrator, Nnanga Pequeña, finds her voice while, one by one, the central male figures, including the titular character, are silenced by dusty death: first, the *abuelo*, [grandfather] synonym of the African 'native' past; then Nfumbaha, the European trained 'post-colonial' future of Africa (from the 1960s on); and, finally, Ekomo, who literally and figuratively embodies the moribund, underdeveloped present of the continent, the fevered legacy of modernity's serial globalization schemes and pretty lies, from the fifteenth through to the twenty-first centuries.

Lest one presume that Bollaín and Nsue Angüe have hit upon a unique formula, it bears noting that non-Hispanic texts hailed as feminist or womanist or Africana womanist treatments disquietingly also follow this paradigm, including the Zimbabwean novel *Nervous Conditions* (c. 1988) by Tsitsi Dangarembga,[22] *Faat Kiné* (2000), a movie by Senegalese director Ousmane Sembene and various North American texts. The novel opens with the statement: 'I was not sorry when my brother died'.[23] Shortly thereafter the now adult narrator Tambudzai explains:

> Therefore I shall not apologise but begin by recalling the facts as I remember them that led up to my brother's death, the events that put me in a position to write this account. For though the event of my brother's passing and events of my story cannot be separated, my story is not after all about death, but about my escape and Lucia's; about my mother's and [aunt] Maiguru's entrapment' and about [cousin] Nyasha's rebellion — Nyasha, far-minded and isolated, my uncle's daughter, whose rebellion may not in the end have been successful.[24]

Accordingly, the first person narrative voice registers insightfully comprehensive about the nervous conditions of the female characters: impoverished mother, bulimic cousin, one defiantly promiscuous aunt and another, educated, demure and precariously poised between native tradition and anglicized modernity. However, that same voice will disingenuously retreat into a childlike mixture of awe and resentment to depict the native male — weak-willed father, arrogant man-child brother, aloof male cousin, and authoritarian uncle, family patriarch for all matters spiritual and financial — whose (heavy-handed) bid to escape their own entrapment is similarly discomfited. Consequently, the narrative sets up a false-positive conflict wherein the narrator must overcome these male figures even when the native condition of both remains over-determined by the selfsame negotiation of cultural expectations, social codes, material disparities and colonial hierarchies. The acknowledgement of those complicated interactions comes most boldly, albeit tardily, at the end of the novel, couched in the paranoid, and hence doubly 'unreliable' ravings of Tambu's self-destructive cousin, Nyasha:

> Do you see what they've [the nebulous white menace] done? They've taken us away.... All of us. They've deprived you of you, him of him, ourselves of each other. We're groveling.... Daddy grovels to them. We grovel to him.[25]

Then there are those whose groveling days are seemingly long past. In Sembene's film, the successful female entrepreneur Faat Kiné snubs the memory of her strictly traditional, poor, native, colonized father and the post-colonial fathers of her out-of-wedlock children. Despite the backward pull of these two mad natives, her commercial triumph at the gasoline franchise she runs unabashedly posits African woman's liberation from patri-local constraints — male pride and polygamy — and her consequent humanity in terms of a slightly more colourful, exotic and loud, but nonetheless faithful replica of *homo oeconomicus*, paragon of middle-class virtues of ownership and self-possession. Similarly, fictional black sisters in United States literature, having likewise excised the offending male member, exorcized in exchange for material stability, find themselves turning the colour purple from waiting to exhale or to be-loved while wondering how to get their groove on. Taken together, the demonization/erasure, whether the motivating premise of the story (*Nervous Conditions, Faat Kiné*) or a series of cumulating deletions which steer the evolving narrative structure (*Flores de otro mundo, Ekomo*), implies the global(ized) dispensability of the (fictional) Black male. Although these female protagonists might want what some women — or men for that matter — can expect, their 'self-cancelling, self assertion' (Wynter) posits a basic contradiction: 'Ain't i a eunuch?' In other words, rife with costly consequences, male erasing texts, distracted it seems by a vexed battle with woman's autonomy in its bourgeois metropolitan aspect, ironically castrate — not entirely in the sense intended by Germaine Greer — the potentiality and relevancy of the woman Black — in flesh and fiction.

The inquiry that motivates this examination of the expendable Black male in Latin America (and beyond) does not assume that Black female autonomy will spell the end of the 'sense of a common life and a common fate' (marital, cultural or political) or of the race. Neither is this an attempt to assuage frail or offended male egos or to excuse the storied mistreatment of the darker sister. Certainly the challenge to the character assassination long practised on the negated, polluted and trod upon African and African descended female protagonist has merit. Rather, in an effort to escape the 'existential weightlessness [of] an always "intellectually indentured" intelligentsia',[26] this analysis represents an attempt to decipher the contexts and presuppositions within which the degradation or the celebration of the woman Black takes place as a 'narrative necessity',[27] reflecting the systemic and imperative functions of her silencing or mouthiness, respectively. Admittedly, the texts juxtaposed as a whole offer a stunning vision of meta-textual migration through the use of rhetorical strategies such as the multiplication of points of view; an inter-textuality of narrative genres (history, literature, popular culture); and a simultaneity which overlaps temporal and spatial regions and ideological territories. Notwithstanding, in the creation of a brave new postmodern world, the reiterated state of unfreedom and the continual fragmentation of this narrative entity requires that she shadow box — while waiting for the real opponent to show him/her/itself, that she take pot shots at her own reflection. This requires a bit of history.

Typically, the representations of the woman Black within the Latin American canon includes stock characterizations of quaint and docile mammy figures; enterprising mistresses, the proverbially tragic *mulata* and a predictable host of degraded femininity: the overly sexualized, the overly masculinized, and the plainly monstrous, not unlike similarly complex and paradoxical North American characterizations. Michelle Wallace observes that:

> From the intricate web of mythology which surrounds the black woman, a fundamental image emerges. It is of a woman of inordinate strength, with an ability for tolerating an unusual amount of misery and heavy, distasteful work. This woman does not have the same fears, weaknesses and insecurities as other women, but believes herself to be and is, in fact, stronger emotionally than most men. Less of a woman in that she is less "feminine" and helpless, she is really *more* of a woman in that she is the embodiment of Mother Earth, the quintessential mother with infinite sexual, life-giving, and nurturing reserves. In other words, she is a superwoman.[28]

Likewise, According to Ann Venura-Young in her study of Hispanic poetry, *negra* and *mulata* are similarly divided: on the one hand, glorified as a steamy collection of swaying, dancing, gyrating body parts; on the other, pedestaled as mother, icon of middle-class respectability, but in the end denied a wholeness within the context she inhabits.[29] Even when honoured for her strength of character, she remains relegated to children's spaces, proscribed from the best social locations, a source of local colour, or — given the paucity of historical data — an anecdote. Taken individually, one might argue that such representations respond to specific historical or national contexts, offering purely symbolic devices or tropes as a shorthand to describe particular social issues or theoretical paradigms: progress-atavism; civilization-barbarism; rationality-irrationality; purity-promiscuity; order-chaos. However, the persistent repetition of this repertoire of images despite temporal or geographic boundaries — and the perennial absence of the African-descended male in the same works — instead points to an underlying and problematic coherency in Latin American racial practices and the ideologies that these spawn.

Of Porches and Plows

Positioned between this or that 'business proposition', the 'race after property and titles' and the 'love game',[30] the prosaic eunuch tacitly underscores a dissonance between acultural universalities and cultural idiosyncrasies. In the introduction to the republication of Greer's *The Female Eunuch*, Jennifer Baumgardner suggests that the second wave feminist 'was writing about autonomy, and she cast the culturally manacled, unliberated woman as a eunuch — her sexuality and will castrated'.[31] In her own introduction to the republished edition, Greer reminisces that her call was for 'freedom to be a person, with the dignity, integrity, nobility, passion, pride that constitute personhood',[32] a goal seemingly not so distant from Wynter's efforts to move toward the *human*. However one must first consider that the idea of autonomy for the woman Black represents a prepositionally nuanced proposition, the difference between freedom to, the aim of consolidating privilege, and freedom from, the aim of escape. Accordingly, since eunuch women could hardly expect the same dubious deference awarded to their counterparts, the 'now capable-of-rationality'[33] Black female protagonist has also to narratively negotiate the standard against which femaleness and female freedom are measured. Such is the case in Zora Neale Hurston's *Their Eyes Were Watching God* (1937/1990) when the 'citified' smooth talking Joe Starks woos Janie Mae Crawford Killicks with promises of 'change and chance':[34]

> You behind a plow! You ain't got no mo' business wid uh plow than uh hog is got wid uh holiday! You ain't got no business cuttin' up no seed p'taters neither. A pretty doll-baby lak you is made to sit on de front porch and rock and fan yo'self and eat p'taters dat other folks plant just special for you.[35]

Later, observing that her current beau 'Tea Cake ain't no Jody Starks',[36] Janie explains her own new-found bid for autonomy:

> [Grandma] was borned in slavery time when folks, dat is black folks, didn't sit down anytime dey felt lak it. So sittin' on porches lak de white madam looked lak uh mighty fine thing tuh her. Dat's whut she wanted for me — don't keer whut it cost. Git up on uh high chair and sit dere. She didn't have time tuh think whut tuh do after you got up on de stool uh do nothin'. De object wuz tuh git dere. So Ah got up on de high stool lak she told me, but Pheoby, Ah done nearly languished tuh death up dere.[37]

Notwithstanding, perspective and position come into play in Pheoby's guarded reply: 'Maybe so, Janie. Still and all Ah'd love tuh experience it for just one year. It look lak heben tuh me from where Ah'm at'.[38] Gray White reasons,

> [An] impossible task confronts the black woman. If she is rescued from the myth of the Negro, the myth of the woman traps her. If she escapes the myth of woman, the myth of the Negro still ensnares her. Since the myth of woman and the myth of the Negro are so similar,[39] to extract her from one gives the appearance of freeing her from both. She thus gains none of the deference and approbation that accrue from being perceived as weak and submissive, and she gains none of the advantages.[40]

Likewise, in *Flores de otro mundo*, the diverging perspectives of Patricia and Milady re-enact the same juxtaposition between 'look lak heben' and slow death. Their supposed emancipation, the shared consequence of their emigration from the Caribbean to Spain assumes a movement from — departure from somewhere not so good — and movement to — arrival to somewhere thought to be better economically or physically. That somewhere is pure pastoral, full of 'health and plenty', and 'humble happiness'[41] — filmically underscored by long and wide pans of breathtaking vistas of rolling hills scored with folkloric melodies. However, not far behind edenic perfection lurks the anti-pastoral: the reality of 'pains and plough', loneliness, racism — overt and proscribed— and life-negating bureaucracies. For Patricia, the pastoral setting represents a welcomed haven/heben from an abusive, hand-extended ex-husband and from the daily humiliations of an illegal alien in domestic service in metropolitan Madrid. She has arrived. Conversely, Milady's excruciating ennui frames the Spanish plains as a hellish respite, an extension of the eco-tourism that landed her there, further constricted by her lover's jealousy and possessiveness. Consequently, she never truly arrives.

The opening scenes of *Flores de otro mundo* sketch a fairly promising arrival for Patricia, replete with welcome, guidance, shift/re-adjustment and renewed commitment. First, a welcoming banner which reads *'Estaís en vuestra casa'* [you are in your house] greets her and the other prospective wives, arriving by chartered mini-bus on a sun-drenched morning set to peruse the rural town's eligible bachelors — and a motley crew they are. A marching band guides the vehicle to the centre of the village through a maze of narrow streets toward the orienting speeches of the festival organizer and the mayor. Later, there is a brief setback when, disillusioned by an unwanted sexual advance, Patricia brusquely steps away from the mass of dancing couples at the evening reception. However, despite her momentarily dashed expectations, she perseveres, attaching herself to a lanky, balding, stuttering suitor who, on the up side, is ploddingly stable and ... grateful. This opening prefigures her efforts throughout the course of the film to situate herself and to adjust the tension between di/con-verging desires: escape from, escape to. Patricia comes to display all 'the virtues of the farmer wife ... who made the home her primary sphere, who was a helpmeet to her husband, who raised her children according to Christian principles, who knew how to cook, sew, and garden'.⁴² Thus farmer wife Patricia's discursive attractiveness resides in her resemblance to another mythological figure who served so well in another context:

> Mammy was the perfect image for antebellum Southerners. As the personification of the ideal slave, and the ideal woman, Mammy was an ideal symbol for the patriarchal tradition. She was not just a product of the "cultural uplift" theory, she was *also* a product of the forces that in the South raised motherhood to sainthood. As part of the benign slave tradition, and as part of the cult of domesticity, Mammy was the centerpiece in the antebellum Southerner's perception of the perfectly organized society.⁴³

Patricia's plight represents the problem with postcolonial, postmodern 'hybrid' autonomy: her escape from the patri-local appeals to feminist discourse; her escape to the patri-global appeals to masculinist paradigms. In the end, the liminality of the woman Black affords her no approbation, nor advantage.

The type of arrival then tells the spectator a great deal about the fitness of the character in their new setting. Spaniard Damian, the accidental beau whom Patricia will eventually marry, never arrives — he does not have to because he belongs. The Cuban Milady arrives, but without fanfare in the small white truck of her would-be consort. She immediately stands out: her height, her blackness made all the more vivid with those star spangled spandex tights and the platform sneakers. Too hip for the confining limits of the sleepy village, she is road bound versus house bound like her friend Patricia. Milady's penchant for drugs and drink, mechanically proficient lovemaking, and *carpe diem* attitude contrast with the demure demeanor and virginal embrace that characterize Patricia. Consequently, she never arrives because she is intent on departure: escape from Cuba, escape to the neighbouring metropolis Valencia (discos and nightlife), escape from the oppressive Spanish pastoral vistas. While both relationships represent at base business arrangements, the Cuban baby doll embodies 'too much fashion and too many leisure pastimes and ornamental attainments':⁴⁴

a person governed almost entirely by her libido, a Jezebel character. In every way Jezebel was the counterimage of the mid-nineteenth century ideal of the Victorian lady. She did not lead men and children to God; piety was foreign to her. She saw no advantage in prudery, indeed domesticity paled in importance before matters of the flesh.[45]

Notwithstanding, Milady is no less desirable to the masculinist discourse as evinced by the salivating males, from pothead teens to toothless old men who follow her every move. She exists as the necessary antithesis/counterimage of 'normalcy'. On the one hand, since the standard is fitness not freedom, she underscores the (material) benefits which accrue to the farmer wife/mammy trope and the dicey prospective of flaunting its ideals, points of interest to feminist discourse. On the other hand, even while hinting at the fissures in the idyllic pastoral scenario, the proposed human order it insinuates, and no less the strings attached to autonomy, the Jezebel figure functions narratively — from the moment of her arrival — as a fail-safe release valve for pent up or dissipating energies, libidinal or otherwise.

For his part, Fran, Patricia's estranged husband, never arrives, he *appears*. On a first level this re-enacts the same magical feat as his alluded to disappearance when he abandoned the family. Since, in the context of the film, the ebony Adonis's unexpected/unplanned appearances are not welcomed, he is not welcome. Not only can he not provide for his spouse and offspring, he is portrayed as abusive, scheming, and selfish. Further, because of him, Patricia must enter into an initially loveless match in order to maintain her children, to safeguard their financial and more critically their juridical well-being (that is, precarious immigration status). Her premeditated rational decision tacitly condemns the predictably hot-blooded irrational sexual passion which presumably brought our heroine to this pass. While her proper arrival demands that the viewer focus her situation, the demonization of the man Black hardly taxes the imagination. Thus, the same elements — migration, legality, poverty — which centralize her plight, dismiss his. Notwithstanding, this seemingly diverging juxtaposition brings into focus their common plight in a racialized — and impoverished — context wherein they are forced to make vexed choices not of free will, but out of necessity.

Doubly manacled to the reality of the plough and the dream of the porch — the long denied status of baby-doll or white madam — eunuch womens understandably express the mimetic desire 'to git dere' — autonomy in its languishing pale bourgeois metropolitan aspect — 'don't keer whut it cost'. And heben comes quite dear. Patricia's bid for domestic security maroons her far from her native Dominican Republic on the lonely Spanish plains under the leery eye of her disapproving mother-in-law. In *Nervous Conditions*, Tambudzai's desire for escape from patriarchy eventually lands her in the midst of the beneficent racism and oppressive matriarchy of the convent school and in the novel's penultimate paragraph, she admits: 'I was beginning to have a suspicion, no more than the seed of a suspicion, that I had been too eager to leave the homestead and embrace the "Englishness" of the mission; and after that the more concentrated "Englishness" of Sacred Heart'.[46] In *Ekomo*, Nnanga Pequeña's odyssey carries her too far afield from those tribal structures which sustain her and within which she makes sense. Faat Kiné's thirst for self-possession threatens to isolate her emotionally, moving her children to instigate a search for a mate for their soon-to-be-empty nest mother. As Soujouner Truth and Neale Hurston's Janie had intuitively recognized, the bittersweet terms of their new-found autonomy — or nervous condition — tacitly calls into question the reach/location of ill-fitting universalist (European) paradigms and eunuch womens' psychic indenture to them.

Tellingly, in the original introduction to *The Female Eunuch*, Greer rightfully advises that 'women must learn how to question the most basic assumptions about feminine "normalcy" suggesting that 'the new assumption behind the discussion is that everything that we may observe *could be otherwise*'.[47] For the Black female protagonist in the works cited, everything is indeed otherwise since her existence refutes what is presented as the standard of 'feminine normalcy' from which women must liberate themselves. On the one hand, Greer contends that the 'normal' feminine 'characteristics that are praised and rewarded are those of the castrate — timidity, plumpness, languor, delicacy and preciosity', coincidentally Pheoby's idea of 'heben' and the basis of Janie's complaint 'Ah done nearly languished tuh death up dere'. On the other, Greer will suggest that 'The chief element in this process [the manufacture of the soul] is like the castration that we saw practised upon the body, the suppression and deflection of *Energy*'.[48] However while Greer focuses the 'sadomasochistic pattern' of 'masculine-feminine polarity'[49] Sojourner Truth had much earlier asserted otherwise: energies dissipated in the negotiation of the racist pattern of plough and porch polarity. In that context, plough not-quite femininity structures the ideal of porch femininity — that trail of signifiers upon which Jody Sparks and Pheoby grasped: a languishing, rocking chair existence tied to whiteness, specialness, ownership, privilege — which conversely exists in relation to its antithesis.

This distinction points to a disquieting partiality which presents itself when the second wave feminist admits that her treatise 'does not deal with poor women (for [she explains] when I wrote it [in 1970] I did not know them) but with the women of the rich world, whose oppression is seen by poor woman as freedom'[50] — clearly the case of Pheoby and Patricia. While such *mésconaissance* seems incredible, Greer moves to correct the oversight, reasoning:

> The sudden death of communism in 1989–90 catapulted poor women the world over into consumer society.... They had freedom to speak but no voice. They had freedom to buy essential services with money that they did not have, freedom to indulge in the oldest form of private enterprise, prostitution, prostitution of body, mind and soul to consumerism, or else freedom to starve, freedom to beg.[51]

Uncharitably, one might suggest that Greer apparently also 'did not know' of the liberation struggles in Africa; the political upheavals, dictatorships and dirty wars in Latin America; and, the history of chattel slavery and civil rights movements in the United States, struggles which all predate and presage the (Eastern) European event and upon which is based its rhetoric of emancipation and economic parity. Further, the woman Black was always *in* consumer society (bought and sold) although not necessarily at the altar before which knelt her western sisters 'of the rich world', a privileged sorority who fill their SUV tanks and expresso cups with products that contributed to (if not insured) the dehumanization and pauperization of the non-West.

Yet, Greer's courageous admission affirms that feminism has unwittingly — and successfully — inverted the paradigm it sought to undermine, putting the 'wo' before 'man'. Wynter notes that:

> [T]he projection of a new mode of extra-human agency represented as directly authoring our present ethno-class or descriptive statement of the human, *[Wo]Man,* not only enables *[Wo]Man's* over-representation as if it were the human itself, but also the over-representation of our present hegemonic imperative of securing the well being, security and overall interests of *[Wo]Man,* as if it were that of securing the well being, security and overall interests of the human species itself.[52]

While deconstructing the tenets of female normalcy, the newly projected mode established a paradigm of *feminist* normalcy, equated with the individualistic, self-possessed consuming middle-class woman. In other words, the impassioned plea for female autonomy dissipates its energies in the over-representation of the well-being 'of the rich world'. Traditionally poor, race women did battle with a draconian matriarchy: a topic that receives the attention of Aída Cartegena Portalatín in 'La llamaba Aurora' and Mayra Santos Febres's 'Marina y su olor' about young Black girls sent out to service who suffer the whims of their white mistresses and the prurient desires of their mistresses's male offspring and relations. Now, rather than being in 'continual revolt against [attempts] to dehumanize man',[53] the plough woman subsumes the needs and interests of the porch woman as her own.

This narrative shift implicit in the emboldened self-assertion of the now capable of rationality woman Black protagonist promises the dramatic rewriting of traditional relations of power. As Greer advises, 'The Ultra-feminine must refuse any longer to countenance the self-deception of the Omnipotent Administrator, not so much by assailing him as freeing herself from the desire to fulfill his expectations'.[54] This logic warns women to not become complicit in their own marginality for the sake of what appears to be security, legality, permanence paid for with frailty and disrupted enunciations. Conversely, right under the noses of the Omnipotent Administrator, right in the midst of folks disinclined to think they have any sense, let alone that they make any sense, 'ultra' woman Blacks like Sojourner and Wynter, with well-mannered mouthiness and belligerence, assail the absurdity of the presuppositions insinuated in the 'Janus-faced contradiction due to the partial and incomplete nature of the emancipatory breakthroughs in cognition, as well as the intellectual revolution of Renaissance humanism which was their seedbed, had set in motion'.[55] These buzzard hawks — and i mean that in a good way — recognize that the celebration of feminine emancipation without the attendant and continual revolt against attempts to under-represent the dynamics of race, class and imperialism often superciliously indulges woman of African descent. Texts patronize, or should I say matronize, their other-raced sisters.

The discursively blindered spot implicit in this over-representation instead re-energizes the 'sadomasochistic pattern' of an,

> economically defined mode of being. As a mode of being whose optimal referent nation-state worlds are logically those of the G7 rich, and so-called "developed countries," as contrasted with the poor and so-called "underdeveloped" countries; at the same time as its optimal referent subjects are the now increasingly incorporated global middle classes, to which as academics we all belong.[56]

Logically, over-representation disallows the otherwise. Understandingly, Tsitsi Dangarembga who also wears hats of scriptwriter and film director admits in an interview: 'I find it difficult to write about race.... Everything I have tried to write about it so far has sounded fantastic, absurd and unreal. I think this is the catch with racism — looked at objectively, it sounds too absurd to be true'.[57] Yet, women blacks inhabit an order within which, on the one patriarchal hand, 'the degradation of [wo]man is part and parcel of the elevation of man' and, on the other racist one, 'the degradation of [the negro] man is part and parcel of the elevation of [the negra and mulata wo]man'.[58] This absurdity — 'the contradiction inserted into the consolidated field of meanings of the ostensibly "universal" theory of feminism by the variable "race"'— underscores the liminality of the woman Black's and the woman native's 'role as the embodiment to varying degrees of an ostensible "primal" human nature'.[59] Thus as Caribbean historian Elsa Goveia notes in another instance, one system contradicts the other in fundamental ways, 'working from two completely different sets of premises: the conflict of directly opposing integrating factors',[60] the particularist and the universalist, and no less the masculinist/feminist, view of freedom from versus freedom to.[61] Consequently, voicing the black female protagonist does not solve or, more to the point, upset anything as Patricia's case proves.[62] Further, the same absurdity which manufactures poster-child eunuch womens and dispenses with the Black man 'by any means necessary', in its most fantastic and unreal aspect, ultimately signals the non-existence of Africa — the invisibility of peoples of African descent.

'Anything is possible with hard work'[63]

Faat Kine and *Nervous Conditions* strive to depict a torrid zone inhabited by ideal(ized) beings: exemplary workers graced by market profits (oil exploitation) or studious consumers-in-training 'who have managed to attain to [the West's] ethno-class criterion'[64] of 'breadwinner/investor/homo oeconomicus'.[65] The display of material prosperity or propensity for the same — pristine gasoline station or missionary compound, elegantly appointed spacious suburban home, monied attire, educational scholarships with the prospect of a bureaucratic position — seek to paint their respective corners of Africa as an infinitely inhabitable (developing) *locus amoenus*.[66] When denizens of the torrid zone invade the 'habitable' regions (whether that is civil service, Europe or a globalized market economy), their success or failure relies on their shedding their predisposed shiftless geographical existence and on their ability to get material. Thus the favoured figures in *Faat Kiné* as well as those in *Flores de otro mundo* possess the endearing non-torrid qualities of homo oeconomicus, accumulator of material goods. Unfitness within the terms of this model is reflected in the ragged grayness, poverty, squalor and sapped energy that engulfs the economically challenged or dependent denizens in *Nervous Conditions*, the majority, and all those in *Ekomo*. In *Flores de Otro Mundo*, the juxtaposition between the diligent Patricia, framed in panoramic pastoral long shot on the one hand and, on the other, the shiftless Milady and the jobless Fran, both captured against truncated glimpses of the urban centre or cramped interior shots which insinuate the constriction of character movement, extends this paradigm into the diaspora.

The favoured amenable subject implicitly subsumes the material standard of 'normalcy', that is the wants and needs of the projected model of economic mobility. A quixotic battle ensues where, on the one hand, the protagonist combats disparaging presuppositions of a needy Africa or disadvantaged diaspora and, on the other, narratively negotiates the standards against which humanness and human orderliness are measured in the brave new world logic of market value. From the fray, a counter-image emerges. Plagued by the instability and insecurity of poverty (migration, joblessness) and weighed down by non-Western tradition (griot, shaman, *curandero*), the native/ex-slave becomes sacrificial lamb just as s(he) had been the 'don't keer whut it cost' offerings to earlier strategies of civilization, progress and modernity.[67] Thus, the fact that the African or the descendent of kidnapped Africans who still suffer the effects of that religious, cultural, political and economic upheaval 'invades' the former empire or its discourses *and* finds idyllic peace there represents a special kind of cynicism.[68] Wynter would suggest that in order for the 'chains-to-autonomy' and 'rags to riches' scenarios to function,

> the processes of their functioning must be *discursively* instituted, regulated *and* at the same time normalized, legitimated.... [W]hat institutes regulates, normalizes and legitimates what then controls us, is the *economic* conception of the human — *Man* — that is produced by the disciplinary discourses of our now planetary system of academia as the first purely secular and operational public identity in human history. While this identity induces us all to behave as producers, traders or consumers, it unifies us as a species in *economically* rather than, as before, in *theologically* absolute terms.... Now, up until the end of the eighteenth century in the West, the conception was primarily *political*; up until the fifteenth century it was primarily *religious*... it is the bioeconomic conception of the human that we inscript and institute by means of our present disciplines and their epistemic order ... that determines the hegemony of the *economic* system over the social and political systems — even more that mandates the functioning of the capitalist mode of production as the everyday expression of that hegemony.[69]

In other words, the hard work of discourse lies in getting everything to fit, under-representing or erasing disparities. Not surprisingly, the vestiges of past conceptions of the human, both ideal and pariah, seemingly denormalized and delegitimized, remain metonymically active within the new conception, thus the emphasis on economic ascendency through education (*Nervous Conditions*) or by acquiescence to a sacrificial contract (by self-imposed celibacy in *Faat Kine* or through advantageous liaison/union in *Flores*).

Accordingly, the bioeconomic standard against which the cited protagonists now unwittingly measure themselves re-energizes an earlier orthodoxy. In that context, Wynter recalls '*the specific presupposition* of the orthodox geography' and the fundamental challenge launched by Columbus as a result of 'his fervent millenarian beliefs'.[70] She observes that:

> In the orthodox geography of the time, the earth was presupposed to be divided into two non-homogeneous areas, those inside God's grace which were habitable [and] those outside it which had to be uninhabitable. So as a result, not only was there the presupposition, at least before the voyages of the Portuguese disproved it, that the Torrid Zone, and therefore Africa, south of the Sahara, had to be *inhabitable*. There had also been another presupposition linked to the first. This was that the land of the Western Hemisphere *had to be*, within the logic of the Christian-Aristotelian physics of the time, under water, in its natural place, rather than being held up above the element of water, by God's providential grace. Therefore, non-existent![71]

Despite this view, Africa wills itself into existence in the works analysed here. Therein lies the problem of the intellectually indentured resistance which, in the attempt to do otherwise, inadvertently legitimizes and normalizes the adept student of Western culture and practices (especially, the missionary zeal of the first generation Christian), the landed political citizen, and the economically invested, therefore, necessarily excluding the invincibly ignorant skeptic or pagan; the dependent colonial native; the landless, non-citizen immigrant-refugee; and the jobless, under/unemployed, and dis-invested subaltern.

In the New World a similar paradigm again sought to erase Africa. The serial globalizations of the narrative of Africa's uninhabitability reproduces itself in the invisibility/erasure of the African descended in the diaspora. Walterio Carbonell explains:

> [at the end of colonialism] Africa became a disturbing word for so-called educated people. Africa was a kind of a Babylon whose name evoked lust. And they were right. Africa was lust in both senses of the word, in the lewdness and material appetites of those Pharysees on the plantations and in the churches. They turned the male into a material thing, a trade object, a commodity; and the female into an object of double possession, a possession for work and a sexual possession.... Africa was the source of wealth on which the bourgeois republic was later built. But its name evoked the abominable origins of bourgeois wealth and as such had to be erased from political and social life.[72]

Aided by feminist and womanist discourse and no less by masculinist paradigms, the black female protagonist re-emerges, phoenix-like. As in the case of mammy, the inclusion of eunuch womens, however paradoxically, represents the ideal centrepiece of a perfectly organized multicultural and globalized discourse. Fittingly, outside the logic of that projected human order, anybody left in the wake becomes, by narrative necessity, expendable: non-existent, and erased. Enter, or rather, exit the man Black.

Whereas arrival represented the telling trope in *Flores*, in *Ekomo* the manner of departure, how each character 'shuffles off this mortal coil' infers his/her fitness for the incoming bioeconomic configuration. At the end of the opening chapter, Fang villagers are on edge because a tribal seer has predicted the deaths of two unnamed victims, an elder and a young man. A series of troubling events represent the basis of this prediction, first the discovery of an adulterous relationship and a menacing sky (eclipse?). The interdependence of cause and effect, sign and meaning, establishes from the beginning the intimate tie between imminent and transcendent, between natural and supernatural. The first person narrative then employs a structure which combines/juxtaposes this motivating prefiguration with flashback memory. Just as the death of Tambu's brother in *Nervous Conditions* puts her in a position to tell the story, so too the death of the tribal elder, of the European educated Nfumbaha and of her husband put Nnanga Pequeña on the storyteller's stool. The deaths of the males then serve narrative necessity while her voicing fulfills narrative destiny.

The elder — *el abuelo 'hombre de hierbas'* [grandfather, shaman] — succumbs soon enough, after having delivered a list of directives to be followed after his death, almost two full pages of detailed instructions.[73] He wastes away and dies — or does he? Once, twice, the villagers think him deceased and undertake funeral preparations, the second time going so far as to bury the man's emaciated body. However, each time, the former warrior shows definite, albeit weak, signs of life, much to the shock and consternation of the would-be mourners. Inexplicably, an aged stranger arrives shouting insults and challenges to the moribund elder:

> Aquel que venía maldiciendo era el enemigo que esperaba el anciano. Insultó y maldijo a nuestros ancestros, exhortando que se enfrentase a él algún valiente del pueblo.[74]

> (That one that came spouting profanities was the enemy that the old man had awaited. He insulted and profaned our ancestors, exhorting some valiant member of the village to confront him).

Since it would be unseemly that warriors and real men die in their beds,[75] a bloody battle ensues and the elder is slain, and, with him, something of Africa's traditional past. Thus it now falls to the newly voiced narrator to explain in luscious detail the ceremonies which were the purview of the fallen warrior — those secrets which accompanied him to the grave.[76]

The narrator wonders if Ekomo, her husband, whose swollen leg daily grows worse, '¿Será el próximo?'[77] (Will he be the next?) A reprieve comes in the guise of the death/disappearance of the European trained Nfumbaha, more palatably presented than the anglicized uncle in *Nervous Conditions*. Flaunting the warnings pronounced by the dying elder, Nfumbaha enters the proscribed jungle:

> Nfumbaha había estado mucho tiempo en Europa, y había perdido el respeto a la tradición. Podia salvarse quizás del embrujo de la selva, porque era ya medio blanco. "Quizás".... La gente continuó cada uno en su quehacer, sin pensar ni mucho ni poco en ello. Al fin y al cabo, Nfumbaha ya no era como nosotros. Dijo que no podía soportar seguir en ese estado y salía a la selva para buscar algún venado.[78]

(Nfumbaha had spent a lot of time in Europe and he had lost respect for tradition. Perhaps he could save himself from the jungle's spell because he was already half white. "Perhaps" .... People continued each one at their task without thinking a lot or a little about it. Whatever the case, Nfumbaha was no longer like us. He said that he could not stand continuing in this state and he left for the jungle in order to hunt for deer.)

Within the context of the novel, Nfumbaha's 'hunting trip' upsets the interdependence of cause and effect, sign and meaning, the tie between imminent and transcendent, between natural and supernatural and serves for a more cosmological source of mourning.

Nfumbaha, el africano de hoy, hombre del mañana, tras estar dos lluvias en Europa, dejó su tradición encerrada entre los libros; dejó allí su personalidad y sus creencias africanas, y el ser sin continente regresó a su pueblo con un disfraz del europeo sin el europeo dentro. Con una máscara de Europa pero sin su rostro en ella. Medio blanco, medio negro. Sus hermanos salieron en su busca porque le amaban, se arriesgaron dos días en la selva porque eran sus hermanos. Las lágrimas de la madres son las del Africa y sus lamentos se esparcen alagados por el aire hasta los confines de la tierra por todos aquellos hijos perdidos y no hallados. ¿Quiénes puede escuchar el llanto de la madre Africa sin sentir compasión por esa mujer que no hace mas que echar hijos al mundo para ver como poco a poco van perdiéndo su personalidad? Y sin embargo, cada vez que cae uno de sus hijos, Africa llora personificandose en cada una de las madres del Nfumbaha. Hijos prefabricados por los supermercados de la evolución histórica, que sin embargo no evolucionan y hablan de política, comercio y religión, que les son ajenos, sin detenerse a examinar el verdadero sentido de las cosas, y mueren con las chaquetas puestas seguros de haber cumplido su misión.[79]

(Nfumbaha, the African of today, man of tomorrow, after having been two years in Europe, abandoned his tradition locked between books, abandoned there his personality and his African beliefs, and the continent-less being returned to his village clad in European trappings without the European essence inside. With a European mask but without his face behind it. Half white, half black. His brothers went searching for him because they loved him, they risked their lives for two days in the bush, because they were his brothers. The tears of the mothers are those of Africa and her lamentations — scattered by air to the ends of the earth — for all those lost and not found children. Who can listen to the cry of Mother Africa without feeling compassion for this woman who has done nothing more than cast her sons to the world to see how, little by little, they would lose their personality? And without exception, each time one of her sons falls, Africa cries personifying herself in each one of the mothers of Nfumbahas. Prefabricated children by supermarkets of historical evolution that however do not evolve and speak of politics, business and religion that is distant from them, without stopping to examine the true sense of things and die clad in suit coats, assured that they have fulfilled their mission.)

Nfumbaha — which is to say, his ghost — returns from the excursion transformed

Unos ojos cubiertos de arrugas, canas y escarhas, pero terriblemente jóvenes en una cara muy viejo. El pelo completamente blanco casi le cae sobre los hombros. Tieso como un palo parece un guerrero al acecho del enemigo.[80]

(Eyes covered with wrinkles, gray hairs and but terribly young in a very old face. The hair completely white falls almost to his shoulders. Thin as a rail he looks like a warrior in search of the enemy.)

The nebulous foe does not appear to put an end to his existential suffering and thus his de-africanized uneasy spirit — poignantly outside European logic and dead to the Fang cosmovision — lingers hauntingly. The spectre's return serves to frame the death of Nfumbaha as a cautionary tale.

The deaths of the *abuelo* and Nfumbaha thus fulfill the 'theologically absolute terms' of the prediction and its 'primarily religious' concept of being. What then discursively institutes them, which is to say their *raison d'être* — both the orthodoxy of the elder and the transgressive liminality of the younger figure — fittingly reflect the Fang tribal sense of cosmic equilibrium, cause and effect. Conversely, Ekomo who will die in bed, evokes a 'purely secular and operational identity', which serves to underscore the non-life affirming aspect and vacuity of the present 'bioeconomic conception of the human ... that determines the hegemony of the *economic* system over the social and political systems'.[81] In the first two cases, there exists an immediacy of cause — the cosmic imbalance wrought by adultery and confirmed by the eclipse — and effect, the richly ceremonial deaths of two men. Ekomo's lingering and worsening infirmity — for which both narrator and reader still hope for a miracle that might spare the young man — points to the unsoundness of the various systems he must negotiate on his odyssey. Accordingly, the passings of *abuelo* and Nfumbaha, in their affirmation of Fang honour and order, evoke sacred meanings, while the slow and painful death march of Ekomo, absent mythical foes and magic forests, remains more mundane — and senseless. The manner of departure then juxtaposes duelling discourses: tradition/transcendence (theologically absolute terms) and modernity/imminence (the bioeconomic concept of being), even as the three, which recall the Christian trinity, remain inextricably bound together.

Ekomo metaphorically represents Africa Present, a composite of struggles with traditional and modern discursive permutations and between theological and bioeconomic orthodoxies. In his posture as *brujo*, the young man recalls the *abuelo, hombre de hiebras*, Africa Past. At the same time he postulates the future, his adulterous adventure in the (national) urban metropolis — root cause of his disabling disease and ultimate demise and first step towards the European metropolis— re-enacts Nfumbaha's misadventure in Europe, root cause of his allegorical extinction and his transgression into the tabooed *selva* (a misadventure akin to Eve's trespass at the tree of knowledge). However Ekomo's tie to non-Western tradition (tribal tradition of bride price and kidnapping and the ritual punishment of widows) and his careless behaviour towards his wife seal his fate in the womanist context while his nativeness and his economic marginality exclude him from masculinist discourse. His illness first takes him to the shadowy encampment of a native *curandero*, then to the sterile whiteness of the hospital across national borders to the French-speaking Gabon, and finally to the less than welcoming confines of the Christian mission. In order to return to health, to become human — 'normalized, legitimized' — according to the tenets of each scenario, he is asked to confess psychic reticence in the first, in the second, to consent to physical amputation; and, in the last, to convert to save his eternal soul but not necessarily his deteriorating body — and always to pay for the privilege. Tellingly, the *curandero*'s solicitous attention the Nnanga Pequeña contrasts with his impatient dismissal of Ekomo. The surgeon bluntly offers his prognosis, failing to understand what the amputation would mean to Ekomo's ability to support himself, literally and figuratively.

Ekomo's worsening physical state or biological unfitness symbolizes his failure to conform to each succeeding requirement and signals his inability to participate in the curative benefits of those discourses, insinuating a more thoroughgoing ontological unfitness. After his death, the unbaptized Ekomo provides the best evidence for the narrative necessity of his own erasure. Not a Christian, his body cannot be interred in sacred ground; or a denizen of the mission, no technicality argues for his burial in that honorary European national territory. Since the couple's limited funds have been exhausted by catastrophic illness, his widow lacks the means to purchase the urban prescribed burial shroud, coffin and plot. Not unlike the uninhabitable Africa he embodies, he remains outside God's grace, the reaches of modern medicine and bureaucratic orderliness. Thus even in death his (in)humanity determines his (dis)placement.

As Ekomo succumbs to the ravages of the infection that courses through his leg and then his entire body, the person who sees him through all his travails is Nnanga Pequeña. Consequently, his (Christian) wife must by default become more vociferous and take more and more responsibility for her once dashing ebony knight — now emaciated and moribund — who will meet the unmanly, unwarriorlike end of dying in his bed (really a pallet on the floor of the mission's infirmary). Thus Nnanga Pequeña becomes fully human: physically stronger and more savvy in terms of negotiations with the outside world. Even while she may not fully understand their meanings, her narrative voice holds together the di/converging universes, the theological and the bioeconomic. Yet, crushed by mourning, she lingers between dream and reality, life and death, observing: 'Mi mente, un poco aturdida no sabe si está en el presente, pasado o en el futuro'[82] (my mind, a bit confused, does not know if it is in the present, past or future). The *Pastor* arrives, *deus ex machina*, to save her from the prescribed tribal rituals and joins her father in suggesting the violation of taboo, thereby rescuing the disgraced widow. Her reintegration into the tribal cosmology require her purification in which her hair is shorn, her clothing discarded and she bathes in the river '*para que el agua, al correr, arrastre todas sus desventuras*'[83] (so that the water, as it flows, might carry away her misadventures). Cleansed, reborn and free after a fashion, Nnanga acknowledges at the end of the book: '*Abro los jos, eso creo, y me encuentro confundida entre la gente, Mas .... ¡qué sola! ¡Qué tremendamente sola estoy!*'[84] (I open my eyes or so I believe and I find myself surrounded. But .... so alone. How incredibly alone am I!). While the reader cannot fault the transformation of this highly sympathetic protagonist, this poignant lament recalls the costly consequences and the unintended and problematic meanings which also surface in the Human Order insinuated in the other texts discussed in this essay.

Conclusion

Thus, just as the discovery/encounter/Middle Passage which inserts the Black into the fact and fiction of the West engenders vexed pronouncements of celebration or condemnation[85], so too the voicing of the woman Black in the texts examined here. On the one hand, the impassioned call for female autonomy brings the buzzard hawk into being as a classed, raced and gendered entity whose inclusion promises, 'to change the reality of all of us'. The ascendency of the Black female protagonist which shifts from the silenced subaltern à la Gayatri Spivak[86] to the proliferation of vocally gifted daughters of Sycorax who vociferously haunt the teleological event-driven narrative which traditionally muzzled and muddled their enunciations, is a good thing. Yet, on the other, the placement that lifts up the buzzard hawk into both hegemonic and contestatory imaginaries, paradoxically central to the situational frame of reference of both, reveals the presence of a contradiction. The black-faced projection of 'specific presuppositions of orthodox systems of meaning' demands the harshest of condemnations no matter its source, not for her figurative serviceability, but rather for the cynical discovery and conquest that attempts to normalize and legitimize the 'stable production and reproduction of our present Western-bourgeois social order', and 'the material conditions of existence' which dehumanize man. The situational frame into which the female Black protagonist has been made to enter comes at the hidden cost of a sacrificial contract and the absence of their phenotypical mate.

Thus in order to get to *after man*, writers and critics must disentangle themselves from the 'absolutism of an earlier order'[87] — the itch to grovel, 'to git dere' — 'don't keer whut it cost', to fulfil the expectations of the current Omnipotent Administrator's mode of being. In just this instance, Wynter suggests the need 'to make opaque to ourselves, the reality of our own agency with respect to the programming and reprogramming of our desires, our behaviours, our minds, ourselves, the I and the we'.[88] For these literary representations to challenge 'everyday practices', they must not lose the 'sense of a common life and a common fate', 'the single history we now live'.[89] Those representations that once confirmed the world of the worldview must now strive to produce an otherwise concept of being human and to secure the well being, not of the falsely universalized individual, but of the village. That 'conception is *the* imperative'.[90]

Notes

N.B. All translations in the text are mine unless otherwise noted. In the fine tradition of e.e. cummings and bell hooks, i do not capitalize the personal subject pronoun.

1. Sylvia Wynter, 'The Prespective Specific to the Post-1492 Caribbean and Post-1444 Black African [Ex-slave and Ex-colonial] Diaspora: As that of the category bearer of a projected Bio-evolutionary dysselected Human Order and therefore liminal, status to our present, Western-bourgeois or ethno-class conception of the human, Man', 10. (Position paper for After Man, Towards the Human. Kingston, Jamaica, June 2002).
2. Sylvia Wynter, 'After/Word: Beyond Miranda's Meanings: Un/silencing the "Demonic Ground" of Caliban's "Woman"' in *Routledge Reader in Caribbean Literature*, eds. Donnell and Lawson Welsh (London: Routledge, 1996), 480.
3. Ibid., 480-481.
4. Addison Gayle, 'Blueprint for Black Criticism', *First World: An International Journal of Black Thought* (January/February 1977): 43.
5. Richard Wright, 'Blueprint for Negro Writing', *New Challenge: A Literary Quarterly* (Fall 1937): 57.
6. The discourse was poorly transcribed thus i use two sources: Margaret Busby, ed., *Daughters of Africa: An International Anthology of Word and Writings by Women of African Descent from the Ancient Egyptian to the Present* (London: Jonathan Cape, 1992), 38-39 and two accounts contained in Foner Phillips and Robert James Branham, eds., *Lift Every Voice* (Tuscaloosa: University of Alabama Press, 1998), 226-229.
7. Margaret Busby, *Daughters of Africa*, 38.
8. Sylvia Wynter, 'After/Word', 476.
9. Foner Phillips and Robert James Branham, *Lift Every Voice*, 229.
10. Sylvia Wynter, 'After/Word', 480.
11. Quotation attributed to Sylvia Wynter at conference in her honour. 'After Man, Towards the Human' (Kingston, Jamaica, June 2002).

12. Asmarom Legesse, *Gada: Three Approaches to the Study of an African Society* (New York: The Free Press, 1973), 114.
13. Ibid., 115.
14. Ibid., 114.
15. Ibid.
16. Foner Phillips and Robert James Branham, *Lift Every Voice*, 229.
17. Hans Blumenburg cited in Sylvia Wynter 'After/Word', 356. See also Hans Blumenburg, *The Legitimacy of the Modern Age* (Cambridge: MIT Press, 1983).
18. Asmarom Legesse, *Gada*, 115.
19. See especially the prickly protagonists in Adalberto Ortiz's *Juyungo* (1943) and Arnoldo Palacios's *Las estrellas son negras* (1949).
20. See for example two Spanish films *Bwana* (Imanol Uribe, 1996) and *Cartas de Alou* (Montxo Armendáriz, 1996) [Letters from Alou] which each feature an African male protagonist and make clear the very different treatment of male emigrés on Spanish soil.
21. See also critical discussions by Maria Zielina Limonta, 'Ekomo: Representación del pensamiento mítico, la magia y la psicología de un pueblo "Fang"', *Afro-Hispanic Review* 19, no.1 (Spring 2001): 93-101 and M'Bare N'gom, 'Relato de una vida y escritura femenina: Ekomo, de María Nsue Angüe', *Journal of Afro-Latin American Studies & Literature* 3, no. 1 (Spring 1995): 77-92.
22. See critical essay Christopher N. Okonkwo, 'Space Matters: Form and Narrative in *Nervous Conditions*', *Research in African Literatures* 34, no. 2 (Summer 2003): 53-74.
23. Tsitsi Dangarembga, *Nervous Conditions* c1988. (New York: Seal Press, 2001), 1.
24. Ibid.
25. Ibid., 200.
26. Sylvia Wynter 'After/Word', 480.
27. 'Adam must have sinned by narrative necessity'. Kenneth Burke quoted by Sylvia Wynter in *Boundary 2* article 12, nos. 3 and 13, no. 1 (Spring/Fall 1984): 19-70, 'The Ceremony Must be Found: After Humanism'.
28. Michelle Wallace, *Black Macho and the Myth of the Superwoman* (New York: Dial, 1979), 107.
29. See Ventura-Young, 'Black Women in Hispanic America Poetry: Glorification, Deification and Humanization', *Afro-Hispanic Review* 1, no. 1 (January 1982): 23-28.
30. Zora Neale Hurston, *Their Eyes Were Watching God* [1937] (New York: Harper & Row, 1990), 108.
31. Jennifer Baumgardner, 'Introduction' in Greer '*The Female Eunuch*' (New York: Farrar, Straus and Giroux, 2001), 3.
32. Germaine Greer, *The Female Eunuch* ([1970] New York: Farrar, Straus and Giroux, 2001), 11.
33. Sylvia Wynter, 'After/word', 113.
34. Zora Neale Hurston, *Their Eyes Were Watching God*, 28.
35. Ibid.
36. Ibid., 108.
37. Ibid., 109.
38. Ibid.
39. '[B]oth blacks and women are characterized as infantile, irresponsible, submissive, and promiscuous. Both blacks and women have generally been dependent politically and economically. Both groups are consigned to roles that are subservient, both groups have shared a relationship of powerlessness ... and both groups, as a matter of automatic response, have been treated as

outsiders and inferiors'. Deborah Gray White, *Ar'b't I a Woman? Female Slaves in the Plantation South* (New York: Norton, 1985), 28.
40. Deborah Gray White, *Ar'b't I a Woman? Female Salves in the Plantation South* (New York: Norton, 1985), 27-28.
41. See Robert Bone, *Down Home: A History of Afro-American Short Fiction from its Beginning to the End of the Harlem Renaissance* (New York: Capricorn Books, Putman's Sons, 1975).
42. Deborah Gray White, *Ar'b't I a Woman?*, 56.
43. Ibid., 58. See also Barbara Neely, *Blanche Passes Go* (Penguin: New York, 2000), where detective Blanche White muses on her own narrow escape from the mammy syndrome:

> She'd been lucky enough to be born without a mammy gene or a case of Darkies' Disease, but she didn't press her luck by trying to befriend her employers' families. Even so, she knew how easy it was to slip into a Darkie crouch, eyes lifted toward the employer as loved one. Darkies' Disease was like any other — nobody planned to get it. It just crept up on some people when their emotional immune systems were damaged from having had to grin at one too many insults or otherwise kiss ass to keep a job they probably didn't want but couldn't live without. Or people caught the disease from their parents, or grew into it out of their own self-hatred. (71)

44. Deborah Gray White, *Ar'b't I a Woman?*, 56.
45. Ibid., 29.
46. Tsitsi Dangarembga, *Nervous Conditions*, 203.
47. Germaine Greer, *The Female Eunuch*, 17.
48. Ibid., 18.
49. Ibid., 19.
50. Ibid., 11.
51. Ibid.
52. Sylvia Wynter, 'The Perspective Specific to the Post-1492 Caribbean and Post-1444 Black African', 10.
53. Addison Gayle, 'Blueprint for Black Criticism', 43.
54. Germaine Greer, *The Female Eunuch*, 21.
55. Sylvia Wynter (David Scott), 'The Re-Enchantment of Humanism: An Interview with Sylvia Wynter', *Small Axe* 8 (September 2000): 119–207, 194.
56. Sylvia Wynter, 'The Perspective Specific to the Post-1492 Caribbean and Post-1444 Black African', 10
57. Tsitsi Dangarembga, *Nervous Conditions*, 205.
58. Sylvia Wynter, 'The Re-Enchantment of Humanism', 195.
59. Wynter, 'After/Word', 476.
60. Elsa Goveia 'The Social Framework', *Savacou: A Journal of the Caribbean Artists Movement* 2 (September 1970): 7-15, 11.
61. Ibid., 14-15.
62. This thought echoes another described by Germaine Greer in *The Female Eunuch*:

> The opponents of female suffrage lamented that woman's emancipation would mean the end of marriage, morality and the state; their extremism was more clear-sighted than the woolly benevolence of liberals and humanists, who thought that giving women a measure of freedom would not upset anything. (26)

63. On The CBS Morning Show, December 12, 2002, Jennifer 'J. Lo' Lopez, promoting her film *Maid in Manhattan*, itself the celebration of the economic mode of being, recalled her parents' advice to her.
64. Sylvia Wynter, 'The Re-Enchantment of Humanism', 160.
65. Sylvia Wynter 'Thematic Outline' (Unpublished presentation for 'After Man, Towards the Human' Conference Kingston, Jamaica, June 2002), 1.
66. Alexander McCall Smith's slightly less problematic mystery series about *The No. 1 Ladies' Detective Agency* (and later installments *Tears of the Giraffe* and *Morality for Beautiful Girls*) tend to repeat this spatial idealization of Botswana.
67. See for example, Chinua Achebe's *Things Fall Apart* ([1959] New York: Fawcett, n.d.)
68. Here Greer gets it right (*The Female Eunuch*):

> The relationships recognized by our society, and dignified with full privileges, are only those which are binding, symbiotic, economically determined. The most generous, tender, spontaneous relationship deliquesces into the approved mould when it avails itself of the approved buttresses legality, security, permanence. (22)

69. Sylvia Wynter, 'The Re-Enchantment of Hunmanism', 160.
70. Ibid., 192.
71. Ibid.
72. Walterio Carbonell, 'Birth of a National Culture' in *AfroCuba: An Anthology of Cuban Writing on Race, Politics and Culture*, eds. Sarduy and Stubbs. Trans. Jean Stubbs (Melbourne: Ocean Press, 1993), 195-203, 196. See also Walterio Carbonell, *Como surgió la cultura nacional* (La Habana: Crítica, 1961).
73. See Nsue Angüe, *Ekomo* (Madrid: Universidad Nacional de Educación a Distanica, 1985), 36-37.
74. Ibid., 39.
75. See also Adalberto Ortiz's *Juyungo* ([1943] La Habana: Colección Literatura Latinoamericana, Casa de las Américas, 1982).
76. These revelations re-enact the recent commercialization of Santeria in Cuba and Candomblé in Brazil, the object of guided tours and cheap souvenirs.
77. Nsue Angüe, *Ekomo*, 49.
78. Ibid., 59-60.
79. Ibid., 85.
80. Ibid., 87.
81. Wynter 'The Re-Enchantment of Humanism', 160.
82. Nsue Angüe, *Ekomo*, 190.
83. Ibid., 194.
84. Ibid.
85. See Wynter 'The Eye of the Other' in *Blacks in Hispanic Literature*, ed. Miriam DeCosta. (Port Washington, NY: National University Press, 1977).
86. See Gayatri Spivak, 'Can the Subaltern Speak?' in *Marxism and the Interpretation of Culture*, eds. Cary Nelson and Lawrence Grossberg. (Urbana: University of Illinois Press, 1988), 271-313.
87. Sylvia Wynter, 'The Re-Enchantment of Humanism', 195
88. Ibid., 194.
89. Ibid., 191.
90. Ibid., 160.

6 | *Reading Said and Wynter on Liberation*

Aaron K. Kamugisha

Introduction[1]

Colonial discourse analysis was initiated as an academic sub-discipline within literary and cultural theory by Edward Said's Orientalism. *This is not to suggest that colonialism had not been studied before then, but it was Said who shifted the study of colonialism among cultural critics towards its* **discursive** *operations, showing the intimate connection between the language and forms of knowledge developed for the study of cultures and the history of colonialism and imperialism.*[2]

—Robert Young

The presentation of Edward Said's *Orientalism*[3] as inaugurating a decisive 'break' with previous understandings of the nature of colonialism is a good place to start a critical reflection on one renowned theorist in what has quickly become the 'tradition' of postcolonial studies; and on another great thinker whose work has been stunningly overlooked in the academy, but is of deep relevance to all people concerned with human liberation. Said's work, *Culture and Imperialism*, attempts on a grand scale to deal with the importance of culture in the conflictual interactions between colonized and colonizer. *Culture and Imperialism* represents not just an additional decade of reflections by Said on this relationship, but is perhaps the most daring, synthetic theoretical perspective on the clash of cultures during colonialism in a generation.[4] In developing the theme of resistance to imperialism, he makes a number of observations on the Caribbean colonial context, and borrows heavily from the ideas of a number of Caribbean theorists of liberation. Conversely, Sylvia Wynter, has emerged in the last 15 years as potentially one of the most important Caribbean thinkers of the twenty-first century. However, only recently has attention been paid to her ever-increasing corpus of critical essays, and her idea of a new pathway to liberation for Africana people worldwide. The need to reflect on themes of liberation seems especially pertinent in contemporary times, given the fact that we are living in an age which some call neo-colonial, and others have suggested might be more appropriately termed one of recolonization.[5]

There are a number of striking similarities in the work of Edward Said and Sylvia Wynter. Both attribute to culture a pivotal role in the institution and reproduction of imperialism. In stark contrast to postmodern disavowals of humanism, Said and Wynter are committed to a revolutionary type of humanism, while at the same time incorporating some post-structuralist arguments into their work.[6] Finally, both heavily mobilize Caribbean theorists in their attempts to find a pathway to liberation for oppressed people worldwide.[7] The aim of my discussion is to interrogate the way the theme of liberation in the Caribbean intellectual tradition is used in the work of Said and Wynter.

Edward Said's *Culture and Imperialism*

Scattered references to the Caribbean can be found throughout *Culture and Imperialism*, but it is in Chapter 3, titled 'Resistance and Opposition', that Said directly engages with Caribbean theorists of liberation and this is the chapter which I believe is the nub of his work.[8] It is at this point — when the colonized disavow the hegemony of the colonizer's appropriation of the word — that we begin to understand Said's vision of postcolonial liberation. A few brief comments on Said's intellectual influences and his position within contemporary debates in the academy are important. Said's *Orientalism* was substantially influenced by Foucault, but in *Culture and Imperialism* his comparison of Foucault with Fanon comes out in favour of the latter, as he suggests that 'Foucault's work moves further and further away from serious consideration of social wholes, focussing instead upon the individual as dissolved in an ineluctably advancing "microphysics of power" that it is hopeless to resist'.[9] Foucault thus 'paradoxically fortifies the prestige of both the lonely individual scholar and the system that contains him', which is further reinforced by his distancing of himself from politics.[10] Such a lack of engagement with the political is anathema to Said, who for many years was one of the most articulate and passionate voices on behalf of the Palestinian people in the United States.[11] The dilemma of the literary scholar, accustomed to close readings of texts and uncomfortable with essentialisms and the activist is one of the more fascinating issues played out within *Culture and Imperialism*, and has a marked effect on a number of Said's insights.

Said identifies three great issues in cultural resistance to imperialism, and the process of decolonization that resulted from it. These are the right to re-imagine the nation as a discrete community; the process of resistance as a new concept of human history; and thirdly — and most directly relevant to my concerns — the move from 'separatist nationalism toward a more integrative view of human community and human liberation'.[12] In a particularly poignant passage, Said suggests where he believes true human liberation might lie. He notes:

> There is also, however, a consistent intellectual trend within the nationalist consensus that is vitally critical, that refuses the short-term blandishments of separatist and triumphalist slogans in favor of the larger, more generous human realities of community among cultures, peoples, and societies. This community is the real human liberation portended by the resistance to imperialism.[13]

Moving towards this new human liberation must result in a thoroughgoing critique of the limitations of previous resistance movements. Here the spectre of Third World nationalism raises its head, and Said's response to the difficulties of nationalism highlights for us his understanding of important issues in the Caribbean colonial and postcolonial condition. His position on nationalism is not quite as severe as Anne McKlintock's, for whom 'all nationalisms are gendered, all are invented, and all are dangerous'.[14] Rather, while acknowledging the 'imagined community' that nationalism creates, Said warns those that might avow a quick dismissal of anti-colonial movements that 'at its best, nationalist resistance to imperialism was always critical of itself',[15] and it was 'only one of the aspects of resistance, and not the most interesting or enduring one'.[16] In a longer comment on his view on nationalism, he makes his position clear:

I do not want to be misunderstood as advocating a simple anti-nationalist position. It is historical fact that nationalism — restoration of community, assertion of identity, emergence of new cultural practices — as a mobilized political force instigated and then advanced the struggle against Western domination everywhere in the non-European world. It is no more useful to oppose that than to oppose Newton's discovery of gravity.[17]

Yet, of course, nationalism has its pitfalls. When we turn to examine Said's position on what Adotevi has called 'the strategy of culture', a stronger engagement with cultural nationalism develops.[18] He suggests that popular Garveyite slogans like 'Africa for the Africans' may be part of a slippage into a dangerous form of 'chauvinism and xenophobia'. This seems an awfully presentist reading, and one that ignores the historical location of Garveyism, at a time in which nearly all of Africa was under colonial domination. In a longer take on nativism, Said would conclude the following:

> Nativism, alas, reinforces the distinction even while revaluating the weaker or subservient partner. And it has often led to *compelling but demagogic* assertions about a native past, narrative or actuality that stands free from worldly time itself. One sees this in such enterprises as Senghor's *negritude*, or in the Rastafarian movement, or in the Garveyite back to Africa project for American blacks, or in the rediscoveries of various unsullied, pre-colonial Muslim essences (emphasis added).[19]

Surely a perspective that locates Rastafari as a seemingly excessive reaction to the tyranny of cultural imperialism, a retreat into an essentialized 'blackness' rather than an embrace of the supposed cosmopolitanism that cultural mixing might bring, should be disturbing for Caribbeanists. There is no need for me to burden myself with refuting this point after four decades of scholarship on Rastafarianism, probably the cultural movement in the post-independence era that has had the most decisive impact on re-imagining Africa in the minds of Caribbean people.[20]

Turning more directly to individual Caribbean thinkers, Said's fulsome praise of C.L.R. James's all-embracing worldview comes with the price of a too-hasty reading of his legacy. James is mobilized by

Said in order to critique (even though not altogether disparagingly) black cultural nationalism in the following manner: 'Well after negritude, Black Nationalism, and the nativism of the 1960s and 1970s, James supported the Western heritage at the same time that he belonged to the insurrectionary anti-imperialist moment'.[21] Said then goes on to quote James from a 1984 interview with the *Third World Book Review*.

> How am I to return to non-European roots? If it means that Caribbean writers today should be aware that there are emphases in their writing that we owe to non-European, non-Shakespearean roots, and the past in music that is not Beethoven, that I agree. But I don't like them posed there in the way they have been posed *either*-or. I don't think so. I think *both* of them. And fundamentally we are a people whose literacy and aesthetic past is rooted in western European civilization.[22]

What Said fails to mention is that James, in his next breath, states that 'we of the Caribbean have not got an African past. We are black in skin, but the African civilization is not ours. The basis of our civilization in the Caribbean is an adaptation of Western civilization'.[23] Puzzlingly, James declares that the relevance of Shakespeare, Beethoven, and Rembrandt extends to *all* people of the world who are willing to appreciate and gain some insight into what they have to offer. The question that arises here is why European civilization is a universal legacy that can be appropriated by all who wish to do so, but Africa is a legacy particular to only Africans on the continent, and not in the diaspora. Nor is this an isolated comment by James. When asked about Kamau Brathwaite's work in a 1972 interview he declared, 'There is something artificial about Brathwaite — he goes to Africa to find out and then writes about it'.[24] James, so comfortable with drawing links between Greek theatre and cricket in *Beyond a Boundary* and the small size of the city state and Caribbean societies in *Modern Politics*, clearly suggests here that Greek 'roots' are legitimate, while African ones are not. The marvelous intellectual contribution to Caribbean thought of the man Paul Buhle has aptly called the 'paradoxical pan-Africanist' seems to contain a strand which might be inimical to an articulation of African diasporic consciousness, and one that deserves a more thoroughgoing critique than Edward Said's quick appropriation for the purposes of praising James's cosmopolitanism.[25]

The Place of Fanon

I have previously noted Said's praise of the work of the revolutionary theoretician Frantz Fanon. Fanon occupies a pivotal place in the history of Third World liberation for Said, as he 'more dramatically and decisively than anyone ... express(ed) the immense cultural shift from the terrain of nationalist independence to the theoretical domain of liberation'.[26] Fanon's rejection of both imperialism and its 'nationalist antagonist' are the reason for the immense value of his ideas a generation after *The Wretched of the Earth*.[27] The difficulty with Fanon for Said is that 'having committed himself to combat both imperialism and orthodox nationalism by a counter-narrative of great deconstructive power ... (he) could not make the complexity and anti-identitarian force of that counter-narrative explicit'.[28] While Said correctly suggests that Fanon may have seen liberation as a *process* rather than a condition reached with flag independence, the search for ways to use Fanon's legacy to counter new forms of global repression of Third World people is not engaged by Said.[29] Instead, in the final pages of Chapter 3, Said utilizes Aimé Césaire's famous *Cahier d'un retour au pays natal*, (*Return to My Native Land*), and C.L.R. James's reading of it. After reading James's take on Césaire's *Cahier*, Said declares, 'I doubt that anyone can take from it some repeatable doctrine, reusable theory, or memorable story, much less the bureaucracy of a future state'.[30] This comment is disappointing as it leaves us to wonder what means, other than poetics, can usher in liberation, at a time when real concerns of cultural hegemony, to say nothing of political-economic hegemony, still exist.

In a salutary review of *Culture and Imperialism*, Benita Parry highlights a number of concerns she has with Said's text.[31] Parry points out the shortcomings of Said's avoidance of a direct engagement with capitalism, and questions also his 'perfunctory references to Césaire, Fanon and Cabral, Walter Rodney and C.L.R. James as *Marxists*'.[32] Said's inability to fully discuss class strikes me as a shortcoming, as, for all his contrapuntal readings, he does not elaborate on what *class* among the colonized did not find the colonizer to be an 'implacable adversary'. Simply put, did Fanon's *damnés* think 'contrapuntally'? Do we know? Parry asks the critical question, 'how ... do we discuss coercion and oppression if we are under the obligation of reading imperialism contrapuntally?'[33] While Said's 'dizzying electicism' may be salutary, as is his 'refus(al) to abandon now unfashionable narratives of human emancipation, and ... (retention of) an affiliation to a politics of fulfillment'[34] his perspective that Fanon was unable to 'make the complexity and anti-identitarian force of ... (the) ... counter-narrative (to imperialism) explicit' seems closer to a prescient meditation on the nature of his own project.[35] Reading Said gives us a brilliant survey of the terrain of liberation, but we still lack the epistemic break that might herald it in. He himself notes that,

> The one place where I feel a tremendous lack on my part, through ignorance, is in failing to make as many connections as I'd have liked between the Western humanists and comparable figures in the non-European world.[36]

Said's typical candour, and forthright appraisal on his relationship to Third-World thought in his above comment, may seem somewhat disingenuous, given his reflections on Césaire, Fanon and James, but he is absolutely correct when one considers his lack of knowledge of the scholarship of Sylvia Wynter.[37] Said's willingness to speak of — and theorize — liberation is, however, refreshing, as is his interest in utilizing Caribbean thinkers as *theorists*, despite my disagreements with him on his interpretation of some of these theorists, and on specific issues. Africana and Caribbean critics are not peripheral to his schema, and *Culture and Imperialism* is not the only example of this. In *Representations of the Intellectual*, Said notes that 'figures like (James) Baldwin and Malcolm X define the kind of work that has most influenced my own representations of the intellectual's consciousness'.[38] This is a shift in Said's position which has been overlooked and *undertheorized* by both supporters and critics of his scholarship alike.[39]

The status of Caribbean critical thought, and the disinterest of a number of metropolitan critics in acknowledging it, has recently been exposed in two penetrating essays by David Chioni Moore and Mimi Sheller.[40] Moore argues that the MLA honorary scholars list is 'terribly Eurocentric', as it excludes any African or Caribbean *theorists*. While Moore does not present a straightforward case of institutional bias, recognizing the presence of a number of African and Caribbean writers on the honorary fellows list, he suggests that it reinscribes the old colonial relationship of the Third World providing raw material (in this case writers) for metropolitan consumption (by its critics). In a meditation on these trends, Sheller advances a consideration of 'what happens when "postmodern" and "postcolonial" theorists consume figurations of intermixture and subaltern agency to claim the Caribbean for "global culture"'.[41] Tracking the movement of terms invented by Caribbean theorists like 'transculturation', 'transversality', and especially 'creolization', is Sheller's concern, as the term creolization has moved from a 'politically engaged term used by Caribbean theorists located in the Caribbean in the 1970s, to one used by Caribbean diaspora theorists located outside of the Caribbean in the 1980s, and finally to non-Caribbean "global" theorists in the 1990s'.[42] This easy adoption of terms indigenous to the Caribbean — often without acknowledging the region of their birth or their creation as a paradigm to interpret patterns of struggle and contention — leaves the 'current "creolization paradigm" with little to contribute to an operative theory of conflict and unequal power relations'.[43] Comments like the following in the well-known text *The Empire Writes Back: Theory and Practice in Postcolonial Literatures* — 'It is ... the Caribbean which has been the crucible of the most extensive and challenging post-colonial theory' — is not matched by supposedly authoritative works like the recent *Norton Anthology of Theory and Criticism*.[44] The question arises if Caribbean theorists' general reluctance to embrace postmodern cultural theory — with the exception of Antonio Benitez-Rojo — licenses a use of their literary and cultural ideas while their provenance in the Caribbean is glossed or forgotten entirely.

In a recent reflection on postmodernism and conservatism in the academy, Lewis Gordon remarked that 'it is difficult to talk about human beings these days' since there exists in so much of contemporary academia the 'preemption of the human in human subjects for the sake of ... pseudopolitical and pseudoethical concerns'.[45] Continuing the theme of this discussion in another essay, and contrasting what the question of humanism means for African-Americans compared to its location in Western thought, Gordon suggests that 'for African-Americans ... humanistic anxieties emerged over the historical reality of a people whose humanity was denied under a specific set of historical circumstances. This denial is well known under the nomenclature of modern slavery and racism'.[46] Postmodernism's 'recent declarations of the death of "man" and humanism' are difficult for self-identified African-American postmoderns like Cornel West and Patricia Hill Collins, who 'consider themselves humanists for obvious reasons; dominant groups can "give up" humanism for the simple fact that *their humanity* is presumed, while other communities have struggled too long for the humanistic prize'.[47] Similarly, in his defense of Fanon's idea of a new humanism, Robert Bernasconi responds to Robert Young's misgivings about whether there really exists a substantial difference between the old humanism and Fanon's new humanism by stating that 'whereas European humanism is differential and survives only so long as the non-European is defined as sub-human, the new humanism liberates both colonized and colonizer'.[48] In a warning to all who would too quickly dismiss radical Third World humanisms, Bernasconi suggests that 'theoreticians should avoid trying to disarm it ahead of time by presuming that they always know where it will lead'.[49]

When one begins to reflect on 'radical Africana humanism' as part of the 'nature of the Black radical tradition' we find it appears in places we might not have previously thought it existed.[50] Consider, for example, Steve Biko's response to the liberal perspective on apartheid:

> Black Consciousness defines the situation differently. The *thesis* is in fact a strong white racism and therefore, the *antithesis* to this must, *ipso facto*, be a strong solidarity amongst the blacks on whom this white racism seeks to prey. Out of these two situations we can therefore hope to reach some kind of balance — a true humanity where power politics will have no place.[51]

Or alternatively, Malcolm X long a militant firebrand with the Nation of Islam, Malcolm X underwent a conversion while on his trip to Mecca that considerably altered his understandings of race, nationalism and culture. His perception of the kind of *human* which was needed to effect the struggle changed dramatically. In his own words, let us hear about an encounter he had the day after the press conference at which he declared his new ideological stance:

> The next day I was in my car driving along the freeway when at a red light another car pulled alongside. A white woman was driving and on the passenger's side, next to me, was a white man. *"Malcolm X!"* he

called out — and when I looked, he stuck his hand out of his car, across at me, grinning. "Do you mind shaking hands with a white man?" Imagine that! Just as the traffic light turned green, I told him, "I don't mind shaking hands with human beings. Are you one?"[52]

The question is, how do we account for a radical tradition that joins Biko, Malcolm X, C.L.R. James, Fanon, Césaire and Wynter?

One way might be to go back to first principles, and ferret out what are their commonly articulated concerns, one of which I want to suggest is a radical demystification of Western man as the universal. It is this which leads me more directly to the scholarship of Sylvia Wynter. No short essay could do justice to the sophistication of Wynter's thought. In sketching her perspective on liberation and the Caribbean intellectual imagination, I will limit my discussion to themes of transcendental liberation that emerge throughout her more than three decades of critical thought. I will further consider her location within a tradition of 'radical Caribbean humanism'. The insights of Paget Henry and David Scott — that she gives us 'more conscious control over the founding and reproduction of liminal categories',[53] and that her work might be best located 'in (the) unevenly overlapping space where the agonistic humanism of Fanon's anticolonialism crosses … the embattled antihumanism of Foucault's archaeological critique'[54] — respectively, are of considerable importance here. One possible interpretation of Wynter is to read her work as a series of critical movements, a type of dialectical progression, towards, to use Elsa Goveia's fine phrase, a better 'understanding of the true nature of our present ambiguous situation'.[55]

From her first essay 'We Must Learn to Sit Down Together and Discuss a Little Culture — Reflection on West Indian Writing and Criticism' in 1968, Wynter suggested that the 'twentieth century revolution must essentially be a cultural revolution; a transformation in the way men see and feel'.[56] While in 'Sambos and Minstrels' she suggests that the 'pain, the angst of those posited as non-norms … compelled examination of the functioning of the Symbolic order itself'.[57] Her fine essay 'Ethno Or Socio Poetics' sees her working through Immanuel Wallerstein's world systems theories and back to the sixteenth century in order to understand the mutation in the concept of the human that was Renaissance humanism. The specific point of this essay is to 'develop

(a) thesis of Western secular ethnocentrism in which the West became the we to the ethnos of all other peoples, who all became the other'.[58] 'The Ceremony Must Be Found: After Humanism', often considered Wynter's landmark essay, argues that the epistemological shift of Renaissance humanism invented secular man, an achievement that was inherently flawed, since the human was invented on the basis of one 'type' — that of Western bourgeois man. In Wynter's words:

> The heresy of the Studia was, therefore, to lie in its break with the higher system of divinely sanctioned identity and with its absolutized world views or ratiomorphic apparatus; in its release of rhetorical man from the margins, orienting his behaviours by a new ordering secular Logos, the Natural Logos of Humanism which took the place of the Christian Theologos.[59]

This newly invented Western man conceived as its other the people of the Americas and Africa, the consequences of which are known all too well. The challenge that Wynter places before us is to effect a transformation of a similar magnitude to that of the Renaissance, and create a body of thought that for the first time can result in the birth of the human:

> The *Studia* must be reinvented as a higher order of human knowledge, able to provide an "outer view" which takes the human rather than any one of its variations as Subject; (and be) ... reformulated as a science of human systems, which makes use of multiple frames of reference.[60]

The problem with previous humanisms is in part that they were only ethno-humanisms, constructed on the premise that Western-bourgeois man was *the* human. Pressed in an interview with David Scott on why we should 're-enchant the human in humanism', Wynter would state that 'we have to recognize the dimensions of the breakthroughs that these first humanisms made possible at the level of human cognition, and therefore of the possibility of our eventual emancipation, of our eventual full autonomy, as humans'.[61] The link to recent defenses of a carefully contextualized universalism here is clear.[62] Wynter proposes nothing less than a "planetary humanism", and these concerns have been the premise behind her major theoretical explorations since, whether during a debate on development in Africa or female circumcision, or the Caribbean intellectual tradition, to which I will now turn.[63]

Radical Humanism in the Caribbean

The Caribbean novelist George Lamming asserts that,

> If we assume man to be man, and his relation to the world to be a human one, then love can be exchanged only for love, trust for trust, and so on.[64]

For Sylvia Wynter, the advent of independence in the Caribbean signalled a shift from a political imperialism to a 'properly epistemological imperialism'.[65] The crisis of the Caribbean at the moment is that while we are aware of, and have been engaged in the past with a battle for political and economic sovereignty, we still have not yet come to terms with the need for 'ontological sovereignty'.[66] It is this crisis, as present today as at the moment of independence, that demands a rethinking of our very understanding of what is the nature of being human, a task which Wynter takes on in one of the most ambitious philosophical projects by a Caribbeanist to date.

Locating Wynter in the tradition of 'radical Caribbean humanism', or 'embattled humanism' is best done via a rereading of the best representatives of this tradition, Aimé Césaire and Frantz Fanon.[67] Césaire's *Discourse on Colonialism* represents one of the greatest, and most withering denunciations of the nature of European imperialism in the anti-colonial struggle. The horror of colonialism renders Europe indefensible in the arena of reason or humanity.[68] While no claim for 'ethnic purity' can be countenanced, and contact between 'civilizations' in and of itself is a salutary enterprise, colonialism resulted not in contact but conquest, racism, and genocide. The question of the break from colonialism becomes not the 'either-or' of a return to a utopian past but the creation of a new society. This society will have to be created by those cast aside by Europe, as 'the West has never been further from being able to live a true humanism — a humanism made to the measure of the world'.[69]

Fanon similarly demonstrates that a move past Europe is critical for the process of national liberation. The 'crisis of European man' for

Fanon, is that Europe has been responsible for only a 'succession of negations of man' which necessitates leaving Europe behind in the need to conceptualize a new man.[70] The Third World must thus attempt to create a

> new *history* of Man, a history which will have regard to the sometimes prodigious theses which Europe has put forward, but which will also not forget Europe's crimes, of which the most horrible was committed in the heart of man, and consisted of the pathological tearing apart of his functions and the crumbling away of his unity (emphasis added).[71]

Wynter's mobilization of Césaire and Fanon is quite different from Edward Said's. The true excellence of Césaire's contribution lies not within the *Notebook*, but in a series of essays published mainly in *Tropiques* in the early 1940s, the most prominent of which is 'Poetry and Knowledge'.[72] After villifying modern scientific knowledge which has led to a man 'depersonalized and deindividualized' from himself, Césaire suggests modern science may be little more than the 'ponderous verification of a few wild images thrown up by poets'. And here Césaire makes his leap, in his speculation that 'Just as the new Cartesian algebra has allowed the construction of a theoretical physics, so the *original handling of the word* can make a new science (theoretical and impartial), of which poetry can already give us a fairly good idea.[73] Césaire's new *science of the word* allows him not only to 'refuse the shadow'[74] cast as his lot by Western civilization, but to propose, in a quest to redefine the human, that we return to the earliest days of the species, during which man was 'closer to certain truths' — a direct link with Wynter's idea of the birth of human consciousness as a 'first emergence'. Conversely, Fanon is engaged by Wynter as the theoretician *par excellence* who extrapolated the idea of ontogeny and sociogeny to the condition of the wretched of the earth. She observes:

> Franz Fanon has pointed out — in his book *Black Skins, White Masks* — that Freud oversaw the fact that at the level of the human life, the organic process of ontogenesis, is always accompanied by the culturally instituted processes of sociogenesis. It is this rupture with the purely organic processes of ontogenesis and its correlation with the always culture-systemic processes of sociogenesis that can be defined as the

first emergence. For this was a process by which all human forms of life, and their languaging living systems, can now be seen to have come into being only on the basis of their rupture with the genetically regulated circuits of organic life, therefore, for the narratively instituted symbolic circuits that were to orient our socialized modes of subjectivity and of interaltruistic symbolic conspecificity, or non-genetically determined variant forms of "kin" recognition and misrecongnition that are defining of human "forms of life".[75]

I have previously mentioned that a central concern for Wynter is the move towards an 'ontological sovereignty'. Wynter suggests that the process towards 'ontological sovereignty' will require an epistemological rupture with contemporary understandings of humanity. Perhaps the best way to approach Wynter's unique contribution to humanism is to quote her in full:

> "Man" is not the human, although it represents itself as if it were. It is a specific, local-cultural conception of the human, that of the Judaeo-Christian West, in its now purely secularised form. Its *'Other'* therefore is not *woman*, as I hope to show. Rather because *Man* conceives of itself, through its origin narrative or 'official creation story' of Evolution, as having been bio-evolutionarily selected, its *'Other'* and *'Others'* are necessarily those categories of humans who are projected, in the terms of the same Origin narrative, as having been bio-evolutionarily dysselected — i.e. all *native* peoples, and most extremely, to the ultimate zero degree, all peoples of African descent, wholly or partly (i.e. *negroes*) who are negatively marked as *defective humans* within the terms of Man's self-conception, and its related understanding of what it is to *be* human.[76]

Speaking on the aims of the cinematic text which she posits as central to the 'representational apparatus of our Western world system', Wynter suggests that the meaning of African cinema will be to 'redefine what it means to *be* human':[77]

> because *Man* further defines itself as *homo oeconomicus*, in the reoccupied place of its pre-nineteenth-century conception of itself as *homo politicus* (political man), as well as in that of its originally matrix

feudal-Christian conception of itself as *homo religious* (religious man), its *'Other'*... is the category of the *Poor*, i.e. the jobless and semi-jobless; as well as, in terms of the global system as a whole, the so-called 'underdeveloped' countries of the world. While because economic *Man* is optimally defined as the *Breadwinner* (with the working classes thereby being defined as secondary Breadwinners to the middle classes, specifically to their investor upper class), the *'Other'* to this definition is, logically, the category of the *jobless, semi-jobless Poor*, together with that of the underdeveloped countries, both of which are made to actualise the negative alterity status of *defective Breadwinners*.[78]

In contradistinction to Said, Wynter does not see Rastafari as a movement that is linked more with a regressive form of 'cultural insiderism' than true liberation. Instead, for Wynter Rastafari is 'transforming symbols, it is re-semanticizing them',[79] since in its 'determined refusal of the "great fictions that pour in upon them from every side"' it is, in fact 'reinventing the imaginaire social, refusing that of Babylon, and creating a new vision of life for the whole body of people'.[80] In a similar, but more complicated, argument, she defends Negritude — or at least Césaire's brand of it — against its critics. For Wynter, Césaire's negritude could never be a retreat into a cultural insiderism that romanticizes blackness, but a 'refus(al) (to accept) the black's role as conceptual other to the representation of Generic man ... (and thus) calls in question our present order of being'.[81] This is truly what Stuart Hall has referred to as 'honour(ing) the moment that I am trying to surpass' — a highly sophisticated series of reflections on Africana intellectual movements that honours them for their contribution to their moment, rather than judging them solely on the basis of our contemporary concerns.[82]

The central purpose in formulating a response to the representation of the West as a universal, rather than a local culture like all others, is the deconstruction of what Wynter refers to as the presentation of Western man as *the* human. The epistemic shift to this understanding by Wynter takes its point of departure:

> from the First Emergence of *fully* human forms of life, as an Emergence that was to be later attested by, *inter alia*, the convergent explosion at multiple sites of the rock paintings of some 30,000 years ago, including

that of the Grotto Apollo of Namibia; as an explosion whose dynamic moving images bear witness to the presence of the representational apparatus inscripting of their 'forms of life', of their culture-specific modes or poeses of being human. This hypothesis, as one which places our origins in *Representation* rather than in *Evolution*, and thereby redefines the human outside the terms of its present hegemonic Western-bourgeois conception as a purely bio-economic being which pre-exists the event of culture, would, of course, call for a new poetics. This poetics, I propose, would be that of the human as *homo culturans/ culturata*, that is, as the auto-instituting ... self-inscripting mode of being, which is, in turn, reciprocally enculturated by the conception of itself which it has created; the poetics, in effect, of a hybrid *nature-culture, bios/logos* form of life bio-evolutionarily preprogrammed to institute, inscript itself, (by means of its invented origin narratives up to and including our contemporary half-scientific, half-mythic origin narrative of *Evolution*), as this or that *culture-centric* (and as also, in our case, *class-centric*) genre of being human.[83]

Wynter's brilliant formulations provide the epistemic break which not only allows us a powerful paradigm for critiquing Euro-class centrism, but points a way forward in our understanding of the conflictual identity formations in the Caribbean 'postcolony'.[84] Her analysis makes meaningful the phrase 'Third World liberation' rather than simply African liberation, as the status of Third World people as 'defective breadwinners' applies as easily to the masses suffering under capitalist exploitation in south east Asia, India, and the native peoples of Australia, New Zealand, the Amazon — and the Caribbean, for Walter Rodney the 'laboratory of racism'. The term 'euro-class centrism' as a continuation of Fanon's 'greedy little caste' critique of the black bourgeoisie centrally places Third World elites desire to attain European cultural capital as a fundamental problem for Third World liberation movements.[85] Her move to a new understanding of the nature of being human demands a turn from the concept of man as a bioeconomic being, to man as a cultural being. Wynter thus answers the suggestion made by Wilson Harris, in his *History, Fable and Myth* series of lectures that 'the structure of intellectual moral protest ... will remain an embalmed posture until immense new disciplines [a new anthropology I would think] can assess original divergences from claustrophobic, political ritual'.[86]

This move to man as *homo culturans/culturata*, and the necessary deconstruction of the privileging of the contemporary culture of the West as universal, can be approached from the perspective of the cultures of Africa. Hence the importance for Wynter of moving our critique of European hegemony and articulation of a new vision of humanity back to 'the first emergence of *fully* human forms of life' as seen in the rock paintings of 30,000 years ago in Africa.[87] A synthesis between this and the understanding that under the current 'order of things' Africana people are the most dysselected from the *status* of humanity truly creates the conditions for a change to our western-bourgeois epistemological order and a powerful argument for the legitimacy of an Africana philosophy. It also points to new pathways by which the vexed 'tradition versus modernity' debates in Africa and the Caribbean might finally be reconciled. The momentous task facing the Third World intelligentsia is to have the moral and intellectual courage, and *epistemic daring*, to ask for the human after man.

Jazz, Cricket, and Final Thoughts on Reading the 'Sylvia Wynter Songbook'

Yet the question quickly arises — does the human exist in the contemporary? Indeed, can it? With the extraordinary power of the 'abductive systems' of Western civilization, in their new guise of neoliberal globalization to manufacture consent in the postcolony and metropolis alike, where are the resources through which we might begin to speak of new possibilities of liberation?[88]

My final speculations here can offer but a partial answer. In the midst of their dizzyingly wonderful duet *Stomping at the Savoy*, Louis Armstrong begs Ella to 'make the break'.[89] It might be too much of an exaggeration to claim that he was referring to breaking with Western epistemological hegemony. However, as Wynter notes on Jazz (and James):

> The great unifying forms of our times are no longer, as in the case of cricket, coded, under the hegemony of middle-class cultural mores. What we are experiencing is a cultural shift of historical magnitude, a

shift that James pointed to in the lectures on modern politics given in Trinidad. The great unifying cultural forms of our times, beginning with the jazz culture and its derivatives, are popular. This is the significance of calypso and Carnival, of the reggae and Rastafarianism. This is the significance of the Jamesian poiesis.[90]

And so, thinking about the Caribbean popular for my conclusion, we can now appreciate why the figure of Matthew Bondman is so important for Wynter, as it earlier was for C.L.R. James. Let us read Wynter's perspective on both Bondman and James: 'Bondman lived next door in Tunapuna to James, the child. "His eyes were fierce, his language was violent and his voice was loud", he refused to take a job but "with a bat in his hand [he] was all grace and style".'[91] Bondman was not one of the 'deserving proletariat'; he was, according to James's aunts, 'good for nothing else except to play cricket'.[92] But — and here Wynter makes her intervention —

> To realize their own powers, to give them full play, the Bondmans had to live in an alternative cosmology, an underground culture which they reconstituted for themselves. In addition, it meant that the total blockage of the realization of their powers, the prevention of their living of their own radical historicity, their subordination, to the historicality of the productive forces would therefore impel the Bondmans of the world (*Les damnes de la terre* as Fanon defines them) to demand, *to desire as that by which alone they can live*, not the liberation of the productive force (Liberalism and Marxism-Leninism) but the "liberation of Man".[93]

Wynter declares that 'Bondman, like the Blacks of the ghetto-prisoner-system-shanty towns archipelago of the modern world system, had not always been useless'. Cricket was not 'play' for Bondman, but an 'alternative life-activity in its own right'.[94] Jazz, cricket and more recent forms of the Caribbean popular-like dancehall may well contain intimations of the human in the contemporary.[95] Or, to put it all much more succinctly — Liberation Jazz! Liberation dancehall! Liberation cricket![96]

Notes

1. *Acknowledgements*: I would like to thank Paget Henry, Mimi Sheller, Greg Thomas and Rinaldo Walcott for their comments on an earlier draft of this paper. While doing the final major edit of this essay, I received the news that Edward Said had died in New York. This essay, in a book in honour of Sylvia Wynter, is dedicated both to her *and* Edward Said.
2. Robert Young, 'Egypt in America: *Black Athena*, Racism and Colonial Discourse' in *Racism, Modernity and Identity: On the Western Front*, eds. Ali Rattansi and Sallie Westwood (Cambridge, UK: Polity Press, 1994), 150.
3. See also Ato Quayson's observation that *Orientalism* was the first to make 'a clear connection between knowledge and power, thereby inserting a poststructuralist problematic into the study of colonialism'. Ato Quayson, *Postcolonialism: Theory, Practice or Process?* (Cambridge: Polity Press, 2000), 4.
4. The previous 'generation' that I refer to is the generation that was actively involved in the anti-colonial struggle. My suggestion is that *Culture and Imperialism* may be the most influential work of its kind from the first 'post-colonial' generation, with Frantz Fanon's masterpiece *The Wretched of the Earth* being the best example from the anti-colonial generation.
5. For use of the concept 'recolonization' as a new form of colonialism as distinct from 'neo-colonialism' see 'Resist Recolonisation! General Declaration by the Delegates and Participants at the Seventh Pan-African Congress' in *Imagining Home: Class, Culture and Nationalism in the African Diaspora*, eds. Sidney Lemelle and Robin Kelley (New York: Verso, 1997); George A.V. Belle, 'Against Colonialism: Political Theory and Re-colonisation in the Caribbean' (presented at the Conference on Caribbean culture, March 3-5 1996, University of the West Indies, Mona Campus); Chen Chimutengwende, 'Pan-Africanism and the second liberation of Africa' *'Race & Class* 38, no.3 (1997). Also see Lewis R. Gordon' use of the term neo-colonial in his collection of essays *Her Majesty's Other Children: Sketches of Racism from a Neocolonial Age* (Maryland: Rowman & Littlefield, 1997).
6. This is clearly apparent in Sylvia Wynter's work, as will be shown. While not establishing what this new humanism might look like in the manner of Wynter, Edward Said has said that 'there is nothing I disagree with in the broad, humanistic tradition'. Said's concern seems to be that humanism has 'always stopped short of national boundaries', denying the humanity of populations not apparently related to the 'us' of nationalism. Edward Said, 'Expanding Humanism: An Interview' in *Wild Orchids and Trotsky: Messages from American Universities*, ed. Mark Edmundson (New York: Penguin Books, 1993).
7. These brief comments by no means exhaust the interesting convergences in the projects of Sylvia Wynter and Edward Said. Questions can also be fruitfully raised about their ambivalence towards Marxism, and (in this case with a greater degree of dissonance) their perspectives on the role of the 'secular intellectual' and religion in liberation struggles.
8. I am not primarily concerned with Said's take on the Caribbean in his reading of Jane Austen's *Mansfield Park*. This is not to suggest that this reading is without merit, for as Benita Parry has observed, 'Said claims that Austen in construing a significant imbalance, offers the Caribbean no status imaginatively, geographically or economically other than that of a sugar-producer permanently subordinated to Mansfield Park'. Benita Parry, 'Imagining Empire: From *Mansfield Park* to Antigua', *New Formations* 20 (1993): 182. While I will discuss Said's perspectives on Caribbean thinkers like C.L.R.

James, Frantz Fanon and Aimé Césaire, he also utilizes the work of George Lamming and Walter Rodney.
9. Edward Said, *Culture and Imperialism* (New York: Random House, 1994), 278.
10. Ibid., 278.
11. In a longer commentary on Foucault, Said states that he 'wouldn't go as far as saying that Foucault rationalized power, or that he legitimized its dominion and its ravages by declaring them inevitable, but I would say that his interest in domination was critical but not finally as contestatory, or as oppositional as on the surface it seems to be.' Edward Said, 'Foucault and the Imagination of Power' in *Foucault: A Critical Reader*, ed. David Couzens Hoy (Oxford: Basil Blackwell Ltd, 1986). These are shrewd words indeed. In a quite astonishing comment in an interview with Mark Edmundson, Said declares that he finds Derrida and Foucault, 'especially in the early seventies and thereafter ... fantastically Eurocentric. They were interested only in Europe — not even Europe, really. They were Franco-centric'. Edward Said, 'Expanding Humanism: An Interview' in *Wild Orchids and Trotsky: Messages from American Universities*, ed. Mark Edmundson (New York: Penguin Books, 1993). Sylvia Wynter herself has noted that despite the 'illuminating nature of his thesis ... Derrida does not himself move, in any fundamental sense, outside the limits of the monocultural field of the west, outside the limits of what it now *calls* human'. See David Scott, 'The Re-enchantment of Humanism: An Interview with Sylvia Wynter', *Small Axe* 8 (2000): 206.
12. Ibid., 215-216.
13. Ibid., 217.
14. Anne McKlintock, 'No Longer in a Future Heaven: Women and Nationalism in South Africa', *Transition* 51 (1991).
15. Edward Said, *Culture and Imperialism* (New York: Random House, 1994), 219.
16. Ibid., 266.
17. Ibid.,218. However, Said could say the following in an interview with Mark Edmundson — 'Nationalism, which is necessary to combat imperialism, then turns into a kind of fetishization of the native essence and identity'. Edward Said, 'Expanding Humanism: An Interview' in *Wild Orchids and Trotsky: Messages from American Universities*, ed. Mark Edmundson (New York: Penguin Books, 1993), 115.
18. I refer here to Adotevi's famous critique of Negritude. Stanislas Adotevi, 'The Strategy of Culture' in *The Ideology of Blackness*, ed. Raymond Betts (Lexington, MA: DC Heath, 1971).
19. Edward Said, *Culture and Imperialism* (New York: Random House, 1994), 219. However, note Said's interesting comment on page 224. Said approvingly quotes Wole Soyinka's well known critique of Negritude from *Myth, Literature and the African World* (Cambridge: Cambridge University Press, 1980). This is a perspective with which Sylvia Wynter would totally disagree. Note her objection to Soyinka's position on Negritude in her essay 'The Pope Must Have been Drunk, The King of Castile a Madman: Culture as Actuality, and the Caribbean Rethinking Modernity' in *The Reordering of Culture: Latin America, the Caribbean and Canada*, eds. Alvina Ruprecht and Cecilia Taiana (Ottawa: Carleton University Press, 1995), 37 n. 18.
20. For a classic statement amidst the impressive scholarship on Rastafari, see Nathaniel Samuel Murrell, William David Spencer and Adrian Anthony McFarlane, eds., *Chanting Down Babylon: The Rastafari Reader* (Philadelphia: Temple University Press, 1998). For a very different perspective to Said's on the contemporary relevance of Ethiopianism, see Erna Brodber, 'Re-engineering Blackspace', *Caribbean Quarterly* 43, no. 1(1997).

21. Edward Said, *Culture and Imperialism* (New York: Random House, 1994), 248.
22. 'An Audience with C.L.R. James', *Third World Book Review* 1, no. 2 (1984): 7.
23. Ibid., 7.
24. C.L.R. James in Ian Munro and Reinhard Sander, eds., *Kas-Kas: Interviews with Three Caribbean Writers in Texas* (Austin: African and Afro-American Research Institute, The University of Texas at Austin, 1972), 31. In fairness to James, he acknowledges that 'many good critics think otherwise', and thus his views may well be idiosyncratic. It does not, however, explain his almost reflexive distaste for the themes raised in Kamau Brathwaite's work.
25. For a take on C.L.R. James and cosmopolitanism, see the chapter on him in Timothy Brennan, *At Home in the World: Cosmopolitanism Now* (Cambridge, Mass: Harvard University Press, 1997). Also see Brennan's fine essay 'Cosmopolitans and Celebrities', *Race & Class 31* (1989). This is certainly not a dismissal of James, as to use but one example, his suggestion that 'to establish his own identity, Caliban, after three centuries, must pioneer into regions Caesar never knew' is brilliantly suggestive from a historicist, and epistemic perspective.
26. Edward Said, *Culture and Imperialism*, 268.
27. Ibid., 269.
28. Ibid., 274.
29. In fairness to Said, the recent explosion of studies on Fanon came after *Culture and Imperialism*. See T. Lewis Gordon, Denean Sharpley-Whiting, Renee T. White, eds., *Fanon: A Critical Reader* (Oxford: Blackwell Publishers, 1996); T. Denean Sharpley-Whiting and Renee T. White, eds., *Frantz Fanon: Conflicts and Feminisms* (Lanham, MD: Rowman & Littlefield, 1997); Lewis R. Gordon, *Fanon and the Crisis of European Man: An Essay on Philosophy and the Human Sciences* (New York: Routledge, 1995); Ato Sekyi-Otu, *Fanon's Dialectic of Experience* (Cambridge: Harvard University Press, 1996). For Fanon from the context of Afro-Caribbean philosophy, Paget Henry 'Fanon, African and Afro-Caribbean Philosophy' in Paget Henry, *Caliban's Reason: An Introduction to Afro-Caribbean Philosophy* (New York: Routledge, 2000).
30. Edward Said, *Culture and Imperialism*, 281. In another reflection on these words, Said states that 'without this concept of "place for all at the rendezvous of victory," one is condemned to an impoverished politics of knowledge based only upon the assertion and reassertion of identity, an ultimately uninteresting alternation of presence and absence'. Edward Said, 'The Politics of Knowledge', in *Race, Identity and Representation in Education*, eds., Cameron McCarthy and Warren Crichlow (New York: Routledge, 1993), 310.
31. Benita Parry, 'Imagining Empire: From *Mansfield Park* to Antigua', *New Formations* 20 (1993).
32. Ibid., 184, 187.
33. Ibid., 185. Parry prefaces this point by pointing out that it 'could be argued that to conceptualize the relationship as mutual and symbiotic, restores agency to the colonized, wiping out the figuration of helpless victims controlled by all-powerful masters', a view that she does not share. I similarly have a deep concern with this perspective as the idea of agency taken too far. To further reinforce her point, she approvingly quotes Christopher Miller's comment that 'Bakhtinian criticism shows how dialogue and polyvocality can be uncovered within apparent hegemonies, and this opens doors towards a better understanding of colonial and postcolonial literatures. Such a fantasy depends on a complete rewriting (or ignorance) of the material conditions of history: colonialism, the centralization of power in European capitals.... All of these are factors which vitiate dialogism within the substance of history'. This

reference is from Christopher Miller, *Theories of Africans: Francophone Literature and Anthropology in Africa* (Chicago: University of Chicago Press, 1990), 27.
34. Ibid., 183, 188
35. Bart Moore-Gilbert critiques Said's failure to critically assess the difference between the humanism that he espouses and previous Western-ethnocentric humanisms with the following words — 'While it is clear that the vision underlying the "new humanism" which Said advances as the premise and goal of a new discourse of liberation is not to be confused with its historical Western counterpart, it is not so clear whether Said's prescriptions are any less vulnerable than (Thomas) Arnold's were in a different epoch and a much more limited cultural frame of reference'. *Postcolonial Theory: Contexts, Practices, Politics* (New York: Verso, 1997), 72.
36. Jennifer Wicke and Michael Sprinkler, 'Interview with Edward Said', in *Edward Said: A Critical Reader*, ed. Michael Sprinkler (Oxford: Blackwell Publishers, 1992), 230.
37. This 1989 interview came five years after the special issue of *Boundary 2* on Humanism, an issue which Said could hardly have missed since it contained an important essay by Abdul Jan Mohammed, and saw the debut of Chandra Mohanty's 'Under Western Eyes: Feminist Scholarship and Colonial Discourses' critique of Western feminism. Sylvia Wynter's contribution, 'The Ceremony Must Be Found: After Humanism', occupied pride of place as the first essay in this collection, which makes Said's lack of knowledge of it all the more startling. See *Boundary 2*, vol. 12, no. 3 &13 (Spring/ Fall 1984), no.1 (Special Issue: Humanism and the University).
38. Edward Said, *Representations of the Intellectual: The 1993 Reith Lectures* (New York: Pantheon Books, 1994), xvii.
39. B. Robbins, M.L. Pratt, J. Arac, R. Radhakrishnan and E. Said, 'Edward Said's Culture and Imperialism: A Symposium', *Social Text* 12, no. 3 (1994): 1-24.
40. David Chioni Moore, 'Where are all the African and Caribbean Critics? The MLA, Honorary Members, and Honorary Fellows', *Research in African Literatures* 32, no. 1 (2001): 110-121; Mimi Sheller, 'Theoretical Piracy on the High Seas of Global Culture: Appropriations of "Creolization" in the Discourses of Globalization' (paper presented at the conference '(Re)Thinking Caribbean Culture', University of the West Indies, Cave Hill, Barbados, June 4-8, 2001), and also her *Consuming the Caribbean: from Arawaks to Zombies* (New York: Routledge, 2003).
41. Mimi Sheller, 'Theoretical Piracy on the High Seas of Global Culture: Appropriations of "Creolization" in the Discourses of Globalization', (paper presented at the conference '(Re)Thinking Caribbean Culture', University of the West Indies, Cave Hill, Barbados, June 4-8, 2001).
42. Ibid.
43. Ibid.
44. Bill Ashcroft, Gareth Griffiths and Helen Tiffin, *The Empire Writes Back: Theory and Practice in Post-Colonial Literatures* (New York: Routledge, 1989), 145, in Carolyn Allen, 'Creole Then and Now: The Problem of Definition', *Caribbean Quarterly* 44, nos. 1&2 (1998): 33-49. Caribbean names absent from the *Norton Anthology of Theory and Criticism* (New York and London: W.W. Norton & Company, 2001) include C.L.R. James, Kamau Brathwaite, Aimé Césaire, Edouard Glissant, Sylvia Wynter and Wilson Harris.
45. Lewis Gordon, *Her Majesty's Other Children: Sketches of Racism from a Neocolonial Age* (Maryland: Rowman & Littlefield, 1997), 89.
46. Lewis Gordon, 'African-American Philosophy: Theory, Politics and Pedagogy', *Philosophy of Education* (1998): 39-46.
47. Ibid.

48. Robert Bernasconi, 'Casting the Slough: Fanon's New Humanism for a New Humanity' in *Fanon: A Critical Reader*, eds. Lewis R. Gordon, T. Denean Sharpley-Whiting, and Renee T. White (Cambridge, MA: Blackwell Publishers, 1996).
49. Ibid., 121.
50. Cedric Robinson, 'The Nature of the Black Radical Tradition' in *Black Marxism: The Making of the Black Radical Tradition* (Chapel Hill, NC: University of North Carolina Press, 2000. [Originally published 1983]).
51. Steve Biko, 'Black Consciousness and the Quest for a True Humanity' in *I Write What I Like*, ed. C.R. Aelred Stubbs (London: Heinemann, 1978), 90.
52. Malcolm X, *The Autobiography of Malcolm X, as told to Alex Haley* (New York: Ballantine Books, 1999).
53. Comment by Paget Henry during his paper 'Wynter and the Transcendental Spaces of Caribbean Thought' at the 'After Man, Towards the Human: The Thought of Sylvia Wynter' Conference (Centre for Caribbean Thought, University of the West Indies, Mona Campus, June 14-15, 2002).
54. David Scott, 'The Re-enchantment of Humanism: An Interview with Sylvia Wynter', *Small Axe* 8 (2000): 121.
55. The full quote by Goveia reads as follows: 'Though they often do not realize it, the West Indians of today cannot afford to go on regarding this region as a tropical estate to be exploited for its economic returns. Whether they like it or not, this is their home. So, we need to face the problems of making the West Indies a more acceptable physical and social environment for ourselves and those who may come after us. *Even now, we often have only the vaguest understanding of the true nature of our present ambiguous situation*'. See Elsa Goveia, 'Past History and Present Planning in the West Indies' (emphasis added). In reading Wynter in this manner, I am thinking of the nature of the reading of Fanon undertaken by Ato Sekyi-Otu. See Ato Sekyi-Otu, *Fanon's Dialectic of Experience* (Cambridge, Mass: Harvard University Press, 1996).
56. Sylvia Wynter, 'We Must Learn to sit down together and talk about a little Culture: Reflections on West Indian Writing and Criticism Pts. 1 & 2', *Jamaica Journal* (1968/1969). An abridged version has been reprinted in *The Routledge Reader in Caribbean Literature*, eds. Alison Donnell and Sarah Lawson Welsh (London and New York: Routledge, 1996).
57. Sylvia Wynter, 'Sambos and Minstrels', *Social Text* (Summer 1979). This perspective by Wynter was undoubtedly due to her location within a North American context, and can be seen in her long quotations in this article from Richard Wright's *Black Boy*. I am reminded here of the wonderful comment by James Baldwin in his front page blurb to this very book — 'Wright's unrelenting bleak landscape was not merely that of the Deep South, or of Chicago, *but that of the world, of the human heart*' (emphasis added). Richard Wright, *Black Boy* (New York: Signet Books, 1951). Wynter would herself note the jarring sense as a West Indian black faced with North American racism. See David Scott, 'The Re-enchantment of Humanism: An Interview with Sylvia Wynter', *Small Axe* 8 (2000): 173. In another incredibly poignant phrase, Wynter would speak of the 'total abjection of being' of the colonized subject. See Scott, 'Interview with Sylvia Wynter', 188.
58. Sylvia Wynter, 'Ethno Or Socio Poetics', *Alcheringa: Ethnopoetics* 2, no. 2 (1976): 79. *Ethno Or Socio Poetics* is of critical importance in tracing her thought, as it precedes what is generally acknowledged to be Wynter's landmark essay, *The Ceremony Must Be Found* by eight years, but in it all of the main features to be found in the later essay are present, including the turn to Renaissance humanism and its connection with the invention of the category of secular man — and what this would mean for the people of the Americas and Africa.

It also demonstrates that while Wynter would later utilize Foucault in her work, he was not central to the formation of her ideas. Indeed, Wynter suggests that it was her considerable work on 15th century Spain that led her in this direction, something which 'Ethno Or Socio Poetics' also confirms. See David Scott, 'The Re-enchantment of Humanism: An Interview with Sylvia Wynter', *Small Axe* 8 (2000): 201, and Wynter on Foucault on page 199. Among Caribbean thinkers, George Lamming has also noted the importance of humanism, its linkages with imperialism, and its effect on knowledge creation in the western academy. George Lamming, 'Caribbean Labour, Culture, and Identity' in *Bucknell Review: Caribbean Cultural Identities* (Lewisburg: Bucknell University Press, 2001).

59. Sylvia Wynter, 'The Ceremony Must Be Found: After Humanism', *Boundary 2* (Spring/Fall 1984): 25
60. Ibid., 56.
61. David Scott, 'The Re-enchantment of Humanism: An Interview with Sylvia Wynter', *Small Axe* 8 (2000): 195
62. Neil Lazarus, Steven Evans, Anthony Arnove, and Anne Menke, 'The Necessity of Universalism', *Differences* 7, no.1 (1995): 75-145. Lazarus et al.'s essay constitute an extended attack on what they see as the 'thoroughgoing unsupportability — politically, ethically, epistemologically — of poststructuralist and postmodernist social and cultural theory', and a 'defense of a radical model of universalism as a philosophical concept and a sociohistorical project'. We can read this in conjunction with Césaire's view of the universal — 'I have a different idea of a universal. It is of a universal rich with all that is particular, rich with all the particulars there are, the deepening of each particular, the coexistence of them all'. Aimé Césaire, *Letter to Maurice Thorez* (Paris: Presence Africaine, 1957), 15.
63. The phrase 'planetary humanism', as a description of Wynter's work, is David Scott's. See David Scott, 'The Re-enchantment of Humanism: An Interview with Sylvia Wynter', *Small Axe* 8 (2000): 121. The articles by Wynter on development and female circumcision are as follows: 'Is Development a Purely Empirical Concept or Also Teleological: A Perspective from "We the Underdeveloped"' in *Prospects for Recovery and Sustainable Development in Africa* ed. Yansane Aguibou (Westport, Connetticut; Greenwood Press, 1996); '"Genital Mutilation" or "Symbolic Birth?" Female Circumcision, Lost Origins, and the Aculturalism of Feminist/Western Thought', *Case Western Reserve Law Review* 47, no. 2 (1997).
64. As quoted by George Lamming in his interview with David Scott. David Scott, 'The Sovereignty of the Imagination: An Interview with George Lamming', *Small Axe* 12 (2002): 180.
65. David Scott, 'The Re-enchantment of Humanism: An Interview with Sylvia Wynter', *Small Axe* 8 (2000): 159.
66. Ibid., 136.
67. The phrase 'embattled humanism' is David Scott's. See Scott, 'Interview with Sylvia Wynter', 153; also his preface to the interview on pages 119-122. Representing this tradition as confined to Césaire and Fanon may be problematic, but these two intellectuals most directly thematized the issue of humanism in their work. However, note Alrick Cambridge's comment that 'C.L.R. James was among the first self-consciously humanist Marxists in the post-war era', as can be seen in James's 1945 essay 'Dialectical Materialism and the Fate of Humanity'. Alrick Cambridge, 'C.L.R. James: Freedom through history and dialectics' in *Intellectuals in the Twentieth-Century Caribbean Spectre of*

the New Class: the Commonwealth Caribbean Vol. 1 (London and Basingstoke: Macmillan, 1992).
68. Aimé Césaire, *Discourse on Colonialism*, trans. Joan Pinkham (New York: Monthly Review Press, 1972). For a recent review of the significance of Césaire's *Discourse on Colonialism*, see Robin D.G. Kelley, 'A Poetics of Anticolonialism', *Monthly Review* 51, no. 6 (1999).
69. Aimé Césaire, *Discourse on Colonialism*, 56.
70. My extremely truncated take on Fanon here is simply due to the summary nature of this paper, rather than my appreciation of the extent of Fanon's legacy. For a summary of the stages of 'Fanon studies', see Lewis Gordon, 'Fanon, Philosophy and Racism' in *Her Majesty's Other Children*. (Maryland: Rowman & Littlefield, 1997).
71. Frantz Fanon, *The Wretched of the Earth* (London: Penguin Books, 1967).
72. Aimé Césaire, 'Poetry and Knowledge', *Tropiques* 12 (January 1945).
73. Ibid. (emphasis added).
74. Aimé Césaire, 'Presentation', *Tropiques* 1 (April 1941).
75. Sylvia Wynter, 'Is Development a Purely Empirical Concept or Also Teleological: A Perspective from "We the Underdeveloped"' in *Prospects for Recovery and Sustainable Development in Africa*, ed. Yansane Aguibou (Westport, Connetticut: Greenwood Press, 1996), 310.
76. Sylvia Wynter, 'Africa, the West and the Analogy of Culture: The Cinematic Text after Man', in *Symbolic Narratives/African Cinema: Audiences, Theory and the Moving Image*, ed. June Givanni (London: British Film Institute, 2000). All italics in the passages quoted from Wynter are her own.
77. Ibid., 25.
78. Ibid., 25-26.
79. David Scott, 'The Re-enchantment of Humanism: An Interview with Sylvia Wynter', *Small Axe* 8 (2000): 145.
80. Sylvia Wynter, 'Beyond the Categories of the Master Conception: The Counterdoctrine of the Jamesian Poiesis' in *C.L.R. James's Caribbean*, ed. Paget Henry and Paul Buhle (Durham: Duke University Press, 1992).
81. Sylvia Wynter, 'Beyond the Word of Man; Glissant and the New Discourse of the Antilles', *World Literature in Review* 63, no. 4 (1989): 647 n. 15. Also see Sylvia Wynter, 'A Different Kind of Creature': Caribbean Literature, the Cyclops Factor, and the Second Poetics of the Propter Nos. *Annals of Scholarship* (1997). Also, see James Clifford's discussion of Rene Menil's effort to distinguish the Negritude of Césaire and Senghor, 'A Politics of Neologism: Aimé Césaire' in *The Predicament of Culture: Twentieth Century Ethnography, Literature and Art* (Cambridge, Massachusetts and London, England: Harvard University Press), 178.
82. David Scott, 'Politics, Contingency, Strategy: an Interview with Stuart Hall', *Small Axe* 1 (1997): 157
83. Sylvia Wynter, '"Africa, The West and the Analogy of Culture": The Cinematic Text After Man' in *Symbolic Narratives/African Cinema: Audience, Theory and the Moving Image*, ed. June Givanni (London: BFI Publishing, 2000), 25.
84. See Anthony Bogues, 'Politics, Nation and Postcolony: Caribbean Inflections', *Small Axe* 11 (2002). The term 'postcolony' is taken from Achille Mbembe's *On the Postcolony* (Berkeley, CA: University of California Press, 2001).
85. Frantz Fanon, *The Wretched of the Earth*, for the phrase 'greedy little caste', see Greg Thomas, 'Reading Fanon and Frazier on the Erotic Politics of Racist Assimilation by Class', *Presence Africaine* 157 (1999). For the best account of this process with respect to the contemporary Caribbean, see Percy Hintzen, 'Reproducing Domination: Identity and Legitimacy Constructs in the West Indies', *Social Identities* 3, no. 1 (1997). Also, the many writings of Rex Nettleford

analysed on this issue in Rupert Lewis, 'Nettleford's Critique of the Black Elite', *Caribbean Quarterly* 43, no. 2 (1997).
86. Wilson Harris, *History, Fable and Myth: In The Caribbean and Guianas* (Wellesley, Massachusettes: Calaloux Publications, 1995), 47.
87. Contemporary anthropology generally agrees that fully human forms of life emerged from Africa. Richard Leakey, *The Origins of Humankind* (London: Orion Books, 1994).
88. I take the idea of 'abduction systems' from Gregory Bateson, mediated through Sylvia Wynter. See Sylvia Wynter, 'Beyond the Categories of the Master Conception: The Counterdoctrine of the Jamesian Poiesis' in *C.L.R. James's Caribbean*, eds. Henry and Buhle.
89. Ella Fitzgerald and Louis Armstrong, 'Stomping at the Savoy' in *Best of Ella Fitzgerald and Louis Armstrong on Verve* (Polygram Records, UPC 731453790926, 1997; originally recorded July 23, 1957). In contrast to Paget Henry's comparison of Wynter to Sarah Vaughn, and his glowing description of her as the 'divine one of Caribbean letters', the link may well be more to Ella Fitzgerald. If Ella was the 'first lady of Jazz', surely Wynter is the 'first human' of Caribbean thought.
90. Sylvia Wynter, 'Beyond the Categories of the Master Conception: The Counterdoctrine of the Jamesian Poiesis' in *C.L.R. James's Caribbean*, eds. Paget Henry and Paul Buhle (Durham: Duke University Press, 1992).
91. Sylvia Wynter, 'In Quest of Matthew Bondman: Some Cultural Notes on the Jamesian Journey' in *C.L.R. James: His Life and Work*, ed. Paul Buhle (London: Allison & Busby, 1986). The quoted sections within this quote are from C.L.R. James's *Beyond a Boundary*.
92. Ibid.,136.
93. Ibid., 137.
94. Ibid., 131.
95. An observation made by Wynter in her keynote response at the conference 'After Man, Towards the Human: The Thought of Sylvia Wynter' (Centre for Caribbean Thought, University of the West Indies, Mona Campus, June 14-15 2002).
96. Beckles and Stoddart will hopefully forgive me for the appropriation of the title of their edited collection, see Hilary Beckles and Brian Stoddart, eds., *Liberation Cricket: West Indies Cricket Culture* (Manchester: Manchester University Press, 1995).

7 | Sylvia Wynter's Hedgehogs: The Challenge for Intellectuals to Create New 'Forms of Life' in Pursuit of Freedom[1]

Neil Roberts

Hedgehog Intellectuals: Some Preliminary Remarks

A series of major events in the pursuit of freedom occurred from the 1940s to the 1960s. From universal adult suffrage in colonial Jamaica (1944) to Aimé Césaire's call for a new science of human systems in his 'Poetry and Knowledge' speech on Haitian soil (1944) to C.L.R. James's *Notes on Dialectics* (1948) to James's draft of *Notes on American Civilization* (1950) to Frantz Fanon's *Black Skin, White Masks* (1952) to the *Brown v. Board of Education* (1954) United States school desegregation case, to the independence of the Gold Coast under Kwame Nkrumah's leadership (1957) to the independence of several British colonies in the 1960s, a foment among Caribbean intellectuals brewed that sought to challenge how the modes of producing the *human* were represented in the world. The year 1953 is of particular importance. Not only was 1953 the date of C.L.R. James's deportation from the United States and the posthumous publication of Ludwig Wittgenstein's *Philosophical Investigations*.[2] It also marked the publication by the late Sir Isaiah Berlin of his essay, *The Hedgehog and the Fox*.[3] The work is ostensibly a study investigating Leo Tolstoy's view of history. When one reads beyond its subtitle, one realizes its greater purpose. Berlin begins by quoting a passage from the Greek poet Archilochus: 'The fox knows many things, but the hedgehog knows one big thing.' He takes this as a framework to investigate the ways intellectuals approach different modes of inquiry. Foxes are individuals who know different individual things well, while hedgehogs seek to formulate a grand theory or grand idea. Berlin gives examples in the Western tradition of thinkers who were hedgehogs and foxes. Dante was a hedgehog, yet Shakespeare was a fox. Plato, Hegel, and Nietzsche were hedgehogs in many degrees, whereas Aristotle, Goethe, and Joyce were foxes. Berlin then claims that Tolstoy by nature was a fox who believed and desired to be a hedgehog.

What does a discussion of hedgehogs and foxes have to do with Wynter, intellectuals, and understanding the Wynterian concept of '*human* freedom' after *man*? I contend Wynter's life and work calls on intellectuals to think and act like hedgehogs. Wynter claims the achievement of *human* freedom after *man* is a task not yet realized. Using the metaphor of the hedgehog, I argue Wynterian thought challenges radical thinkers to become what I call *hedgehog intellectuals*. Various shades of Liberalism and Marxism have dominated discourse in political theory for over a century, each purporting to offer a lens for *human* emancipation. Wynterian thought provides a heretical model for achieving *human* freedom that breaks out of both the paradigm of Liberalism and Marxism.

My foci in this chapter will be the role of intellectuals, the concept of freedom, and the relationship of these concepts to Wynterian thought. I develop my argument in four stages: (1) discuss what the phrase hedgehog intellectuals means within the context of the crisis of secular *man*'s over-representation as the *human*; (2) in contrast to the materialism of Karl Marx's eleven *Theses on Feuerbach*, situate the genesis of Wynterian thought in search of new 'forms of life' by naming 11 figures central to Wynter's insights; (3) illustrate how Wynterian freedom is distinct from freedom in the Marxist paradigm by contrasting the Hegelian-Marxist dialectics of Fredric Jameson with the Liminal Dialectics of Wynter; and (4) conclude with brief reflections on what imagining a political theory of *human* freedom means for Wynter and the role hedgehog intellectuals play in this quest. This essay addresses in particular why achieving Wynter's heretical concept of *human* freedom can only occur by emancipating ourselves from the present concept of material economic freedom.

The Crisis of Secular *Man*'s Over-representation as the *Human*

Fifty years after the founding of the United Nations and its endorsement of 'universal' human rights, political theorist Anthony

Bogues investigates the radical Caribbean intellectual tradition.[4] He points out an important distinction between Western liberalism's concept of freedom and the notion of freedom in the Caribbean from the vantage point of the Caribbean's black populations. To illustrate this claim, Bogues invokes the work of Berlin. His discussion, focuses on Berlin's well-known essay 'Two Concepts of Liberty' and the distinction Berlin makes between negative liberty and positive liberty.[5] Negative liberty is the freedom of an individual from coercion, whereas positive liberty deals with autonomy and the freedom of an individual to determine what he or she seeks to do. Berlin was afraid that positive liberty would trump negative liberty. For Berlin, twentieth-century totalitarianism exhibited an extreme form of positive liberty, with Stalinism and Nazism as examples of his greatest fears. As a result, Berlin only acknowledges negative liberty as the valid realm of freedom. Bogues intervenes and persuasively argues that this negative/positive liberty distinction does not pertain to the Caribbean especially in the case of the Haitian Revolution. The struggle to achieve freedom for black slaves manifest in the actions of Toussaint L'Ouverture, Henri Christophe, Jean-Jacques Dessalines, Boukman, and the black Haitian masses cannot be explained in terms of Berlin's value-pluralism or the variants of Western liberalism's notion of freedom. Looking at the Haitian Revolution brings us back to the thought of C.L.R. James, and looking at Western civilization's over-representation of a universalistic European Man brings us back to the thought of Wynter. Recognizing a need to go beyond the important phenomenological contributions of Edmund Husserl's cartesian meditations and Maurice Merleau-Ponty's phenomenology of perception, we must acknowledge that our current crisis is not simply that of the European sciences or European Man. Rather, the crisis is *man*'s over-representation of itself as the *human*.[6]

Wynter wants us to achieve what it means to be *human*, and she argues our pursuit for freedom and understanding the role of intellectuals must confront the reality that we have not properly conceived this concept. This is similar to James's concern in *Notes on Dialectics* that interpretations of Marx such as V.I. Lenin's theory of the vanguard party and Leon Trotsky's notion of permanent world revolution were merely forms of understanding/*verstand*. Wynter therefore holds concerns that world civilization is stuck in the paradigm of various concepts of the *human* but have not come to grips with how to represent modes of producing the *human*.⁷

Clyde Taylor speaks of the mask of art and breaking the aesthetic contract privileging a certain notion of Euro-American beauty above others. Enrique Dussel's constant chanting of liberation catalogues the emergence of those in Latin America and the Caribbean situated at the 'underside of modernity' as a result of the brutal slaughter of indigenous persons, the transatlantic slave trade, and the indentured servitude of labourers. Charles Mills points out how the raceless social contract central to modern Western political theory masks the unwritten contract and hitherto unnamed political system of the modern Western world — white supremacy — thus maintaining a system of *Herrenvolk* ethics privileging whites/persons over non-whites/subpersons (*Untermenschen*).⁸

Wynter conceives of two major evolutions in the concept of *man* following the advent of the Renaissance and its resultant secular humanism. Each of these evolutions accounts for the insights offered by Taylor, Dussel, and Mills. Figure 1 illustrates these evolutions:⁹

MASKING OF THE HUMAN	TIME PERIOD
Medieval Christian	Middle Ages
Man (1)	Late 15th/C to Late 18th/C
Man (2)	19th/C to the Present

Figure 1: Wynterian Understanding of Prior Attempts to Offer a Concept of the Human

Each concept of *man* masks and over-represents itself as the *human*. The masking of the Human by Man (1) refers to the late fifteenth-century to late eighteenth-century period in which *man* is represented in terms of *homo politicus*/political man. Due to a process of secularization, the intellectual authorities no longer were the clergy of the Middle Ages. Instead, the intellectuals were the lay humanists of the Renaissance. The *human others*/outcasts/liminal group of the mad becomes the Indians and Negros, and the order of *being* transforms into the political.

A major shift occurs in the nineteenth century. Adopting and modifying the discussion by Michel Foucault of shifts in *epistemes*/orders of knowledge among the order of things, Wynter refers to Man (2) as the notion of *man* from the nineteenth-century to the present.[10] This second post-Renaissance over-representation of *man* conceives of the masked *human* in terms of *homo economicus*/economic man. The liberal humanists and bourgeois intellectual authorities operate within a bioeconomic concept of what it means to be *human*. The liminal category of *human others* in this over-representation of the *human* contains the natives, niggers, and the global poor.

In the list of enclosures Wynter provided participants in the June 2002 seminar on her work at the University of the West Indies, Mona, was a copy of a flyer inside an edition of Charles Darwin's *The Descent of Man* found by Jason Ambroise in the library of the University of California at Berkeley.[11] Darwin writes in the wake of Copernicus's then heretical argument for the Earth revolving around the sun, the Western Copernican Revolution; of Immanuel Kant's *Critique of Pure Reason* and his third antinomy outlining man's autonomy in search of freedom; Kantian deontological moral philosophy and anthropology, and recently documented examples of racist anthropological works composed out of the Enlightenment and German Romanticist eras which do not acknowledge the ability of liminal Africans and Caribbeans to reason.[12] Darwin's writings on evolution became a foundation for the creation of Social Darwinism.

The flyer copy shows a picture of two seemingly ape-like entities looking at one another face-to-face. These beings in fact are supposed to represent people of African descent. The caption reads, 'The Negro ... Animal or Human? Which do they act like? You decide.' The deduced implication of this flyer is that the niggers/*human others*/liminal blacks are no more than animals ontologically. Blacks are non-human. Returning to the ideas of Charles Mills — the racial contract narrates the unnamed Western political system of white supremacy that masks the human as Western *man*. Carrying this idea further, the state of Man (2) makes the claim that blacks are normatively non-human since Man (2) does not conceive of blacks as a part of humankind within a bioeconomic framework of social Darwinism and genetic determinism.

Regarding Wynter's description of the evolution in the concept of freedom, some important remarks are in order. Fanon's heretical insight in *Black Skin, White Masks* lies in the revolutionary declaration separating himself methodologically from the psychoanalysis of Freud:

'Besides phylogeny and ontogeny stands sociogeny.' Whereas ontogeny deals with the individual organism and phylogeny with the structural dimensions of the species, sociogeny engages the manner in which the social world mediates our behaviours. Fanonian sociogenesis takes into account the social elements of a society and how the social affects those who embody the condemned of the earth. At the core of Fanon's innovation remains a desire to figure out 'truly what is to be done to set man free'. We must stay preoccupied with understanding freedom's meaning in Fanon's view because, as he states, we must always say '*No to the butchery of what is most human in man: freedom.*'[13] Thus, Fanon, like Wynter, seeks to explore the meaning of *human* freedom as distinct from the freedom of *man*.

Fanon's ideas about sociogenic processes lead Wynter to formulate her *sociogenic principle*.[14] The sociogenic principle argues that the social order or episteme of an era conditions the normative beliefs of those living in that era. The concept of freedom that individuals and collective groups hold in an order arises from the normative beliefs shaped by the actualities of social life. The Gnostics, for example, approached fellow humans in order to spiritually free humans from the significant ills of their days. Medieval thinker St Augustine did not believe sin lay in the material universe or natural scarcity. Rather, he felt significant ills in the City of God lay in a person's enslavement to original sin. The process of attaining Augustinian freedom through spiritual redemption came from baptism by the clergy and Augustinian freedom became a founding matrix in the Medieval Christian era.

Through the lay humanism process of secularization, a shift occurs with the creation of a secularized version of Original Sin and Spiritual Redemption. During the era of Man (1), debates emerge over the value of using a universalistic notion of rationality. The French Enlightenment *philosophes* (Enlightenment philosophers and political theorists) and the *physiocrats* (Enlightenment political economists) were the intellectuals who dualled over these ideas and Enlightenment rationality reached its triumphant height in the bourgeois French Revolution. Unfreedom is seen as existing in a state of irrationality, while freedom for Man (1) resides in rationality.

The era of Man (2) transforms the dialectic of unfreedom and freedom. The theories of Ricardo and Malthus on comparative advantage and population respectively give rise to concerns about poverty, wealth, and population growth. An emphasis on genes replaces rationality as the dominant view in freedom discourse. Unfreedom for Man (2) deals with enslavement to natural scarcity, and the road to freedom resides in possessing the correct genes. The excitement among many in the global capitalistic world order surrounding the mapping of the Human Genome Project exemplifies this current state of freedom discourse. Freedom within this matrix manifests itself in the desire for attaining material redemption. Theories of Liberalism and Marxism usher in thought debating how best to live in a globe conditioned on a normative bioeconomic materialistic worldview. Natural Scarcity creates the category of the jobless poor/new poor, and the transitions from emphasizing God to rationality to that of genes creates a demarcation between the genetically selected and dysselected. It is this latter concept of freedom, namely Man (2), that Wynter seeks to break out of with the help of hedgehogs. The following chart summarizes these ideas:[15]

MASKING OF THE HUMAN	UNFREEDOM	FREEDOM
Medieval Christendom	Original Sin	Spiritual Redemption
Man (1)	Irrational	Rational Redemption
Man (2)	Natural Scarcity/ Dyselected Genes	Material Redemption/ Selected Genes

Figure 2: Wynterian Understanding of Prior Concepts of Unfreedom and freedom

Having outlined in theory Wynter's understanding of prior concepts of unfreedom and freedom, what does her own notion of freedom look like? Put differently, how can humankind overcome what Theodor Adorno calls the 'world's own unfreedom' by adopting the Wynterian framework for freedom beyond Man (2)'s in order to solve the crisis of *man*'s over-representation as the *human*?[16] Before answering these central questions, I shall invoke an interlude offering an itemized genealogy of influences on Wynterian thought. Once one comprehends the genealogical influences on Wynter, one may better understand the genesis of Wynterian heretical freedom and her reasons for diverging from the materialism of Marx.

Influences on Wynterian Thought: Foundations of a Political Theory

Wynter and Marx

Wynter does not hate Marx. In fact, Wynter adopts the ideas of Marx after shunning a mélange of theories promulgated under the banner of Liberalism and Liberal Humanism that in her opinion fail to pay attention to the needs of the colonized and oppressed globally. Wynter possesses a love for the literary art form of writing manifestos so exquisitely displayed in Marx's oeuvre.[17] Marx plays a major role in the evolution of Wynter's own path to heretical theorizing from the mid-twentieth century through the late 1970s and up until the toppling of the revolutionary government in Grenada during the early 1980s. Marx and Wynter both occupy the position of radical hedgehog intellectuals. They each develop a theory of freedom with the belief that their own innovation is the lens leading to the emancipation of the earth's condemned. In the case of Marx, his hedgehog theoretical ideas put forth a concept of freedom locating socialism as the solution to the alienation of those exploited in the capitalist world system. Marxism attracts Wynter for a substantial time period because it helps explain in many ways the plight of the condemned of the earth. After a series of cataclysmic world events during the Cold War, however, Wynter had an epiphany. She came to realize the epistemic box Marxism encased its hedgehog thinking in as it operated within the framework of Man (2)'s bioeconomic concept of freedom.

Wynter does not abandon all the innovative dimensions of Marxist thought. Rather, Wynter moves beyond its overall epistemological understanding of freedom recognizing it provides as radical a theory as can be expected. In an interview with David Scott at the turn of the millennium, Wynter discusses the limitations in Marx's notion of modes of production and idea that those who control the modes of production control the unfreedom and freedom of mankind. She states:

> This leads me to another point, a very slippery, difficult point to make. For what I'm going to suggest is that in the world in which we live today, it is not primarily the mode of production — capitalism — that controls us, although it controls us at the overtly empirical level through the institution of the free market system, and the everyday practices of

its economic system. But you see, for these to function, the processes of their functioning must be *discursively* instituted, regulated *and* at the same time normalized, legitimated. So what I am going to suggest is that what institutes, regulates, normalizes and legitimates, what then controls us, is instead the *economic* conception of the human — *Man* — that is produced by the disciplinary discourses of our now planetary system of academia as the first purely secular and operational public identity in human history.[18]

Later in the interview, Wynter admits the usefulness of Marx's original interpretations of activity, productivity, and instituting in ways that the projects of anti-Marxist liberal humanists concerned with the human condition such as Hannah Arendt cannot.[19] Nonetheless, although Marx conceptualizes class consciousness in powerful terms, the fact of race and racism holds negative social realities in the present order of things which Wynter believes Marxism improperly addresses. The theoretical premises of Marxism, in her opinion, have incorrectly constructed the 'Negro Question' or the question of black misery as a subsidiary question to the 'Class Question' instead of isolating focus on the realities of the Negro Question, race, and racism in the world system. The Fanonian fact of blackness, or the lived experience of black misery, haunts Wynter in the sense of a Marxian spectre. This pushes Wynter to create another framework for thinking through freedom and unfreedom. Again she observes:

> Why, as [Elsa] Goveia asked, did the fact of blackness *have* to be a fact of inferiority, the fact of whiteness, vice versa? What linked these two questions to each other? Now, once I realized, after trying for many years, to find an answer to these questions in terms of the Marxian explanatory model, I saw that I would have to find an alternative one. Yet what I knew from the beginning was that I would still need some concept that could carry over Marx's formidable insights, like his ideas of *activity*, of *productivity*, of something that one is *instituting*. What was this something, I asked myself, that needed as its own condition of existence the systemic impoverishment of the darker peoples of the world? The no less systemic inferiorization of the black and of the other non-white peoples of the earth?[20]

For these reasons, Wynter makes the break with Marx. Wynter's response to Marx's revolutionary call to action may be found in the eleven revolutionary figures central to her theorizing. These people collectively buttress the hedgehog call of Wynter for a theory of *human freedom* to play a transformative role in world society. The term theory in its etymological origins (*theoria*) deals with the unique ability of one to see or to view. The ideas of seeing and viewing beg the question, 'For what purpose does theory have?' Marx and Wynter agree on the purpose of theory leading to praxis. That agreement along with shared hedgehog thinking allows them to hold a common belief in the duty of intellectuals to create new 'forms of life' in pursuit of freedom. Their methods of revolutionary praxis differ, and those differences drive a wedge between their theories of freedom.

While sharing Marx's desire for revolutionary change manifest in the last Thesis of the *Theses on Feuerbach*, Wynter objects to the limited theoretical framework of Marx's freedom. Wynter lays the foundations for her political theory by synthesizing various concepts from a diverse range of figures. These figures provide Wynter a foundation. As we shall see later, Wynter jumps off from this foundational platform in order to implement her own hedgehog intellectual thinking.

Wynter's Revolutionary Eleven

In my view the collective impact of eleven key figures, their concepts, and their influence has shaped significantly the core of Wynter's notion of freedom. These figures include[21]: (1) Frantz Fanon's idea of *sociogenesis*; (2) Christopher Columbus and the meanings of both *1492* and *discovery*; (3) Gregory Bateson's *descriptive statements*; (4) Giambattista Vico's *New Science* and *poetic wisdom*; (5) Aimé Césaire's *discourse on colonialism* and call for a *new science of human systems*; (6) Asmaron Legesse's description of *liminality*; (7) Elsa Goveia's clear illustration of the race/class paradox in the postcolonial Caribbean *social framework*; (8) Michel Foucault's *episteme* and construction of the centrality of *power/knowledge*; (9) Zygmunt Bauman's articulation of the *intellectuals as legislators and interpreters*, the *New Poor*, and ruminations on the *sociogenesis of freedom*; (10) Karl Marx's notions of *ideology, activity*, and *modes of production*; and (11) C.L.R. James's *rejection of the New Class, analysis of intellectuals*, and desire for *freedom*.

Wynter draws upon the thought and impact of these eleven figures in order to postulate the causes and solutions to our world's misery. The misery resulting from our misdiagnosis of the *human* also results in our misdiagnosis of the causes and outcomes of freedom and unfreedom in our world. Consider the hypothesis formulated by Wynter in the aftermath of the tragic September 11 attacks on the World Trade Center in New York City and the Pentagon in Washington, DC. She notes:

> The hypothesis here is that what was being fought out from Marcus Garvey's "Race first", not "Class first", postulate of the twenties, to [C.L.R.] James' thirties revolutionary answer, to [Aimé] Césaire's 1956 letter [resigning from the French Communist Party], as well as the clashes of Wright, Ellison, later Harold Cruse, with the Marxian answer to the Negro Question was and is the following fundamental question. Is the ultimate cause of all the ills of our contemporary world — including that of the system of economic apartheid which ensures that roughly 20% of the peoples of the earth (the North, the First World) controls and consumes 80% of its resources, and is responsible for 75% of its pollution, while the remaining 80% must make do with the leftovers of 20% — that of the Marxian mode of production? ... Or instead, is the ultimate cause that of our ongoing collective productions and reproductions of our present mode or genre of the human Man?[22]

These revolutionary eleven each in their own way contribute to Wynter's rethinking of the questions put forth in the above hypothesis and in my own explorations into her thought. In relation to theorizing freedom, Columbus, Foucault, and Legesse provide Wynter with the fundamental groundings of her hypothetical inquiries. Their lives and works illustrate Copernican shifts among different orders of knowledge. With shifts in orders of knowledge, transformations occur between those dictating the normative belief systems of the order and those occupying the position of heretics. Spinoza's heresy in seventeenth-century Europe, for example, involves a monistic push for the freedom to philosophize in a European world dominated by a Cartesian notion of rational Man (1). The heretical Spinozist push, lands him an order of excommunication from within his own Amsterdam Sephardic Jewish community. The European normative order of Cartesian dualism cannot incorporate the heresy of Spinoza, and as such Spinoza gains the label of a liminal heretic.[23] Wynter's discussions about the arrival of Columbus in the Caribbean, colonialism, modernity, and the wretched of the earth cannot be understood without questioning the groundings of orders of knowledge and the positioning of norms and heresies within different orders.

Bauman and Bateson highlight the role of intellectuals, the workings of the mind and environment, the consequences of modernity, and the meanings of words and actions undertaken by intellectuals. Bauman holds a place for Wynter in challenging the role of intellectuals. Intellectuals should never become blind to their complicity in their roles as legislators constructing the world we have lived in and presently reside. Intellectuals have not always been interpreters of knowledge, nor are they divorced from the role of legislators. The educational background of a large number of leaders in the contemporary Caribbean proves this claim to be true. Bateson's brilliance lies in the ability to decipher meanings, texts, and contexts in the ecologies of the mind. Bateson's deutero-learning, or meta-learning, issues an introduction in rethinking how humankind comes to learn acquired information. Bateson inspires Wynter to look deeply into areas as seemingly esoteric as etymology and as complex as the process of deciphering the meaning of aesthetics altogether. The two combined move attention away from the modernity/postmodernity pseudo-crisis as the crisis is not between these notions but rather the larger debate of Man (2)'s over-representation as the *human*.

Fanon and Goveia bring to the fore the lived experience of the black within the context of a global system of racial Manichaeism that has created a race/class paradox in the social framework of many places including the Caribbean. Fanon's influence in Wynterian thought seems omnipresent, and it is not too much to say that he may be the leading thinker impacting Wynter's most recent writings on the *human* condition. That said, Goveia's influence on Wynter has been amazingly neglected by critics. Goveia, like Fanon, was born in 1925. Unlike Fanon, Goveia was born in Guyana, studied history rather than psychiatry, and lived nearly 20 years longer than her Martinican brethren. Goveia mentored several Caribbean intellectuals such as Walter Rodney. Rodney's *A History of the Guyanese Working People, 1881–*

1905 acknowledges Goveia's long-term guidance in shaping Rodney's historical narratives. Yet, Wynter's reasons for considering the work of Goveia stem not from Goveia's historical brilliance. Instead, Wynter sees Goveia as a pioneer illustrating the social dynamics leading the mid-to-late twentieth-century Caribbean being embroiled in the paradox of race and class. Goveia's question — Why is the fact of blackness a fact of inferiority? Why does the fact of whiteness or near-whiteness correspond to the fact of superiority? Should those seeking freedom from oppression adopt a class-first position, race-first position, or a mixture of the two? Goveia opens the eyes of Wynter to race/class dynamics that then merge onto Fanonian explorations into the sociogenic elements of our world's own unfreedom and freedom.

Vico and Césaire are the clearest examples of thinkers articulating entirely 'new' paradigms of thought, which radical hedgehog intellectuals must adopt if they are to continue being hedgehogs instead of foxes. When one thinks of words to describe Wynter, 'new' appears as one of the adjectives. Vico's new science appeals to looking at poetic wisdom as a venue for implementing radical, hedgehog ideas in the way the world functions. Successful implementation of the new science for Vico has implications on the nature of *human* institutions. Vico's genius mirrors the genius of other hedgehog intellectuals that feel temporally displaced in their own time period. By appealing to the wisdom of poetic knowledge, Vico brings out the importance of words. Césaire embodies the archetype of the hedgehog Caribbean intellectual with a global vision of emancipating the black masses along with the masses of people unable to imagine actualizing their visions of freedom. Césaire's appeal focuses on the science of words. Similar to Vico, Césaire looks towards poetic wisdom. What distinguishes Césaire from Vico is his knowledge of the Afro-Caribbean condition, of the black condition, of the colonized condition that Vico does not. For Wynter, Césaire's archetypal role hovers around the science of words serving as a mechanism for achieving *human* freedom.

The Influence of Marx

We now reach the influence of Marx and the Caribbean Marxist, C.L.R. James. Marx's impact on Wynter has already been discussed and will gain further attention when we turn to the work of Fedric

Jameson. Whereas Fanon arguably influences Wynter the most in her current theorizing of the *human*, James is the thinker Wynter has written about and lectured more extensively on over the last few decades.[24] Part of the reason why Wynter has contributed so much to Jamesian scholarship has to do with the explosion of scholarship examining James for the last quarter century. Another reason has to do with the similarities in their own personal and intellectual biographies. James and Wynter come from the Caribbean during colonialism, spent significant time in England and the United States, participated in Independence movements taking place in Africa and the Caribbean, and mentored numerous black intellectuals in the process. A final reason has to do with the fact that James represents one of the most radical hedgehog intellectuals to emerge out of the Caribbean with a dual focus on the Caribbean and the global stage. Jamesian freedom from the 1950s until his death in 1989 locates itself in a stream of independent Marxism distinct from classical Marxism. The Jamesian concept of freedom from the 1950s attracts Wynter greatly. From his narrations on cricket to interpretations of the Hegelian dialectic, James takes into account the race/class paradox of the Caribbean, thus shifting the gaze from orthodox Marxism's emphasis only on class to engaging the role of race in the modern world. James's influence continues to grow globally, and those from the Caribbean such as the late Tim Hector of Antigua incorporate Jamesian thought into their own politics inside the region. In the end, James remains a Marxist and his grand idea for freedom involves giving primacy to Marxian beliefs in the analysing modes of economic production. I close the section with Marx and James because the next section on Jameson's freedom and Wynter's freedom focuses on, in a narrower sense, the Jameson/Wynter connection, the applied political theories of Jameson's form of Marxism, Hegelian-Marxism, Wynter's reading of the heretical aspects of C.L.R. James's freedom, and Wynter's move to applying her own political theory of freedom.

In the initial portion of the essay, I introduced my own political theory of hedgehog intellectuals. In the next portion, I gave an overview of some differences between Marx and Wynter through immersion into intellectual history. Now, I return to political theory in order to differentiate Jameson's freedom from Wynter's. I outline their notions of freedom, focusing on one main work for each thinker. Although their concepts of freedom contrast, they share a crucial conceptual tool: dialectic thinking. How they use the dialect differently will be a topic of discussion.

Wynter and Jameson: Competing Dialectical Concepts of Freedom

Sylvia Wynter and Fredric Jameson are two of the leading hedgehog intellectuals of our time. Despite her humble reservations against seeking fame, Wynter's stature in the Caribbean intellectual tradition now stands high alongside other hedgehog Caribbean theorists such as Césaire, Fanon, and James. For an equally humble living theorist, Jameson's fame has grown to almost mythical proportions. Jameson is known as the leading American Marxist critic writing today, and his notoriety in the last 20 years comes from being known as the main theorist globally of postmodernism. Postmodernism's emphasis on ending grand narrative theories of emancipation presents the classic case for the fox, rather than hedgehog, theorist. While Jameson's *Postmodernism, or, the Cultural Logic of Late Capitalism* may in fact hold a special place in the hearts of devout fox postmodern theorists, Jameson is no fox. Above all, his intellectual and political ties for the last several decades remain closest to Hegelian-Marxist hedgehog thinking. One sees Jameson's hedgehog thinking at work from his first book *Sartre: Origins of a Style* to *Late Marxism: Adorno, or, the Persistence of the Dialectic* to his numerous books, essays, and interviews.[25] Jameson's connection to key Caribbean theorists over the years such as Wynter, George Lamming, and Roberto Retamar has been a highly neglected topic of discussion as these connections have influenced his own thought much the same way his investigations into Sartre have done. But why bring up Jameson at all? In Wynterian scholarship, the relationship, convergence, and divergence between Wynter and Jameson are another in a series of hitherto unstudied phenomena. Explaining their relationship in addition to contrasting their dialectical notions of freedom shall make understanding Wynter's concept of freedom clearer.

Wynter spent significant time at the University of the West Indies (UWI), Mona during the 1960s lecturing in Spanish and publishing articles and books in both Spanish and English. In the early 1970s, after a brief visiting professorship at the University of Michigan, Wynter officially leaves UWI, Mona and assumes her first full-time professorship in the United States at the University of California (UC), San Diego. She teaches there until moving to Stanford University in the late 1970s to both teach in the Department of Spanish and Portuguese and also to take over directorship of the programme in African and Afro-American Studies from the previous director St Claire Drake. At UC, San Diego, Wynter teaches literary criticism specializing in the work of literature coming out of the Third World. The political term 'Third World' itself emerges not too long before Wynter's move to the US as it became a political tool and creation of national leaders of countries in the Non-Aligned Movement. During her time at UC, San Diego, Wynter's close colleagues include the writer Shirley Anne Williams, radical philosopher Herbert Marcuse, and Jameson.

Wynter and Jameson help to found in 1979 the journal *Social Text*, which devotes itself explicitly to varieties of Marxist thought. The inaugural issue features Wynter's essay 'Sambos and Minstrels' and Jameson's 'Reification and Utopia in Mass Culture'.[26] The socialist revolution in Grenada two decades after the Cuban Revolution serves as one of the backdrops, and those organizing the journal believe strongly in versions of Marxism providing solid frameworks for freedom. They overtly reject Stalinism and totalitarian Marxist theories, yet provide an open forum for versions of Marxist thought from structural Marxism to Hegelian-Marxism. Moreover, the editorial collective adopts dialectical thinking as a central tool of analysis. The inaugural prospectus of *Social Text* reads:

> This is to announce the publication of a new journal devoted to problems in theory, particularly in the area of culture and ideological practices .... The framework of this journal is Marxist in the broadest sense of the term. It should be possible today, now that Marx's own writings are becoming more fully available, now that the rich oppositional currents of the various non-Stalinist Marxisms are being rediscovered, to free this term from sterile Cold War overtones .... For us, the vitality of dialectical thinking lies in the power to re-historicize methods and positions and resuscitate them in the immense life history of human society from its tribal origins to multinational consumer capitalism and beyond. . . . Thus, the thrust of *Social Text* cannot be conveyed through the usual oppositions such as that between structural

Marxism and Hegelian Marxism, but must be defined by the problems and issues we feel it is most urgent to address.[27]

The collapse of the socialist revolution in Grenada in 1983 culminating in the United States invasion and murder of Marxist-Leninist Prime Minister Maurice Bishop with his government ministers by Stalinist followers on the island is one turning point in Wynter's relationship to Marxism. The amount of years between the formation of *Social Text* and Wynter's break with Marxism are not that long. Wynter becomes traumatized by the lack of outcry among Caribbean Marxist intellectuals regarding the events in Grenada. She realizes the benefits of Marxism as well as its limitations. Jameson, though, does not give up on the Marxist project. In his view, the tragic events in Grenada can be explained as the implementation of a perversion of Marxist thought that should not be interpreted as representing all versions of Marxism.

Thus, Wynter and Jameson diverge on their overall political theories of freedom. An analysis of Jameson's *Marxism and Form* and Wynter's essay 'After the New Class: James, *Les Damnés*, and the Autonomy of Human Cognition' will provide a closer look at these two thinkers' competing dialectical concepts of freedom.

Jameson's Freedom

Jameson's *Marxism and Form* presents a classic statement on freedom within the Hegelian-Marxist tradition.[28] The book is an analysis of dialectical theories of literature in the works of Theodor Adorno, Walter Benjamin, Herbert Marcuse, Ernst Bloch, Georg Lukács, and Jean-Paul Sartre. On a more fundamental level, this work is also an investigation into political theory. Jameson presents his case for the central role that dialectical thinking has for theorizing the attainment of freedom. For centuries following the deaths of Hegel and Marx, many theorists tended to separate the dialectical thinking of Hegel's idealism from the later transformation of Hegelian thought by Marx into his own materialistic form of Marxist dialectics. Jameson, however, forges his own space in Marxist thought which seeks to utilize the insights of both Hegel and Marx. He wants to retain Marx's revolutionary focus on class consciousness while at the same time turn to a central source of Marx's own inspiration, namely the thought of Hegel. He forecasts in the early chapters a goal that he hopes results from those reading this work on dialectical criticism when he writes:

> In the final chapter of the present work we will try to redefine the role Hegelianism is called upon to play in a Marxist framework: the problem is clearly one with the relationship between the values of the older middle-class revolutions and the revolutionary consciousness and needs of the present day. Yet it is at once evident that the very principle at work in dialectical analyses which we have described above — that of the adequation of subject and object, and of the possibility of reconciliation of I and Not-I, of spirit and matter, or self and world — is itself the very premise of Hegel's system and may be claimed to be virtually Hegel's intellectual invention.[29]

Jameson begins by noting the revival of Hegelian-Marxism in early twentieth-century Germany and France. Hegelian-Marxism opposes itself to the tragic aspects of the Soviet tradition of Marxist thought exemplified by the fact of Stalinism. *Marxism and Form* seeks to bring German and French dialectical thinking into the Anglo-American tradition, which contains a lineage of thought dominated by political liberalism, empiricism, and logical positivism. The trajectory of the Anglo-American tradition at the time of Jameson's writing is not dialectical, and it is within the Anglo-American tradition that Jameson brings the German and dialectical renaissance in order to make the case for why the Anglo-American tradition should adopt dialectical thinking.

Dialectical thinking dominates one stream of the German intellectual tradition. Theorists within this tradition such as Marcuse put dialectical thought to work by fusing the ideas of Hegel, Marx, and Freud in order to produce a 'hermeneutics of freedom'.[30] In the French tradition, while one finds the presence of dialectical thinking in the areas of French phenomenology, and applied Marxism through the movement of existentialism spearheaded by Sartre. Reading dialectically poses challenges to the reader. Yet Jameson, like Wynter, abhors the instant sentence that may be easily digested and quickly forgotten.[31] Jameson terms the Western world in which he dialectically writes the postindustrial monopoly capitalistic world. This world creates new modes of production and organization. Though there are different types of Marxism, Jameson engages Hegelian-Marxist thought in order to address the realities of postindustrial society. Twentieth-century Marxism calls on the great themes of Hegel's political theory, which include the relationship of part to whole, concrete versus abstract, totality, dialectics of appearance and essence, and the subject/object interaction.

What is so important about freedom for Jameson, and how does this emphasis on articulating a concept of freedom relate to Jameson's own use of the dialectic? Dialectical thinking involves a relationship between two forces that on the one hand may be polar opposites from one another, while on the other hand exist as forces that seemingly cannot exist without the existence of the other. Thesis, antithesis, and synthesis poorly illustrates the Hegelian method for understanding the leap from dialectical tensions between two ideas to the creation of a third state and the formation of another form of dialectical tensions once reaching the third state. With regards to Marxism, the dialectical relationship between labour and capital fundamentally constructs the tensions in the postindustrial monopolistic capitalist system. That being true, one must understand how the tensions among labour and capital and how the tensions between these two different concepts shape one's understanding of unfreedom and freedom. Jameson employs a dialectical method of politically interpreting the six thinkers under study in *Marxism and Form*, piecing together aspects of each of these thinkers in ways that further his own interpretation of freedom.

Jameson states the importance of coming to grips with the political understanding of freedom this may:

> Indeed, it is the concept of freedom which, measured against those other possible ones of love or justice, happiness or work, proves to be the privileged instrument of a political hermeneutic, and which, in turn, is perhaps itself best understood as an interpretive device rather than a philosophical essence or idea. For wherever the concept of freedom is once more understood, it always comes as the awakening of dissatisfaction in the midst of all that is — at one, in that, with the birth of the negative itself.... From the physical intimidation of the Fascist state to the agonizing repetitions of neurosis, the idea of freedom takes the same temporal form: a sudden perception of an intolerable present which is at the same time, but implicitly and however dimly

articulated, the glimpse of another state in the name of which the first is judged. Thus, the idea of freedom involves a kind of perceptual superposition; it is a way of reading the present, but it is a reading that looks more like the reconstruction of an extinct language.[32]

Jameson says he views freedom as an interpretive device rather than a philosophical essence or idea. For him, freedom as a practice takes primacy over freedom as a normative ideal. Since unfreedom and freedom change over time, encountering for the first time a type of unfreedom or freedom can shock individuals. It seems, though, that Jameson states a case against freedom as a normative ideal even though he holds as normative Hegelian-Marxism to be the lens leading one to freedom in the era of postindustrial monopoly capitalism. Despite the tension between articulating freedom as a practice and freedom as a normative ideal, Jameson believes articulating the formal character of a concept of freedom allows one to overcome some of the most fundamental contradictions in modern existence that imprison the human to a fragmented double life. He notes:

> It is not too much to say that the concept of freedom thus permits us to transcend one of the most fundamental contradictions in modern existence: that between the outside and the inside, between public and private, work and leisure, the sociological and the psychological, between my being-for-others and my being- for-myself, between the political and the poetic, objectivity and subjectivity, the collective and the solitary — between society and the monad. It is an opposition which the confrontation between Marx and Freud dramatizes emblematically; and the persistence of this attempted confrontation (Reich, the Surrealists, Sartre, left-wing Structuralism, not to speak of Marcuse himself) underlies the urgency with which modern man seeks to overcome his double life, his dispersed and fragmentary existence.[33]

The chapter on Sartre's *Critique of Dialectical Reason (Vol. I)* presents Jameson at his best.[34] Not only does he render a first-hand analysis of Sartre's *Critique* to an English-speaking audience before the *Critique* becomes translated into English from the French. He also finds in Sartre a theorist adopting the works of Hegel and Marx in order to forge a dialectical concept of freedom that takes into account the role of history. Jameson's now popular common utterance 'Always historicize!' finds a kindred comrade in Sartre. Sartre delves into freedom's meaning by posing the problems of mediation in which one looks at how we move from one level of social life to another such as the shift from the psychological to the social and the social to the economic. Sartre confronts head on the problem of scarcity. In the Marxist framework, struggles to overcome alienation by those lives as the condemned of the earth involve struggles to overcome material scarcity in search of freedom. Jameson views Sartre addressing the role of Marxist thought in the emancipation of workers and the colonized from the pervasive bourgeois humanism dominating the world. The notion of a 'project' so prominent in Sartre's *Critique* puts forth the idea of having a projected goal towards achieving freedom. This notion of having a projected goal is essential to the thinking of hedgehog intellectuals.

Lastly, Jameson's fascination with Sartre emanates from Sartre's fusion of Marxism with other modes of thought. Sartre fuses Marxism, existentialism, and phenomenology. Jameson fuses Marxism, phenomenology, Hegelianism, and literary criticism. Sartre's vision of praxis, dialectical thinking, and the reciprocal processes involved between dialectical oppositions leading to a state of freedom becomes central for Jameson. In the end, Jameson forges a dialectical literary criticism constructed towards the problems unique to the Western world such as the problems of postindustrial monopoly capitalism and the lack of exchange between the global North dominated by the Unites States and the global South of the Western Hemisphere containing the areas of Latin America, Central America, and the Caribbean.

The thinkers under analysis in *Marxism and Form* inform Jameson's thought, but Jameson ultimately develops his own Hegelian-Marxist dialectical creation. The Hegelian dialectic of 'identity and difference' informs most of Jameson's thought. Negotiating the tensions among identity and difference within the context of a materialistic world ruled by modes of economic production determines if one shall continue to live in a state of unfreedom or if they shall be set free.[35]

Wynter's Heretical Freedom

Sylvia Wynter's essay 'After the New Class' details her new, heretical concept of freedom that she calls 'the autonomy of human cognition'. This notion of freedom distinguishes itself from the paradigm of Liberal Humanism that includes thinkers such as Isaiah Berlin as well as from the paradigm of Marxism that includes thinkers such as James and Jameson. Wynter's esay which details her dialectical concept of freedom was written in honor of the death of C.L.R. James within the context of the collapse of Marxist projects in Eastern Europe and the Gulf crisis in the Middle East of the early 1990s. Wynter analyses two works of James: the Hegelian-Marxist theoretical tract *Notes on Dialectics* and the lecture *From Du Bois to Fanon*. Through engaging the heretical aspects of James's own concept of Hegelian-Marxist freedom and fusing it with the Fanonian concern for *Les Damnés* (the condemned of the earth), Wynter is able to critique Stalinist Marxism as well as point out the limitations of the attempted heresies enacted by James, Hegelian-Marxists, and the various thinkers devoted to strands of Marxism. She writes in the beginning:

> In this paper, I want to identify what I see as the major aspects of C.L.R. James's intellectual legacy to us. I shall do this in the context of the cataclysmic collapse in Eastern Europe of Marxism as a viable alternative "world perception" and order of knowledge, to that of Liberal Humanism. But I shall do it as well in that of the context too of the recent Gulf crisis which has equally, if more implicitly so, called in question the viability of the Liberal-Humanist world perception itself.... In order to do so, I have selected two scriptural texts from the range of James' works. I shall relate these in turn, to a major formulation made by a contemporary thinker so as to show that these texts, both of which are emblematic of James' thought, whether contesting or reinforcing the formulations of these present-day thinkers, clearly   provide us with the outlines of a new world perception that I see both as his major intellectual legacy and of the still to be completed task that he left for us to complete. Since it is a world perception, whose outlines if filled out and pushed to its complementary heretical conclusions, can enable us to carry over and transform the still dynamic inter- and counter-textuality, of the epochal but still only partial conception of human freedom put forward by Liberal Humanism on the one hand,

and Marxism on the other, into a new conception of freedom that I have defined in my title as that of the "autonomy of human cognition".[36]

In the process of her critique, Wynter details her own notion of Liminal Dialectics in contrast to Hegelian-Marxist dialectics such as that of James and Jameson. Furthermore, Wynter provides a clear illustration of the differences between understanding freedom as a practice and freedom as a normative ideal. Lastly, Wynter's critique of the New Class intellectuals of Stalin's Soviet Union, Marxist-Leninist vanguard party bureaucrats, and Grenada serves as a nexus linking the development of her notion of freedom to her call for hedgehog intellectuals to create new 'forms of life'. Although she rejects the Liberal Humanism of persons such as Berlin, I maintain that Berlin's usefulness especially to her own thought lies not in his theory of freedom but in his metaphor of the hedgehog that provides an optic for thinking about the role of intellectuals in theorizing freedom in search of change. Wynter's notion of the autonomy of human cognition maps onto her project of moving beyond Marxism's emphasis on modes of economic production towards understanding that battling the crisis in our contemporary era necessitates looking at the conflicting modes of producing the *human* in existence between different orders of knowledge.

In *Notes on Dialectics,* James makes use of Hegel's *Science of Logic* in order to explain the following problem: how did Marxism as a political theory of liberation lead to the empirical dystopia of Stalinist purges, Gulags, and pervasive bureaucratization of the state? James concluded that the New Class notion of socialism as nationalized property led inevitably to the Gulags, Stalinism, and advent of Nazism. But who were the New Class and how did their notion of socialism ultimately lead to heightened states of unfreedom rather than freedom? The New Class represented intellectuals with 'certified degrees of knowledge'. Operating within the framework of socialism, these intellectuals sought as their goal not the acquisition of material wealth but the consolidation of power roles inside the hierarchy of the political state structure.[37] The New Class constructed the administrative dimensions of the state in the form of a bureaucracy. As such, the New Class developed as an elite group outside the prism of social class distinctions based on economics. This was the moment of intellectual hegemony. That is, instead of Marxist or state socialist calls for the dictatorship of the proletariat, the dictatorship of the New Class over the proletariat ensued. Wynter describes the New Class:

> Rather this New Class as the administrative and techno-bureaucratic class par excellence, had as its goal the monopolization not of wealth, but of state and societal power .... That as a class that comprised, as the authors of the 1970s Eastern-European study points out, of the only group in society which has no other title to its societal statuses except on the basis of its certified degrees of knowledge, it must necessarily, whenever it seeks to take state political power in its own name and right, subordinate its "cognitive" activity and, with it the interests of cognition, to its group-empowering interests, a paradox that might therefore be defined as the untruth of the New Class, i.e. in its Stalinist or Nazi variants.[38]

James's *Notes* traces the evolution of the New Class as socio-historical phenomenon from its modern origins in English Civil War of the seventeenth century to its historical formation in the 1789 French Revolution through the 1917 Bolshevik Russian Revolution and the Revolution's aftermath. Lenin's concept of the vanguard party marked a new moment in the evolution of the New Class. With the vanguard party, Lenin brought into being the centrality of the political party as a central organism for attaining and maintaining the proletarian Revolution. James not only rejects the existence of the New Class in its Stalinist and Nazi forms. James also denounces Marxism-Leninism's championing of the vanguard party and the New Class elite of the political party as the main thrust for political organizing. The primary thesis of the *Notes* is the creation of an independent Marxism championing the abolition of the political party as the central form of organization for Marxist political theorists. This turn represents James's 'Copernican' insight in relation to Marxist theory.[39]

For Wynter, the essence of James's insights in *Notes* reached its most prophetic tragic culmination in the Caribbean, resulting in the 1983 collapse of the Revolution in Grenada. Wynter observes:

> It was in Grenada, paradoxically that the overall unraveling of the New Class notion of Marxian socialism, against which James had warned,

was first set in motion with the execution of the less hard-line believers in the notion of socialism-as-equalling-nationalized-property, by the more hard line ones. So that, as a result, the Stalinist "murderous cast" who James had powerfully attacked in the *Notes* would appear again in his very own Caribbean; and again in many instances as men and women hardliners who, once their thinking had come to be heteronomously controlled by a Notion of socialism, projected from their group-perspective and represented as the very apex of the autonomy of human self and societal cognition, had acted in good and righteous faith to precipitate the tragedy which heralded in turn the undoing of the "nationalized property" Notion of socialism.[40]

The collapse of the New Class in Grenada points to a flaw in Marxist analyses regarding the roads to freedom from unfreedom. James forges an independent path of Marxism even though he cannot see flaws in his own insights. Marxism champions a class-first approach as opposed to Garveyism's race-first approach. Despite Caribbean Marxists like James who give primacy to the class-first approach while paying attention to race, there is an epistemological gap resulting from the modern Manichaean racial state that in Wynter's view simply does not allow the Marxist paradigm to explain all of the significant ills or all of the world's own states of unfreedom.

Wynter's move towards analysing James's lecture during the 1960s, *From Du Bois to Fanon*, details further some Jamesian narratives while at the same time shifting the geography of reason towards constructing her own concept of freedom. The line of black intellectual thinking from Du Bois to Garvey to Fanon concerns itself with the needs of black people. The race question to the Pan-African question to the anti-colonial national question all deal in their own ways with such needs. For James, these are all fundamental topics central to Western civilization and the Western world system as a whole. Wynter notes that in James's eyes Fanon exemplifies the 'fullest development' of the movement of autonomous black intellectual to engage the struggles blacks face globally. James concludes his talk by saying that he does not like the English translation of Fanon's work *Les Damnés de la terre* as *The Wretched of the Earth*. Instead, James proposes the translation *The Condemned of the Earth* to signify the ongoing struggles of black people fighting for freedom. Black intellectuals must pay attention to the sociogenic needs of black people.[41]

Wynter here ushers in the break from James. Having reached the break, one may now return to contrasting Jameson and Wynter with spectres of James. So enamoured by Hegel's idealism and Marx's materialism, James and Jameson cannot let go of seeing the limitations to viewing human emancipation solely through the prism of modes of economic production. How can it be that an island in the Caribbean governing itself under socialist principles derived in large part by Hegel, Marx, and Caribbean Marxism would allow its revolutionary project to implode? Moreover, why did other Caribbean Marxists outside of Grenada remain silent to the Grenada tragedy? Wynter's answer: look to those occupying the state of liminality and the workings of Liminal Dialectics.

Liminal dialectics refers to the dialectical tensions among those who are liminal heretics and others representing the non-liminal status quo. The lived experience of the black for Wynter exposes the fact that Marxism in its variants and Liberal Humanism in its strands cannot address the epistemic problem of the inferiority of the black and the superiority of the white. Understanding the fact of blackness and the fact of whiteness is not linked solely to Garvey's race-first proposition or Marx's class-first proposition or Feminism's gender-first proposition. The task of solving the problems of liminal blacks, Caribbean citizens at the underside of modernity, and other liminal groups involves coming to terms with the dialectics of liminal categories. Conflicts between these categories generate the tensions between unfreedom and freedom. If one now looks at modes of producing the *human* instead of modes of economically producing Man (2), then one can next look into the ways liminal dialectics operate in relation to freedom. Isolating the liminal dialectical tension solidifies hope in achieving *human* freedom. Wynter's use of her revolutionary eleven as opposed to the thought of only Hegel and Marx gives Wynter more extensive grounding in developing a robust freedom theory. Remember, Wynter does not reject Marx. She goes beyond Marx. Wynter remarked in public not too long ago that her thought is 'post-Western, not anti-Western'.[42] To extrapolate, Wynter's thought is post-Marx, not anti-Marx. Consider Wynter's words in the latter portion of 'After the New Class':

It is in the naked starving fellah, Fanon had written in *Les Damnés de la terre*, and in him alone, that the truth resides. He is the truth! It is from the perspective of the systematic category of the *damnés*, and therefore of, in Asmaron Legesse's terms, of the *liminal* category of Negation, of Lack ... on whose basis each human order erects itself at the same time as it prescribes an imperative cognitive blindspot to that which is the condition of its own existence and autopoetic functioning as a living system, that access to the higher level systemic truth of which we are participant subjects can alone be had.[43]

Finally, Wynter's heretical concept of freedom makes the case for why theories of freedom must be understood in terms of an evolving practice rather than as a normative ideal. Theorizing freedom as a normative ideal does not allow for discussions of different concepts of freedom from one order of knowledge to another. This is the reason that the earlier discussion of Jameson's articulation of a Hegelian–Marxist concept of freedom can never truly lead to human emancipation because it remains stuck to the idea that there is a norm of freedom in existence within the Hegelian–Marxist framework. To be fair to Jameson, he spends time in *Marxism and Form* talking about the ways one may be both a Hegelian–Marxist as well as a proponent of an alternative political theory. Nevertheless, when discussing freedom, Hegelian–Marxism serves as Jameson's route to emancipation.

Wynter, in contrast to Jameson, sees freedom as a political practice that evolves. Hence, returning to the original Wynterian genealogy of evolutions detailing the concept of freedom from the medieval Christian concept to Man (1) to Man (2), one may now see how Wynter's concept of freedom unmasks the *human* from these prior over-representations of it. Wynter's freedom sheds itself of the fake over-representations of the *human* and focuses on a theory of freedom emanating from the tensions between the liminal and the non-liminal. The truth of an order may be found at the site of an order's liminal, heretical fringes. Only through a heretical intervention can the new Wynterian concept of freedom — the autonomy of human cognition — be born.

Reimagining Freedom: Concluding Reflections for Hedgehog Intellectuals

I want to conclude with a series of citations by Wynter, Marley, Césaire and Simone.

How then shall we reimagine freedom as emancipation from our present ethno-class or Western bourgeois conception of freedom? And therefore, in human, rather than as now, Man's, terms? ... beyond those of Man's oppositional sub-versions — that of Marxism's proletariat, that of feminism's woman (gender rights), and that of our multiple multiculturalisms and/or centric cultural nationalisms (minority rights), to that of gay liberation (homosexual rights), but also a conception of freedom able to draw them all together in a synthesis? One in which the 'rights' of the Poor/Jobless and increasingly criminalized category to escape the dealt cards of their systemic condemnation will no longer have to be excluded?[44]

—Sylvia Wynter

Emancipate yourself from mental slavery
None but ourselves can free our minds...
Won't you help to sing, these songs of freedom
Cause all I ever had, redemption songs
All I ever had, redemption songs
These songs of freedom, songs of freedom[45]

—Bob Marley

In this disowning town under the sun this desolate crowd which rejects everything expressive, affirmative, or free in the daylight of the earth which is its own earth. Which rejects Josephine, Empress of the French, dreaming high above the niggers. Rejects the liberator bound in his liberation of white stones. Rejects the conquistador. Rejects this contempt, this freedom, this daring.[46]

—Aimé Césaire

Black is the color of my true love's hair.

—Nina Simone

What implications does Wynter's heresy have for hedgehog intellectuals? Let us reflect on three important ones. First, hedgehog intellectuals must come to terms with their own complicity in our present state of global affairs. The lack of outcry among many Caribbean intellectuals with respect to the tragedy in Grenada exemplifies this complicity. Complicity need not involve direct involvement in a tragic event. Silence alone may paint the negative fates of many.

Second, Wynter's heresy calls upon those theorists wedded to specific disciplines such as political science, anthropology, philosophy, sociology, literature, history, physics, chemistry, and mathematics to think beyond disciplinary bounds. Lewis Gordon correctly identifies the 'disciplinary decadence' pervading the current age.[47] The late hedgehog Stephen Jay Gould understood the false divide between the humanities and the sciences. Wynter herself has written and lectured widely in the last decade about 'disciplinary decadence'. But unlike Gordon and Gould, Wynter's articulation of the crisis of disciplines maps onto her larger quest highlighting the evolutions in concepts of freedom.

Lastly, Wynter's heretical, dialectical notion of freedom calling for emancipating ourselves beyond the entrapments of materialism brings us back in touch with Bob Marley's prophetic words in 'Redemption Song' chanting for an end to mental slavery. Grand theorizing must take into account the psychic as much as the material or physical. Sylvia Wynter's hedgehogs must do no less in order to reimagine freedom beyond *man*'s oppositional sub-versions. The goal of creating new 'forms of life' in pursuit of freedom cannot come to fruition unless this is done. The future of the *human* after *man* depends on it.

Notes

1. This chapter was originally presented in 2002 at the conference, 'After Man, Towards the Human: The Thought of Sylvia Wynter' at the University of the West Indies, Mona, Jamaica. I wish to thank Sylvia Wynter above all for sharing her life and work with me, Lewis Gordon and Paget Henry for introducing me to Wynter's thought, Stefan Wheelock for comments on an earlier draft of the chapter, and Anthony Bogues, Rupert Lewis and Brian Meeks for putting this series together. I dedicate this essay to the memory of Jim Murray, founding Director of the C.L.R. James Institute, whose constant energy made the lives of many around the globe better each day.
2. Ludwig Wittgenstein, *Philosophical Investigations* (New York: Macmillan, 1953).
3. Isaiah Berlin, 'The Hedgehog and the Fox: An Essay on Tolstoy's View of History' in *The Proper Study of Mankind* (New York: Farrar, Straus and Giroux, 1997 [1953]), 436-498. The scientist Stephen J. Gould's recent work *The Hedgehog, the Fox, and the Magister's Pox* (New York: Harmony, 2003) uses Berlin's metaphors of the hedgehog and the fox in order to address the ways in which the present divide between the sciences and the humanities should be

conceptually reduced. Incidentally, though Gould finished the manuscript of his work shortly before the draft of my essay was complete, I and the rest of the world did not see his text in print until nearly a year after his death in May 2002. My utilization of the hedgehog and fox metaphors differs from Gould's. Nonetheless, my use of these metaphors along with Gould's provide useful heuristic devices for understanding Wynter's argument in favour of '*human freedom*' beyond the current disciplinary divides inherited in the Western tradition from the times of Plato's Academy to the era of Medieval Christendom to the present era of *man* with its bioeconomic notion of freedom.

4. Anthony Bogues, 'Investigating the Radical Caribbean Intellectual Tradition', *Small Axe* 4 (1998): 38-43. Bogues investigates aspects of the radical Caribbean intellectual tradition in other works of his such as *Caliban's Freedom: The Early Political Thought of C.L.R. James* (London: Pluto Press, 1997) and *Black Heretics, Black Prophets: Radical Political Intellectuals* (New York: Routledge, 2003).

5. Isaiah Berlin, 'Two Concepts of Liberty' in *Four Essays on Liberty* (Oxford: Oxford University Press, 1979), 118-172.

6. Maurice Merleau-Ponty, *Phenomenology of Perception* (New York: Routledge, 1958); Edmund Husserl, *Phenomenology and the Crisis of Philosophy* (New York: Harper Torchbooks, 1965). Lewis Gordon's *Fanon and the Crisis of European Man* (New York: Routledge, 1995) is a welcome attempt at using existential phenomenological thought in order to understand the crisis of European Man through the prism of the Human Sciences as opposed to simply the sciences of Man. For more details on the Human Sciences, see Roger Smith's well-documented *The Norton History of the Human Sciences* (New York: W.W. Norton & Co., 1997).

7. C.L.R. James, *Notes on Dialectics: Hegel, Marx, Lenin* (London: Allison & Busby, 1980).

8. Enrique Dussel, *The Underside of Modernity* (Atlantic Highlands: Humanities Press, 1996); Charles Mills, *The Racial Contract* (Ithaca: Cornell University Press, 1997); Clyde Taylor, *The Mask of Art* (Bloomington: Indiana University Press, 1998); Charles Mills, 'Race and the Social Contract Tradition', *Social Identities* 6, no. 4 (2000): 441-462; Neil Roberts, 'Colonialism & Its Legacies: New Directions in Contemporary Political Theory', *Philosophia Africana* 7, no. 2 (2004): 89-97.

9. Figure 1 is a visual adaptation of ideas presented by Wynter in her essay, 'Un-Settling the Coloniality of Being/Power/Truth/Freedom: Toward the Human, After *Man*, Its Over-Representation' (paper prepared for the Annual Coloniality Working Group Conference, SUNY Binghamptom, April 27–29, 2000).

10. Michel Foucault, *The Order of Things: An Archaeology of the Human Sciences* (New York: Vintage Books, 1973).

11. See Wynter's 'List of Enclosures Plus Comments on to Point of Enclosures' from the June 2002 conference.

12. David Theo Goldberg, *Racist Culture: Philosophy and the Politics of Meaning* (Oxford: Blackwell, 1993); Emmanuel Eze, ed., *Race and the Enlightenment: A Reader* (Oxford: Blackwell, 1997); Paget Henry, *Caliban's Reason: Introducing Afro-Caribbean Philosophy*, 2000.

13. Frantz Fanon, *Black Skin, White Masks*, 1967 (New York: Grove Press, 1967), 9, 11, 222.

14. Sylvia Wynter, 'Towards the Sociogenic Principle: Fanon, the Puzzle of Conscious Experience, of "Identity" and What Its Like to be "Black"' in *National Identity and Sociopolitical Changes in Latin America*, eds. M. Durán-Cogan and A. Gómez-Moriana (New York: Garland Press, 2001), 30-66.

15. Figure 2 represents my own interpretation of Wynterian notions of unfreedom and freedom in her overall political theory.
16. See Theodor Adorno's *Negative Dialectics* (New York: Seabury Press, 1973) for his explanation of the 'world's own unfreedom'.
17. An example of Wynter's penchant for composing manifestos is Sylvia Wynter, 'A Black Studies Manifesto', *Forum NHI* 1, no. 1 (1994): 3-11.
18. David Scott, 'The Re-Enchantment of Humanism: An Interview with Sylvia Wynter', *Small Axe* 8 (2000): 159-160.
19. See Hannah Arendt's *The Human Condition* (Chicago: University of Chicago Press, 1998 [1958]) for a discussion of the Arendtian notions of activity, natality, plurality, and productivity. Arendt declares that this text, like her later *On Revolution* (New York: Penguin, 1965) is an attack on the insights of Marx. What is quite interesting is that, while Wynter and Arendt disagree about the usefulness of Marxist thought, they each concern themselves with theorizing the *human* condition beyond *man*.
20. David Scott, 'The Re-Enchantment of Humanism: An Interview with Sylvia Wynter', 200.
21. A selection of the most relevant works by or about the eleven key figures influencing Wynter includes: Frantz Fanon, *The Wretched of the Earth* (New York: Grove Press, 1963); Frantz Fanon, *Black Skin, White Masks* (New York: Grove Press, 1967); Giambattista Vico, *The New Science of Giambattista Vico* (Ithaca, Cornell University Press, 1968); Aimé Césaire, *Return to My Native Land* (Middlesex: Penguin Books, 1969); Elsa Goveia, 'The Social Framework', *Savacou* 2 (1970): 7-15; Aimé Césaire, *Discourse on Colonialism* (New York: Monthly Review Press, 1972); Gregory Bateson, *Steps to an Ecology of Mind*, 1972 (New York: Ballantine Books, 1972); Michel Foucault, *The Order of Things* (New York: Vintage Books, 1973); Asmaron Legesse, *Gada* (New York: The Free Press, 1973); Karl Marx, 'Theses on Feuerbach' in *Marx-Engels Reader*, ed. R. Tucker (New York: W.W. Norton & Co., 1978), 143-145; Gregory Bateson, *Mind and Nature* (New York: Dutton, 1979); Michel Foucault, *Power/Knowledge* (New York: Pantheon Books, 1980); C.L.R. James, *Notes on Dialectics: Hegel, Marx, Lenin* (London: Allison & Busby, 1980); C.L.R. James, *From Du Bois to Fanon* (n.d.); Zygmunt Bauman, *Legislators and Interpreters* (Ithaca: Cornell University Press, 1987); Zygmunt Bauman, *Freedom* (Minneapolis: University of Minnesota Press, 1988); Aimé Césaire, 'Poetry and Knowledge' in *Aimé Césaire: Lyric and Dramatic Poetry, 1946-82*, eds. C. Eshleman and A. Smith (Charlottesville: Caraf, 1990); C.L.R. James, 'Freedom Today' in *American Civilization* (Oxford: Blackwell, 1993), 106-117; Sylvia Wynter, 'Columbus, the Ocean Blue, and Fables That Stir the Mind' in *Poetics of the Americas*, eds. B. Cowan and J. Humphries. (Baton Rouge: LSU, 1997), 141-164.
22. Sylvia Wynter, 'September 11, Its Aftermath, "The World's Unfreedom" and the Crisis of Secular "Man": Explorations Towards the Human', Course Syllabus (Spring 2002).
23. Baruch Spinoza gains the label of heretic before publishing his two most famous posthumous tracks, *Ethics* (Indianapolis: Hackett, 1992) and *Theological-Political Treatise* (Indianapolis: Hackett, 2001). See Spinoza's *Theological-Political Treatise* for his views on the 'freedom to philosophize'.
24. Some of Sylvia Wynter's writings and lectures on C.L.R. James include: Wynter, 'In Quest of Matthew Bondman: Some Cultural Notes on the Jamesian Journey' in *C.L.R. James: His Life and Work*, ed. P. Buhle. (London: Allison & Busby, 1986), 131-145; Sylvia Wynter, 'Beyond the Categories of the Master Conception' in *C.L.R. James's Caribbean*, eds. P. Henry and P. Buhle. (Durham: Duke University Press, 1992), 63-91; Sylvia Wynter, 'James, *Les Damnés*, Notions

of Freedom and the Absolutism of Man's: On the Production of Our Modes of Being Human, of Mind' (paper prepared for the Conference *C.L.R. James Scholarship: Old and New*, Brown University, April 14–16, 2000).

25. For a selection of Fredric Jameson's hedgehog intellectual thinking, see Fredric Jameson, *Sartre: The Origins of a Style* (New York: Columbia University Press, 1984); 'Foreword' to R. Retamar, *Caliban and Other Essays* (Minneapolis: University of Minnesota Press, 1989), vi-xii; *Late Marxism: Adorno, or, the Persistence of the Dialectic* (London: Verso, 1990); *Postmodernism, or, the Cultural Logic of Late Capitalism* (Durham: Duke University Press, 1991); 'Culture and Finance Capital', *Critical Inquiry* 24, no. 1 (1997): 246-265; *Brecht and Method* (London: Verso, 1998). Key secondary writing on Jameson's thought include: Clint Burnham, *The Jamesonian Unconscious* (Durham: Duke University Press, 1995); Roland Boer, *Jameson and Jeroboam* (Atlanta: Scholar's Press, 1996); Sean Homer, *Fredric Jameson* (New York: Routledge, 1998); Michael Hardt and Kathi Weeks, eds., *The Jameson Reader* (Oxford: Blackwell, 2000).

26. Fredric Jameson, *Marxism and Form: Twentieth-Century Dialectical Theories of Literature* (Princeton: Princeton University Press, 1971). For other important writings dealing with dialectical thinking in relation to Hegelian-Marxism, see G.W.F. Hegel, *The Science of Logic* (London: Macmillan, 1951); Herbert Marcuse, *Reason and Revolution: Hegel and the Rise of Social Theory* (Atlantic Highlands: Humanities Press, 1954); Theodor Adorno, *Negative Dialectics* (New York: Seabury Press, 1973); Jean-Paul Sartre, *Critique of Dialectical Reason (Vol. I)* (London: Verso, 1976); G.W.F. Hegel, *Phenomenology of Spirit* (Oxford: Oxford University Press, 1979); C.L.R. James, *Notes on Dialectics* (London: Allison & Busby, 1980); Robert Pippen, *Hegel's Idealism* (Cambridge: Cambridge University Press, 1989); Fredric Jameson, *Late Marxism* (London: Verso, 1990); Tony Smith, *Dialectical Social Theory and Its Critics*, 1993 (Albany: SUNY Press, 1993); Bertell Ollman, 'Marxism, This Tale of Two Cities', *Science & Society* 67, no. 1 (2003): 80-86.

27. Fredric Jameson, *Marxism and Form*, 44.

28. Ibid., ix-xix. Compare Jameson's views rejecting the easy digestible instant sentence (1971), xiii with Wynter's rejection of the easily digestible instant novel in Sylvia Wynter, 'The Instant Novel—Now', *New World Quarterly* 3, no. 3 (1967): 78-81.

29. Fredric Jameson, 'Reification and Utopia in Mass Culture', *Social Text* 1 (1979): 130-148; Wynter, 'Sambos and Minstrels', *Social Text* (Winter 1979): 149-156.

30. 'Prospectus', *Social Text*, (Winter 1979): 3-4.

31. Fredric Jameson, *Marxism and Form*, xix, 111.

32. Ibid., 84-85.

33. Ibid., 85.

34. Ibid., 206-305.

35. Ibid., 325.

36. Sylvia Wynter, 'After the New Class: James, *Les Damnés*, and the Autonomy of Human Cognition' (paper prepared for the International Conference on *C.L.R. James: His Intellectual Legacies*, Wellesley College, April 19–21, 1991), 1.

37. One may consult the following sources surrounding the New Class, intellectuals, and the crisis of intellectuals in the Caribbean and the globe: Gyorgy Konrad and Ivan Szelenyi, *The Intellectuals on the Road to Class Power* (New York: Harcourt, Brace and Jovanovich, 1979); C.L.R. James (1980); C.L.R. James, *From Du Bois to Fanon* (n.d.); Zygmunt Bauman, *Legislators and Interpreters* (Ithaca: Cornell University Press, 1987); Ivan Szelenyi and Bill Martin, 'Three Waves of New Class Theory', *Theory and Society* 17 (1988): 645-667; Aimé Césaire, 'Poetry and Knowledge' in *Aimé Césaire: Lyric and Dramatic*

Poetry, 1946-82, eds. C. Eshleman and A. Smith (Charlottesville: Caraf, 1990); Sylvia Wynter, 1991; Alister Hennessy, ed. *Intellectuals in the Twentieth Century Caribbean*, vols. 1 & 2 (London: Macmillan Education, 1992); Isaiah Berlin, 'The Hedgehog and the Fox: An Essay on Tolstoy's View of History' in *The Proper Study of Mankind* (New York: Farrar, Straus and Giroux, 1997 [1953]), 436-498; Anthony Bogues, (1998): 38-43; Brian Meeks and Folke Lindahl, eds., *New Caribbean Thought* (Kingston: University of the West Indies Press, 2001).
38. Sylvia Wynter, (1991): 8.
39. Ibid., 9. In *Caliban's Freedom* (London: Pluto Press, 1997), Anthony Bogues discusses James's claim in *Notes on Dialectics* that Marxists should abolish their allegiance to the political party as viable political organism. In Hegelian terms, James called on the negation of the political party. For a different interpretation of *Notes*, see John McClendon III, *C.L.R. James's* Notes on Dialectics (Lanham: Lexington Books, 2005).
40. Sylvia Wynter (1991): 15.
41. Ibid., 92-93.
42. Statement by Wynter during her keynote address at the conference, 'After Man, Towards the Human: The Thought of Sylvia Wynter' (June 2002, University of the West Indies, Mona, Jamaica).
43. Sylvia Wynter (1991): 106. See also Legesse, *Gada* (New York: The Free Press, 1973).
44. Sylvia Wynter, 'Africa, the West and the Analogy of Culture: The Cinematic Text After Man' in *Symbolic Narratives/African Cinema*, ed. J. Givanni. (London: British Film Institute, 2000), 41-42.
45. Lyrics from Bob Marley's song 'Redemption Song'. See Bob Marley and The Wailers, 'Redemption Song' in *Uprising* (Tuff Gong: Island Records, 1980).
46. Aimé Césaire, *Return to My Native Land* (Middlesex: Penguin Books, 1969), 39.
47. Lewis Gordon, 'The Human Condition in an Age of Disciplinary Decadence', *Philosophical Studies in Education* 34 (2003): 7-25; Stephen J. Gould, *The Hedgehog, the Fox, and the Magister's Pox* (New York: Harmony, 2003).

8 | Notes on the Current Status of Liminal Categories and the Search for a New Humanism

Nelson Maldonado-Torres

In *Gada: Three Approaches to the Study of African Society*, Asmaron Legesse defines the liminal person as the 'conceptual antithesis' to any given social order.[1] Legesse argues that the liminal person plays a generative role in respect to the society that qualifies him or her as liminal. The liminal person 'generates conscious change by exposing all the injustices inherent in structure, by creating real contradictions between structure and anti-structure, social order and man-made anarchy'.[2] As it is well known, Sylvia Wynter adopts Legesse's ideas of generative anthropology and asymmetric dialectics and uses them to make sense of epistemologically emancipatory social processes.[3] Wynter conceives liminal subjects as primary motivators of social and conceptual change. Among the recent social movements that defy the central liminal categories of the modern Western episteme Wynter highlights the struggles of the 1960s in the United States.[4] African-Americans, Chicana/os and Latina/os, native Americans, women and other people identified with their struggles destabilized in different ways the solid bedrock of the liminal categories in United States society. For Wynter their struggles represented in many ways a progressive step in the direction of formulating a more expansive concept of the *human*.

To be sure, emancipatory politics are hardly welcome in our traditional modern societies. Instability is often met with the force of edicts, rules, regressive propositions, reforms, imprisonment, or even bullets. It is very significant that in this our twenty-first century, more than 30 years after the social upheavals that shook the United States and other countries in the 1960s, condemnation of the 1960s and their legacy have increased. The liminal categories are now being reinforced through a moralistic and quasi-religious discourse that makes subjects who distrust the conceptual framework of liberal politics and neo-liberal economics the targets of discrimination and persecution. The context of the 'war against terror' has only increased animosity toward the legacy of the 1960s and facilitated all kind of claims under the banner of patriotism and devotions to the central values of Western civilization. I will examine here the nature of this opposition to the legacy of the 1960s as well as proposals to counter their force. My aim is to show that both condemnations and celebrations of the 1960s and their legacy usually miss the transgressive character that Wynter identifies in these movements. In the final section of this essay I suggest a more Wynterian conception of the legacy of the 1960s through the work of Frantz Fanon, whose writings played a major role in such struggles and have been so influential in Wynter's thinking.

Pierre Bourdieu and the Utopia of Neo-liberalism

Pierre Bourdieu, who has been referred to as a sixty-eighter 'pur et dur', once referred to neo-liberalism as 'the utopia (becoming reality) of unlimited exploitation'.[5] For him neo–liberalism represents the implementation of a utopia converted into a *political programme*.[6] Like all utopias, neo-liberalism generates a faith, in this case, the faith in 'free trade'. But neo-liberalism easily exorcizes the possible accusation of fundamentalism by dressing itself up in the garments of mathematical reason. The economist is elevated to the status of a public intellectual — only matched up by psychologists who specialize in self-help. One thing is clear in this scenario, for the economic system to work we should preserve our sanity — even though we may lose our humanity in the process. Economic efficiency is what matters. In this context quantity takes over quality and extension over depth.

In addition to the genius of mathematical reason, that elevates the faith in the market to the status of logic, Bourdieu also considers what he refers to as the 'negative intellectual'. The 'negative intellectual' is in charge of 'symbolic policing', which has as its ultimate aim to break the bonds of solidarity with certain kind of subjects or certain kind of struggles. The work of the 'negative intellectual' aims to 'give satisfaction to superficial pity and racist hatred' but is 'masked as humanist indignation'.[7] With the collaboration of 'the cream of the media intelligentsia and the political class' it brings advances of critical scholarship back to zero.[8] What we see today unfolding according to the distorted logics of a 'clash of civilizations' was anticipated by Parisian intellectuals who criticized the feeble forces of a politics of hospitality. They portrayed Algerian immigrants as '"murderers and rapists", as "madmen of Islam", enveloped under the abominated name of Islamicism, the quintessence of all Oriental fanaticism'. According to Bourdieu all this is 'designed to give racist contempt the impeccable alibi of ethical and secular legitimacy'.[9] This form of thinking clearly anticipated what was to become the core of the current 'war against terror'.

The rhetoric of opposition to terrorism has proven to be insatiable. It consumes opposition wherever it finds it: in the present and in the past; in the United States and everywhere where its interests are affected that is, in this our global context, virtually everywhere. The success of the rhetoric of opposition to anti-Western terrorism is partly due to fear, to hate, to the legacy of Western modes of approaching non-Western peoples, but also, as Bourdieu suggests, to the sense of an almost realized utopian project that should not be contested. The 'war against terrorism' has allowed neo-liberalism and market democracy to present themselves once again as the desired dream of humankind or the utopia of all. While during the 1990s the reasons to comply with these forces were mainly tied to self-interest (loans and national 'development'), now they seem to have acquired a moral dimension of their own: one complies in order to fight terror and evil. The morality of opposition to all evil, as Jean Baudrillard pointed out in his comments about the 'war on terror', can only produce more evil.[10] In this situation the world turns upside down: the search for peace produces terror and the claims for justice turn into injustice.

Just a few years before the beginning of the 'war against terror' Bourdieu made a double call: a call to pursue 'symbolic struggle against the incessant work of the neo-liberal "thinkers" aimed at discrediting and disqualifying the heritage of words, traditions and representations associated with the historical conquests of the social movements of the past and the present', and a call to defend in an intelligent way institutions like labour law, social welfare, social security, and the state, which for him can be construed as forces of resistance and not merely as conservative forces that belong to an old geo-political and economic order. I would like to focus here on the first of these two calls: on the call for 'symbolic struggle'. This call for a 'symbolic struggle' invites both artists and intellectuals to fight for the value of the heritage of 'historical conquests of the social movements'. To be sure, as Wynter and others make clear, perhaps no other recent period than the decade of the 1960s, and within it, the events of 1968, have unsettled the tranquil waters of political authority and the values of capitalist civilization in the Western world. The sixties have been condemned in many ways by revisionist historiography since its inception. But this critical trend perhaps has not been as strong as today when it is both denounced and commodified in mass media and culture. Many young people today in the United States do not know much more about the sixties than what they learn from Britney Spears in a Pepsi commercial, or what they are exposed to in films like Austin Powers.[11]

Bourdieu's call for 'symbolic struggle' becomes very pertinent today. Perhaps he did not imagine how pertinent it was to become: the legacy of the sixties has been demonized once more, now more than ever before in the context of yet another war. This context makes clear that the need for reflections on the sixites responds to interests that go beyond historical revisionism or the defense of memory. They partly respond to the need of looking for an-other utopia in the midst of war.

The Sixties

In a recent article entitled '1968 and all that' Michael Watts revisits 1968 and portrays it as a global 'great rehearsal' aimed to 'enlarge the field of the possible'.[12] Watts is aware of the many different interpretations of the sixties, yet, for him 1968 cannot be reduced to any of its demonizing interpretations. For him, they ignore the extent to which 1968 advanced a project of building counter-institutions and of 'working against the institutions while working within them'.[13] In their hybridity and their diversity 1968 provides for Watts 'a striking illustration of what Hardt and Negri call the multitude against empire'.[14]

Watts makes an excellent job in showing how the radical democratic 'great rehearsal' of 1968 had global, regional, and local dimensions. The year 1968 is a transnational phenomenon whose different expressions responded to geo-political dynamics and to local particularities. This year did not occur in exactly the same way in the East and in the West, in North and South.[15] It also had different manifestations in India and Japan, Ethiopia and England. Watts shows that there were not one, but multiple 1968s. Yet, for this very reason it is most intriguing that he labels his exploration of the continuities between 1968 and the present as 'Three roads from Paris'. While Watts conceives the struggles of the 1960s as diverse and multifarious, he maintains the notion of a solid and firm genealogy with Paris at its centre. It would probably have been more interesting and more politically progressive at the same time to show how the struggles that occurred in the United States and other places defy the already traditional genealogy that can only find the traces of pertinent political and conceptual change in Europe. Following Wynter, one could try to discern what were the unique forms of thought and political activity that emerge in the 1960s. Instead, Watts followed Marshall Bennan in believing that the innovations of the sixties can be traced back to 'a political struggle to unite two logics of different provenance, one Marxist, the other libertarian'.[16] In this way, the 'grammar of dissent' of many different groups and upheavals is automatically deciphered and articulated. The erasure of specifics and the imposition of a Eurocentric genealogy also appear in Watts's article when he dilutes the need for uncovering multiple tactics and contributions to political thought by unambivalently relying on Hart and Negri's concept of the anonymous 'multitude'. What Watts misses here is the peculiarity of the challenges and the tactics that emerge from positions of liminality, as Legesse and Wynter understand them. I will elaborate this idea below.

The centrality of Paris in his analysis of the upheavals of 1968 is reaffirmed in the concluding part of Watts's essay when he firmly endorses the view of whom he describes as a French sixty-eighter 'pur et dur', Pierre Bourdieu. Watts's strongly favourable mention of Bourdieu at the end of his article illustrates an interest coincidence. Thirty years after 1968 Bourdieu calls us to fight against the neo-liberal negative intellectual by reaffirming our commitment to past struggles. The very same year Watts engages in the activity of retrieval by revisiting 1968. Watts then concludes his essay with a celebration of Bourdieu, whom he portrays as a 1968er. I do not mean to suggest that Bourdieu and Watts were necessarily in direct communication with each other, or that Bourdieu is not a 1968er. What is interesting to me is that by looking at this equation at first sight it seems that Bourdieu's call for 'symbolic struggles' ultimately collapses into a call to himself, the Parisian philosopher and sociologist of 1968. Put differently, the idea is that the call to engage in 'symbolic struggle' culminates in Bourdieu himself, who calls us to engage in 'symbolic struggle'. This apparent product of fortune or pure contingency points to limits in the way in which 'symbolic struggle' is carried out. Here symbolic struggle seems to lose any dialectical character and rather collapses into the form of a tautology. The tautology is structural in character. It is like a constant sense of *déjà vu*, a repetition that seeks to re-establish order in the modern/colonial *matrix* of meaning and significations. Symbolic struggle is radically limited by a structural tautology. It becomes clear in Bourdieu and Watts's texts that such struggle does not necessarily entail the defense and articulation of critical and creative positions that emerge from liminality. And if they do, they are subordinated under the dominant narratives of modernity. Before spelling out the difference between these forms of engagement I would like to explore another possibility. To see if we can liberate ourselves from the close circle or tautology that was forming itself above, let's explore a critical account of the Parisian of 1968 and of Bourdieu himself.

I would like to focus now on Luc Ferry and Alain Renaut's virulent critique of the thought of 1968 in their *French Philosophy of the Sixties: An Essay on Antihumanism*.[17] According to Ferry and Renaut, French intellectuals in the 1950s and 60s invested much time in a critique of the modern world, inspired by Marx and Heidegger. The camps were divided between Marxists and Heideggerians, with a few people in between, but as Marxism was each time more identified with authoritarianism and economism the balance ended up increasing with the Heideggerians critique of the subject. Marxism did not disappear completely, but was put in the service of the critique of *Man*. While Marxists pointed out the ideological character of humanism, Heideggerian took care of the metaphysical aspects. In short, both ended up advocating the death of the subject or the Death of Man. The subject appears in this light as the expression of either a monadic bourgeois egoism or as the invention of modern metaphysics. It is seen as Consciousness or Will, as a means of representation or as the ultimate ground of decision. Ferry and Renaut sympathize with the critique of the excesses of humanism. Yet, for them reducing the legacy of humanism to ideological expressions or to a vicious metaphysics can only lead to a repetition of the proverbial act of 'throwing out the baby with the bathwater'. And this is precisely for them what took place in the thought of 1968. The thinkers of this time gave credence to the radical individualism and the economies of desire that unfolded in Western societies only two decades after 1968. Declaring the death of the subject was indeed liberating, but in its turn came an egoistic and indifferent self.[18] At the end, the right to difference turned into the right for indifference — a right alternatively claimed by some groups in society and by the state.

Ferry and Renaut claim that in great part because of its indebtedness to Heidegger (rather than to Marx), the thought of 1968 exploded only one dimension of the ambiguous heritage of the historical moment: individualistic freedom was emphasized over comradeship, institutional transformation, and action. Ferry and Renaut believe that the total rejection of modern humanism and the discourse on the 'Death of the Subject' or the 'Death of Man' are too excessive and ultimately lead to indifference or to a restatement of the 'law of the fittest',[19] where might makes right. In order to oppose this problematic tendency, outlined by Lipovetsky in his *L'Ere du Vide: Essais sur 1 'individualisme Contemporain*, they call for a 'nonmetaphysical humanism'.[20] And this consists in 'conferring a coherent philosophical status on the promise of freedom contained in the requirements of humanism that it's metaphysical development led it to betray'.[21] They make clear what kind of modernity they are thinking about when they praise the virtues of democracy and human rights. It is the modernity of the French Republic. Ferry and Renaut's intent is to oppose the problematic influence of German anti-humanism, which is seen by them as a virus that consumed the French spirit from 1968 on, with a defense of the French Republican tradition.[22] They want, as it were, to combine what is for them the best of 1789 with the best of 1968. I believe, in contrast, that they ended up reproducing some of the worst features of both. The centrality of France's contribution to modernity and French civilization serves in their work to erase the crucial interventions to the project of modernity that have emerged from the darker side of France, its own colonies. It is as if the Haitian Revolution were not sufficiently connected with France or did not make any contribution to the critical engagement or to the rearticulation of the Rights of Man.[23] It is also as if Fanon, who called for a new humanism in his native Martinique and later in his second home the other French colony of Algeria, did not have anything to contribute to the task of rethinking humanism. I suspect that for Ferry and Renaut it is not so much that they do not think that Fanon does not have anything to contribute. For them Fanon is simply invisible, invisible to them as invisible to the French Republic. Ferry and Renaut expand the circle that begins and ends with Bourdieu. They expand it and maintain its epicentre intact. At every moment glorious France remains at the centre. Theirs is a French centric critique of French and German anti-humanism.

In their respective admiration and criticism of 1968, both Watts on the one hand, and Ferry and Renaut on the other, leave untouched the basic coordinates of legitimate critical theorizing. The coordinates are well known to all of us. In this case they take the form of a dramatic tension between Marx and Heidegger, French humanism and French anti-humanism, Marxism and libertarianism, 1789 and the Parisian 1968. Watts, Ferry and Renaut, along with the French theorists of the 'Death of Man' still leave untouched the fundamental primacy of European *man*. Compare these gestures with Fanon's call:

> Leave this Europe where they are never done talking of Man, yet murder men everywhere they find them, at the corner of every one of their streets, in all the corners of the globe.... So, my brothers, how is it that we do not understand that we have better things to do than to follow that same Europe? For Europe, for ourselves, and for humanity, comrades, we must turn over a new leaf, we must work out new concepts, and try to set afoot a new man.[24]

Fanon's call contrasts sharply with both humanist and antihumanist European currents, for he calls not for the 'Death of Man', but more particularly for the Death of European Man.[25] Different from Ferry and Renaut, Fanon challenges us to formulate, not merely a non-metaphysical humanism, but a non- Eurocentric humanism. Fanon makes clear that the critique of metaphysics and the critique of ideology are not by themselves conducive to the radical critique of Eurocentric privilege that he calls us to abandon.

Fanon's critical gesture toward Europe also radicalizes Bourdieu's posture: for him Eurocentrism appears as a sort of an unacknowledged 'symbolic capital' of Western academe. Eurocentrism becomes what could be referred to as the 'intellectual capital' of Western *homo academicus*. He may be culturally decrepit or poor, but as long as he has Kant, Nietzsche, Foucault, or Bourdieu on his side he feels comfortable. There is an investment of value in the tradition of Western thought. What must be maintained at all costs is the *monopoly of theory*. Unlike economicism, which, as Bourdieu points out, collapses the time of giving and receiving into immediate and calculable transactions, Eurocentrism recognizes temporality, but only in the form of the history of Europe as exclusive giver of the gift of reason and theory. European Man is not merely *homo academicus*, he is more precisely *homo academicus imperiosus*, the one who has the right to know and the duty to give, but who never receives. For 'symbolic struggle' to be effective it has to take the form of a decolonization of knowledge.[26] This involves an elucidation of the challenges and contributions made by liminal subjects to the overcoming of modernity/coloniality[27]. A critique of Eurocentrism, but also a critique of racism and sexism are central here. One must not forget that the discourse of the 'neo-liberal negative intellectual' embodies some very definite characteristics: it carries the traces of whiteness, maleness, and Eurocentrism, all of which inhibit the possibility of generous interhuman contact, of giving and receiving the gift that is the self.

The critique of capitalism has to provide an alternative to the logic of accumulation and it cannot do so without criticizing the ways in which economic, symbolic, and intellectual capital work. Our version of 'symbolic struggle' should include an explicit engagement with all this. It must become a project of decolonizing knowledge 'against the incessant work of the neo-liberal [White Male European] "thinkers" aimed at discrediting and disqualifying the heritage of words, traditions and representations associated with the historical conquests of the social movements of the past and the present'. And for this it is convenient to turn to the sixties, but not only to the sixties of Derrida or Foucault in Paris, but to the sixties of Third World intellectuals and activists who visited Paris but who never settled there intellectually, intellectuals like Fanon and others.[28] It is from this point that we begin a more systematic alteration of the geography of reason.[29] But reactions against this move abound, and even more so in the last decade, particularly after September 11. The context of the Vietnam War is quite different from that of the war against Afghanistan. What are the challenges of talking about the sixties today?

Outcome of the Sixties

There are many ways in which the 1990s appear very much as the inversion of the 1960s. Immanuel Wallerstein described the movements of the 1960s as anti-bureaucratic, anti-authoritarian and anti-Western.[30] The post-cold war, or what looks to some as the information age, has seen the subsumption of anti-bureaucratic and anti-authoritarian demands to a new form of despotism: the brutal forces of transnational capital. Conservatives in the United States oppose intervention of the government in the regulation of their lives, but very easily endorse the intervention of the state in the affairs of other peoples. They want the protection and respect of their way of life, the American way of life. They do not want the state intervening with their lives, but they do not want to see international organs intervening with the plans and actions of their state. Anti-westernism has turned into a strong sense of Americanism.

Even the left has taken a nationalist turn. We did not have to wait until the publication of Richard Rorty's *Achieving Our Country* to realize this.[31] Already in 1989, the very year of the collapse of the Soviet Union, a once student of Rorty, Cornel West, was calling intellectuals in the United States to question the 'American obsession with theories from continental Europe' and to embrace their 'own nationalist traditions of thought'.[32] Cornel West argues that this obsession was one of the intellectual legacies of the sixties. And in fact, the sixties generated a strong critique of the United States, as it was testified in the protests against the Vietnam War. The incidents of the decade led to the idea, as Rorty puts it, that America was unachievable.[33] The period was followed by a massive import of French theory.[34] Rorty's and West's can be seen as late responses to the sixties. If Ferry and Renaut make French centric critiques of the French theory of the sixties, Rorty and West, very much in the spirit of the 90s, offer United States-centric critiques of European thought. Although both Rorty and West have important considerations in mind, for example, that the cultural left becomes political — what they do very much seems like another episode in the tension between the Old World Europe and the country that has appropriated the virtue of itself being entirely the New World, that country known to many as America. The problematic tendencies of this Americanism are evident in Rorty, who castigates Habermas for his praise of the 'unfinished' project of the Enlightenment, while he calls for the 'unfinished' business of America. What makes America redeemable and the Enlightenment not is hardly evident in his reflections, particularly considering that to a great extent they are both outcomes and protagonists of the drama of modernity/coloniality.

After September 11, calls for intellectual patriotism in the United States have only increased. Elizabeth Cobbs Hoffman, a professor of American foreign relations at San Diego State University states:

> I understand modern historian's dilemma. As a forty something person, I grew up with Che Guevara, Bob Dylan and the Vietnam War. I come from the activist left, and I am proud of that heritage. I remain a liberal [that she includes Che in her liberalism is by itself interesting here]. Like many of my colleagues, I hesitate to write books or give lectures that might appear to whitewash America's character flaws or its choices as a superpower.
>
> But it is time to admit that this generation of historians — with some notable exceptions — has yet to deliver to students, and to the public, a usable and balanced interpretation of the past.
>
> Too many researchers have done a better job documenting the republic's weaknesses than revealing its strengths.
>
> If some American intellectuals are not as prepared to defend the nation as they are to criticize it, they may deserve the accusations of "unpatriotic" that we have parried for 30 years. The political right will capture the American flag only if we hand it to them.
>
> Last, it would not hurt professional skeptics to meditate — only briefly, if it hurts too much — on the nature of American goodness.[35]

I have been discussing so far the limits of the modes of critique that emerged in the 1960s in the north. Much to the contrary, Hoffman argues that the critique has gone too far and that it has been too one-sided. I agree that it has been too one-sided, but not so much because it was too critical of the United States, but simply because it was never critical enough. Either France or the United States remained at the centre after the critique. Always devalued were the intellectuals of the South, not to mention the (im)migrant population who redefined the very meaning of what it was to be an 'American'. With this I mean that the critique of the United States was still relative and did not question the dominion of theory by the North. On the contrary the one-sidedness of the critique increased, and it was each time easier to simply dismiss the contributions of Third-World intellectuals. As an example of this, consider the following statement about Fanon's work published a few months before September 11:

> Fanon was very much a figure for the 1960s: only in that decade could he have achieved his fame, which was almost entirely posthumous.... His evident hatred of Europe fitted in well with the exhibitionist self-loathing of the era: a hatred and self-loathing based largely on ignorance. When in Rome, for example, Fanon displayed no interest whatever in the monuments of that marvelous city, in case — I suspect — he were confronted with the astonishing glory of Europe as well as its degradation, a confrontation which would have required him to moderate his views.... The ruins of Rome threatened his world view, and therefore his justification for the violence he lauded.
>
> In the last analysis, Fanon is more interesting as a sociological phenomenon — both for himself and for the reaction he called forth in the parts of the world he excoriated — than as a thinker.[36]

Anthony Daniels is hardly making an original conclusion here. He is simply restating in one of the most stupid ways ever seen a general consensus: that the life of intellectuals of colour is of more value than their intellectual production.[37] What is characteristic of our times is this concession to the lack of arguments, which shows a desire not merely to continue the repression of radical critical voices, but to actually make them entirely vanish. The utopia of neo-liberalism is giving birth to a proto-fascism that masks itself with celebration of a skewed democracy and with the defense of a very selected set of freedoms.

Toward a Different Utopia

Elsewhere I have articulated the idea of a weak utopian project as bringing about the Death of European Man.[38] I think that the peculiar intricacies between 'estadounidense' patriotism, Eurocentrism, the propensity to war, and the continued subordination of the theoretical contributions of peoples from the South call for a reformulation of this idea. Today, after the post-1989 and post-September 11 patriotism we shall call more directly simply for the Death of American Man. By American Man I mean a concept or figure, a particular way of being-in-the-world, or else, the very subject of an episteme that gives continuity to an imperial order of things under the rubrics of liberty and the idea of a Manifest Destiny that needs to be accomplished. American Man, as its predecessor and still companion European Man, are unified under an even more abstract concept, Imperial Man. Many of the struggles of the sixites and their outcomes have put into question these concepts of the human. They have partly done so by going against the grain from within but also by proposing alternative futures, utopias, or ways of being human.

The 'they' to which I allude here does not refer to 'we' the people or to the postmodern multitude, but to the liminal 'they', that is, those whom Frantz Fanon called the wretched or condemned of the earth (*damnés de la terre*). The Fanonian concept of damnation, articulated in the context of decolonization struggles against French imperialism (before 1968), continues to be of relevance today for it refers precisely to the positions of liminality that Legesse and Wynter have in mind.[39] The concept of *damnés* (of modernity/coloniality), different from the people (of the nation) or the multitude (of Empire), makes reference to the invisibilized and radically abject subjects of modernity (subjects who are no subjects; neither self nor other).[40] It is their agency which for Fanon has the capacity of subverting the rules of dominant rhetorical forms and institutions. Agency here refers, to be sure, to political activity, but not only to it. It primarily refers to the very condition of possibility for political activity. Agency alludes to the transition from no-self/no-other to self, which requires a process of 'despojo' and the emergence of new coordinates for *being-human*. It is primarily in this sense that the agency of the damné brings forth a new world (a new set of meanings, significations, attachments, desires).[41]

The damné is not only a victim. The damné is a category that enunciates the condition of subjects who are locked in a position of subordination. The damné lives in a hell from which quite literally there is no escape. When history passes and the dialectic advances the damnés usually remain as recipients of still new orders of injustice, degradation, dehumanization, and suffering. The damné is, as it were, a liminal subject at the second or third degree. It is often the liminal of the liminal or the almost permanently liminal subject. From her perspective the dialectic seems almost frozen. In the far side of oppression, domination, and coloniality there is thus no such thing as a dialectic of the subaltern. What begins to emerge at the extreme point of irritation, frustration, and desire for conceptual and material transformation is a renewed sense of agency that seeks an-other understanding of the human.[42] This is the meaning that I propose for Fanon's often misunderstood words:

> Leave this Europe where they are never done talking of Man, yet murder men everywhere they find them, at the corner of every one of their streets, in all the corners of the globe.... So, my brothers, how is it that we do not understand that we have better things to do than to follow that same Europe? For Europe, for ourselves, and for humanity, comrades, we must turn over a new leaf, we must work out new concepts, and try to set afoot a new man.[43]

Fanon proposes postcolonial agency as an antidote to the non-dialectics of damnation. The concept of agency that Fanon proposes is intrinsically tied to the confrontation with the realities of damnation. That is to say, what stands as the background of his concept of agency is not the achievement of a modern bourgeois or socialist revolution or the ethereal insights of any given classical text in political theory. What informs his understanding of agency is an acute perception of coloniality and what is needed to overcome its pernicious effects.

As Fanon's work suggests, and as the very etymology of the term damné makes clear, the damned is the one who wants to give but who cannot give because what he possesses has been taken from him.[44] The damnés are the subjects who by virtue of their gender or skin colour are not seen as subjects who can participate in generous intersubjective contact with others. Fanon's characterization of the damné includes not only systematic and long-standing dehumanization, but also a particular kind of desire to establish generous human contact. In her most consistent attempts to elevate herself beyond the struggle for recognition that takes place within the dialectics of lordship and bondsman, the colonized, wretched or condemned, engages in a struggle for non-sexist human fraternity that involves, both self-critique and an ethics of receptive generosity.[45] When Fanon referred to the colonized as the damné he was not only describing a situation but also raising a challenge to colonized subjects. This challenge was to set afoot a new ideal of the human, one that would take us beyond the limits of modernity/coloniality as incarnated in its European expressions and elsewhere.

For Fanon it was clear that the utopia of the colonized would remain within the horizons of modernity/coloniality and its masculine charged ethno-class conception of the human if it were based on rights of possession. Beyond obtaining property rights or social equality the utopia of the damné consists in giving birth to a world where human subjects could give themselves as who they are to others while others would recognize them as givers. The damné does not merely desire to possess (to have or to be), but to give and receive as well. Fanon pointed out that what the master resists most is not a formal recognition of rights or the equal division of property. Concession of property rights does not end racism. What the master resists most is to recognize the slave as someone who can give something to him. This alone challenges his status as absolute owner and absolute giver. The radical suspension of this privilege is what I have in mind when I call for the Death of Imperial Man, both in its European and American expressions. Calling for the Death of European and American Man means to divorce ourselves from the ideas, feelings, and actions that inhibit the generous transaction of gifts. This is a call to engage in a praxis of liberation which is also an ethics of risk and of generous encounter articulated from the position of the damné. Against the utopia of neo-liberalism, which functions as a reification of economism to the point of making authentic livelihood a constant preparation for a 'war against terror', it is possible to conceive and fight for a non-imperial, non-sexist, and non-racist way of engaging with different subjects, with different cultures, and with different ways of thinking. The 'negative intellectual' should be opposed by a 'decolonizing intellectual', by someone who is neither patriot nor universal cosmopolitan and who promotes epistemic and cultural decolonization. This 'decolonizing intellectual' must be ready to engage in a project of decolonization (previously 'symbolic struggle') that well surpasses the dreams of the Parisians of 1968, including Bourdieu. The task is particularly difficult now, since the United States mainland has been attacked. Many 'estadounidenses' are thirst for revenge and armed conflict. It will probably be harder today than it was in the sixites to oppose the war machine. Yet the fight must be fought and the decolonizing intellectual must learn how to fight it in solidarity with those who are standing against it. As Edward Said has so elegantly put it, it is time to speak truth to power.[46] And as Sylvia Wynter reminds us there is no truth more resisted than that which is brought for by the damnés.

Notes

1. Asmaron Legesse, *Gada: Three Approaches to the Study of African Society* (New York: The Free Press, 1973).
2. Ibid., 271.
3. See, for instance, Sylvia Wynter, 'On Disenchanting Discourse "Minority" Literary Criticism and Beyond,' in *The Nature and Context of Minority Criticism* (New York: Oxford University Press, 1990), 461-2.
4. See Paget Henry, *Caliban's Reason: Introducing Afro-Caribbean Philosophy* (New York: Routledge, 2000), 130.
5. See the short essay with the same title in Pierre Bourdieu, *Acts of Resistance: Against the Tyranny of the Market*, trans. Richard Nice (New York: The New Press, 1999), 94-105.
6. Ibid., 94.
7. Ibid., 92.
8. Ibid., 92.
9. Ibid., 92.
10. See Jean Baudrillard, 'L'esprit du Terrorisme', *Le Monde* (November 3, 2001).
11. It is revealing that the same actor, Mike Myers, plays the role of both Austin Powers and his nemesis, Dr Evil. In some way he anticipates the thesis of Tariq Ali that Bush and Bin Laden represent two sides of the very same coin. See Tariq Ali, *The Clash of Fundamentalisms: Crusades, Jihads, and Modernity* (New York: Verso, 2002).
12. Michael Watts, '1968 and all that', *Progress in Human Geography* 25, no.2 (2001): 175.
13. Ibid., 167.
14. Ibid., 176.

15. Ibid., 171-2.
16. Ibid., 182.
17. Luc Ferry and Alain Renaut, *French Philosophy of the Sixties: An Essay on Antihumanism*, trans. Mary Schnackenberg Cattani (Amherst, MA: The University of Massachusetts Press, 1990).
18. Ibid., 227.
19. Ibid., 229.
20. Gilles Lipovetsky, *L'ere du vide: essais sur l'individualisme contemporain* (Paris: Gallimard, 1983), xxviii.
21. Ibid., xxviii.
22. Ibid., 121.
23. For a contrasting vision about Haiti see Michel-Rolph Trouillot, *Silencing the Past: Power and the Production of History* (Boston, MA: Beacon Press, 1995).
24. Frantz Fanon, *The Wretched of the Earth*, trans. Constance Farrington (New York: Grove Press, 1968), 311-12, 316.
25. For an elaboration of the term 'Death of European Man' see Nelson Maldonado-Torres, 'Post-imperial Reflections on Crisis, Knowledge and Utopia: Transgresstopic Critical Hermeneutics and the Death of European Man', *Review* 25, no.3 (2002): 277-315.
26. The idea of 'decolonization of knowledge' is articulated in, among others, the compilation by Edgardo Lander, *La Colonialidad del Saber: Eurocentrismo y Ciencias Sociales. Perspectivas Latinoamericanas* (Buenos Aires: CLACSO, 1993). See also *Revista del Centro Andino de Estudios Internacionales* 2 (2001), and the Special Dossier 'Knowledges and the Known: Andean Perspectives on Capitalism and Epistemology', *Nepantla: Views from South* 3, no.1 (2002). The concept is also key in Walter D. Mignolo, *Local Histories/Global Designs: Coloniality, Subaltern Knowledges, and Border Thinking* (Princeton, NJ: Princeton University Press, 2000). For an exploration of decolonization within the field of Western philosophy see Nelson Maldonado-Torres, 'Latin American Thought and the Decolonization of Western Philosophy', *The American Philosophical Association Newsletter on Hispanic/Latinos Issues in Philosophy* 100, no.1 (Spring 2001).
27. For a recent and important effort in this direction see Sylvia Wynter, 'Unsettling the Coloniality of Being/Power/Truth/Freedom: Towards the Human, After Man, Its Overrepresentation: An Argument', *The New Centennial Review* 3, no. 3 (2003): 257-337.
28. For an analysis of the epistemological contributions of Fanon and other Third-World intellectuals see the work of Chela Sandoval, *Methodology of the Oppressed* (Minneapolis: University of Minnesota Press, 2000).
29. I owe the term 'geography of reason' to Lewis R. Gordon. See among others his *Existentia Africana: Understanding Africana Existential Thought* (New York: Routledge, 2000).
30. Immanuel Wallerstein, 'Antisystemic Movements' in *Transforming the Revolution: Social Movements and the World-System*, eds. Samir Amin, Gunder Frank Arrighi and I. Wallerstein (New York: Monthly Review Press, 1990).
31. Richard Rorty, *Achieving Our Country* (Cambridge, Mass: Harvard University Press, 1998).
32. Cornel West, *The American Evasion of Philosophy: A Genealogy of Pragmatism* (Madison, Wis: The University of Wisconsin Press, 1989), 239.
33. Richard Rorty, *Achieving Our Country*, 38.
34. Cornel West, *The American Evasion of Philosophy: A Genealogy of Pragmatism*, 239.
35. Elizabeth Cobbs Hoffman, 'What Intellectuals Owe to America', *North Carolina Herald Sun*, (January 13, 2002), A-11.

36. Anthony Daniels, 'Frantz Fanon: The Platonic Form of Human Resentment', *The New Criterion* (http://www.newcriterion.com/archive/19/rnayO1/fanon.htm) 7. Access March 2, 2002.
37. For an analysis of this point see Lewis Gordon, *Existentia Africana*, 23-40.
38. See Nelson Maldonado-Torres, 'Post-imperial Reflections on Crisis, Knowledge and Utopia: Transgresstopic Critical Hermeneutics and the Death of European Man', *Review* 25, no.3 (2002).
39. See Frantz Fanon, *The Wretched of the Earth*, trans. Constance Farrington (New York: Grove Press, 1968).
40. For the concept of modernity/coloniality see Walter Mignolo, 'José de Acosta's *Historia natural y moral de las Indias*: Occidentalism, the Modern/Colonial World, and the Colonial Difference' in *Natural and Moral History of the Indies by José de Acosta* (Durham: Duke University Press, 2002),: 451-518. For the idea of what I call the 'sub-alter' as no-self/no-other see Lewis R. Gordon, *Existentia Africana: Understanding Africana Existential Thought* (New York: Routledge, 2000); and Nelson Maldonado-Torres, *Against War: Views from the Underside of Modernity* (Durham: Duke University Press, forthcoming).
41. See Nelson Maldonado-Torres, *Against War*.
42. I follow Walter Mignolo in giving the adjective 'an-other' both the sense of disruption from the genealogy of European thought and the opening to a diversity of views that emerge from the perspectives of histories marked by the colonial experience. The difference between what Mignolo refers to as 'an-other paradigm' and a genealogy of critical movements and thought like the one proposed by Watts is evinced in that while for Warts the political thinking of the Zapatista movement is explained by tracing it back to Paris, Mignolo interprets it in the context of similar uprisings by colonized peoples, like those of many indigenous movements in South America and other struggles in Africa, the United States, and elsewhere. Mignolo does not argue that the Zapatista uprising is not related to Paris in any way. His point is rather that the coordinates of the movement are best explained in relation to struggles that do not assume Paris as their centre. See Walter Mignolo 'Prefacio ala Edicion Castellana. Un "Paradigma Otro": Colonialidad Global, Pensamiento Fronterizo y Cosmopolitanismo Critico' ['Preface to the Spanish edition. An-other paradigm: "Global coloniality", Border Thinking, and Criticial Cosmopolitanism']. *Historias Locales/disenos Globales: Colonialidad, Conocimientos Subalternos y Pensamiento Fronterizo*, trans. Juan Maria Madariaga y Cristina Vega Solis (Madrid: Ediciones Akal, 2003), 22. For a more comprehensive analysis of the Zapatista movement see Walter Mignolo, 'The Zapatista's Theoretical Revolution: Its Historical, Ethical, and Political Consequences', *Review* 25, no. 3 (2002): 245-75. For an expanded exposition of some of the main arguments in these essays see Walter Mignolo, *Local Histories/Global Designs: Coloniality, Subaltern Knowledges, and Border Thinking* (Princeton: Princeton University Press, 2000).
43. Frantz Fanon, *The Wretched of the Earth*, trans. Constance Farrington (New York: Grove Press, 1968), 311-12, 316.
44. See Emile Benveniste, 'Gift and Exchange in the Indo-European Vocabulary' in *The Logic of the Gift: Toward an Ethic of Generosity*, ed. Alan D. Schrift, trans. Mary Elisabeth Meek (New York:Routledge, 1997) 33-42. For a full analysis of the ethical component of the meaning of *damné* see Nelson Maldonado-Torres, *Against War* (forthcoming). See also, Nelson Maldonado-Torres, 'The Cry of the Self as a Call from the Other: The Paradoxical Loving Subjectivity of Frantz Fanon', *Listening: Journal of Religion and Culture* 36, no. 1 (2001): 46-60.

45. For an elegant and creative exposition and analysis of the ethics of reciprocity see Rornand Coles, *Rethinking Generosity: Critical Theory and the Politics of Caritas* (Ithaca, NY: Cornell University Press, 1997). For a development of these ideas in connection with the work of feminists of colour see Romand Coles, 'Contesting Cosmopolitan Currencies: The Nepantlist Rose in the Cross(ing) of the Present', *Nepantla: Views from South* 4, no.1 (2003): 5-40. Important in this regard is also Chela Sandoval, *Methodology of the Oppressed* (Minneapolis: University of Minnesota Press, 2000).
46. See Edward Said, *Representations of the Intellectual* (New York: Pantheon Books, 1996).

9 | *Biocentrism,* Neo-Ptolemaicism, and E.O. Wilson's *Consilience*: A Contemporary Example of 'Saving the Phenomenon' of *Man,* in the Name of the Human

Jason R. Ambroise

This essay takes its point of departure from a seminal thesis of Sylvia Wynter. Building off of Maurice Godelier's contention that what disappears with the sacred word of religious thought is 'man as the author of his social way of existing', Wynter makes an analogous point with respect to the sacralized — because supposedly purely objective word of *biocentrism* — as the thought coterminous with our own.[1] That because of its projection of an extra-human origin of and basis to our contemporary, Western-bourgeois mode of socio-human existence — doing so *on* the biological process of evolutionary natural selection — biocentrism erases the role assumed in the production and replication of this ethno-class mode of existence by all its members — in particular its mainstream intellectuals.[2] In exploring this notion, the paper takes as its primary object of investigation the most recent work of the United States biologist E.O. Wilson entitled *Consilience: The Unity of Knowledge.*

Wilson argues in his 1998 text (as well as in a series of articles for the March and April 1998 issues of *The Atlantic Monthly*), that whereas 'humanity overall is improving per capita production, health, and longevity', such 'improvement' has come at the expense of 'eating up the planet's capital, including natural resources and biological diversity millions of years old'.[3] Seeing such a Janus-faced dynamic and its ensuing crisis — one that as well threatens the long-term viability of the human species — as correlated with a contemporary crisis of knowledge, Wilson argues that transcending this social situation will necessarily calls for a *consilience* of all knowing.

BIOCENTRISM, NEO-PTOLEMAICISM, AND *CONSILIENCE*

Taking the word 'consilience' from the nineteenth-century Western thinker William Whewell in the latter's 1840 book, *The Philosophy of the Inductive Sciences,* Wilson means a '"jumping together" of knowledge by the linking of facts and fact-based theory across disciplines to create a common groundwork of explanation'.[4] The realization in our contemporary epistemological situation of such a 'common groundwork' Wilson believes is possible only on the basis of the 'fact-seeking' paradigms and methods of the natural sciences — in particular the discipline of biology. This privileging of biology results from his correlated major premise that the human is a purely 'organic machine' subject to the laws of 'organic space and time'.[5] Two such laws he terms *epigenesis,* or the 'inherited regularities of development in anatomy, physiology, cognition, and behaviour', and *gene-culture coevolution.*[6] With an understanding and application of these laws, Wilson proposes to bridge the gap between what C.P. Snow defined in 1959 as the two cultures of the natural sciences on the one hand, and the social sciences and humanities on the other, making possible a 'common groundwork of explanation'. And this unanimity will at the same time enable mankind to free itself from the cultural baggage, moral and spiritual collapse, and species-potential destruction of contemporary, modern-industrial civilization, bringing into being a new golden age of human harmony and perfection.

This essay is divided into two parts. Part I summarizes the major aspects of Wilson's position in *Consilience.* Part II explores these arguments and those of other related works within the context of this collection's major theme of 'After Man, The Human' and correlated hypotheses as formulated by Sylvia Wynter. In this second context, a central point made by Samuel Sambursky is relevant.

In his text *The Physical World of Late Antiquity,* Sambursky elucidates a central dilemma that confronted Western astronomers beginning with the ancient Greeks. This dilemma was that of how to 'save the phenomenon' or 'account for' the geocentric conception of the universe whereby all heavenly bodies were presumed to revolve around a stationary earth in uniform, circular motion. Although a relatively simple undertaking in the earlier days of Greek astronomy, this enterprise grew more complicated with the 'steadily increasing precision' of analysis of later astronomers. One such observation was the apparent 'retrograde motion of the planets' or the fact that certain heavenly bodies at times reverse their motion across the earth's horizon. Sambursky notes that this effort to 'save the phenomenon', one in which the 'physical content' of the universe was sacrificed to a series of then 'appropriate geometrical assumptions', culminated in the work of a sect of Greek astronomers, the most renown being that of Ptolemy. These astronomers put forth the theory that the 'planets moved on the circumference of small epicycles whose centres themselves moved along the circumference of the main circle with the earth as its centre'.[7] Such a theory preserved the belief in the 'earth as the centre' of both 'planetary motion' and the universe and was harnessed by Judaeo-Christian theologians during the Middle Ages to reinforce their belief in a theocentric world enacted by the presumed supernaturally-determined drama of human sin and salvation.[8]

The objective of this essay is to show the way in which E.O. Wilson's alleged project of human emancipation, although far-reaching and insightful, nevertheless functions to 'save the phenomenon' in its own right. That which is 'saved' this time is not a geocentric conception of the physical universe, but a *purely* biocentric conception of the human, one enacted by the this-wordly drama of evolutionary natural selection and dysselection. Wilson does so by drawing new insights and partial attempts to posit new ways of knowing the human species formulated throughout the twentieth century — ones which challenged the very validity of the purely biocentric worldview — back within the latter's natural-scientific terms. In consequence (and in the context of this collection's major themes), Wilson's work:

1) denies that the human is, in Wynter's terms, a 'third level of existence' beyond the purely physical and biological, based on Frantz Fanon's hybridly *ontogenetic* and *sociogenetic* description of the species;[9]
2) following Godelier, continues to make opaque both the central role of humans in the authorship of their own societies, as well as the specific social technologies through which such authorship is mediated;[10]
3) masks the central role of mainstream intellectuals as, in Asmarom Legesse's terms, the 'grammarians' of socio-human existence, including both the role that Wilson assumes in

our contemporary society, as well as that which he would assume in his *projected* own;[11] and

4) 'saves' the disciplines of the social sciences and humanities by anchoring their models and paradigms within his epigenetic and gene-culture coevolutionary description of the human. In doing so, he reinscribes *man*, what Wynter defines as our contemporary ethno-class and purely biocentric conception or *genre of the human*.[12] Such a reinscription thereby closes off any possibility of resolving our contemporary social crisis outside the terms of this genre, since the point of Wilson's neo-Ptolemaic humanist project is not to 'erase *man*', but to 'save its appearance'.[13]

Part I:
A Summary of Wilson's *Consilience*:
From Chaos and Confusion in Knowledge and the Undermining of the Foundations of Science and Traditional Philosophy, to Chaos and Confusion in Contemporary Society and the Undermining of the Viability of the Human Species

Wilson begins his text *Consilience* by arguing that our present organization of knowledge is in a state of 'chaos'. This chaos he in large part attributes to the 'atomization' of reality originally introduced by the French Enlightenment thinker René Descartes the years 1637–1649 with the latter's method of 'reductionism', the 'study of the world as an assemblage of physical parts that can be broken down and analyzed separately'.[14] As a method, Wilson suggests, reductionism became 'the most powerful intellectual instrument of [the] modern sciences', one, that has led to the discovery and manipulation of atomic and subatomic particles and the human genome.[15] Yet although for Descartes this method was considered a mere first stage in his attempt to create an 'overarching vision... of knowledge as a system of interconnected truths . . . abstracted into mathematics', for contemporary scientists and social thinkers, reductionism has, according to Wilson, become an end unto itself.[16] The result is that attention has been drawn away from formulating a 'big picture' or systemic view of reality. In consequence, Wilson writes that, 'Professional atomization afflicts the social sciences . . . humanities [and the natural sciences]'.[17] He continues:

> The faculties of higher education around the world are congeries of experts. To be an original scholar is to be a highly specialized world authority in a polyglot Calcutta of similarly focused world authorities. . . . Professional scholars in general have little choice but to dice up research expertise and research agendas among themselves. To be a successful scholar means spending a career on membrane biophysics, the Romantic poets, early American history, or some other such constricted area of formal study.[18]

The end result of this atomization is that the two cultures of knowledge of both physical and socio-human reality 'are no longer on speaking terms'.[19] 'Each has its own practitioners, language, modes of analysis, and standards of validation. . . . The result is confusion'.[20]

The confusion resulting from this atomization is as well reinforced by what he defines as 'philosophical postmodernism' and 'its more political and sociological expressions'.[21] Within these expressions he includes 'Afrocentrism, constructivist social anthropology, "critical" (that is, socialist) science, deep ecology, ecofeminism, Lacanian psychoanalysis, Latourian sociology of science, neo-Marxism', and the 'bewildering varieties of deconstruction techniques and New Age holism'.[22] All of these theoretical approaches are problematic for the United States biologist because they 'challenge the very foundations of science and traditional philosophy', foundations that he holds in high esteem and which form the basis of his consilient worldview.[23]

This intellectual chaos and confusion within knowledge and undermining of the foundations of science and traditional philosophy, for Wilson is paralleled by a contemporary social chaos and confusion that is undermining the viability of the planet's bio-diversity, including the human species. An environmental crisis, he rightfully argues, is already underway with the greenhouse effect, where the level of carbon dioxide gas (or CO_2) in the earth's atmosphere 'stands at 360 parts per million, the highest measure' in a 160,000 year period. This increase in CO_2 levels is 'tightly correlated' with a rise in the 'global average temperature', such that for the past 130 years alone, the 'global average temperature has risen by one degree Celsius (or 1.8 degrees

Fahrenheit)'.[24] The Intergovernmental Panel on Climate Change, a global community of 2,000 scientists studying the issue, has projected '[an] additional rise of global average temperature of 1.0 to 3.5 degrees Celsius (1.8 to 6.3 degrees Fahrenheit)' by the year 2100.[25] In consequence of this heating of the earth and the subsequent melting of polar ice caps, the sea level is expected by the same date to rise some 30 centimeters (12 inches), potentially obliterating small islands and intensifying coastal erosion. Rainfall patterns will change. . . Tropical cyclones will increase in average frequency. Entire natural ecosystems and the life-forms that comprise them, may disappear. Indeed, this bio-diversity is already in jeopardy in some areas, with mass extinction already commonplace. In the United States alone, an estimated one per cent of all species are extinct and another 32 per cent are in jeopardy.[26] And the failure of the 1991 'Biosphere 2' project, where eight volunteers attempted to build a self-contained and self-sustaining ecosystem, showed that, according to project reviewers Joel E. Cohen and David Tilman, (as cited by Wilson),

> No one yet knows how to engineer systems that provide humans with the life-supporting services that natural ecosystems produce for free. . . [and] despite its mysteries and hazards, Earth remains the only known home that can sustain life.[27]

This human catastrophe linked to the *environment* is paralleled, Wilson argues, by another ongoing human catastrophe. Presently, the world's population totals around six billion. 'Roughly', Wilson writes,

> 1.3 billion people, more than a fifth of the world's population, have cash incomes under one U. S. dollar a day. The next tier of 1.6 billion earn $1–3. Somewhat more than 1 billion live in what the United Nations classifies as absolute poverty, uncertain of obtaining food from one day to the next. Each year more than the entire population of Sweden, between 13 and 18 million, mostly children, die of starvation, or the side effects of malnutrition, or other poverty-related causes. In order to gain perspective, imagine the response if Americans and Europeans were told that in the coming year the entire population of Sweden, or Scotland or Wales combined, or New England would die of poverty.[28]

And yet, he continues, to raise the 'living standards of the rest of the world . . . to that of the most prosperous countries, with existing technology and current levels of consumption and waste, is a dream in pursuit of a mathematical impossibility'.[29] For this would 'require 2 more planet Earths'.[30] And the attempt 'to level out present-day income inequities' or to redistribute the fruits of the system, 'would require shrinking the ecological footprint of the prosperous countries. That is problematic', he continues,

> in the market-based global economy, where the main players are also militarily the most powerful, and in spite of a great deal of rhetoric largely indifferent to the suffering of others. Few people in industrialized countries are fully aware of how badly off the poor of the world really are.[31]

If this social chaos and confusion, one which threatens both the biodiversity of the planet and the viability of the human species itself, is in turn correlated with the intellectual confusion and chaos within knowledge, then the resolution of the former crisis in society is for Wilson linked to the resolution of the latter crisis in thought. Thus, the purpose of his text *Consilience* is to spearhead a unification of knowledge, thereby giving humanity a 'big-picture' view of the world we inhabit in order to transcend it. On what basis, according to Wilson, can such a unification and transcendence be effected?

Recapturing the Enlightenment Spirit, Transcending Chaos and Confusion through Modern Biology

The 'central idea of . . . [Wilson's] consilient worldview', one that he believes will allow contemporary humanity to unify knowledge, is to recapture the 'spirit of the Enlightenment'.[32] This intellectual spirit he characterizes as the 'shared . . . passion to demystify the world and free the mind from the impersonal forces that imprison it', a belief in the 'unity of all knowledge', human 'perfectibility' and 'progress', and a faith in 'science' as the primary 'engine' for achieving such ends.[33] And just as the 'Promethean thrust' of the Enlightenment allowed for the creation of a kind of knowledge that 'liberate[d] mankind by lifting it above the savage world', Wilson believes that recapturing this thrust can have the same effect on humankind in its attempt to deal with the chaos and confusion of our contemporary, socio-human predicament.[34]

This recapturing for Wilson is based on the premise that 'all tangible phenomena, from the birth of stars to the working of social institutions, are based on material processes that are ultimately reducible, however long and tortuous the sequences, to the laws of physics'.[35] Thus the *apparent* gap in reality between the natural and socio-human worlds is in reality a bridge held together on the basis of purely natural-scientific processes. Knowledge must therefore be reconceptualized to mirror this presumed reality. Yet unlike his Enlightenment forebears, who allegedly achieved such unanimity on the basis of a mechanistic natural philosophy (even if intertwined at times with theology), Wilson, from his post-nineteenth-century, late modern perspective, posits 'biology as the most proximate and hence relevant of the scientific disciplines'.[36] This privileging of biology logically derives from Wilson's assumption that the human is a purely biological being in a relation of pure continuity with organic species.[37] In consequence, he takes phenomena that he identifies as unique to the human — that is, culture, the mind, consciousness, and language — and argues, within the terms of his purely biocentric premise, that biology has all of these phenomena 'on a leash'.[38] And because his text is formulated in the wake of attempts throughout the twentieth century to take these unique qualities as a sign of the limits of biological explanations of human behaviour, *Consilience* carries with it a central concern. This concern is that of how biology and these uniquely human features interact in a transocietal manner to constitute a single human nature.

Within the context of Wilson's desire to create a transsocietal perspective of the human is where his dually related principles of explanation — epigenesis and gene-culture coevolution — come to the fore. For through these principles, he hopes to provide a ground from which all human behaviours can be explained. How do these principles function?

'Epigenesis', he writes,

> originally a biological concept, means the development of an organism under the joint influence of heredity and environment. Epigenetic rules... are the innate operations in the sensory system and brain,...

rules of thumb that allow an organism to find rapid solutions to problems encountered in the environment.[39]

This 'prepared learning' is programmed in us by our genes and 'predispose[s] individuals to view the world in a particular *innate* way and automatically to make certain choices as opposed to others [emphasis added]'.[40] In consequence, such rules, according to Wilson, are able to explain the origins of and reason for two classes of human phenomena — biological phenomena resulting from the hardwiring of the human body and brain and cultural phenomena linked to socio-human behaviours. So the fact that humans are genetically programmed to see only 400–700 nanometers of radiation (meaning we see 'a rainbow in four basic colors' as opposed to 'in a continuum of light frequencies') and that our range of hearing is '20 to 20,000 Hz, or cycles of air compression per second' (in contrast to bats who hear at higher frequencies), are phenomena that Wilson holds to be of the same level of existence and, therefore, accountable through the same process of functioning as the culture-human phenomena of art, ethics, morality, beliefs, and values. And because epigenetic processes only have meaning within the context of the Darwinian fitness that they confer, that is to say, of the extent to which they improve the ability of the genes to reproduce and survive, then cultural phenomena and processes, because presumed to be of the same order as epigenetic ones, for Wilson function as 'environmental tracking devices' that find their reason-for-being solely within this purely biocentric context.[41] How, then, do biology and culture interact?

Gene-culture *coevolution* is the name Wilson gives to this process of interaction. This process functions as follows. The 'genes prescribe epigenetic rules'. These rules, because determining how we see the world, 'animate and channel the acquisition of culture'. Since culture has as both its condition and basis the 'genetically structured human brain', its (culture's) function is purely Darwinian in that it has the power to 'determine which of the prescribing genes survive and multiply from one generation to the next'.[42] Genes that have reproductive success in turn 'alter the epigenetic rules of populations'. And these newly 'altered epigenetic rules', in consequence, both change the way in which we see the world and 'the direction and effectiveness of the channels of [new] cultural acquisition'.[43]

As an alleged description of a process ostensibly responsible for all human thought, meaning, and action, Wilson believes that gene-culture coevolution will provide a 'theory of causality that' can stretch 'across the various disciplines', making possible his goal of a consilience of all knowing. The social and natural sciences he sees as already converging with the fields of cognitive neuroscience (or the brain sciences), human behavioural genetics, evolutionary biology, and the environmental sciences. An 'enduring theory of the arts', he as well holds, will likewise call for 'stepwise and consilient contributions from the brain sciences, psychology, and evolutionary biology'.[44] And ethics, religion, and moral reasoning in general, will all be brought within an empiricist worldview that elucidates their purely biological roots. The end result will be a rearranging of the two cultures into two great branches of learning, the humanities, particularly 'the creative arts', on the one hand, and the natural sciences, on the other. 'Social science', he writes,

> will split within each of [these branches] ... with one part folding into or becoming continuous with biology, and the other fusing with the humanities.... In the process, the humanities, embracing philosophy, history, moral reasoning, comparative religion, and interpretation of the arts, will draw closer to the sciences and partly fuse with them.[45]

This resulting consilience of knowing, one generated from Wilson's purely biocentric understanding of the human, will presumably allow the species to transcend the chaos and confusion that characterizes our modern epistemological condition, of how we know and experience ourselves and the world.

How, then, can such a consilience on the basis of biology make possible the transcendence of the chaos and confusion of our contemporary socio-human predicament, one that threatens the human species with extinction? This argument by Wilson will be explored within the context of issues related to Part II of the paper, which interrogates the way in which Wilson's project saves the phenomenon of biocentric *man* in the name of the human. In this context, as aforementioned, part II builds off of the work of Sylvia Wynter in order to show the way in which Wilson's work,

1) denies that the human is, in Wynter's terms, a 'third level of existence' beyond the purely physical and biological;
2) continues to make opaque the central role of humans in the authorship of their own socio-human existence;
3) masks the central role of mainstream intellectuals as the 'grammarians' of each such existence; and
4) 'saves' the disciplines of the social sciences and humanities by anchoring their models and paradigms within his epigenetic and gene-culture coevolutionary description of the human. In turn, his work reinscribes *man*, what Wynter defines as our contemporary ethno-class, biocentric conception of the human, thereby closing off any possibility of resolving our contemporary social crisis outside the terms of this genre of the human.

Part II:
'Saving the Phenomenon' of Biocentric *Man*? Or a Science of the Human as Sylvia Wynter's 'Third Level of Existence'

The first way in which Wilson 'saves the phenomenon' of biocentric *man* is that, because seeing our origins as purely in evolution he denies that the human is, in Wynter's words, a 'third level of existence' based on Frantz Fanon's hybridly *ontogenetic* and *sociogenetic* premise. Wilson most explicitly does so by arguing that certain unique features of our species — that is, culture, the mind, consciousness, and language — only have relevance within the context of the realization of the biological imperatives of genetic reproduction and survival. The knowledge politics of his work is made clear when he explicitly attempts to draw back within the paradigms and methods of biology the attempts of past and contemporary intellectuals to de-biologize socio-human existence, even if these attempts were/are partial in nature. These attempts include those of the early twentieth-century anthropologists Franz Boaz, Ruth Benedict, and Margaret Mead with respect to the phenomenon of *culture*, and the more far-reaching, late twentieth-century ones of the Australian David Chalmers and the American Frank Jackson with respect to *subjective experience*.[46] And yet because these thinkers had/have not worked out a viable explanatory connection between these unique features of the human and the obvious biological aspects of the species, then they left/leave themselves open to Wilson's attempt to draw their partial and/or *new* insights into his neo-paradigm.

Sylvia Wynter, building off a tradition of thought contestatory to this biocentric description of the human — including centrally that of intellectuals of black Africa and the black diaspora — has worked out such a redefinition, one which preserves the uniqueness of the species. This re-definition cuts against Wilson's purely biocentric premise that no essential break occurs with the purely biological world by the emergence of human life. It proposes that the above uniquely human features emerged because of the insufficiency of the fixed codes of biology to orient and motivate behaviours. The end result was the emergence of a form of life that no longer knew and experienced itself and the world purely within the objective terms of its species-specific biology. Instead, this species — that is, the human — would also come to know and experience itself and the world within the subjective terms of a culturally-induced way of knowing and experiencing, a genre of the human — yet one that we normally know and experience as 'objective'.[47] Thus, unlike Wilson, who views *culture* (as well as the mind, consciousness, and language) as a *pure* extension of biology, 'culture' for Wynter, while having as its *condition* the genetic codes of biological existence, has as its *basis* verbal, semantic, and other forms of symbolic representation. As a result, unlike purely 'organic machines', whose lives are solely determined by the information encoded in their genes/DNA, human lives are determined dually by this genetic information on the purely biological level, and on the socio-human level by systems of symbolic representation as information encoded in a specific culture. In consequence, Wilson's *nature-nurture, gene-culture* discourse is rightfully deemed a false one whose will to truth is derived from the terms of his purely biocentric understanding of the human. In contrast, Wynter proposes, humans are by nature programmed to be nurtured, not merely by a physical environment (as the *only* kind of environment that exists for Wilson's purely biological self), but as well within the terms of a specific cultural environment. Within such a specific cultural environment, humans not only see, experience, and behave upon the world (including the physical) within the epigenetic terms outlined by Wilson, but also within the symbolic terms of Fanon's proposed sociogenetic self.[48]

As such symbolically coded beings, Wynter writes in a recent essay, 'humans are transformed from being purely biological *males/females* into hybridly biological and cultural [symbolic] *men/women, husbands/ wives, fathers/mothers, sons/daughters, brothers/sisters, uncles/aunts, nephews/nieces*, and so on'.[49] In the process, our lives are not oriented solely about the realization of the biological imperatives of genetic reproduction and survival, as Wilson assumes, but also by symbolically or culturally-induced imperatives, imperatives that we alone, in her words, 'auto-institute'. So that the Aztec empire's goal of maintaining the 'flow of life', one which called for human sacrifice, and our contemporary goal of maintaining the 'flow of capital' through 'economic growth and development', one which calls for the sacrifice of the bio-diversity of the planet, including humans via institutionalized poverty and joblessness, are not of the same level of existence as the biological goal of the reproduction and survival of the genes.[50]

To sum up, humans do not merely live *natural* lives, but also *symbolic* lives; nor do we merely die *natural* deaths, but also *symbolic* deaths. This *governing code of symbolic life and death*, through which we realize ourselves as a specific mode or genre of being human — whether Yoruba, Aztec, or Western-bourgeois — is also Wynter's resolution to a central concern posed by Ernesto Grassi in the context of his discussion of the 'distinctly human phenomenon' of the 'absence of an immediate [biological] code for deciphering' reality. This central concern is 'whether there is actually a governing code for human beings, and if so, how it actually takes effect and how is it structured'.[51] How does this resolution by Wynter then further disenchant Wilson's project of 'saving the phenomenon' of biocentric *man*?

In connecting the functioning of this governing code of symbolic life and death to the functioning of what the medical scientist Avram Goldstein and other neurobiologists like James F. Danielli have identified as the opiate, neuro-chemical reward and punishment system of the brain and the neuro-physiological network of the body, Wynter closes off Wilson's attempt to draw culture and the unique features of the human back within biology's natural-scientific terms. For Wynter, following the insights of Danielli, has suggested that with the emergence of this uniquely human governing code, this biological mechanism of opiate reward and punishment — and, therefore, our behaviours in general — are re-harnessed by culture to the realization of symbolic, as opposed to purely biological, imperatives and ends. Thus, rather than biology having culture on a leash, as Wilson has proposed with his gene-culture coevolutionary theory, *culture instead has biology on a leash*. That is to say, culture harnesses those aspects of biology which mediate socio-human behaviours towards the realization of symbolic ends, making possible the third level of existence that we humans are.[52] A fairly recent article by Sandra Blakeslee reaffirms this insight.

In her article 'Highjacking the Brain Circuits With a Nickel Slot Machine', Blakeslee writes that neuroscientists are beginning to uncover a 'common thread' within behaviours as diverse as 'compulsive gambling', 'exuberance while at sporting events', to 'investing in stocks'. This 'common thread', she notes, is that 'such behaviours . . . rely on brain circuits that evolved to help animals assess rewards important to their survival. . . . [T]hose same circuits', in turn, 'are used by the human brain to assess social rewards', rewards that are chemically secured by the firing of 'dopamine' by the middle region of the brain.[53] '[T]hese midbrain dopamine signals', she continues, 'are sent directly to brain areas that initiate movements and behaviour. . . . In humans, though, the dopamine signal is also sent to a higher brain region called the frontal cortex for more elaborate processing'.[54] In this context, Blakeslee writes that,

> Some people [even] seem to be born with vulnerable dopamine systems that get hijacked by social rewards. The same neural circuitry involved in the highs and lows of abusing drugs is activated by winning or losing money, anticipating a good meal or seeking beautiful faces to look at.[55]

But whereas this process of 'hijacking' is characterized in the article as an aberration, Wynter's elaboration shows that this process is indeed part of the normal, everyday functioning of the motivation and regulation of socio-human behaviours, but one that we are unable to normally see as such because of our contemporary culture's purely biocentric description of the species. 'In consequence', as Wynter writes in a recent essay,

> where for all purely organic species, it is the *biochemical event* of reward and punishment which directly motivates and is causal of each species'

ensemble behaviours, the fundamental distinction for human forms of life is that it is the *culture-representational event* which motivates and is causal of (by means of the functioning of the opiate reward/punishment system which it verbally recodes) *our uniquely human* behaviours.[56]

Thus, if it is the '*culture-representational event* which motivates and is causal of *our uniquely human* behaviours', then E.O. Wilson's gene-culture coevolutionary discourse, where the genes have culture on a leash, collapses in front of our very eyes. Furthermore, if the way we humans see, experience, and behave upon the world is also always already a culturally-induced way of seeing, experiencing, and behaving enacting of a particular genre of the human, then Wilson's purely epigenetic conception of the species also falls apart. Such a concept of the self is still relevant in the context of purely biological phenomena where humans are normally programmed to see only 400–700 nanometers of radiation or hear between 20 to 20,000 Hertz of sound waves. However, it is only partially relevant in the context of socio-human existence, as an existence that has as its basis the 'cultural-representational event'. And while analogies between the purely natural and socio-human worlds can be made, a true consilience of knowledge would ultimately be premised on a relation of both continuity and discontinuity between these different levels of existence. In consequence, Wilson's own epigenetic self — at the socio-human level — should be both complimented and *conditioned by* Fanon's sociogenetic self, together constituting Wynter's scientific description of the species as a 'third level of existence'.

Against the Erasure/Denial of Human 'Auto-Institution'

Secondly, because Wilson's purely biocentric premise denies the human the right to its uniqueness as a third level of existence, the United States biologist is likewise unable to see the central role that we as a species assume in the authorship or, in Wynter's terms, *auto-institution* of our social existence. The central theoretical move that blinds him to this fact is his own projection of human agency onto a presumed bio-evolutionary cosmos, as allegedly the immediate cause of socio-human existence, of how we see, experience, and behave upon the world. This projection of human agency then allows him to posit that 'outside our heads there is a free-standing reality [both natural and socio-human]. Only madmen and a scattering of constructivist philosophers, doubt its existence'.[57] While maybe correct with respect to purely natural phenomena that are themselves able to function independently of human motives, this is not so with respect to socio-human phenomena, which are never independent of auto-instituting processes. For if no social reality can pre-exist human beings, and if no human can pre-exist the process of its own auto-institution, then no social reality exists that can pre-exist human invention or auto-institution of that specific reality. This premise holds in the case of Okonkwo's Umuofia in Chinua Achebe's *Things Fall Apart*, to our contemporary Western-bourgeois, global system.[58]

Yet Wilson's belief in a 'positive' social reality that is purely the result of evolutionary processes, allows him to then posit the existence of an objective truth 'out there'. This truth, he writes, impinges on our senses and is reconstituted by the 'inner representations' of the brain. But, he continues, the 'alignment of outer existence with its inner representation has been distorted by the idiosyncrasies of human evolution. . . . That is, natural selection', by some paradox which he does not explain, 'built the brain to survive in the world and only incidentally to understand it at a depth greater than needed to survive'.[59] And here Wilson allows us to transition to the third erasure that his culture-specific, purely biocentric reductionism induces and compels — that of the masking of the central role of mainstream intellectuals as, in Legesse's terms, the 'grammarians' of each socio-human order, including the role that Wilson both assumes in our contemporary one and would assume in his *projected* own.

Against the Erasure/Denial of the Mainstream Intellectual as 'Grammarian'

The 'proper task of scientists', Wilson writes, is 'to diagnose and correct the misalignment' between 'outer existence' — both natural and socio-human — and the 'inner representations' of the brain. In turn, his understanding of the world-task of mainstream intellectuals is restricted to merely assuring that socio-human existence conforms to the rules and prescriptions of his purely biocentric understanding of the human. The paradox is that in making this assumption, Wilson is unable to see the way in which his descriptive statement of what the human ostensibly is, based on his twin laws of epigenesis and gene-culture coevolution, actually functions as a *prescriptive* statement of what the human ought-to-be. His role as Legesse's 'grammarian' — that is, as producer and reproducer of the epistemological ground of a specific genre of the human and mode of socio-human existence — is therefore a non-conscious one. Thus, the outwardly political nature of his project is masked by his mis-recognition of his role of auto-institutor as being a mere function of some bio-cosmic process. In consequence, his 'scientists' are called upon to function more like 'prophets' — this time, not as revealers of the eternal word of his old Protestant faith, but of the objective word of his new faith of evolution. In other words, *the genes are speaking through him/us*. What are they saying?

Answering this question allows us to revisit an issue that was put on hold early in this essay. This issue is that of how Wilson believes the laws of epigenesis and gene-culture co-evolution will allow humankind to transcend the chaos and confusion in society and bring into being a golden age of human harmony and perfection. 'Throughout prehistory', Wilson writes, 'particularly up to a hundred thousand years ago, by which time the modern *Homo sapien* brain had evolved, genetic and cultural evolution were closely coupled'.[60] But as a result of some peculiar process, during the 'advent of Neolithic societies, and especially the rise of civilizations . . . cultural evolution sprinted ahead' of 'genetic evolution'.[61] In this context, a number of 'cultural variations' and 'combinations' emerged that 'no longer contribute to health and well-being'.[62] These variations and combinations induced behaviours that ran 'wild', effectively reducing the Darwinian fitness of both individuals and societies, to the point of destroying them at times.[63]

Such is the case, he proposes, with our contemporary, Western culture and its human inhabitants. On the one hand, this culture in its present form is destructive of both the bio-diversity of the earth and the environmental life-support system on which humanity depends for its survival, and, on the other, has intensified the process of human destruction by placing man in competition with man. And whereas the social Darwinists of the late nineteenth century saw this ethic of competition as the natural functioning of the laws of biology, for Wilson this ethic is antithetical to his understanding of our alleged purely biological nature. Instead, as Howard Kaye writes in a critique of one of Wilson's earlier works, this ethic for Wilson is a sign that 'the human "biogram" and the modern cultural environment have drifted dangerously far apart. . . . [H]uman survival', in turn, 'depends on planned changes in human nature, ethics, and society in order to reestablish harmony between human biology and human culture'.[64]

To understand this subtle yet important difference between the social Darwinism of the late nineteenth century and the late twentieth and now twenty-first century, bio-philosophy of E.O. Wilson, is to return to this earlier and probably more controversial work critiqued by Howard Kaye. This work — *Sociobiology: The New Synthesis* — provides the conceptual background and building blocks for the specific argument made by Wilson in *Consilience*. Although *Sociobiology* was criticized as an 'ideological defense of the modern capitalist status quo' by other distinguished biologists like Richard Lewontin and the now deceased Stephen J. Gould, Kaye notes that such a stance missed out on the moral and spiritual component of Wilson's work — his 'social goal of encouraging more encompassing forms of altruism'.[65]

Taking the modern synthesis of biology and population genetics as his starting points, Wilson attempted to construct a unified picture of the history of life, both human and non-human. Unlike the social Darwinists of the late nineteenth century, who took *competition* to be 'the central theoretical problem' to be bio-centrically explained, Wilson inverted their paradigm by making *altruism* the central issue to be bio-centrically explained by sociobiology.[66] As such, Wilson wanted to show how the evolutionary process creates 'other-benefiting or self-sacrificing' behaviour, from that of single-celled slime moulds to termite colonies, to 'turkey brotherhoods' to humans societies.[67]

What made his apparent resolution of this phenomenon possible was the work of the biologist W.D. Hamilton, whose concept of 'inclusive fitness' allowed Wilson to argue the following.[68] That because now the survival of the highest number of a population's genes takes precedence over that of any individual member of that population, then at times, nature compels an individual organism to perform 'altruistic acts' that will increase the frequency of specific genes within that population, even requiring an individual organism to sacrifice its own life for the common good. In other words, Wilson reduced all social behaviour to a 'single thread of "enabling devices" for the increase of inclusive fitness'.[69] He then constructed a narrative of human history to go along with his sociobiological understanding of the species, a narrative that legitimized his desire to induce higher forms of human altruism in order to transcend our modern predicament. In this story, Wilson made use of the nineteenth-century, bourgeois discourse of social evolution, yet brilliantly inverted for his own purposes. That narrative goes as follows.

The human mind/brain (the two are synonymous for Wilson) was programmed by evolution for an Old World, 'Ice-Age hunter-gatherer' existence. These hunter-gatherers lived during a golden age of human altruism, when the species emerged with the full-flowering of 'other-benefiting' behaviours that rivalled those of the social insects like bees and ants. From then on, gene-culture coevolution took over, as the process by which mankind moved away from this hunter-gatherer existence, tamed the soil through agriculture, invented religion, the arts, and then later science and technology, and now finds itself in a modern, industrial-economic organization of reality. That is to say, humanity now finds itself displaced from its original, altruistic biological roots by a modern, competitive civilization that is in imminent decline, potentially taking the species and the bio-diversity of the planet with it. 'This decline', writes Kaye in summary, 'will take the form of a "loss of moral consensus", a loss of passionate human effort in the service of the group, and a steady regression towards self-indulgence that will be hastened by the atrophy [or wasting away] of kin altruism'.[70] Yet because biology has culture 'on a leash', this decline can be averted by an appeal to the laws of sociobiology.

And it is in this context that Wilson's biocentric descriptive statement of the human becomes a *prescriptive* statement for future action. For a knowledge of such laws will enable humanity to reign-in or pull our contemporary culture back in-line with our biological, Old World roots — that is to say, back in-line with more 'other-benefiting' behaviours that are the hallmark of a being programmed by evolution for an Ice-Age, hunter-gatherer existence. In this sense, Kaye notes, sociobiology takes the place of the other-worldly religious narratives, including his old Protestant faith. But in this case, sociobiology makes of '"cardinal value" the individual's service to the survival of the gene pool'.[71]

The decline alluded to by Wilson in his 1976 work was then spelt out by him 22 years later in *Consilience*, as the social confusion and chaos that threatens both the bio-diversity of the planet and the continued existence of the human species. And only on the basis of his proposed understanding of the human can such a crisis be averted. The unity of human knowledge on the basis of biology, that is, the goal of *Consilience* is therefore premised on the stance that such knowledge must be made consistent with this self-understanding, else 'we will render everything fragile . . . impoverish our own species for all time . . . [and] become nothing'.[72]

In analysing this argument, the important points to remember are that with Wilson, we are still here dealing with a representation of the human in purely biological terms, one based not on the social Darwinism of the late nineteenth century, which argued that humans were innately *competitive*, but on Wilson's inverted purely biocentric reading of the human, where we are now innately *altruistic*. In turn, the competitive culture of contemporary Western modernity is retroped as a 'culture run wild', as opposed to the way it was represented in the nineteenth century by social Darwinists, as a logical functioning of the laws of nature. For Wilson, therefore, the sole function of the intellectual is to initiate and see through the process of harmoniously reconciling human culture and human biology. Only on this basis can humankind avert the social and intellectual crisis made possible by culture's 'running wild' on us.[73] And yet, without the purely biocentric conception of the human where our genes prescribe the way we see, experience, and behave upon the world — that is, epigenesis — and that biology therefore has culture 'on a leash' — that is, gene-culture co-evolution — then none of the above assumptions by Wilson would be posable as discourse in the first place.

Sylvia Wynter has also specifically taken to task another central aspect of the sociobiology of Wilson and other like thinkers. This aspect is their belief that both human altruism and the solidarity of human societies are based on the degree to which the individual members of a human collective share a critical number of the same genes. Such a belief then carries with it the correlated premise that such communities have as their reason for being the maintaining of or increase of this gene frequency, by any means available — including the extreme other-benefiting act of self-sacrifice. Wynter, in contrast, holds that human altruism and solidarity are not a function of a shared gene pool, but of a shared order of consciousness. Yet this order of consciousness, while having as its condition the fixed codes of biology, has as its basis the governing code of symbolic life and death of a culture-specific genre of the human, as this code is mediated by a verbally recoded, opiate reward and punishment system. Thus, as Wynter argues, if it is 'the culture-representational event' which 'motivates and is causal of' individual human behaviours, thereby constituting a symbolic *I*, then the same culture-representational event also 'motivates and is causal of' a specific collective of human behaviours, constituting a symbolic *We*. The primary goal of a specific *We* is not the reproduction and survival of the collective gene-pool, but always a function of the realization of the governing genre of the human and its symbolic imperatives — including the genre of Western-bourgeois *man* and its imperative of maintaining the 'flow of capital' through 'economic growth and development'.[74]

The ability to transcend genetic constraints in cohesiveness and altruism is *the* reason for the display of a degree of cohesiveness and altruism in humans that rivals those of the purely genetic groupings of the social insects. Yet this *symbolically* induced cohesiveness and altruism in humans also carry with them limitations if the culture-specific genre of the human organizing of a specific collectivity has nothing to ultimately do with the empirical well-being of the species. Such is the case with our contemporary genre, as Wynter has proposed, which emerged in the late eighteenth and nineteenth centuries to give primacy to economic and techno-industrial processes. E.O. Wilson has done a commendable job pointing out the empirical effects that this genre of the human has wreaked on the planet, its bio-diversity, and humanity. But contrary to his opinion, the cause of this social crisis and confusion is not 'culture run wild' from his part scientific, part imagined understanding of the human biogram, a view which limits the role of the intellectual to that of reconciling human society with this imagined human nature. Instead, as Wynter has proposed, *the* primary cause of this social chaos and confusion is the order of consciousness of this specific genre of the human *man* and the Western bourgeois, economically-organized collectivity to which *it* — that is, *man* — gives rise. The role of contemporary intellectuals therefore, should be to take seriously their role as 'grammarians'. In this context, to feel empowered by a new science of the human as a third level of existence to refashion a new genre of the human (married to an already emerging counter-culture of the human to that of *man*) that takes as its overarching goal the empirical and symbolic well-being of the species.[75]

Against the 'Saving the Appearance' of *Man*, of *Its* Epistemological Order

This line-of-thinking leads us to the point of the fourth and final section, that in attempting to 'save' the disciplines of the social sciences and humanities by anchoring their models and paradigms within his epigenetic and gene-culture coevolutionary description of the human, Wilson reinscribes our contemporary ethno-class conception or genre of the human, *man*, which these disciplines elaborate. In turn, he closes off any possibility of resolving our contemporary social crisis outside its terms, since his point is to 'save *man's* appearance'.

As Michel Foucault elucidates in *The Order of Things*, the configuration of our present epistemological order emerged in the late nineteenth century on the basis of the elaboration of the premise that the human is a 'purely natural organism'.[76] Wilson takes theories generated from his own descriptive statement of sociobiology in order to rethink some of the assumptions of this biocentric ground, as his critique of nineteenth-century social scientists who were either too Darwinian on the one hand, or Marxist-Leninist on the other, illustrates.[77] An example of such a rethinking occurs with his discussion of 'economics', which he characterizes as both the 'Queen of the Social Sciences' and the one discipline best able to 'bridge the gap' with the natural sciences.[78] However, economics in his opinion suffers from two afflictions — it is both too 'Newtonian and hermetic'.[79] Yet by no means does he consider it 'Ptolemaic'.[80] Rather, to correct or 'save' itself, the discipline merely needs to incorporate a knowledge of 'the complexities of human behaviour and constraints imposed by the environment'.[81]

In this context, he discusses the emergent sub-field of ecological economics, a field initiated because of what he and others have characterized as the failure of mainstream economics to take into account the human subject in relation to its physical environment. The end result of this failure, he continues, has been that this discourse's goal of material growth and development has come at the cost of the ongoing destruction of our human life-support system, species biodiversity, and so on. 'In national balance sheets', Wilson writes,

> economists seldom use full-cost accounting, which includes the loss of natural resources. A country can cut down all its trees, mine out its most profitable minerals, exhaust its fisheries, erode most of its soil, draw down its underground water, and count all the proceeds as income and none of the depletion as cost.[82]

Placing economics within the context of his purely biocentric reading of the human he believes will allow us to see that no organism can survive without its natural environment. In doing so, he hopes to make possible 'new indicators of progress' from which the economy can be monitored, in order to give the 'natural world and human well-being', and not just 'economic production', 'full measure'.[83]

But this blindspot of economics with respect to its inability to account for the costs of environmental destruction, does not result from an error in the alignment of the 'inner representations of the brain' with 'external reality', as Wilson believes. Instead, this blindspot is one instituted by our present genre or mode of being human. This genre of the human — and its master disciplinary paradigm of economics — induces us to realize ourselves at the public level of existence as hegemonically economic beings possessing 'unlimited' yet 'unsatisfiable', 'material wants'.[84] Within this worldview, the 'environment' is indeed taken into account, but only as the natural resource to be exploited/negative externality way in which *man* — our ethno-class conception of the human — must know the environment in order to realize itself as a specific genre or mode of being human.[85] But because of Wilson's purely biocentric premise, *he is unable to think in terms of genres of the human*. In consequence, he believes that it is *Homo sapien* who is destroying the planet through consumption and deforestation, and not *a specific genre of the human* enacted by all of us as subjects of our contemporary world-system — subjects socialized, that is, to realize ourselves within the terms of ethno-class *man*. In turn, Wilson's diagnosis of the cause of the problem of the environment necessarily degenerates into the genocidal, Malthusian and biocentric discourse of *overpopulation*, of there being too many *Homo sapiens* on the planet, as opposed to their being too many of us socialized to realize ourselves within the terms of this specific Western bourgeois, genre of the human, of its goal of 'material redemption' or higher standards of material well-being.[86] What is required, therefore, is our collective fashioning of a new genre of the human, one that can detach our notion of true humanness from such species destructive ends, to one that can make possible the higher forms of altruism that Wilson seeks, without 'saving the phenomenon' of biocentric *man*.

In Conclusion:
Sylvia Wynter's New Science of the Human as an Entrance Into the 'Noncommonsensical'

Such a new definition of the human, in erasing the purely biocentric premise of our contemporary globalized, Western-bourgeois cultural system, which induces us to know and experience ourselves as if we were purely flesh-and-blood beings, would necessarily appear to us to be as 'noncommonsensical' as the then new, post-Copernican physics would have appeared in its own cultural-historical context. For Copernicus revealed that the observed retrograde motions of certain heavenly bodies had nothing to do with those bodies themselves, but of how their motions must appear from the perspective of a moving earth. As a result, as Stephen Shapin writes, in the wake of the publication of the Copernican model of the universe,

> The human experience of inhabiting a static platform, diurnally circled by the sun and stars that were subject to their own annual motions, was denied. If common sense testified to the earth's stability, this new astronomy spoke of its double motion, daily about its axis and annually about the now static sun. Common experience was here identified as but "appearance." If common sense expected that such motions, were they real, would cause people to hold onto their hats in the resulting wind or fall off the earth, then so much the worse for common sense. And if stones thrown straight upward tended to fall back to earth at the point they started from, then a new, noncommonsensical physics would be needed to show why this should happen on a moving earth.[87]

In proposing that the way we know and experience ourselves and the world is not merely the consequence of the unfolding of a purely biological self, but also determined by our socialization into a culture-specific genre of the human, Sylvia Wynter's deciphering of the third level of existence that is the human is an analogous movement into the 'noncommonsensical' for our times. And if the 'common sense' of our present, culture-specific genre induces us to believe that we are purely flesh and blood beings, then so much for this genre-specific 'common sense'. And just as a new noncommonsensical physics was called upon to explain how certain physical phenomena could occur while on a moving earth, then Wynter's new noncommonsensical science of the human must necessarily be called upon in order to explain *how* socio-human phenomena are derived from our own auto-instituting processes, for both tremendous 'good' and tremendous 'ill'. Only then can we as a species be conceptually empowered to create a new and ecumenically human social order, one projected from a new understanding, a new conception, after *man*, the human.

'At this juncture', Wynter writes, 'you find yourself caught up in an enormously revalorized sense of what it is to be human'.[88]

Notes

1. Maurice Godelier, *The Enigma of the Gift*, trans. Nora Scott (Chicago: The University Chicago Press, 1999), 171.
2. Sylvia Wynter, 'In the Great Silence of Scientific Thought: After Man, Towards the Human', ('After Man, Towards the Human' Conference, University of the West Indies, Mona, June 14, 2002). Also see David Scott, 'The Re-Enchantment of Humanism: An Interview with Sylvia Wynter', *Small Axe: A Journal of Criticism 8,* and 4, no. 2 (September 2000): 203-204.
3. E.O. Wilson, *Consilience: The Unity of Knowledge* (New York: Belknap Press of Harvard University Press, 1998), 280. See also his articles 'Back from Chaos', *The Atlantic Monthly* 281, no. 3 (March 1998): 41-62; and 'The Biological Basis of Morality', *The Atlantic Monthly* 281, no. 4 (April 1998): 53-70.
4. Ibid., 8.
5. Ibid., 82.
6. Ibid., 150.
7. Samuel Sambursky, *The Physical World of Late Antiquity* (New York: Basic Books, 1962), 137.
8. David Scott, 'The Re-Enchantment of Humanism: An Interview with Sylvia Wynter', *Small Axe: A Journal of Criticism 8,* and 4, no. 2 (September 2000): 183.
9. Ibid., 183.
10. Maurice Godelier, *The Enigma of the Gift*, 171.
11. Asmarom Legesse, *Gada: Three Approaches to the Study of African Society* (New York: The Free Press, 1973).
12. David Scott, 'The Re-Enchantment of Humanism', 183.

13. The phrase and concept behind 'erase man' is taken from Michel Foucault in *The Order of Things: An Archaeology of the Human Sciences* (New York: Vintage Books, 1973): 387. The phrase 'saving its appearance' is adapted from Owen Barfield's *Saving the Appearances: A Study in Idolatry* (London: Faber and Faber, 1957).
14. E.O.Wilson, 'Back from Chaos', *The Atlantic Monthly* 281, no. 3 (March 1998): 49.
15. Ibid., 49.
16. E.O.Wilson, *Consilience: The Unity of Knowledge* (New York: Belknap Press of Harvard University Press, 1998), 28.
17. E.O.Wilson, 'Back from Chaos', *The Atlantic Monthly* 281, no. 3 (March 1998): 55-56.
18. Ibid., 56.
19. E.O.Wilson, *Consilience: The Unity of Knowledge*, 40.
20. Ibid., 9.
21. E.O.Wilson, *Consilience: The Unity of Knowledge*, 40.
22. Ibid., 42-43.
23. Ibid., 40.
24. Ibid., 285.
25. Ibid., 285.
26. Ibid., 292.
27. Ibid., 280.
28. Ibid., 282-283.
29. Ibid., 282.
30. Ibid., 282.
31. Ibid., 282.
32. Ibid., np.
33. E.O.Wilson, 'Back from Chaos', *The Atlantic Monthly* 281, no. 3 (March 1998): 44.
34. Ibid., 54.
35. E.O.Wilson, *Consilience: The Unity of Knowledge*, 266.
36. Ibid., 266.
37. Ibid., 266. 'In support of this idea', Wilson writes, 'is the conclusion of biologists that humanity is kin to all other life forms by common descent. We share essentially the same DNA genetic code, which is transcribed into RNA and translated into proteins with the same amino acids. Our anatomy places us among the Old World apes and monkeys' (266). '[W]hether we like it or not', he writes in another context, '*Homo sapiens* is a biological species' (157).
38. Ibid.,163. As he writes, 'culture has arisen from the genes and forever bears their stamp'. However, he continues, 'with the invention of metaphor and new means, it has at the same time acquired a life of its own' (163).
39. Ibid., np.
40. Ibid., np.
41. Ibid., 150.
42. Ibid., 157.
43. Ibid., 157.
44. Ibid., np.
45. E.O.Wilson, 'Back from Chaos', *The Atlantic Monthly* 281, no. 3 (March 1998): 62.
46. E.O.Wilson, *Consilience: The Unity of Knowledge*, 115-116, 184.
47. David Scott, 'The Re-Enchantment of Humanism: An Interview with Sylvia Wynter', *Small Axe: A Journal of Criticism 8,* and 4, no. 2 (September 2000): 183.

48. Sylvia Wynter, 'Africa, the West and the Analogy of Culture: The Cinematic Text after Man' in *Symbolic Narratives/African Cinema: Audiences, Theory and the Moving Image*, ed. June Givanni (London: British Film Institute, 2000), 45-56.
49. Ibid., 45-46.
50. By *laws of Auto-Institution*, Wynter argues that human beings 'auto-institute' themselves as a specific genre of the human, as this genre is encoded in a specific 'culture'. This auto-institution is alone made possible by the third level of dually biological and symbolic existence that is the human, and is always adaptive to a specific geo-political, ecological, and epistemological context. See Sylvia Wynter. 'Africa, the West and the Analogy of Culture: The Cinematic Text after Man', 23-76.
51. Ernesto Grassi, *Rhetoric as Philosophy: The Humanist Tradition* (University Park: Pennsylvania State University Press, 1980), 108.
52. Sylvia Wynter, 'Africa, the West and the Analogy of Culture: The Cinematic Text after Man', 49-56.
53. Sandra Blakeslee, 'Hijacking the Brain Circuits with a Nickel Slot Machine', *The New York Times*, February 19, 2002, F5.
54. Ibid., F5.
55. Ibid., F5.
56. Sylvia Wynter, 'Africa, the West and the Analogy of Culture: The Cinematic Text after Man', 53.
57. E.O. Wilson, *Consilience: The Unity of Knowledge*, np.
58. Sylvia Wynter, 'Africa, the West and the Analogy of Culture: The Cinematic Text after Man'.
59. E.O.Wilson, *Consilience: The Unity of Knowledge*, 157-158, 193.
60. Ibid., 157.
61. Ibid., 157-158.
62. Ibid., 193.
63. Ibid., 158.
64. Howard Kaye, *The Social Meaning of Modern Biology* (New Brunswick: Transaction Books, 1997), 101.
65. Ibid., 127.
66. E.O.Wilson, *Sociobiology: The New Synthesis* (Cambridge: Harvard University Press, 1975), 3.
67. E.O.Wilson, *Sociobiology: The New Synthesis*, 129.
68. Howard Kaye, *The Social Meaning of Modern Biology* 96-97. 'Inclusive fitness', as Kaye writes, 'differs from Darwinian or individual fitness in that it includes the effect of an individual organism's behaviour on the fitness of its relatives, weighted by the degree of genetic relationship. Thus even if an individual's organism is reduced, social behaviour may still be "adaptive" and can evolve (assuming that it is under genetic control) provided that it increases the individual's *inclusive* fitness' (96).
69. Ibid., 107.
70. Ibid., 128.
71. Ibid., 132.
72. E.O.Wilson, *Consilience: The Unity of Knowledge*, 298.
73. Howard Kaye, *The Social Meaning of Modern Biology*, 101.
74. Sylvia Wynter, 'Africa, the West and the Analogy of Culture: The Cinematic Text after Man', 46, 52.
75. Ibid., 46, 52.
76. Michel Foucault, *The Order of Things: An Archaeology of the Human Sciences* (New York: Vintage Books, 1973), 310.
77. E.O.Wilson, *Consilience: The Unity of Knowledge*, 182.

78. Ibid., 195.
79. Ibid., 197.
80. Ibid., 202.
81. Ibid., 197.
82. Ibid., 292.
83. Ibid., 292.
84. For these assumptions with respect to the discipline of economics, see any elementary economics textbook.
85. Sylvia Wynter, 'Is "Development" a Purely Empirical Concept or also Teleological?: A Perspective from "We the Underdeveloped"' in *The Prospects for Recovery and Sustainable Development in Africa*, ed. Aguibou Y. Yansané (Westport, CT: Greenwood Press, 1996), 311.
86. For Wilson's argument on overpopulation, see E.O.Wilson, *Consilience: The Unity of Knowledge*, 288.
87. Steven Shapin, *The Scientific Revolution* (Chicago: University of Chicago Press, 1996), 25.
88. David Scott, 'The Re-Enchantment of Humanism: An Interview with Sylvia Wynter', *Small Axe: A Journal of Criticism 8*, and 4, no. 2 (September 2000): 206.

10 | *Is the Human a Teleological Suspension of Man? Phenomenological Exploration of Sylvia Wynter's Fanonian and Biodicean Reflections*

Lewis R. Gordon

No attempt must be made to encase man, for it is his destiny to be set free.[1]
—Frantz Fanon

Sylvia Wynter is an intellectual who, similar to many other great Caribbean intellectuals, challenges the limits of being and the being of limits. She approaches life with outstretched hands, reaching, always, to the beyond while taking seriously that she could only do so by remembering that her feet must stand on foundations, however fleeting. Hers is a way of approaching the life of the mind that has been a hallmark of her illustrious predecessors and recently deceased contemporaries who include José Martí, Frantz Fanon, Elsa Goveia, C.L.R. James, and her living colleagues, such as Aimé Césaire, George Lamming, Stuart Hall, Kamau Brathwaite, and V.S. Naipaul. It is an understanding and sense of the self whose closest North American and European counterparts were the circle of friends and critics that constituted that special moment in European intellectual life that occasioned North American émigré intellectuals Gertrude Stein, F. Scott Fitzgerald, and Ernest Hemingway in one period, and French intellectuals Jean-Paul Sartre, Simone de Beauvoir, Raymond Aaron, Albert Camus, and Maurice Merleau-Ponty shortly after. I speak, of course, of the designation *writer*.

An unusual feature of the Caribbean writer, as with the French writer, is the inconceivability of limited scope. For such an individual, there may be initial interest — say, philosophical, fictional, poetic, historical, or natural scientific — but in the end, the concern is more about what needs to be said than on the credentialing or locating of disciplinary identities of who says it. Thus, the sociologist, historian, philosopher, economist, psychiatrist, or dramatist becomes, ironically, more temporary clothing for the salient body of *thought*. I mention this because of the difficulty and inappropriateness of determining exactly what Sylvia Wynter *is* and what she *does*. She has, in effect, transcended the collapse of means-and-ends argumentation by literally making disciplinary formation a mere *tool* for her greater set of projects.[2] True, she has a degree in Medieval Spanish literature, and it is also true that she has worked as a dancer, an actress, and she has written plays and a novel, and it is also true that she is Professor Emerita of Spanish and Portuguese Studies and Black Studies at Stanford University.[3] These designations are for her opportunities with which she had to work through her struggle to comprehend things greater than herself, which are, in effect, greater than all of us. Heavily rooted in the currents of social life, she is attuned to the value of transcendence as what Karl Jaspers would call a *cipher* of where we are.[4] Put differently, we must stay attuned to a 'there' in order to understand what it means to be 'here.'

In the course of such attunement, Wynter has sought many guides. Hers is a world of multiple thinkers from multiple perspectives. In some, she finds a kindred spirit. One of them is Frantz Fanon.

Sylvia Wynter on Frantz Fanon

Fanon is brought to the fore in several of Wynter's writings, ranging from her critique of development studies to those on the black self. Her work in the latter has produced her most detailed engagement with Fanon's thought — namely, her essay 'Toward the Sociogenic Principle: Fanon, Identity, the Puzzle of Conscious Experience, and What It Is Like to Be Black.'[5] In that essay, she explores the question of 'being black' as a conscious mode of constitutive being. In effect, the condition of being is posed in terms of 'being-like' precisely because of the subjective possibility of standpoints. To imagine 'being the other' requires the self's and the other's subjectivity, for if the other or the self were devoid of such self-apprehension, then there would be no distinguishing upsurge, no moment of emergence. If the relation was purely asymmetrical, there would simply be the imposition of consciousness. To imagine 'being' a stone, for example, is patently not that of a stone, nor even the prerogative of a stone, but the imposition of the self onto or into an anthropomorphized or noetically conditioned stonelike object. Wynter uses the thought of analytical philosopher Thomas Nagel, from his famous essay, 'What Is It Like to Be a Bat?,' as a guide for this problematic, but the genealogy of the problem has roots in the Husserlian phenomenological tradition — a tradition Nagel borrows from greatly in his work without acknowledgement.[6] The problem posed by Husserl was not simply the question of, say, other minds or other selves, but also the question of what is involved in analogical reasoning where, in thinking about that other's standpoint, one is in touch with that other as, first, a subjectivity, which one realizes as a *human, embodied* subjectivity.[7]

The problem of apprehending the subjective standpoint of another species is a matter in which a bit of humility is a sign of respect for rigour, but there are good reasons to expect the possibility of more than the intersubjective moment of eye-contact or realized utterances in encounters between human beings; *empathy* stands as the condition whose denial entails a collapse into *self-denial*. Criticisms of this form of self-denial are shared ironically by Jean-Paul Sartre and Emmanuel Levinas. Sartre realized that denying the subjective life of others requires *suppressing* that encounter both outwardly and inwardly.[8] The outer–inner distinction militates against the solipsism occasioned by the denial, for, in effect, such denial exemplifies a desire to be the only point of view, to be, literally, the world. How can there be inner–outer relations when there is nowhere beyond the self? But such a self could not emerge as self except where distinguished from an *other* self. Sartre's word for this phenomenon is *mauvaise-foi*, 'bad faith.'[9] The Levinasian model relies on appreciating the infinite set of problematics posed by the *other* as uncontainable but realizable in the flesh, or more specifically the face, as another human being.[10] It is that transcending subjectivity — what Sartre would call its 'metastability,' its refusal to stand still — that initiates a relationship marked by a series of interrogatives. Our limited knowledge of each *other*, occasioned by enough shared knowledge, as Kwasai Wiredu has shown, for communication, stimulates processes of questions and disclosure.[11] In both the Sartrian and Levinasian instances, the outer-directed act of apprehending an *other* involves a leap outward through and into an inner reality.

An insight from African thought is that the resources by which people are capable of evading the inner-life of whole groups of people are nearly endless. If an *other*'s subjectivity is denied, then, so, too, is his or her *being*. In effect, such a denial amounts to the (false) claim that, in encounters with such people, there is no *other* there.

The reader may be wondering what all this has to do with Fanon. Wynter is here elaborating Fanon's taking on of a task first formally identified by W.E.B. Du Bois in 1897 but made most poignantly in 1903 in *The Souls of Black Folk,* that from the standpoint of a culture premised upon anti-black racism, black people have no point of view.[12] In its most radical form, the anti-black standpoint lays claim to the view that black people lack an inner life. The implications are severe if we consider what it would mean for such a lack to be operative.

Fanon's insight, shared by Du Bois, is that where there is no inner subjectivity, where there is no being, where there is *no one there,* and where there is no link to another subjectivity as ward, guardian, or owner, then *all is permitted*. Since *in fact* there is an *other* human being in the denied relationship evidenced by, say, anti-black racism, what this means is that there is a subjectivity that is experiencing a world in which all is permitted against him or her. The conclusion, marked in red over half a millennium, is ineluctable: structured violence.

The problematic of a denied subjectivity means that the Fanonian black faces a structured situation in which his or her struggle is more than material reconstruction. That black faces, also, the question of appearance *as a subjectivity,* which means a struggle for epistemic relations emerges. We could call this struggle the dialectics of recognition. Fanon argues that such projects within the confines of the signs and symbols that constitute the modern world, what Wynter prefers to refer to as the modern *episteme* or order of knowledge, suffer from structural failure. For the paths they offer blacks are those that already set whites as the standard of human *being*. In effect, this creates a relational semiosis with at least two consequences. The first has theological reverberations: should blackness be asserted as a *human* location, then we face depending on a standard that is below a standard. In effect, that would make whites a standard above the human, which would make whites gods. Since to be human is by definition to fall short of the divine, then whites would function simultaneously as the impossible wish in the face of their lived reality of its achievement in themselves. Here, the obvious consequence is akin to Freud's observation of children's fantasy in 'The Relation of the Poet to Day-Dreaming,' that the child has but one wish: to be an adult.[13] The black faces but one ultimate desire: to be white. The effect is white normativity, where whites are the presumed standpoint of human maturation. Whites become what it means for human beings to grow up. The second semiotic turn collapses into narcissism. Whites as the standard live as originality, as *the original*, as Adam. What this means is that blacks can at best hope to be *like* whites, to be their *imitation*, since to be black here means to be that which seeks typicality, seeks being, from the prototype. The problem with being an imitation, however, is that it is just that — an imitation. The 'real' or the 'authentic,' as the standard, already achieves what it is. The imitation, depending on the original as its standard, lacks a standard of its own — that is, lacks itself as its standard. In effect, it faces a negative relation of *not being the original*. That is what it means to be an imitation, to be that which is trying to be what it is not. We need simply think of the slew of presumed white types for which there are black imitations in popular culture, the most controversial of which is 'Black Jesus.' Narcissism emerges where the imitation attempts to be the original. To be such, the imitation must convince itself that it is not an imitation, which means that it must regard itself as an original. But the problem is that the original that it lays claim to being is the original that it is not by virtue of a standard that it cannot be. Thus, the claim to originality becomes an effort to see a lying reflection. There are many concrete examples of this phenomenon. One could think of the Queen in *Snow White*, who seeks her being in *the words* of her mirror. Why did the image require the addition of words? Why was it necessary for the mirror to tell her that she was the most beautiful, and therefore the epitome of beauty — in fact, *beauty itself*. As the story shows, the subsequent existence of the girl Snow White creates a crisis in which the Queen needed to make the mirror *say* what she wanted to believe — that it was she, not Snow White, who exemplified beauty, which requires not only for Snow White not to exist, but for her *never to have existed*. In effect, it requires pretense, which lays bare the deceptive feature of narcissistic desire: It is not only for the world to be as one desires it, but also for it never to have been against one's desire. It requires defying reality. At the heart of narcissistic retreat, then, is failure as with divine desire: in both instances, the Black never emerges as standard because standard itself has been saturated with white normativity.

There is an existential objection that should immediately be made here. Blacks are, after all, *presumed* to be imitation whereas whites are simply granted prototypical status. In effect, whites' existence is treated as self-justified whereas blacks' existence is treated as requiring justification. But if a process of justification is what constitutes justification, how could whites justify their being justified without having gone through such a process? What whites could claim is that, as the standard, they also are the processes of justification itself. In effect, what this would mean is that blacks suffer even in the process of justification as well, for their process lacks the legitimating condition of being white. In effect, it requires being white in order to become white. Blacks lose here before they have started. In truth, the best way out of this 'Catch 22' is not to engage it. Seeking white recognition is itself a failure.

There is another objection. To articulate it, we must, however, clarify our position on an often misread concept: *double consciousness*. The simplest formulation of double consciousness comes from our discussion of imitation. Blacks face two worlds — theirs and those of whites. The former is the world of imitation and the latter is the world of the standard. When blacks are with one another, lost in the world of imitation, we live as though we are the standard (white face), but it is when we realize that we cannot be white, when we encounter whites, we realize that our white faces were masks and that we are, underneath, black and imitation. This is the standard read of both Du Bois and Fanon. What is often not taken into account, however, is that Du Bois and Fanon speak of these cases as *pathological* cases, and they do refer to another sense of doubling that challenges the imitative status of blackness. The notion of white prototypicality is a function of the white world, a world in which such standards are already presumed. Such a world presumes its scope as ontological, as absolute being, where there is literally no outside. But there are those who live the contradiction of such a view of the world. They do live outside, and because they do not deny the subjectivity of those on the inside, they know the answer to the question, What is it like to be white? They thus live with the knowledge that the world is larger than the white one, and they know that the ascription of being is not granted to that wider world — that world of, as it were, dark matter — but they also know that they live in that world, it is their lived experience. Whiteness exemplifies a kind of blindness. It is a patronizing view of blackness as a limit, a limit of being, a point of lack. What this creates is an internal consistency of whiteness that makes it appear as complete. The insight from blackness, as the contradiction, and therefore as incompleteness, is that whiteness is complete only at the level of delusion. As complete, it becomes nature and, consequently, what it means to be natural. To be such is an axiology of perfection, which means that all imperfection must be extraneous. So there is a performative contradiction of a denied outside, solipsism, that depends on its dirty laundry being outside of itself. This outside, being an illegitimate outside, is what it means to be a problem. Wynter refers to such location, such mode of non-being, as 'the liminal.'

Double consciousness, epistemologically understood, is the realization of the contradictions of one's society. Such realization is truth. That means that double consciousness is a subversion of white normativity *through identifying white normativity as normativity*. For internal to white normativity is its absence of boundaries, its radicalization of scope. This means that white normativity lives itself as 'universal,' 'complete,' and 'absolute.' But its contradiction renders it particular by virtue of *seeing* beyond it. This seeing is both epistemological and phenomenological. It is phenomenological because it is a form of *consciousness,* and as a form of consciousness it has an intentional structure that presents, by virtue of its simultaneous ability to make distinctions, even white normativity as an object with which it is not identical. This observation suggests that double consciousness is not an apprehension that should be overcome. It suggests that it is a form of critical consciousness that should be understood. In a later essay, Sylvia Wynter agrees when she in effect argues that Black Studies is such an epistemic practice.[14] Du Bois also agreed more than a century ago, for he devoted the rest of his career to building thought and history from that troubled world of being a problem.[15]

The contradictions that emerge from blackness are not simply regarding the political relationships between black and white. That the world is larger, both spatially and temporally, than the white world claims it to be opens the door to empirical work that undermines white legitimacy yet brings to the fore the pervasiveness of a whiteness that sees but still does not see, as Kierkegaard once reflected.[16] I mentioned earlier the ideological force of imitation implicit in the term 'Black Jesus.' I recently viewed a documentary on Jesus in which forensic scientists' reconstruction of typical skulls from Judea during that period reveal what would today be considered brown and black people. In spite of this admission on a scientific television programme, the dramatizations returned to contemporary Eastern European images of these ancient people, including Jesus, whose time in the sun would have surely meant melanoma had they been such.[17] That Jesus was literally brown or black means that the Aryan and, for that matter, even the contemporary European Jewish image of him and other ancient Jews, is in fact the imitation, not the original. A claim of double consciousness, then, could be one in which the notion of originality is identified as having been subverted, and double conscious insight is to put things historical in their proper place. This need not be restricted to the embodied god of two billion people. Think of Ralph Ellison's famous essay, 'What Would America Be Like Without Blacks?'[18] After listing the features of things peculiarly American, Ellison showed that many of them emerged from *black* America. What this form of double consciousness reveals is that white originality is narcissistic; it is a function of white domination, not always white creativity. The question raised, then, is this: If *reality* is on the side of black double consciousness, why does the world in which blacks live continue to support white normativity?

Fanon's response, affirmed by Wynter, is that the notions of whiteness and blackness are functions of the social world. The social world produces normative categories and serves as the basis of the generation of meanings by virtue of which new varieties of life enter the world and others disappear from it. The significance of this insight, for Wynter, is that it raises the question of reality beyond the confines of its ontogenetic and phylogenetic imperatives.[19] This transcendence of the phylogenetic–ontogenetic models signal the limits of the biological one.[20] The biological model, linked to the naturalism of the modern episteme, encounters *its* limits in the social world. That reality — social reality — raises the question of the human being beyond the confines of even sscience itself, which, for Wynter, is a source both of hope and inspiration, from the liminal, for the limits of the modern formulation of the human, of which she writes as the emergence and reign of *man*. Writes Wynter:

> *Man* as a new (and ostensibly universal because supracultural) conception of the human had in fact been invented by a specific culture, that of western Europe, during the sixteenth century..., the anthropologist Jacob Pandian notes that this invention had been made possible only on the basis of a parallel invention.... This had been so, he explains, because while western Europe was to effect the transformation of its medieval religious identity of the *True Christian Self* into the now secularizing identity of *Man*, it was confronted with the task of inventing a new form of binarily opposed Otherness to *Man*, one that could reoccupy, in secular terms, the place that its conception of the *Untrue Christian Self* had taken in the matrix of the religio-cultural conception of the human, *Christian*. In consequence, where the Other to the *True Christian Self of medieval Europe had been the Untrue Christian Self* (with the external Others being *Idolaters* and/or *Infidels*), with the invention of *Man* in two forms (one civic humanism, the other in the context of that of Liberal or economic humanism which took place at the end of the eighteenth and during the nineteenth century), Europe was to invent the Other to *Man* in two parallel forms. And, because *Man* was now posited as a supracultural universal, its Other had logically to be defined as the Human Other.[21]

A central feature of Wynter's argument here is that the process of secularization does not shed with it the grammar of Christo-centrist values. Along with these values come theological rationalization and legitimation practices in secular form.[22] Because of this, old problems, such as theodicy, return with proverbial vengeance. Theodicy is the effort to account for the ultimate goodness and justice of God in the face of evil and injustice. How could an all-powerful, all-knowing, all-good, and perfect God exist who does not do anything to prevent the emergence of such wrongs? Is God ultimately responsible for all that happens? The classic response has been to place evil and injustice 'outside' of God's causal nexus in two ways. The first is simply to say that such problems are a consequence of the freedom of angels and human beings. The second is to remind us of our epistemological limitations. We do not ultimately know what God knows, which means that what may appear to us (finite beings) as unjust might not be so for God (an infinite being). Secularized, God is replaced by the knowledge systems and social systems in which we live. If those systems are treated as perfect, then the two lines of rationalization take the form, as we have seen in our earlier discussion of Du Bois, of identifying 'problem people,' people whose contradictory nature is a consequence of being outside the system, and people who fail to see that the ultimate justice of the system makes them incompatible with the future. In her more recent formulation, she develops the linkages between this theodicean rationalization and Darwinian concepts of life itself, which, she argues, has the consequence of a *biodicy* in which the preservation of *man* as life is the latest sleight of hand of late modernity.[23]

Man – Fanon and Wynter

Fanon comes to Wynter's *man* as *white man* in different ways but with a shared consequence: 'White civilization and European culture have forced an existential deviation on the Negro. I shall demonstrate that what is often called the black soul is a white construction.'[24] Fanon's is paradoxically a Lacanian formulation that ironically relativizes Lacanian psychoanalysis. This relativizing enables him to transcend Lacan into the location of a radical critical reflection.[25] In his discussion of Mayote Capecia's autobiographical novel *Je suis Martiniquaise*, Fanon showed that Capecia sought not words of love from her lover André, a white military man, but words of whiteness — words of loving her *as he would a white woman* and that *he could only love white women*. Such words would assure her that she must not really be a black woman, and *as words* they produce the undercurrent of communicable reality, social reality, through which 'truth' is generated. In effect, Capecia wants a lie that she could accept as truth. It could not be just *her* truth, because she wanted to *be* white, which means it must also be a truth for André or *others*. Our discussion of the Queen in *Snow White* returns here. What is André but her mirror whom she demands to give her the words she most desires? That André is a man maintains the patriarchical relations of language in the Lacanian system, wherein woman is lack, the silence that makes language speak. But Fanon shows, as well, that the troubled black man, Jean Veneuse/René Maran, in love with a white woman though he may be, could not rest till he, too, procured from a white man, those precious words of whiteness:

> In fact you are like us — you are "us". Your thoughts are ours. You behave as we behave, as we would behave. You think of yourself — others think of you — as a Negro? Utterly mistaken! You merely look like one. As for everything else, you think as a European. And so it is natural that you love as a European. Since European men love only European women, you can hardly marry anyone but a woman of the country where you have always lived.... André Marielle, whose skin is white, loves Jean Veneuse, who is extremely brown and who adores Andree Marielle. But that does not stop you from asking me what must be done. You magnificent idiot![26]

The white man grants Veneuse this gift of a transition from black to 'extremely brown' and with it a claim of being 'one of us [whites].' That Veneuse is, at least, male challenges his relation to the female of his affection, for where are his valuable words for the affirmation of her desire? What Fanon is showing here is that Veneuse is not a man, for man has been subdued in his consciousness into *man* as *white man*. This *man* is the one that haunts all of the black's failures in *Black Skin, White Masks;* he is there in the assailing force of a child screaming, 'Look, a Nigger!'; there in the Reason that plays cat and mouse until Fanon realizes its habit of walking out the door whenever he walks into a room; there in the jubilee of Fanon's retreat into the irrationalism of rhythmic escape in the name of *Nègritude;* there in the coldness of the sky and the concrete that lay beneath the black's feet; claustrophobic, saturating, he is there in full biocentric force as he stimulates the secretion of the alien black self.[27]

Yet, in the midst of all this, is the underlying realization of a physical world from which, if there could be a 'from which', all this appears to be the source of much ado about nothing. That world, a world that is not in fact a standpoint at all, a world in which there is no meaning, is one in which *man* as white invests himself as real, and because of this, he evades the reality that both constitutes him and the subjects by which his various relations emerge in the world. This *man*, who depends as everyone else does on the social world for his being, sees himself as independent of it precisely because he expects it as conditioned by him and for him. Such entitlement leads to the luxury of boundlessness, as we have already observed. It is, however, because of this investment in a 'real' as against the social (which, he at times, may even consider fictional) that puts him in conflict with social reality. His model becomes, in a word, himself, and in such an identity relation, there is only degenerative difference, which issues the return of a contradictory solipsism — the self as world by virtue of a denial of *others* without whom the self could not have been posited in the first place. It is this inhibition that constitutes an obstacle to the emergence of the human.

The social world holds out its outstretched arms and beckons us to reach into its bosom in which there continues to be the proliferation of meanings that promise a new humanity. Since Wynter sees Fanon's advancement of sociogenesis as key, let us now turn to a more detailed examination of that concept.

Sociogenesis as a Phenomenological Notion

Fanon did not devote any energy to elaborating the concept of sociogenesis, although it is a concept on which his main arguments for social transformation are based in his early and final works.[28] In *Black Skin, White Masks,* he announces:

> Reacting against the constitutionalist tendency of the late nineteenth century, Freud insisted that the individual factor be taken into account through psychoanalysis. He substituted for a phylogenetic theory the ontogenetic perspective. It will be seen that the black's alienation is not an individual question. Beside phylogeny and ontogeny stands sociogeny. In one sense, conforming to the view of Leconte and Darney, let us say that this is a question of sociodiagnostic.
> What is the prognosis?
> But society, unlike biochemical processes, cannot escape human influences. Man is what brings society into being. The prognosis is in the hands of those who are willing to get rid of the worm-eaten roots of the structure.[29]

Fanon's reminder of human influences is his existential critique of reductionistic structuralism. Just as society constitutes forms of life, we should remember that the constitution of society is a human affair. It is, in other words, a constructed construction, which means it can be constructed differently. But constructing a society differently, Fanon's opus cautions us, is not a simple or easy endeavour. It is a political project wrought with violent upheavals. It is also an effort saturated with much irony, where success could be failure and failure could be success. Take, for instance, the course of his naive protagonist in *Black Skin, White Masks*, who marches on in good faith, hope of becoming an 'assimilated black' versus those blacks who realize the inherent failure of that project. If the former never woke up, his 'success' would affirm the system's verdict of his elimination. *He* would not have succeeded in his success. For those who fail, however, their failure is *theirs*. Having failed in their failures, they have paradoxically also succeeded in those failures; their unhappiness is much healthier than the fate of the happy slave. Theirs require confronting the scope of their situation, which means moving from intrasystemic obedience to extrasystemic critique.

At the extrasystemic level, what is 'seen,' so to speak, is a world whose breath is entirely dependent on human actions. At the behavioural level, there would be no reason to think of human collectives as any different from other living collectives such as ants and bees. But at the actional level, we find the proliferation of meanings that constitute the social world. Here, what is important is that meanings must be understood, negotiated through, and not simply asserted, but asserted *as meant*. Such an activity is also known as *intentionality*. We are now on phenomenological terrain, where intentionality refers to the structure of consciousness marked by the preposition *of*: consciousness is always consciousness *of* something. This relationship pertains to all activities premised upon consciousness — experience, for example, is always *of* something. Within the structure of such intentions is also their reflective apprehension; they are, in other words, *lived*. This is so by virtue of all intentions being a here–there relation. To intend, one must intend from somewhere. But somewhere for living beings is an originary point of their own unsurpassability; no living creature can, in other words, surpass its own location except as an analogical positing of that location at another point ('there'). This originary point is *the body*. If consciousness were not embodied, it would not be somewhere, and not to be somewhere is to be nowhere. One could retort with the example of being everywhere, but such a move would eliminate the points from which a *there* could make sense. To be everywhere eliminates a point of view, the effect of which is to *be* nowhere.[30] Because we are also animals, the body amounts to the expression *consciousness in the flesh*.[31]

As body, we are locatable. We are either here or there. Our locatability is, however, a source of anxiety for some of us. Some attempt to be unlocatable through convincing themselves of really being a form of disembodied consciousness. The problem is that they would have to assert their perspective on the world not only as the only perspective, but also not as a perspective at all. The inherent contradiction is the same as that which flows from the notion of a self constituted without others. The other extreme amounts to a similar contradiction — claiming that we are not only locatable but incapable of locating others renders us as points without perspectives. The problem of having a perspective that denies our perspective is the result.

Reductions in the form of pure transcendence or a pure thing collapse into their opposites because the conditions that make even their assertion possible require them to be in tension with the ambiguous reality of living, intending, being. Put differently, intentional activity always has with it the negation of one state in the positive intention of another. When applied to things that are not conscious, such activity takes the form of surface relations. There is not an 'inside' to which to appeal, which makes the epistemological project one of thematizing how such things appear. With another consciousness, however, the 'inside' becomes the intentional apprehension of the rest of the world, including us. A lone consciousness is insufficient, however, for the stock of possibilities that could be presented to it as objects of its intention. At such level would only be the sensory-perceptive matrix. Other consciousnesses present multiperspectives on the world and, with them, multiple arrangements that can be *communicated* in an array of signs and symbols through which language manifests itself. To be conscious of another human being brings with it ever-evolving situations, and these situations, marked by intersubjective relations, set the framework for the layers and layers of concepts and practices that constitute the social world.[32]

The phenomenon of social evasion, briefly discussed as flights from embodiment and efforts to drown in one's physical presence, carries the implication of attempting to flee human reality. Why *human* reality? The best example is the plight of feral children. Studies have shown that although such children achieve intersubjective relations in the sense of knowing there are other consciousnesses in the world, an entire world of relations is shut off from them by virtue of the absence of synaptic development for language in their brains.[33] In that crucial window of opportunity through which language is learned, the path from the biophysical hominid to the human being is built. Although language in itself is not necessarily human, it is clear that the one that is a consequence of human interaction is such. A human social world is, then, a transcendental — that is, necessary and universal — condition for the emergence of individual human beings. But this emergence is never a completed tale. If it were so, then the human organism and the social world would be isomorphically suited to the former's environment. The human being would be maximally adapted and, consequently, cease to learn and to grow.

The social world is, therefore, an *opportunity* of human possibility. The implications of this insight are manifold.

The Human – Disciplinarily Decadent Models versus Teleologically Suspended Ones

Of course, 'What is it like to be black?' is not a black question, and even more, it is a question without the answer of a single black consciousness. What is key is that it is about a *consciousness* at all, which brings to the fore the question of a subjectivity that beckons intersubjectivity. That the question is raised signals a collapse in human relations — what Fanon often calls the death of the human — since there are easily recognized evidential differences between intersubjective relations with other human beings versus non-human consciousnesses. The mechanisms of language that afford the interplay of the stock of human meanings require a process of *dehumanization* for their denial to be maintained at institutional levels. This dimension suggests an emendation of Wynter's claim that the consequence of the system of *man* is a *human other*. Such an *other* entails a social relationship through which ethical problematics can be formed. The dehumanizing practices that constitute racism are the denial of a *human* relationship, which means also the denial of an *other*. It is the claim of a non-*self*-non-

other relationship. A liberation struggle involves, then, not a fight against *otherness* but laying the groundwork for the claim *to* being an *other* — an *other human being*. The subversive side of such a struggle is, however, as we have seen in our discussion of double consciousness, one in which the in-advance claim of the white world to human status is brought into question. Think, for example, of Leopold Senghor's claim that modern man — *man* — builds himself on overly rationalistic foundations. Lost are the passionate sides of his soul through which he could emerge as more fully human. This critique could be taken further to the very conception of rationality at work in modern life — a concept that attempts, through the hegemony of natural science, to force reason under the yoke of instrumental rationality. A similar critique applies, as well, to historicist science.

In such discussion, we find ourselves, along with Wynter, moving from purely archaeological concepts of framing the question of the human to genealogical–existential ones. Although there are many models, premised as they are on questions of power relations and practices of de-centring, we should also consider the symptomatic features of recalcitrance that mark decaying practices against which we should build a living and livable future. At the level of disciplinary knowledge, wherein the human sciences have evolved and with them the portrait of the human as *man* that has dominated us in the modern world, decadence emerges as a failure to realize the openness *of* the human subject. When these disciplines ontologize themselves, treat themselves as complete, a form *of* epistemological closure occurs with a consequence *of* a theodicy *of* technique, *of* pure application. The life-blood *of* knowledge is thus drained from the discipline in nihilistic hubris — where there is supposedly nothing substantive to learn because such practitioners have themselves ceased to learn. Their social and epistemological retraction are advanced by them as the limits of the world. Such a path is deontological in form. The discipline becomes an obligation without having to be consequential.

The question of consequence is more than a practical matter, for ironically even the conceptual basis of practicality is not an empirical one. Usefulness *of* knowledge is, after all, not simply a function *of* application. In the realm of theory, a useful idea could be one on which to build greater theoretical insight. The insight of phenomenological treatments *of* the human subject is the insight that in studying the human subject, we also contribute to its constitution. Such a consequence transcends the purely deontological and presents itself with the paradox of an open teleology.

Our age has been marked by a profound distrust *of* teleological reason. Whether avant garde postmodernist or liberal political theorists, both seem to condemn the teleological as a totalizing reality *of* false consensus.[34] Yet, as Kierkegaard has shown more than a century ago, the efforts to work along purely deontological claims to universality encounter a collapse into a universal that falls short of an absolute.[35] The internal appeal to rules or laws render the collapse of meaning onto itself, and we would see here the *fait accompli* of formalism. That human beings can suspend the universal, however, in the name *of* something higher than the universal raises the question of the ultimate value of universal decrees. For Kierkegaard, faith answers to a calling that provides life with meaning, with purpose, that cannot be met by mere adherence to the consistency of rules. For him, the individual is higher than the universal, but this is so because the individual can live not only as obedience to rules but also as disobedience to such rules for the sake of values that transcend such values.

Ours need not be Kierkegaard's search for a religious absolute, but we would be deluding ourselves if we expect instrumental rationalities and the disciplines constituted by them to make our lives more meaningful. And if the human after *man* is more valuable than the deontological *man* that has enmeshed our ways of knowing and constituting human reality, then Fanon's call for setting the human free requires suspending such practices. But such suspension would be meaningless without the purpose for which it could be initiated. In effect, then, in spite *of* the suspicions against teleological reason, a teleological suspension of *man* is a necessary condition for the creative practices that could constitute the human.

We May Wonder What Those Creative Practices May Be?

In one sense, the outline of such practices before they are performed would, in effect, be to put the proverbial cart before the horse. It is the task of each generation, as Fanon has argued in *Les Damnés de la terre*, to find its mission. Building the future also requires building its infrastructure. It is clear from Fanon's and Wynter's meditations that such a future requires epistemic as well as material foundations, which is ironic in an age of anti-foundationalism. It is not for the generation to *know* its mission in advance; it is for each generation to find it. The organizations *of* knowledge that have been constituting both the centred and liminal points *of reflection will, too, go through their process of* decay, and in their midst has already begun the process of organizing thought differently. Beyond the postmodern preface is also the challenge of what Kenneth Knies calls the *post-European sciences,* and in geographical terms, Nelson Maldonado-Torres has already initiated his project of *post-continental* reason.[36] Unfolding, as I write this essay, is a process of shifting the geography of reason, and this shift is taking place at a time, no less, when the human 'perspective' is no longer earthbound as our eyes look out at the stars and, through our technology, back at us from our neighbouring red planet. This moment of ours, marked by competing visions of a global world, faces its dramatic unfolding in a compression of space and time, which makes the ultimate threat of implosion a genuine one.

Fanon closed *Black Skin, White Masks* with a prayer for his body to make of him 'a man who questions!' What, in the end, is a teleological suspension of *man* but *the question* for which our troubled times now struggle?

Notes

1. Frantz Fanon, *Black Skin, White Masks,* trans. Charles Lam Markmann (New York: Grove Press, 1967), 230.
2. The use of intellectual tools is an essential feature of her thought and normative conviction, for her goal is not the elimination of the West's master narratives but of the *mastery* in those narratives. By decentring them, they no longer function as ends but as means. In this sense, she is genuinely interested in the question of epistemological postcoloniality. For discussion of this concept, see Lewis R. Gordon, *Fanon and the Crisis of European Man: An Essay on Philosophy and the Human Sciences* (New York: Routledge, 1995), *passim,* and Lewis R. Gordon, *Existentia Africana: Understanding African Existential Thought* (New York: Routledge, 2000), chapter 4. Michel Foucault advances the formulation of 'tools,' which can be found in *Society Must Be Defended: Lectures at the College de France, 1975-1976,* edited by Mauro Bertani and Alessandro Fontana; general editors, Francois Ewald and Alessandro Fontana; translated by David Macey (New York: Picador, 2003).
3. All this can be found in David Scott's insightful interview, 'The Re-Enchantment of Humanism: An Interview with Sylvia Wynter,' *Small Axe,* no. 8 (September 2000): 119-207.

4. See the third volume of Karl Jaspers, *Philosophy*, trans. E.B. Ashton (Chicago: University of Chicago Press, 1969–1971). For discussion in relation to my arguments here, see Lewis R. Gordon, 'Irreplaceability: An Existential Phenomenological Reflection,' *Listening: A Journal of Religion and Culture* 38, no. 2 (Spring 2003): 190-202.
5. Sylvia Wynter, 'Towards the Sociogenic Principle: Fanon, Identity, the Puzzle of Conscious Experience, and What It Is Like to Be "Black",' in *National Identities and Sociopolitical Changes in Latin America*, ed. Mercedes F. Duran-Cogan and Antonio Gomez-Moriana (New York: Routledge, 2001), 30-66. See also 'Is "Development" a Purely Empirical Concept or also Teleological?: A Perspective from "We the Underdeveloped"' in *Prospects for recovery and sustainable development in Africa*, ed. Aguibou Y. Yansane (Westport, CT: Greenwood Press, 1996), 299-316 and 'On How We Mistook the Map for the Territory, and Re-Imprisoned Ourselves in Our Unbearable Wrongness of Being, of Desêtre: Black Studies Toward the Human Project,' in *Not Only the Master's Tools: African-American Studies in Theory and Practice*, eds. Lewis R. Gordon and Jane Anna Gordon (Boulder, CO: Paradigm Publishers, 2005).
6. Thomas Nagel, 'What Is It Like to Be a Bat?,' *The Philosophical Review* LXXXII, no. 4 (October 1974): 435-50. Nagel concludes the article with some phenomenological speculations on the nature of objective explanation; compare also Nagel's *The View from Nowhere* (New York: Oxford, 1989), which borrows heavily from Maurice Merleau-Ponty's *The Phenomenology of Perception*, trans. Colin Smith (New York: Routledge, 1962), see especially Merleau-Ponty's reflections in his preface.
7. See, for example, Edmund Husserl, *Cartesian Meditations: An Introduction to Phenomenology*, trans. Dorion Cairns (The Hague: Martinus Nijhoff, 1960), the Fifth Meditation.
8. See Sartre's discussion of sadism and the body in Part III, chapters two and three of *Being and Nothingness*, trans. Hazel Barnes (New York: Washington Square Press, 1956), and for commentary see my discussions in *Fanon and the Crisis of European Man*, chapter 2 and *Existentia Africana*, chapter 4. See also the discussion of the body in bad faith in Lewis R. Gordon, *Bad Faith and Antiblack Racism* (Amherst, NY: Humanity Books, 1995), Part I.
9. See *Being and Nothingness*, Part I, chapter 2, 'ad Faith,' and *Bad Faith and Antiblack Racism*, Part I.
10. See, for example, Emmanuel Levinas, *Alterity and Transcendence*, trans. Michael B. Smith (New York: Columbia University Press, 1999). For discussion, see David Ross Fryer, *The Intervention of the Other: Levinas and Lacan on Ethical Subjectivity* (New York: Other Press, 2004).
11. See Kwasi Wiredu, *Cultural Universals and Particulars: An African Perspective* (Bloomington, IN: Indiana University Press, 1996).
12. For Du Bois's 1897 formulation, see his 'The Study of the Negro Problems,' *The Annals of the American Academy of Political and Social Science* 568 (March): 13-27, originally published in the same journal in 1898. He returns to it in the first chapter of *The Souls of Black Folk* (New York: Knopf, 1993), originally published in 1903.
13. Sigmund Freud, 'The Relation of the Poet to Day-Dreaming,' in *Character and Culture*, with an introduction by Philip Rieff (New York: Collier Books, 1963), 36.
14. See Wynter's essay, 'On How We Mistook the Map for the Territory, and Re-Imprisoned Ourselves in Our Unbearable Wrongness of Being, of Desêtre.'
15. I am referring, of course, to his life's work. For his reflections, see *The Autobiography of W.E.B. Du Bois: A Soliloquy on Viewing My Life from the Last*

Decade of Its First Century, edited by Herbert Aptheker (New York: International Publishers, 1968).

16. See Soren Kierkegaard, *Works of Love: Some Christian Reflections in the Form of Discourses*, trans. Howard and Edna Hong; preface by R. Gregor Smith (New York: Harper & Row, 1964).
17. See the Discovery Channel's website: *http://dsc.discovery.com/news/briefs/20030414/jesus.html*. See also Charles S. Finch, III, MD, *Echoes of the Old Darkland: Themes from the African Eden* (Decatur, GA: Khenti Inc, 1991).
18. In Ralph Ellison's, *Going to the Territory* (New York: Random House, 1986).
19. See 'Towards the Sociogenic Principle,' 35.
20. Ibid., 51.
21. Ibid., 43. The Foucault reference is *The Order of Things* (New York: Vintage Books, 1973) and the Jacob Pandian reference is *Anthropology and the Western Tradition: Toward an Authentic Anthropology* (Prospect Heights, IL: Waveland Press, 1985).
22. I have written on this phenomenon recently in the context of Fanon's thought in 'A Questioning Body of Laughter and Tears: Reading *Black Skin, White Masks* through the Cat and Mouse of Reason and a Misguided Theodicy,' *Parallax* 8, no. 2 (2002): 10-29, the full-length version of which appears as 'Through the Zone of Nonbeing: A Reading of *Black Skin, White Masks* in Celebration of Fanon's Eightieth Birthday', *The C.L.R. James Journal* 11, no. 1 (Summer 2005): 1-43. For Wynter's comments, see 'On How We Mistook the Map for the Territory, and Re-Imprisoned Ourselves in Our Unbearable Wrongness of Being, of *Desêtre*.'
23. See 'On How We Mistook the Map for the Territory, and Re-Imprisoned Ourselves in Our Unbearable Wrongness of Being, of *Desêtre*.'
24. *Black Skin, White Masks*, 14, translation revised.
25. For discussion of this concept of radical critical reflection, see *Fanon and the Crisis of European Man*, especially chapter 3, and *Existentia Africana*, introduction, chapters 1-4.
26. *Black Skin, White Masks*, 68-69.
27. Fanon speaks of secreting blackness as a biochemical transformation that many blacks develop when they come in contact with the white world. For discussion, see Kelly Oliver's *The Colonization of Psychic Space: A Psychoanalytic Social Theory of Oppression* (Minneapolis, MN: University of Minnesota Press, 2004).
28. In each instance, from *Black Skin, White Masks* to *Les Damnés de la terre*, known by its English translation of *The Wretched of the Earth*, Fanon demonstrates that the social world can be changed by its subjects becoming what he calls *actional*. For discussion, see Lewis R. Gordon, *Fanon and the Crisis of European Man* and 'Fanon and Development: A Philosophical Look,' *African Development/Development Afrique* 29, no. 1 (2004): 65-88.
30. The classic discussion of this problem is in Merleau-Ponty's *Phenomenology of Perception*, a work that, by the way, influenced Fanon's thought on the body. See, for example, *Black Skin, White Masks*, chapter 5.
31. It may well be possible that all life, including plant life and fungi, is conscious. Since we are talking about human beings, I restrict my analysis here to animal life.
32. For a more developed account, see Alfred Schutz, *Collected Papers*, volume 1, *The Problem of Social Reality*, edited and introduced by Maurice Natanson, with a preface by H.L. van Breda (The Hague: Martinus Nijhoff, 1962).
33. See, e.g., Michael Newton, *Savage Girls and Wild Boys: A History of Feral Children* (New York: Thomas Dunne Books/St. Martin's Press, 2003); and Russ Rymer,

Genie: An Abused Child's Flight from Silence (New York: Harper Collins Publishers, 1993). See also the website, 'Studies of Feral Children': *http://www/ ling.lancs.ac.uk/chimp/langac/LECTURE4/4feral.htm.*

34. Two recent and classic formulations are those of Jean Francois Lyotard, *The Postmodern Condition: A Report on Knowledge*, trans. Geoff Bennington and Brian Massumi; foreword by Fredric Jameson (Minneapolis, MN: University of Minnesota Press, 1984); and John Rawls, *A Theory of Justice* (Cambridge, MA: Harvard University Press, 1971).

35. See Kierkegaard's *Fear and Trembling* in *'Fear and Trembling' and 'Repitition,'* edited and trans., with introduction and notes by Howard V. Hong and Edna H. Hong (Princeton, NJ: Princeton University Press, 1983).

36. See Kenneth Knies, 'The Idea of Post-European Science: An Essay on Phenomenology and Africana Studies' and Nelson Maldonado-Torres, 'Toward a Critique of Continental Reasoning: Africana Studies and the Decolonization of Imperial Cartographies in the Americas,' both in *Not Only the Master's Tools*, eds. Lewis R. Gordon and Jane Anna Gordon (Boulder, Colorado: Paradigm Publishers, 2005); and Lewis R. Gordon, 'Africana Thought and African Diasporic Studies,' *The Black Scholar* 30, nos. 3–4 (Fall–Winter 2000): 25-30.

11 | Wynter and the Transcendental Spaces of Caribbean Thought

Paget Henry

Introduction

The thought of Sylvia Wynter must be approached with a firm grasp on the future of all of humanity, and not just that of Africana people. Anything less will fail to give it the justice that it so richly deserves. Rising from the particular crises of the racialized poor of the Caribbean, Wynter's thought moves out on powerful wings of poetic analogy to embrace the universal conditions of human self-formation and the global patterns of human domination of other human beings. Wynter brings these universal conditions and global patterns together in a powerful discourse of epistemic historicism to explain why so many in the Caribbean and other parts of the world are impoverished, racialized and condemned as lost or expendable. Like C.L.R. James and Frantz Fanon, it is the ongoing global production of this group, 'the condemned of the earth', that remains the persistent focus of Wynter's thought. No matter how far above or below, how far to the left or to the right her thought goes it is always in the service of clarifying some aspect of the conditions that are responsible for the condemned being a necessary part of our world. This paradox of the persistence of the condemned of the earth in spite of our ideals of freedom, justice, equality, and brotherhood/sisterhood is the knot that Wynter will attempt to untie. In the course of this undertaking, she has challenged the global scholarly community as profoundly as it has ever been.

For us in the Caribbean, Wynter has insisted that we enter regions of ourselves and our social world that we have neglected or overlooked in our search for a way out of the crisis of the condemned in the postcolonial order that we have been attempting to create. This order was supposed to have been a new beginning, a radical break with its colonial past, but instead has been derailed by that past which has now left it with only neo-colonial options. More than any other Caribbean thinker, Wynter has insisted that we turn our attention to the epistemic foundations of our discourses and social orders. This is not an area to which the Caribbean intellectual tradition has given a great deal of attention. Consequently, Wynter's insistence on exploring the transcendental spaces of Caribbean thought is the source of the originality of her contributions to the crisis of the condemned in our neo-/postcolonial order.

This transcendental turn has brought into clearer focus the hidden foundations of the discourses that we routinely use. It exposes and thematizes these epistemic depths that we take for granted when engaged in a particular exercise of knowledge production. Wynter's interest in the transcendental ground of knowledge production was not motivated by a desire to account for the success of the natural sciences as in the case of Kant. Rather, it was the repeated failures and ongoing production of systemic errors in the humanities and social sciences that motivated her transcendental turn. Particularly important, were the systemic misrepresentations of subordinated, oppressed and condemned groups in these disciplines. As crises of technification in the European natural sciences drove Husserl to explore their transcendental foundations, in a similar way, the crises of misrepresenting the condemned of the earth forced Wynter to explore the transcendental grounds of the European humanities and social sciences. However, Wynter does not bring her crisis of the humanities and social sciences into a critical engagement with Husserl's crisis of the natural sciences. The primary reason for this is Wynter's claim that the European natural sciences have achieved a cognitive autonomy that still eludes the social sciences and humanities.

The primary purpose of this essay is an examination of Wynter's epistemic historicism and the ways in which it has opened up the transcendental spaces of Caribbean thought. I will show that her examination of these spaces has produced three important results. First, it has identified and outlined some of the major contours of the field of Caribbean transcendentalism. Second, she has used these contours to radicalize the transcendental discourses of Kant, Husserl,

Habermas and Foucault. Third, Wynter's transcendental focus has enabled her to rework the Caribbean Marxist tradition in a very innovative way. Of these three results, our primary concern will be with the last. Consequently, this essay will be organized around four basic sections: first, the autopoetic foundations of Wynter's historicism; second, her theory of epistemes and epistemic change; third, her epistemic reading of James; and fourth, the consequences of that reading for Marxist discourses.

The Autopoetic Foundations

Wynter is in the best sense of the term a radical thinker. She goes to the roots of things in her search for the levers and mechanisms of change. Yet the question with which she always begins is one that has been at the centre of conservative sociological and political thought: the question of social order. How are social orders established? What are the mechanisms, the glue, or the centripetal forces that integrate societies and hold them together? In radical traditions of thought, the answer has consistently been force, power, authority or some combination of the three with culture playing a legitimating role. In conservative traditions, the answer has consistently been myth, religion, norms, mores, values or some combination of these cultural factors, with force, power and authority playing secondary roles. Wynter's approach shares the cultural focus of the conservative tradition but does not move at the level of already established cultural and discursive practices such as norms, mores or religious beliefs. Rather, it moves below such specific cultural practices and links the problem of social order to a more general set of a priori conditions that make cultural and discursive practices possible. These always presupposed conditions carry within them the order-producing codes and patterns that inform and frame the self-organizing capabilities of individuals and groups. In turn, these self-organizing capabilities make 'self-speciation'[1] possible. However, this ability of life forms, both human and non-human to establish and realize their particular mode *of* being is one that comes with inherited codes and inherited coding processes. Thus in the animal kingdom, these codes *of* self-speciation are genetic in nature. In the human world, they are autopoetic in nature. Thus in our self-speciating or society creating activities, genetic codes have been significantly replaced by autopoetic ones. Following Fanon, Wynter refers to this shift as the move from phylogeny to sociogeny.[2]

Autopoeisis is thus Wynter's answer to the problem *of* social order and not the particular norms, values or discourses that it may subsequently make possible. It is responsible for the distinct species life *of* humans and also for the different social orders that we find in human societies. Consequently, autopoeisis is the process by which human self-organization has been able to establish and maintain internally coded social orders while at the same time adapting to changes in the surrounding environment. At its core, autopoeisis is a set *of* encoded creative possibilities that can be discursively mobilized and deployed in the service *of* human self-formation. In more deterministic language, it is the encoded manner in which human self-organization is 'bio-evolutionarily pre-programmed' with the shift from phylogeny to sociogeny.[3]

This pre-programmed aspect of the autopoeisis of human social orders is important for two reasons. First, it points to the hidden status of the basic codes of social orders. They dwell in opaque spaces of constitutive otherness, and thus are beyond our immediate grasp. As we intervene in physical nature with the aid of scientific discourses, we can, with the aid of poetic discourses, intervene in these constitutive spaces of order-producing codes to lessen opaqueness, to adjust them to our needs, and to increase our levels of autonomy in relation to them. However, in spite of these interventions, we will never really transcend this mode of coded inscription or gain full control over it. The second importance of this autopoetic pre-programming by inaccessible, and as we shall see, epistemologically compromised codes, is that it constitutes a foundational layer of Wynter's philosophical anthropology. Here we see the beginnings of Wynter's view of the human as a being whose formation is embedded in codes from which it must be partially extricated. In short, autopoeisis is ontological writing. Through its coded possibilities it allows humans to write different versions of themselves into being.

In creating social orders, autopoeisis must write into being three dimensions of human speciation that are largely absent in the genetically coded speciations of the animal kingdom. First, human autopoeisis requires symbolic representations of the individual self or

'I'. Through these representations, the individual should be able to say to self and other who he/she is in reasonably definite terms. Second, human autopoeisis must include symbolic representations of the collective self or 'we' of the social group. Again, through such representations, the group must be able to consciously affirm itself to itself and to others. Third and finally, human autopoeisis must include symbolic representations of the surrounding environment. These three sets of representations, linked together by narratives of origin and end, will frame the basic vision of existence that is the cultural heritage of the group. Such visions of existence and the human capacity to produce them is the crucial difference that separates autopoetic from genetically coded social orders.

However, this striking advantage of human autopoeisis brings with it some major epistemological responsibilities. Our visions of existence must accurately and truthfully represent self and world. If they do not, this advantage will quickly turn into a major disadvantage. Wynter thinks it is right here that the first major problems of human autopoeisis emerge. Throughout the evolutionary history of order-producing codes, their knowledge-producing processes have always been intensively and extensively shaped by the conditions necessary for securing the self-organization of the group. Consequently, all earthly organisms must necessarily know themselves and their environments in the terms needed to ensure the conservation and replication of its order-producing codes. Wynter argues that this is true for us as well as the organisms of the animal world. Thus, we too know reality in species— specific terms which may not coincide with the way things are outside of our particular viewpoint. Echoing Kant, Wynter concludes from this that the cognition made possible by our 'governing' or order-producing codes is 'cognition of things for us and not cognition of things in and for themselves'.[4] This 'for us' knowledge, Wynter refers to as adaptive truths or ethnoknowledges as they are subject to and conditioned by the self-replicating needs of our autopoetic governing codes. In short, the shift to sociogeny and its autopoetic codes, has not freed our knowledge-producing practices from species-specific constraints that they continue to share with the genetic codes of phylogeny.

For Wynter, the primary reason for these epistemological problems of human autopoeisis is the binary oppositional manner in which it produces its representations of self, other and world. Thus, in representing the 'I', sociogenic autopoeisis cannot directly grasp the self but only indirectly through some type of trope that is semiotically linked to its opposite. These tropes and their abductive extensions become tape measures of being and non-being, of desired and undesired modes of the subject. These patterns of indirect representation through systems of binary oppositional tropes draw on prior classificatory systems of sameness and difference which serve as basic templates for processes of autopoetic production. For Wynter, different cultures rest on different semiotic organizations of these templates of sameness and difference. Thus it is the different scripts that can be semiotically extracted from these templates that make possible the systems of oppositional tropes by which specific modes of the 'I' or the 'We' are ontologized or written into being. However, it is this binary mode of inscription that raises Wynter's doubts about the truth-producing capabilities of autopoetically conditioned knowledge. The full implications of all this will emerge much more clearly when we take up the nature and limitations of epistemes. Here we need only to note that these are the autopoetic foundations that for Wynter shape both social and epistemic orders.

Autopoeisis and Epistemes

Although primarily linked to the problem of social order, the autopoetic templates of human sociogeny also serve as a transcendental or discourse-constitutive underside of human knowledge production. It is this underside of everyday discursive activity that Wynter theorizes in terms of epistemes and their transformation. Epistemes are pre-theoretical, self-organizing, discourse-constitutive formations that make routine knowledge production possible. They ground such knowledge-constitutive practices as induction, deduction, abduction, the troping of self and other. Epistemes are coherently organized sets of analogies, categories, images, concepts, and rules of statement formation that rest upon the classificatory schemes of autopoetic codes and templates. Hence they are able to draw on the semiotic creativity and auto-instituting powers of the latter. As in the autopoeisis of social orders, the autopoeisis of epistemes rests on the semiotic manipulation of the signifiers of sameness and difference contained in the governing template. In the case of epistemic orders, these templates must be re-centred around binaries such as truth/error, founding/unfounding concepts, inside the order/outside the order. With such signifiers to be semiotically manipulated, abductively extended and deployed in a self-organizing manner, epistemes can be established.

Given this mode of formation, epistemes, like other autopoetic creations, also have very clear binary patterns of internal organization. Thus, very often it is quite clear what is inside an epistemic order and what must be kept on the outside. However, for Wynter the most important binary pattern of an episteme is the polarization between its founding category and its semiotic opposite. She refers to the latter as the 'liminal' or 'chaos' category of the episteme. For example, in the Christian episteme of medieval Europe, spirit constituted the founding category, while its semiotic opposite, the flesh, constituted the liminal category of this episteme.[5]

In addition to these founding/liminal dynamics, the knowledge-constitutive creativity of epistemes is also profoundly shaped by what Wynter calls knowledge-constitutive goals. These are ordinary everyday goals that quite often are related to the social order that has been established. Thus salvation through the church, or fulfillment through political action are examples that Wynter has given of knowledge-constitutive goals. These goals help to orient the more formal aspects of epistemes to particular domains of reality, and thus aid in the production of specific kinds of knowledge whether spiritual, social or natural. Consequently, the organization of an episteme is never just a matter of the formal relations between categories, conceptual schemes and arguments, as in Kant's portrayal of the transcendental domain of the natural sciences. Rather, this organization must include definite socio-historical elements such as those goals that are definitely needed for epistemic closure. However, it is important to note that once epistemically selected this ordinary social goal is elevated and transcendentalized by the autopoetic powers of the episteme and thus becomes knowledge-constitutive in nature. Wynter's goals function a lot like Habermas's knowledge-constitutive interests.[6] The latter also historicize Kant's fonnalism by opening two-way connections between the transcendental and social realms.

With this account of epistemes, Wynter then raises the question of their truth-producing capabilities. Although very necessary for human knowledge production, Wynter argues that epistemes are prone to systemic error from three basic sources. First, the dynamics between founding and liminal categories create significant truth-producing problems for epistemes. In Wynter's view, founding categories tend to inflate or 'over-represent' the people, events and things assigned to them. In other words, whatever figure, claim or principle that is selected to serve as the centre or ground of the episteme must at least have the appearance of an indefinite capacity to explain, and sufficient generality to subsume the contributions of other discourses. In securing these inflations, founding categories often make use of the 'absolutization strategies' of epistemes. These include abductive moves such as mapping the contents of founding categories onto the cosmos itself or its eternal cycles and laws. In this way the significance of these contents are semiotically increased. These a priori or autopoetically prescribed features of epistemic centres are imposed on quite ordinary concepts and claims after they have been selected for this crucial role. Consequently, the built-in errors of founding categories are those of magnification and inflation in representational practices.

In contrast, liminal categories are marked by problems of systemic devaluation and minimalization in representation. This category and its contents are semiotically mapped onto negatives such as death, decay, evil and impermanence. Given such inscriptions, the question becomes how truthful or how adaptive will be the representations of this category? Will it be able to represent without being unduly influenced by the reproductive needs of its founding category? Wynter's answer is a clear no. Liminal categories distort and misrepresent their contents to the extent that they are semiotically read as threats to the autopoetic installing of the founding category. In short, they deflate and under-represent the objects, events and people assigned to them. Together, these dynamics between founding and liminal categories constitute the first major source of the tendencies of epistemes to systemic error.[7]

The second source derives from the incorporating of transcendentalized social goals into the semiotic logics of episteme fonnation. Like founding categories, knowledge-constitutive goals are inflated and over-represented because of their necessity to the internal order of the episteme. Very often they are absolutized to the degree that they are figuratively connected to the self-organization of the episteme. Correspondingly, whoever or whatever represents the opposite of these goals is deflated and under-represented. They cannot be read semiotically in an objective or positive light. They must be stigmatized, devalued and negated in the interest of the order of the episteme. So once again we have a necessary element in the constitution of epistemes that is prone to the systematic generation of error.[8]

The third and final source of systemic error in epistemes is the conditioning and orienting of their self-organizing activities by the larger autopoetics of social orders. Earlier we examined the epistemological problems of these poetics. There we saw that they could only generate knowledge of an adaptive or 'for us' nature. Wynter thinks that this basic pattern is reproduced on several levels of episteme formation and related discourse-constitutive activities. In short, because of this autopoetic inheritance epistemes are also unable to represent self, other and world without being unduly influenced by the self-organizing imperatives of the social orders in which they arise.

This error prone view of epistemes could easily lead to a position of skepticism that could take us back to Hume or to some version of postmodern relativism. However, this is not the outcome that emerges from Wynter's historicizing of epistemes and the larger transcendental domain. Indeed, Wynter's autopoetic reading of Kant's transcendental a priorism makes some very distinctive contributions here. In this regard, Wynter's semiotic inscription of the transcendental domain can also be usefully compared to those of Charles Sanders Pierce and Karl Otto Apel.[9] Both have brought a semiotic dimension to the reading of transcendental activity that was largely absent in Kant and Husserl, and to a large degree also in Habermas. However, the socio-historical dimensions that are so evident in Habermas's transcendental analyses are much weaker in the cases of Pierce, Husserl and Apel. Consequently, the distinctness of Wynter's transcendentalism is the unprecedented degree to which it has both semioticized and historicized this knowledge-constitutive domain, and the ways in which it links the latter to the production of the condemned of the earth. Given this originality, it follows that Wynter's transcendentalism should lead to outcomes that are quite different from those of the above philosophers. The most important of these is of course Wynter's epistemic historicism.

Epistemic Historicism

Epistemic historicism is an approach to history as a medium of human self-formation (and not just as a discipline) that rests on the dynamic relationships that Wynter sees between epistemic change and the transformation of social orders. It is a view of history from the perspective of the epistemologically compromised autopoetic process of instituting and de-instituting social orders. In other words, it approaches history from the standpoint of the sociologically creative and founding activities of governing codes and templates. However, it is the representational instabilities of this epistemologically compromised sociological creativity that produces what I will call the epistemic motions that, for Wynter, drive the historical process. From this perspective, liminal and other epistemic crises do not lead to skepticism but to a revolutionary concept of historical possibilities that both challenges and engages those of Marxism.

Epistemic change is the complex process by which an individual or a group substantially transforms or moves beyond the episteme of its day by changing the binary oppositional orderings of its governing template and thus is able to think new thoughts in new discourses. For Wynter, the key to this process of change is the magnitude of errors generated by an episteme representation or misrepresentation of the people, objects, and events that are outside of its boundaries of inclusion. These errors will increase in magnitude as we approach the objects and subjects that the episteme semiotically reads as directly antithetical to its founding categories. This systemic mobilizing of error and mis-representation creates the most vulnerable area in the internal order of an episteme that may eventually lead to its decline. These representational instabilities of epistemes are part of the larger category of epistemic motions referred to earlier that constitute the wheels of history.

In cases of major errors of misrepresentation, the contrary signals or claims coming from the object or subject may force a shift in the organization of the episteme or its eventual overthrow and replacement by another episteme. The latter produces epochal changes while the former results in less dramatic changes in the existing social and epistemic orders. Thus the vulnerability introduced into the structure of an episteme by liminal strategies of representation arises out of the resistance of the liminalized to its portrayal and evaluation. The liminal other will persistently say, do, or achieve things that challenge and contradict its representation within the episteme. Such challenges create crises of credibility for the episteme and confront it with the need for change.

The nature and depth of these challenges will determine the extent to which the foundations of the episteme are shaken, or just some discursive formations on its upper surfaces. Clearly to achieve the former a challenge must be to have the semiotic power expose and re-order the binaries of the governing template on which the episteme was auto-instituted. In other words, the challenge must be to have the autopoetic power re-organize the episteme or write a new one into being. It must be able to get to the depths of the governing template, identify the sources of misrepresentation, propose and execute its rewriting. Only such a process will bring about revolutionary epistemic change and thus dramatic shifts in the representation of the condemned. Such shifts in the representation of this group could be the basis for major changes in the social order. This is the autopoetic link between epistemic and social orders that is at the heart of Wynter's epistemic historicism.

For Wynter, the paradigmatic example of a revolutionary epistemic shift remains the rise of the modern bourgeois episteme out of the spiritual episteme of medieval Christianity. Indeed this epochal shift serves as one of the key founding analogies of Wynter's discourse of epistemic historicism. On the abductive wings of this analogy her thought expands to reach other themes such as race, gender, cinema, female circumcision, and specific authors such as Lamming, Glissant and James. Wynter has examined this shift in breathtaking detail, showing the ways in which challenges from lay humanists uprooted the founding flesh/spirit binary of the Christian episteme.[10] This is followed by equally detailed analyses of their reworking of the oppositions of its template that produced the bourgeois episteme. The latter was now re-centred around oppositions such as reason/lack of reason and property/lack of property. This was the secular episteme out of which the worlds of capitalism and socialism arose. As imperial extensions of the former, our colonial and post/neo-colonial societies have been profoundly shaped by the governing template and codes of this episteme. In the anti-colonial and anti-racist discourses of Africana people, Wynter sees the possibility of an epistemic shift of epochal proportions. These discourses have exposed the systemic errors of the modern bourgeois episteme and hence have created crises of credibility for it.

Because of these *counter* impulses Wynter has called these Africana discourses 'post-Western'.[11] However, Wynter remains deeply concerned about the fate of this Africana challenge as it does not appear to be decoding and rewriting the fundamental oppositions that have auto-instituted the Western bourgeois episteme. The Africana challenge has been unable to get to those depths because the discourses in which its alternatives are framed remain rooted in the bourgeois episteme and its governing template. As we will see, this is the context in which Wynter locates the current postcolonial/neo-colonial impasse of Caribbean societies.

Looking at Caribbean societies from the perspective of Wynter's epistemic historicism, three broad epistemic periods emerge. First, a period governed by the pre-colonial episteme of African religions; second, a period governed by the spiritually hybrid Afro-Christian episteme; and third, the current period of our postcolonial episteme. In the first it was the codes, templates, and autopoetics of African sociogeny that informed the sociological creativity of Africans in the Caribbean. The second was the result of the replacing of some of these African codes and binary oppositions by Christian ones. Such changes in the governing codes and templates help to explain the rise of a distinct Afro-Caribbean subject. Finally, since the late nineteenth century there have been growing secular shifts that have culminated in our current postcolonial episteme. These have re-centred the latter around binaries such as colonized/colonizer, black/white, freedom/domination, and developed/underdeveloped. These binaries in turn have made possible the articulating of important counter discourses that have guided major postcolonial transformations. However, these alternatives drew heavily on Western discourses such as Marxism, liberalism, positivism, and developmentism, which indicated the extent to which our postcolonial alternatives were still rooted in the bourgeois episteme. Wynter's concern here is that with our currently mixed governing codes and templates, sociological creativity may be such that we are unable to write into being a genuinely post-Western social order in which the need for the condemned will be eliminated.

This in brief is Wynter's epistemic historicism. For the region it offers a new approach to the problems of historical action. Because of its theories of the auto-instituting of epistemic and social orders, it is an approach that demands of us a well developed poetics. In particular, an interventionist poetics that is capable of rewriting the governing codes and templates that inscribe the a priori condition of epistemic and social orders. As intellectuals, we must become the rewriters of codes and so be able to change the current directions and velocities of epistemic motion in the interest of reclaiming the humanity of the condemned. As such, this poetics opens up revolutionary possibilities for social change at the same time that it challenges us to explore more deeply the repairing of liminal and other tendencies to systemic error that still continue to plague our sociological and epistemic creativity. We will return to these themes in our discussion of Wynter and James. But first, a brief phenomenological detour in which we examine more carefully the nature of the discontinuities that exist between the transcendental and everyday levels of discursive activity. This will also be important for our examination of the Marxian model of dialectical synthesis from the perspective of Wynter's epistemic historicism.

Epistemic Historicism, Phenomenology and Poetics

Throughout our exposition of Wynter's epistemic historicism we have made several references to the hidden foundations of discourses. We have referred to that domain of otherness in which governing codes, templates and epistemes work to establish the a priori conditions that make routine knowledge production possible. We've also suggested that this sub-textual level of activity was not available or accessible to us in the same way that the results of more conscious efforts at textual or discursive production are. What we have not made clear is the nature of this sub-textual hiddenness, the discontinuities it creates between episteme and discourse, and how Wynter and other transcendentalists have been able to get around these difficulties in moving between the textual and sub-textual levels.

In examining this problem of sub-textual unavailability, the key observation that must be kept in mind is that we are often unaware of the epistemic foundations upon which our discursive practices rest, and thus are unable to articulate them. This suggests two important features of the relationships between episteme and discourse. First, epistemes are not established in the same symbolic registers as the discourses we routinely manipulate or produce. Epistemes are produced in autopoetic registers that are unconscious, semio-linguistically organized systems of symbolic creativity. The discourses that we normally produce on the a priori foundations established by epistemes are constructed within the creative registers of self-conscious subjects. These are two very different sets of creative codes and between them there is often little that is immediately or automatically translatable. Think of the cases of the language of physics or sociology on the one hand and that of the transcendental or epistemic on the other. There are significant problems of commensurability here. Hence Wynter's insistence that we 'silence' or step out of our everyday discursive practices and learn the autopoetic language of epistemic and social orders.

Second, our inability to directly reach the epistemic from routine discursive locations suggests the possibility of a mutually displacing relationship between the two. If epistemes were always present, they would get in the way of normal knowledge production as we only make conscious use of small portions of them. To create knowledge with them, we must be able to lose sight of them, to let them go. The more we consciously focus on them the less we are able to engage in routine knowledge production. Indeed the relationship between episteme and live acts of knowledge production is a lot like Heisenberg's uncertainty principle. We cannot have both at the same time. The more we have of one, the less available becomes the other. Another way of thinking about this mutually displacing aspect of the relationship between episteme and discourse is to view it as one in which the contributions of both must be written simultaneously in their different registers on opposite sides of the same sheet of paper. Thus, when we are writing, we are unable to access the epistemic inscriptions that are being made on the other side of the sheet. Indeed, we must forget them if we are to produce commonly desired forms of knowledge. This discursive forgetting of the epistemic is an integral part of most of our modes of knowledge production. To gain access to the epistemic from one of our normal discursive locations we usually have to interrupt our knowledge-producing activities, turn the sheet over and shift to the register of autopoetics. In other words, one has to be silenced or suspended for the other to emerge and be heard. In Wynter's language, it is in 'the great silence' of the epistemic that live discursive production is born; and conversely, it is in the great silence of live discursive production that the epistemic is reborn or remembered.

These two factors, the need for silence and translation between episteme and discourse, points to the qualitatively different nature of the relations between these two as compared to relations between one discourse and another. Epistemes are absent presences, while discourses are present presences. There are imperatives that come with the former type of presences that are absent in the case of the latter. Modes of discursive silencing must be cultivated as well as practices of translation if absent presences are to be recovered. This recovery of the epistemic domain through the silencing or suspending of everyday practices brings us very close to the world of phenomenological self-reflection. Phenomenology, particularly as practised by Husserl, can be viewed as a form of discursive remembering that is an antidote to the necessary forgetting of the epistemic foundations that human knowledge production requires. Thus phenomenological self-reflection is one way in which we can navigate the discontinuous transcendental terrain between discourse and episteme.

However, this phenomenological recovery of the transcendental domain can take place with the aid of different discursive searchlights. The subject who is returning to the transcendental ground will do so from some point inside of the discourse in which he/she is currently inscribed. Thus it is through the prism of that discourse that the transcendental domain will be perceived and not necessarily that of philosophical logic as in the cases of Kant and Husserl. As we have already seen it is through the prism of poetics that Wynter approaches the transcendental domain. This is why she is able to return from her explorations of this domain with epistemic gifts that are quite different from those of Kant and Husserl. The primary gifts with which Wynter returns are those of transcendental codes and templates and not that of the transcendental subject.

As novelist, playwright and critic, Wynter's roots are in the Caribbean poeticist tradition along with George Lamming, Wilson Harris, Derek Walcott, Jamaica Kincaid and others.[12] However, what is distinctive about Wynter's intellectual development is the extent to which she has been able to suspend normal processes of poetic composition and reach the epistemic ground of her own poetic creativity. Consequently, Wynter's approach to the transcendental has been through effective suspensions of the conditions of producing poetic knowledge rather than those of producing scientific, logical, moral or mathematical knowledge. It is out of this self-reflection of the poet, this turning over of the sheet upon which her poetic compositions were written, that Wynter's distinctive poetics arises and at the same time acquires its phenomenological dimensions. It is the extensive and intensive development of this poetic phenomenology that has given Wynter the ability to overcome the discursive discontinuities and inaccessibilities that normally keep the transcendental realm hidden. Thus if we too are going to be able to overcome these difficulties, then we are going to have to develop phenomenological practices that are appropriate for suspending the normal routines of discourses in which we are inscribed.

Out of her poetic phenomenology, Wynter has produced the important concept of ceremonies. Wynter's ceremonies address the autopoetic dimensions of the discontinuities between episteme and discourse. To engage these aporias or discourse resistant gaps, semiotic ways must be found to recode and de-institutionalize this very opposition and abductively related ones, so that processes of suspension, translation and loosening of auto-instituted epistemic boundaries can begin. Semiotic recodings such as these are at the core of Wynter's ceremonies. They are the reality behind the title of Wynter's classic essay, 'The Ceremony Must Be Found: After Humanism'. Ceremonies or appropriate semiotic recodings of binaries and their abductive extensions must be found and performed at the sites of autopoetically instituted divides, absolutizations, closures and liminal categorizations. This is the only way in which these discourse-constitutive formations can be undone or de-instituted. Everyday discursive critiques may shake but not change the epistemic foundations on which these discourse-constitutive elements are reproduced on an ongoing basis. Perhaps the divide between the creativity of transcendental subjects and that of transcendental templates persists because the appropriate ceremonies have not yet been found to de-institute the autopoetic inscriptions that keep it in place. For the more scientifically inscribed, Wynter's call for a science of signs to unlock autopoetically established divides may be more appealing. For the still more technically inscribed, I suggest thinking of these ceremonies as epistemic engineering. This is important as we should be able to reach these epistemic foundations from the various discourses in which we are inscribed. As we will see, this call for ceremonies will be extremely important for Wynter's reading of Marxism.

Wynter, James and Marxism

Working at these subtextual depths, there is the real danger that Wynter could become so entangled in an autopoetic textualism that she would lose sight of the pressing social concerns of the Caribbean and beyond. This was the concern that Brian Meeks raised so forcefully at the end of the presentation of this paper at the conference, 'After Man, Towards the Human'. Because of the poetic coherence and the comprehensive scope of her work, there is no such forgetting or losing sight of the social on Wynter's part. The social occupies two ineliminable places in Wynter's poetics. First the creation of social orders is the primary function of autopoetic processes. Second, Wynter's subtextual explorations have been consistently motivated by the misrepresentations of the condemned in the European social sciences and humanities. It is the latter social concern that has brought Wynter's epistemic historicism into its critical engagement with Marxism. This engagement has been a mutually influencing one, with each leaving definite marks on the other.

As a discourse of the European social sciences, Wynter approaches Marxism with an awareness of the compromised and error prone epistemic foundations upon which it rests. But at the same time Marxism is openly critical of much of European social scientific knowledge. Much of this opposition was directed at the way in which the condemned working classes of Europe were represented in that tradition. Not only do these two philosophies converge here, but there are also important overlaps between their historical frameworks. Thus the crucial points of divergence will be over the roles of epistemicism and materialism in explaining the status of the condemned.

In Wynter's view, Marx made the mode of economic production the governing template and hence the foundation upon which his discourse rested. This materialism with the economic as its founding category was discursive produced by setting it in liminal opposition to the idealistic domains of spirit, art, ideology and so on. As such, it was a very distinctive move within the secular episteme of European modernity that definitely made possible new ways of economic seeing. This episteme had already de-transcendentalized spirit as a knowledge-constitutive and self-troping category, and replaced it with bio-economic ones. Consequently, both knowledge production and self-constitution could be done in these terms. Marx's transcendentalizing of the mode of production deepened and extended this bio-economic restructuring of the spiritual episteme of medieval Europe. Indeed it was upon these foundations that Marx erected his labour theoretic concept of the human as worker/direct producer. The critical power of Marxism, its ability to recognize the exploited status of the European working classes, has a lot to do with its distinct location within the modern episteme of European social science. Given this distinct location, the key question for Wynter is whether or not this oppositional discourse within the Western episteme could adequately represent the condemned of the colonies who had also been racialized. Her doubts about Marxism in this regard were raised by two crucial factors: the needs that motivated James's repeated reworking of classical Marxism; and second, Wynter's concern that the dynamics of founding and liminal categories that had already compromised the modern Western episteme, were continuing to affect Marxism in spite of its distinct location and oppositional stances.

Wynter's entry into James's corpus is through what she calls his 'poeisis'. By this she means the discursive strategies through which James was able to reach the foundations of both Marxism and liberalism in order to restructure them. At this sub-textual level, Wynter sees the aim of James's poeisis as a 'constant and sustained attempt to shift the "system of abduction" first of colonial liberalism, later of Stalinist and Trotskyist Marxism, and overall, of the bourgeois cultural model and its underlying head/body, reason/instinct metaphorics'.[13] In short, what interests Wynter in James's poeisis is the series of displacements and re-incorporations, or de-instituting and re-instituting activities around the labour theoretic foundations of Marxism in which he was constantly engaged.

In Wynter's view, these subtextual transformations of epistemic foundations made James's Marxism pluri-conceptual rather than mono-conceptual. In addition to the transcendentalizing of the mode of economic production and its labour theoretic concept of the human, James found it necessary to find epistemic spaces for categories of race and gender. Indeed the biological elements in the modern European concept of the human had already transcendentalized racial and gender categories, making possible the unprecedented production of racial discourses. To generate the necessary counter discourses to this massive racial misrepresentation, James had to make subtextual adjustments in his Marxism.

Wynter suggests that James felt the need to make these adjustments because he had been racialized as a 'negro'. As such this identity was an integral part of a larger template that shaped an intricate permutation of colour, levels of education, levels of wealth, and levels of 'culture'.[14] This permutation of values derived from 'the a priori categories'[15] of an ego-constitutive template that included head/body, reason/instinct analogies. Because of their fluidity and plurality, these permutations gave rise to multiple identities that carried different ratios of value and associated measures of misrepresentation and domination. Consequently, a 'system of color value existed side by side with capital value, education value, merit value, and labor'.[16] Each of these had their own variations on the underlying themes of modes of coercion and domination. As a result, the factory model of domination was only one of many that were generated by this governing template of identity formation. Hence it could not be singled out and epistemically centred in the exclusive way that it had been in classical Marxism. For Wynter, 'the quest for a frame to contain them all came to constitute the Jamesian poeisis'.[17]

This pluri-conceptual framework produced by James's poeisis, Wynter refers to as the pieza conceptual framework. The pieza was 'the name given by the Portuguese, during the slave trade, to the African who functioned as the standard measure, the general equivalent of physical value against which all others could be measured'.[18] He was a man of about 25 years who was also in good health. In the Jamesian poeisis, 'the pieza becomes an even more general category of value, establishing equivalences between a wider variety of oppressed labor power'.[19] With this pieza conceptual framework in place, the epistemic foundations of James's Marxism now had not one but a number of founding categories that were engaged in relations of mutual displacement and reincorporation. Consequently, labour theoretic concept no longer had an exclusive hold on the a priori role of founding category. This now had to be shared with race theoretic and gender theoretic concepts that could displace and reincorporate labour theoretic concepts in a changed epistemic architecture. This was the pieza complexity that distinguished James's Marxism.

In addition to changing the conditions and possibilities of knowledge production, the pieza conceptual framework also changed the conditions and possibilities of self-troping. Within the pieza framework, as opposed to that of classical Marxism, it was not just the human as worker/direct producer that was in need of liberation. There were also other registers and social practices in which humans were condemned. Among these are the racialized and the jobless. For the latter, 'the identity of labor is not the norm'.[20] Indeed, the jobless can become the liminal category of labour theoretic discourses. Thus in the pieza conceptual framework, the category of human beings to be liberated is a greatly expanded one that takes in the lumpen proletariat, peasants, the racialized, and women. In this context, there can be no one revolutionary subject or no single correct line. Rather, there must be multiple revolutionary subjects and multiple lines. This de-centring and reincorporating of the revolutionary potential of the proletariat into a larger whole is for Wynter 'the great heresy of the Jamesian poeisis'.[21] This was the move on James's part that convinced Wynter that Marx's transcendentalizing of the mode of economic production was not radical enough of an epistemic change to make possible the adequate representation of the condemned in the colonies.

As noted earlier, Wynter's second concern about Marxism was its location within the error prone Western episteme in spite of its reorganization of the latter. What this reorganization did not engage were the liminal dynamics that Marxism inherited from this episteme. Hence the likelihood that these dynamics were still compromising Marxist processes of knowledge production. Again, it was James's reading first of Stalinism and later of Trotskyism that convinced Wynter of the relevance of these liminal dynamics to the crisis that had overtaken Marxism.

The liminal dynamics of Marxism can be seen on several levels of its discursive structure. As we saw earlier, the auto-instituting of the mode of production as founding category was in part achieved through the semiotic manipulation of binaries such as materialism/idealism as well as their abductive extensions and absolutizations. Linked to the material by relations of sameness, the economic can be epistemically centred by semiotically privileging materialism and its extensions over idealism and its extensions. In conjunction with a similar pattern of privileging between other relevant binaries, it was possible to establish the economic as a founding category. However, this necessarily entails the liminalization of the ideal and its figurative extensions that are linked to the economic as founding category by relations of difference. Hence, Wynter is not surprised by Marxism's difficulties in adequately representing the role of culture in social life.

This epistemically restricted view of the role of culture is an important factor motivating Wynter's reordering of relations between modes of economic production and modes of social speciation. This inversion is not between the economic and any specific cultural practice of everyday life, but between the former and the autopoetic instituting of the a priori conditions upon which such practices rest. This is the level at which Marxism's liminal reading of idealism runs into trouble. In other words, the cultural practice that Wynter demands of Marx is that of the explicit thematizing of those semiotic manoeuvres by which he was able to secure the centring of the economic. Only from such an examination of its own foundations will Marxism take control of its liminal dynamics, and come to a better knowledge of the founding powers of culture.

Much more significant are the liminal dynamics associated with the representation of both the social goal of Marxism and its opposite. The former is of course the liberation of the proletariat. Thus we should look for liminal dynamics in relation to whoever is semiotically represented as binary opposites of the proletariat. The most obvious of such relations of difference are those with the capitalist. But there are others. Wynter's entry into these liminal dynamics of Marxism is through James's category of the 'millions in the forced labor camps'.[22] Wynter is disturbed but not floored by the emergence of this Stalinist category. Her response is to locate its roots in the semiotic economy of Marxism. In doing this, she follows James in trying to identify what he called 'the laws of thought'[23] that could make necessary the use of such a category. For Wynter, the laws of thought are autopoetically established. Hence it is to the founding template that provided the initial categories for self-troping that she turns. These categories are inscribed in the chain of signifiers and origin narratives that made possible the discursive production of the proletarian genre of the human as the desired mode of the subject. Wynter explains the rise of this discursive possibility by linking it to the foundations laid by liberal bourgeois notions of the human that were 'encoded in the metaphysics of the privatized ownership of mobile property'.[24] The proletarian concept of the human was a variant of the liberal one, and was encoded in 'the metaphysics of nationalized property'.[25] Remaining within the Western episteme and unable to thematize its own liminal dynamics, the proletarian concept of the human could only become a desired mode of the subject by creating and deploying undesired modes of the subject. Wynter suggests that into the latter category was placed all those who were read as representing the danger of a historical regression and a slide back into the dictatorship of private ownership of property. In addition to the capitalist, the Zek, still inscribed in the private/peasant mode of being, was also put into this category. Semiotically, the latter was seen as 'a capitalist roader who sought to hold back the emancipation of the proletariat'.[26] Consequently, he could be condemned and interned as expendable and discardable forced labour.

This role of the Zek, Wynter links to the status of other liminalized groups who make up the condemned of the earth. She makes them semiotic equivalents of the workers and 'negroes' of the liberal discourses based on private property. Wynter writes:

> we can therefore generalize the systemic role of James's "millions in the labor camps" to that of all such parallel group categories, to whom the generic name of les damnes, as defined by Fanon and translated by James as the condemned, can now be given. We can also, in the wake of both James and Fanon, generalize the definition of the systemic function played by their proscribed and interned status as ... that of verifying the specific mode of over-representation by which the interests of the ruling group are made equitable with projected interest of the "common good" of their system-specific collectivity.[27]

Along with these cases of the former Soviet Union and Eastern Europe, Wynter has pointed to similar dynamics in the Grenadian

Revolution of 1979. In short, it is these liminal dynamics that Wynter thinks are responsible for the crises and contradictory outcomes that have overtaken Marxism both in the Caribbean and abroad. Without a more radical and explicit thematizing of its own autopoetics, Marxism will not be able to avoid these liminal disasters that have their roots in the larger Western episteme in which it is embedded.

Wynter's Ceremonies and Post-Marxian Syntheses

The revolutionary project that Wynter's epistemic historicism holds up before us is a multi-dimensional one. It requires us to engage multiple logics of domination and coercion, to recognize multiple revolutionary subjects, and also to be deeply involved in the explicit thematizing of the autopoetics of the governing codes and templates by which the above logics are instituted as the a priori foundations of both discursive and social practices. More specifically, it means recognizing the distinct liminal logics that operate to condemn the humanity of women, blacks, workers, the jobless, Zeks, Jews and others so that particular elites can auto-institute and stably replicate their social projects and their own 'ethno-class' concept of the human. Consequently, the intellectual challenge here is to find a pluri-conceptual or pieza framework that is even more inclusive than James's. This we can attempt by making its concept of the human none of the local genres listed above, but a more genuinely universal one in which they could all participate: a concept of the human that takes explicit account of the autopoetic processes by which all of these local or ethno-class concepts are discursively established. This transcendental concept of the human as a self-constituting agent, but one whose constituting activities are mediated by epistemologically problematic governing codes, templates and epistemes is the most comprehensive view that we get of Wynter's philosophical anthroplogy. In Wynter's view, such a concept of the human and its related episteme could be the basis for the first social order without a liminal other and hence truly human. This new episteme could also be one in which the representational problems of the humanities and social sciences would be solved. Such a freeing of these disciplines from current levels of subjugation to the adaptive needs of our autopoetic reproduction would put them on par with the natural sciences, which achieved their liberation with the emergence of the modern Western episteme. This liberating of the social sciences and the humanities would be the real basis for what Wynter has called the 'post-Western' discourses or 'the rewriting of knowledge'.[28] In short, these are the dimensions of the powerful vision of the future to which Wynter's epistemic historicism calls us.

For Caribbean Marxists in particular, it means advancing the project begun by the Jamesian poeisis as well as that of Fanon's. For feminists, it means developing the ability to displace gender as an exclusive founding category of knowledge production and self-troping, and to reincorporate it into a more inclusive epistemic formation. However, this expansion must be secured by making its process of auto-instituting the feminine an integral part of its concept of the human. In this way it could become pluri-conceptual and at the same time establish control over its discourse-constitutive need to create and deploy a category of the conceptual other. For Pan Africanists, black nationalists, and other race theoretic discourses, Wynter's epistemic historicism means the de-centring of racial categories and their reorganization in an expanded epistemic framework in which their founding status would be shared with class and gender. Again, an epistemic change of this type could only be achieved by drawing on a concept of the human as a being that is capable of auto-instituting these and many other genres of the human. In short, we all have transcendental work to do, for which we are going to need a poeisis or a poetics that will empower us and supply us with the ceremonies by which our current local concepts of the human and their liminal others can be de-instituted and reincorporated in new and more inclusive epistemes.

However, it is precisely at this point that we encounter some of the major intellectual obstacles in the way of Wynter's project of rewriting epistemes and changing social orders. These difficulties arise because the ceremony 'that will wed Desdemona to the huge Moor',[29] the feminist to the womanist, or the proletarian to his jobless brother have not yet been found. The absence of these ceremonies are evident in the splits that continue to divide these groups, and leave them open to the co-opting strategies of an increasingly plutocratic capitalism. Establishing genuine discursive syntheses and bonds of human solidarity or co-speciation across these divides is indeed the crucial cultural and intellectual challenge before us. Overcoming them will require finding new ways and new ceremonies by which currently separated analytic discourses can be wed to constitute new discursive totalities or syntheses. On this point, a further examination of Marxism in the mirror of Wynter's epistemic historicism will be very rewarding.

In Marxism, the dialectical synthesis created around the political as a modality of the economic holds a very central and privileged position. This synthesis is perceived as a paradigm for other dialectical totalizations. In this case, the coming together of these two analytic domains clearly reinforces the explanatory power of the economic, making the advantages of the synthesis very clear. The crucial question that arises here is whether or not this classic Marxian synthesis can be a model for the ones that a pluri-conceptual and autopoetically self-conscious epistemic framework would require. Given all that has been said about the discontinuities between episteme and discourse, this question must be answered in the negative. To see this more clearly, let us take a closer look at the relation between economic discourse and the epistemic in Marxism.

The most likely response of Marxism to Wynter's epistemicism would be to include it as a partial cultural formation within its economically centred dialectal totalization. In other words, it would see the epistemic as another cultural modality in which the economic can be lived. Wynter's concept of knowledge-constititive goals, by opening up epistemes to historical influences lends some truth to such a reading. However, if at the same time epistemes are the autopoetically established a priori foundations of economic knowledge production, this status places severe limitations on the above reading for two basic reasons.

First, as a priori foundations, epistemes are not available for economic knowledge production in the same way that political and everyday cultural practices are. The latter are also written on the upper side of the page as the economic, just in different scripts. To reach them from inside an economic discourse it may not be necessary to turn over the page as in the case of reaching epistemes. Here a shifting of the gaze and some translating between knowledge-producing codes may be all that is necessary. Consequently, there is a sharper break separating the economic from the epistemic as compared to the economic and the political.

Second, there is greater incommensurability between the knowledge-producing codes of transcendental and economic discourses than between the latter and political discourses. Economic and political discourses share strategic and instrumental orientations as well as institutional concerns that are largely absent in the case of transcendental discourses. Between economic and political discourses the working out of what Charles Mills has called 'intertheoretical inconsistencies'[30] have been much easier to achieve because of this greater similarity in discursive codes. In short, because we do not have to turn over the economic page to find the political and the high level of commensurability between their creative codes, a classic dialectical synthesis is possible. However, between the economic and the epistemic/transcendental these ideal conditions do not hold. Consequently, a dialectical synthesis of similar discursive quality cannot be forged between the two. The result would of necessity be a synthesis that was more formal, abstract and with less explanatory power.

This difference in the discursive quality of epistemic/economic syntheses as compared to political/economic ones, raises questions about dialectical constructions of race/economic, gender/economic, gender/race and other syntheses that would have to emerge from Wynter's pluri-conceptual framework. Is it likely that they would have the discursive quality and explanatory power as the politico-economic one that stands at the heart of Marxism? I do not think so. I take this position because, as in the case of the epistemic, the discourse-constitutive conditions for such a synthesis will not be met in most of these cases. For example, mutual recodings of texts between the economic and the political have been much easier than those between economic and religious texts, or between semiotic and political texts. In other words, because of differences like these, more radical displacements of the centred discourse will be necessary for a seeing of the other than in the case of political economy.

These are the dynamics that Jean-Paul Sartre's *Search For A Method*[31] gestured toward but did not really find. In my view, these are also the dynamics that make Hart and Negri's, *Empire*,[32] a very problematic work. Its conceptual framework is a dialectical synthesis of the political and the semiotic. In this regard, it has attempted to shift the epistemic ground of Marxism by forging a new synthesis of the type that should emerge from Wynter's pluri-conceptual framework. However, as a synthesis it definitely does not cohere as well as the politico-economic one, and hence does not have its explanatory power. The intertheoretical inconsistencies that result from different creative codes are not well worked out. This attempt at a synthesis between the political and the semiotic is not as successful as Cornelius Castoriadis's, *The Imaginary Institution of Society*,[33] or Jean Baudrillard's, *The Mirror of Production*.[34] One feels throughout Hart and Negri's text the unresolved tensions between political and semiotic codes. Further, the loss in explanatory power is evident in the fact that Marxian political economy allows for a better thematizing of the semiotic than this political/semiotic synthesis allows for a thematizing of the economic. Indeed, the economic becomes almost invisible and unthematizable within the framework of this synthesis. This stands in sharp contrast to Negri's solo work, *Time For Revolution*,[35] which rests on a synthesis of political economy and phenomenology. The failure of *Empire* raises the question of the appropriateness of a dialectical model of synthesis for bringing together these two distinct analytical registers.

Given these wide variations in the discursive quality of non-politico-economic dialectical syntheses, it is very likely that the problem resides in the dialectical framework that these totalizing attempts have inherited from classical Marxism. This model needs to be seen as being unique to the marrying of the political and the economic, and not paradigmatic for other discursive marriages. Marxism did indeed find the ceremonies by which its two key analytic discourses could be wed. It did not find the ceremonies by which others could be similarly joined. Consequently the discovery of these ceremonies is the challenge before us.

To find these ceremonies, we will need a new or post-dialectical model of synthesis. Borrowing a term from the Caribbean poet, Kamau Brathwaite,[36] I will call this new model of synthesis tidalectical. The major difference between a dialectical and a *tidalectical* synthesis is that the latter will not be epistemically grounded in a single fixed centre, but in multiple centres that are mutually displacing and reincorporating of each other. These fluid, back and forth currents are the epistemic motions that will distinguish tidalectical syntheses from dialectical ones. In the case of classical Marxian political economy, the epistemic centre is primarily occupied by the economic with the political being its most important masked modality. The reverse is not really possible in this epistemic framework. Consequently, there can be no major back and forth tidalectical currents as in the case of James's race/economic synthesis. The suggestion that I am making is that in the cases of political/semiotic, gender/race and other syntheses, a tidalectical model may be more appropriate than the classical dialectical one. This more fluid framework is necessary as the comparative ease with which the political can exist as a modality of the economic is not repeated in the cases of these syntheses. It is thus more difficult to reach one of these discourses from within the knowledge-producing field of the other. A result of this difficulty is that there has to be a greater displacing or silencing of one for the contributions of the other to be seen than in the case of political economy. Further, when one is reworked in the codes of the other, the quality of the reproductions are a lot poorer. Thus the only solution in these cases is a more fluid or tidalectical model of synthesis in which analytic discourses mutually displace and reincorporate one another.

If indeed the tidalectical model of synthesis is the more paradigmatic, then we must recognize that the autopoetic and epistemic ceremonies by which such syntheses can be established have not yet been found. These we must now work to uncover. For Caribbean Marxists, it will mean advancing the pluri-conceptual (race/political economy) tendencies found in James, Padmore, Fanon, and Du Bois in particular. In our search for these ceremonies, we will have to pay close attention to at least four sets of factors. First, we must note carefully the distinctive strategies of discursive forgetting by which the epistemic is silenced, and the corresponding patterns of phenomenological remembering by which it can be recovered within the categories of that discourse. As the work of Habermas and Wynter clearly suggest, these patterns of forgetting and remembering vary widely between discourses. Thus to the extent that these patterns are autopoetically prescribed, ceremonies will have to be found for their de-instituting, the flipping over of the page on which both episteme and discourse have been inscribed, and their re-instituting.

Second, as already noted, we will have to pay close attention to differences in incommensurability in the epistemic and discursive codes that figure prominently in the production of knowledge in the fields that are being synthesized. These will determine the magnitude of the intertheoretical inconsistencies that must be worked out for the totalization to be mutually beneficial. At the discursive level, the solution to recoding problems may be readily available and hence may not require any special ceremonies. However, in the case of codes that are epistemically prescribed, such ceremonies will be necessary. Thus the discursive crossing of categorical breaks or aporias that are epistemically inscribed, becomes a prohibition that is very difficult to remove from within the framework of any of the discourses being synthesized. We will have to become skilled at recognizing such aporias and other discourse-constitutive patterns that have been established a priori.

Third, finding these Wynterian ceremonies will require discursive techniques for reaching and engaging the governing templates that provide the classificatory systems of sameness and difference around which epistemes are auto-instituted. These techniques will in turn require the cultivating of a poetics or a science of signs that will be more inclusive than James's poeisis, and better able to control founding and liminal dynamics.

Fourth and finally, we will have to think more carefully about the relationships between the epistemic and the organizational structures of societies studied by sociologists. For Wynter, the governing categories of epistemes, through both knowledge-producing and cultural practices, are encoded in the organizational structures of societies. These 'structural encodings of cultural conceptions are made possible by the fact that the structure serves as the abduction system for the thought systems and vice-versa'.[37] Thus the cultural and epistemic aspects of social organizations such as the state are as original as its structural aspects. In other words, each can serve as a code for the other's development. This 'equiprimordiality' of structure and cultural concept points to three relatively autonomous levels of institutionalization in Wynter: the epistemic, the discursive and the sociological. The epistemic reaches the sociological or organizational level by making its codes and patterns of binary opposition constitutive analogies within the instrumental and functional logics of social organizations. Consequently, the social institutions that make up human societies are triply established by autopoetic/epistemic codes, discursive legitimation and social organizing. This suggests that institutions cannot be fully grasped at just the sociological and discursive levels as we often attempt to do. Their autopoetic and epistemic roots must also be recognized. Thus to unlock the autopoetic or epistemic connections that may be helping to keep an institution in place, new ceremonies will have to be found. In other words, to really change an institution we must 'call into question both the structure of social reality and the structure of its analogical epistemology'. [38]

Without the discovery of ceremonies that are capable of undoing and redoing autopoetic and epistemic inscriptions we will not be able to produce the new tidalectical syntheses required by Wynter's pluri-conceptual framework. Without these syntheses the new discourses and new bonds of co-speciation needed for concerted mass action in the present period will continue to elude us.

Conclusion

The above ceremonial challenges are important consequences of the pluri-conceptual and tidalectical directions in which Wynter's epistemic historicism takes us. It lays bare the transcendental foundations of our discourses and the epistemic restructuring that we must carry out if we are to get going again with our postcolonial project of liberating the condemned through the establishing of a new social order. Although Wynter's historicism emphasizes the importance of the epistemic wheels of history, she is well aware that epistemic motion alone will not be enough to produce the overthrow of the bourgeoisie and its bio-economic concept of the human. Both have also been triply instituted. Consequently, uprooting its founding codes and destroying its discursive legitimation will often leave its sociological levels of institutionalization as viable bases from which to fight back. It is here that Wynter's epistemic historicism must seek sociological supplements from Marxism. Epistemic motion must be supplemented by social motion if real historical change is to be effected. Both are needed for the realization of a post-bourgeois social order. Marxism needs epistemic supplements if it is to uproot autopoetic codes and aporias. As Baudrillard has pointed out, 'you cannot defend against the code with political economy or "revolution"'.[39] The ceremonies must be found that will link these two — code and political economy — if we are to move beyond our present bourgeois order. Wynter's epistemic historicism is a crucial step in the making of these important discoveries.

Notes

1. Sylvia Wynter, 'Unsettling the Coloniality of Being/Power/Truth/Freedom: Towards the Human: After Man, its Over-Representation' (paper presented at the Coloniality Working Group Conference, SUNY, Binghamton, April 27–29, 2000) 20.
2. Ibid., 12.
3. Ibid., 19.
4. Ibid., 19.
5. Sylvia Wynter, 'The Ceremony Must Be Found: After Humanism', *Boundary 2*, no. 12 (Spring 1984).
6. Jurgen Habermas, *Knowledge and Human Interests* (Boston: Beacon Press, 1971).
7. Sylvia Wynter, 'The Ceremony Must Be Found', 39–41.
8. Sylvia Wynter, '1492: A New Worldview' (paper presented at the Smithsonian Institute, Oct. 31–Nov. 1, 1992), 27.
9. Charles Sanders Pierce, *Collected Papers* (Cambridge: Harvard University Press, 1931), 227.
10. Sylvia Wynter, 'The Ceremony Must Be Found', 28-29.
11. Sylvia Wynter, 'After the New Class: James, *Les Damnes* and the Autonomy of Human Cognition' (paper presented at Wellesley College, April 19–21, 1991) p. 88.
12. For an analysis of this tradition, see my *Caliban's Reason* (New York: Routledge, 2000), 91-114.
13. Sylvia Wynter, 'Beyond the Categories of the Master Conception: The Counterdoctrine of the Jamesian Poesis', in *CLR James' Caribbean*, eds, P. Henry and P. Buhle (Durham: Duke University Press, 1992).
14. Ibid., 68.
15. Ibid., 68.
16. Ibid., 69.
17. Ibid., 69.
18. Ibid., 81.
19. Ibid., 81.
20. Ibid., 75.
21. Ibid., 75.
22. Sylvia Wynter, 'After the New Class', 61.
23. Ibid., 67.
24. Ibid., 67.
25. Ibid., 67.
26. Ibid., 80.
27. Ibid., 68.
28. Sylvia Wynter, 'The Ceremony Must Be Found', 43.
29. Ibid., 19.
30. Charles Mills, 'Prophetic Pragmatism as Political Philosophy', in *Cornel West: A Critical Reader*, ed. George Yancy (Oxford: Blackwell, 2001), 206.
31. Jean-Paul Sartre, *Search For A Method* (New York: Vintage Books, 1968).
32. Michael Hart & Antonio Negri, *Empire* (Cambridge: Harvard University Press, 2000).
33. Cornelius Castoriadis, *The Imaginary Institution of Society* (Cambridge: MIT Press, 2000).
34. Jean Baudrilliard, *The Mirror of Production* (St. Louis: Telos Press, 1975).
35. Antonio Negri, *Time for Revolution* (New York: Continuum, 2003).

36. See Elizabeth DeLoughery, 'Tidalectics: Charting Caribbean "Peoples of the Sea"', *Span* 47 (Oct. 1998).
37. Sylvia Wynter, 'Beyond the Categories of the Master Conception', 67.
38. Ibid., 67.
39. Mark Poster, ed., *Jean Baudrillard: Selected Writings* (Stanford: Stanford University Press, 1988), 122.

12 | *Legitimizing Africa in Jamaica*

Nicosia Shakes

History has mainly been about the European superstructure of civilization. Yet in the interstices of history we see in glimpses, evidences of a powerful and pervasive cultural process which has largely determined the unconscious springs of our beings: a process which we shall identify and explore as the process of "indigenization" — a process whose agent and product was Jamaican folklore, folksongs, folk-tales, folk-dance.

To rise on the social scale, one danced the quadrille but turned ones back on the shay- shay. One claimed all that was Europe and denied Africa. Africa would not be denied. The African gods were too pervasive, too tangled with the unconscious roots of our being. They were the roots.[1]

—Sylvia Wynter

In these excerpts, Wynter sums up the most prevalent and arguably most controversial part of Afro-Jamaican, and by extension, Afro-West Indian existence. This is the primacy of Africa, its pervasiveness, its unwillingness to go away even in the face of denial, of de-legitimization, of outright oppression. Africa will not go! Any accurate definition of being Jamaican must embrace this primacy of Africa in our culture, existing not only as a part of *Afro-Jamaican* life, but in essence, *Jamaican* life.

I remember having a conversation once with someone about Black Nationalism. One perspective coming out of the argument was that we should explore the possibility that the application of black race consciousness tends to result in a certain type of over-analysis of the degree to which race affects not only the relationship between black people and the other races, but also basic facets of human life such as decisions, food preference, romantic preference and so on.[2] Another element to my interlocutor's perspective was that race consciousness should be a means to an end and not an end in itself. The ultimate goal should be a condition where being 'black' is not seen as a virtue within itself but rather being 'human'. Put simply, it is a situation where black is seen as neither 'ugly' nor 'beautiful', but merely 'black'. This ideal of course cannot be achieved without the cooperation of the other races, since black race consciousness in the form that it has taken has been a response to 'white race consciousness' and 'white supremacist' ideologies. Had there not been a doctrine of *black is ugly*, then there would be no need for a counter-doctrine of *black is beautiful.*

To achieve this ideal one has to contend with the fact that definitions of what is considered 'human' are intertwined with race and culture. Can a definition of 'human' be based solely on biological criteria ; the fact that all humans regardless of race are *homo sapiens?* Even though colour and external features such as hair texture have been used to categorize humanity, there are also the non-genetic criteria: those differences in society, geographical location, history and ultimately, culture.

Wynter has written about the equiprimordial relationship between humanity and culture. This perspective is brought home in her statement: 'Culture in my view is what a human being creates and what creates a human being at the same time. In culture the human being is simultaneously creator and creation'.[3]

This concept of humanity and culture will be my point of departure. While culture is dependent on human creation, it also assumes an independent and deterministic role in defining humanity. It is for this reason that though conscious negation of a culture or a specific part of a culture may prevail, its prevalence will not cease as long as it continues to be preserved in the day-to-day existential reality of the humans who practise it. African culture within Jamaica, and by extension the Caribbean, while it exists practically, is faced with the challenge of proving its worth, its legitimacy operating alongside the hegemonic European culture.

There is a difference between *recognition* and *legitimization*. To recognize a phenomenon is to acknowledge that it exists. Thus we have a well-accepted creole definition of Jamaican life, which identifies the mixture between Europe, Africa and other cultures. Rex Nettleford has poetically described Jamaican/Caribbean culture as the *'melody of Europe and rhythm of Africa'*.[4] In Jamaica, this perspective takes on patriotic symbolism in the motto 'Out of many one people', which while accommodating African ethnicity along with others, exaggerates the level of ethnic and racial diversity in the country almost creating an illusion of a raceless Jamaica.[5]

Legitimization is a much more sophisticated process. It involves an acknowledgement of the value of a culture and its equality with other cultures. Secondly, it involves an acceptance of this culture on its own merit, without it having to be twinned or 'hybridized' by another more acceptable culture.

There is a fundamental problem here if our definition of being *human* is completely different from the actual existential reality of it. It creates the contending existence of a universal identity and an *other* identity — a sub-identity, which is rendered inferior by virtue of its existence outside the universal. The practical blend of Europe and Africa contrasts with the separation of both in our ideological definition of 'high culture', with Africa losing out. This contention of identities is a psychosis manifesting itself almost in a type of 'split personality disorder'.

Maureen Warner-Lewis in her article 'African Continuities in the Rastafari Belief System',[6] brings to light the epistemic retention of Africa by drawing on a number of examples of African cultural retentions in Jamaican day-to-day life. The spiritual significance of salt as a disempowering substance is one such example. What is interesting is that this particular retention is not only consciously manifested in the avoidance of salt in the diet of some Rastafarians, but by the cross section of Jamaica in language. The saying of 'Yuh salt' or 'Mi salt' to connote bad luck is one very good example. Likewise, the pouring of libations in acknowledgement and honour of the ancestral spirits is done even by those who reject ancestral veneration. The practice of the 'nine-night' ceremony still very prevalent in Jamaica exists both among Afro-Christians and orthodox Christians who reject the very basis of the nine-night. All these are examples of the split-personality, human/sub-human, cultural/sub-cultural, ego/alter-ego identity issue, which forms a large part of what it means to be a black Jamaican.

Paget Henry in *Caliban's Reason* speaks of the need to acknowledge African orders of knowledge within the diaspora and to admit the existence of an African philosophy in our lived reality that is rarely promoted to the intellectual sphere. In *Caliban's Reason* Henry locates Sylvia Wynter's intellectual contributions within a post-structuralist framework. He examines her thinking on culture as deconstructive of humanism. Conversely, David Scott, does not exempt Sylvia Wynter from the genre of humanism; rather he describes her thinking as an effort to establish a humanism *made to the measure of the world*.[7] These two perspectives are however not mutually exclusive. It is through post-structuralist deconstruction of the European-biased brand of humanism that we can establish a humanism made to the measure of the world. As far as philosophy and knowledge are concerned in the context of the Caribbean, the only real truth, the only *real philosophy* is that belonging to the Euro-Christian tradition. Anything else is just a *belief system*.

I will explore three issues in this chapter. Firstly, with direct reference to Wynter's writings on culture and its role in shaping humanity, I will examine the ways in which Africa as an *other* identity, was initially de-legitimized during the initial phase of European conquest and continues to be de-legitimized, not only through the definitions used in assessing its cultural manifestations in Jamaica but also the religio-rational interpretation of its order of knowledge in the eyes of the West.

Secondly, I will elaborate on what I think should be the approach taken in the study and legitimization of Africa, arguing that whilst intellectual studies of Afro-Jamaican culture have served to legitimize its existence, there is another task at hand — that of examining it on the level of culture and not *sub-culture*. I argue that the word 'sub-culture', while it might define a specific part of a culture, also connotes inferiority; much in the same way that *sub-human* is definitive of an 'inferior being'. However, not only should there be an acknowledgement of the worth of African culture as it exists in Jamaica, but also the acknowledgement of the legitimacy of efforts to create a 'black space',[8] in the country by using African orders of knowledge. The task at hand is therefore not to challenge the European concept of knowledge, but to totally deconstruct the notion of it as the only valid knowledge source.

Thirdly, with reference to my own research on Rastafari, I am suggesting that the movement be studied within the framework of the legitimization of African orders of knowledge and not just as a movement which glorifies Africa on the physical and spiritual levels. This will not be a detailed examination of Rastafari but one that points to features of its worldview as worthy of exploration.

On the Lack of, or Errors in, Reason and Cultural Alterity

In her article, 'On the Relativity, Nature-Culture Hybridity and Auto-Institutedness of Our Genres of Being Human', Wynter makes the case for a transcultural understanding of the Caribbean. Transculture is defined as a *space in or among cultures, which is open to all of them*.[9] The post-1492 Caribbean gave birth to the creation of a space of transculture, with the coming together of three main cultures. These were the culture of Judaeo-Christian Europe, the culture of the Amerindians who inhabited the Caribbean long before the Europeans came, and the culture of Black Africa. Later on, other cultures would enter into the picture. Wynter sees this initial coming together of the three as more of a *re-encounter* than an *encounter*, as these three language groups, cultural matrices and their correlated genres of being human now different, had a common origin in Africa. Of course in the battle for power, these groups laid the negotiations of the terms in which they would coexist. This negotiation, according to Wynter, was carried out on military, religious-spiritual and secular-intelligent terms. In the end, it was Judaeo-Christian Europe that became hegemonic along with its genre of the *human*. The others were to be relegated to the status of the *other*, the inferior. This hegemony was of course maintained even with the influence of other cultures that entered the picture through further immigration in the post-slavery period.

Wynter, in her two articles on Bartolomé de Las Casas,[10] examined the way in which religion and rationalism during the European conquest of the Indies, and their interpretations of *sameness* and *otherness* served to create the binary oppositional chains of European/Non-European, thus Christian/non-Christian, thus civilized/uncivilized thus good/evil. The Europeans in their own eyes, through their possession of culture and civilization, became *human*, while their chattels who supposedly possessed no culture and no civilization became *sub-human*.

There were two types of European conquerors displaying different attitudes toward their subjects and in essence a different interpretation of the latter's level of humanity. The first group of conquerors consisted of the malevolent ones hungry for riches, and eager to exploit the natives to secure it. In their eyes the Amerindians and the enslaved Africans who came afterwards were uncivilized *sub-human* savages who lacked natural reason. Thus, there was no wrong in treating them accordingly.

The benevolent perspective, emerging from the clergy and other 'less cruel' Europeans, articulated strongly by Bartolomé de Las Casas and later the missionaries who came during black slavery, was that the 'natives' did not have a 'lack of reason'. Rather, what characterized their unusual customs and practices was an 'error in reason'. They unfortunately had not been exposed to the true reason, or the true god. It was thus the duty of the 'enlightened' Europeans to correct their error and instruct them otherwise. This patronizing religio-rational perspective was later advanced by the missionaries who came in the period of Christian penetration during slavery as well as among the abolitionists. Of course in the grand scheme of things, the lack of or error in natural reason had placed the Amerindian natives and later the African slaves outside the redemptive grace of God. Where one group chose to leave them there, the other saw it as its Christian duty to 'save' them.

These two perspectives were articulated in the debates at Vallodolid, Spain, which took place from 1550 to 1551 between Juan Ginés de Sepúlveda, the theologian-humanist scholar and official royal historian, and Bartolomé de Las Casas, the priest and reformed *encomendero*. Las Casas, after recognizing his own 'error' in reason of initially enslaving Amerindians, spent the rest of his life campaigning for their rights under Spanish rule and illuminating the brutality of the Spaniards. Juan Ginés de Sepúlveda in *Democrates Alter: Or On the Just Causes of War Against the Indians*, wrote:

> Compare then, these gifts of prudence, magnanimity, temperance, humanity, and religion with those possessed by these half-men (homunculi), in whom you will barely find the vestiges of humanity.... Although some of them show a certain ingenuity for various works of artisanship, this is no proof of human cleverness for we can observe animals, birds and spiders making certain structures.... I believe the barbarians can be conquered within the same right which makes them compelled to hear the words of the Gospels. [11]

Las Casas counter-argued, in his most famous work *A Short Account of the Destruction of the Indies*, that the Amerindian natives were in fact rational beings with alert, intelligent minds, docile and meek by nature and 'devoid of wickedness'. He wrote:

I have time and again met Spanish laymen who have been so struck by the natural goodness that shines through these people that they frequently can be heard to exclaim: "These would be the most blessed people on Earth if they were given the chance to convert to Christianity!" [12]

He went on to further this argument in *Apologetic History of the Indies:*

Not only have they [the Indians) shown themselves to be very wise peoples and possessed of lively and remarkable understanding, prudently governing and providing for their nations (as much as they can be nations without faith in, or knowledge of the true God) and making them prosper in justice; but they have equaled many diverse nations of the World, past and present that have been praised for their governance, politics and customs; and exceed by no small measure the wisest of all these, such as the Greeks and Romans, in adherence to the rules of natural reason.[13]

Where Sepúlveda supported the enslavement of the Amerindians and later using similar arguments, the Africans; Las Casas called for drastic reforms. His proposals were for the abolition of Amerindian slavery, then their settlement into communes, in which they would continue to provide a labour pool for the Spaniards who would collect their share of the profits but also ensure their (the Amerindians') financial, physical and religious well-being. Officials would be employed to see to their religious and educational instruction. They would be taught to read and write Spanish while at the same time be converted to Christianity.[14]

The decision as to who won the debate was left up to how each perspective was materially manifested in the actions of the Council of the Indies. By all accounts it was the Sepúlvedan perspective that essentially won. Sepúlveda's argument was more in line with the well-ingrained humanist religio-rational perspective that categorized non-Europeans as *sub-human*, which was essentially a perspective that was much more financially profitable to Spain. Las Casas's radical reform proposals were not adopted and while he was appointed 'Protector of the Indians', moderate reform measures were put in place and the 'destruction of the Indies and the Indians', continued. Las Casas was later to go on to propose the total abolition of the *encomienda* system and the alternative of importing African slaves who were in his thinking, more justifiably civil slaves since a number of Africans were 'justly' captured in war. Later on Las Casas, after realizing the methods by which the Africans were captured, expressed regret for making this decision, seeing it as an error in *his* natural reason.

Wynter describes Las Casas as a man before his time who, by a great conceptual leap made thinkable the possibility of a universally applicable law of human identification, in whose context the errors of specific forms of natural reason and behaviours are law-like and rule-governed.[15]

I argue, that Las Casas was at the same time *a man of his time,* to the extent that he believed that rationality was based upon the inevitable attainment of the universal knowledge order, which was that of Europe. While he applauded the intelligence of the Amerindians he was also highly preoccupied with the fact that they were not Christian and that their culture was in need of European injection. Thus, in his view, while the Amerindians were rational and intelligent there was also the need to direct this rationality and intelligence towards learning and acquiring European culture. Las Casas was also informed by the concept of the universality of the European Word a notion he and his ideological opponent, Sepúlveda did in fact share.

Neither Sepúlveda's nor Las Casas's perspective saw the culture of the Amerindians and Africans as representing a 'difference' in reason. This would in effect negate the concept of the Euro-Christian truth as universal and would cancel out the binary oppositional chains. It would be on the part of Sepúlveda, humans conquering humans, civilized conquering and civilizing civilized, good against good, and on the part of Las Casas — enlightened instructing enlightened. That makes no sense!

A *malevolent conqueror* is as much a redundancy as a *benevolent conqueror* is oxymoronic. Both approaches are, regardless of their manifestations, those of domination. The fact is, whether they settled in the West Indies and the Americas to exploit the natives or to campaign for their rights while instructing them in Christianity and European culture, the Europeans never left. They stayed. To reiterate the old adage: 'They came, they saw and they conquered!' While the benevolent masters did not enslave or destroy physically, they conquered with their culture, religion, philosophy: their Word.

Las Casas points out that the Amerindians were not whipped into Christian conversion. According to him they were eager to acquire that which was rightfully theirs by virtue of the fact that they were humans; to re-inhabit that place within the Redemptive Graces of God, which by a critical error they had initially rejected. As he stated they were:

> particularly receptive to learning and understanding the truths of our Catholic Faith and being instructed in virtue. Once they begin to learn of the Christian faith they become so keen to know more, to receive the sacraments, to worship God, that the missionaries who instruct them do truly have to be men of exceptional forbearance.[16]

From Las Casas's perspective, they chose to be converted, but choice is a very tricky word. It connotes 'free will'. What really is free will? Is it a prerequisite for choice; does it have to do with the absence of physical barriers or rational-spiritual barriers? Did the Amerindians have free will to adopt Christianity given the fact that they had already been conquered, already been placed in a subservient position by the time the priests got there, already been led to believe that their religion was either inferior or non-existent because it had, like its adherents, been disempowered by the more powerful Christian religion? The philosophical hegemony of Europe in the Caribbean has relied heavily on Christianity. As such throughout this chapter a great deal of attention will be paid to this religion and the powerful effect it has had in de-legitimizing African culture, even while being co-opted by people of African descent in liberation struggles. This will be examined later on.

This debate between the two perspectives on natural reason and culture, both of which originated from the Euro-Christian conception of the human, was to continue into the days of African slavery and endures today. The Sepúlvedas and Las Casases of the initial period of European conquest were to be later reincarnated in the plantocracy, the missionaries and abolitionists of the Black Slavery era. This debate about the so-called sub-culture of the Amerindians and Africans versus the culture of Europe is in essence, a debate about the lack of, or error in natural reason and has been expanded in the latter part of this century with postmodernist and post-structuralist support to include 'difference' in reason.

With the increasing challenge to it by Pan-Africanists and reformers in general, explicit racist ideology has entered the realm of political incorrectness though it is still very much alive. It continues epistemically, because it was merely challenged and not destroyed. What prevails more than ever now is the debate about error in reason as opposed to difference in reason and this debate is not limited to whites. Now those whose ancestors were considered inferior based on their strange *other* culture asserting their humanity, hold that 'Negroes', rational beings like the whites have a space within the definition of civilized men and can occupy that space by correcting an error in reason inherent in a cultural legacy that they inherited. Those whose ancestors were considered inferior also assert their worth based on re-educating themselves about black history and thus filling gaps that have been intentionally created in historical writings for centuries.

One of the breakthroughs in the study of black history has been the discovery of evidence that Africa was at the forefront of what we know as 'civilization'. The illumination of this element of our history has been promulgated by Pan-Africanism as a worldview and supported not only in the research of intellectuals such as Martin Bernal[17] and John Henrik Clarke[18] but also paleoanthropologists such as Louis and Mary Leakey who discovered numerous fossils of hominids (human-like species) at the Oldupai (also called 'Olduvai') Gorge in Tanzania between the 1940s and 1970s; and Donald Johanson and Thomas Gray who in 1974 discovered the oldest most complete remains of a human ancestor in Ethiopia. This hominid, a female dubbed 'Lucy', is believed by some to be the mother of all humankind. One of the ways in which we challenge white racist ideology and its promulgation of blacks as 'backward beings' with no history is with the dissemination of information on Africa's role in the making of what we now know as the West (besides of course, its unwilling provision of a labour pool that would provide the economic support for what the West was to become).

Marcus Garvey urged black people:

> Be as proud of your race today as our fore-fathers were in the days of yore. We have a beautiful history and we shall create another in the future that will astonish the World.[19]

Are we however, going to choose to recognize sections of our history based on what is considered valuable in the eyes of the modern West? Are we as cognizant of Egypt's ancient religion, which included what came to be known as 'pagan worship', its burial rites and rituals as we are of the fact that it was an early practitioner of what would be adapted into Athenian democracy and later be developed into representative democracy?

What follows is a series of 'What ifs?' What if there had been no ancient kingdoms in our history? No Mali, no Songhay, no Moorish conquest of Spain? What if the only ancestors of whom we could boast were those belonging to the much less-recognized tribal civilizations? Would we then really believe what white racism has been telling us for centuries — that we are history-less, backward and savage? Are we as proud of the San ('Bushmen'), the Ibo, and the Maasai, as we are of the Moors, the Egyptians, the Ethiopians? Are we going to reject the side of our history that we *think* supports the racist belief that we are inferior?

Cultural Sanitization

It is not enough to celebrate the manifestations of a heritage without celebrating the foundations of these manifestations. One of the ways in which we have shown appreciation for African culture is through 'cultural sanitization'. It is important that we not confuse 'sanitization' with 'creolization,' though the latter has a profound psychological influence on the former. Sanitization is a more pre-meditated occurrence. It involves the 'selective exclusion' of a particular element of the culture, not because of ignorance about its existence but because the sanitizer is simply ashamed of that element. Sanitization involves an acknowledgement of a culture accompanied by an effort not to fully present it in its raw, uninhibited or supposedly less sophisticated forms. There are various ways in which this sanitization is manifested. One manifestation can be seen in a conscious effort to 'dilute' the culture to make it more accessible. Hence there might be the application of a European melody to a drum-accompanied chant, in an effort to make it sound more like *music*.

Another manifestation can be seen with the concentration on an element(s) of the culture seen as indifferent, respectable or harmless.

Thus we may concentrate on the entertainment value of the drum beat but not its spiritual value. We may also advance the worth of Kumina, Ettu, Naggo, Dinki Mini and other African inspired religious/cultural practices by simply concentrating on their dance forms while rejecting their philosophical foundations. In fact, where a number of African-influenced practices have been accepted is in the realm of the creative arts. While a number of traditions can penetrate the 'harmless' realm of entertainment, their foundations have not been allowed to enter the realm of cultural politics or philosophical discourse.

Within the ambivalent psychosis of being black in the West is what David Scott refers to as an 'embattled humanism'.[20] Paget Henry, refers to the same thing as 'entrenchment in European sign systems', while railing against Europe, against the *colonizer*, the enslaver in *his* language. Here humanism as it has already been defined by Europe is being used to challenge the negative manifestations of this humanism. Indeed C.L.R. James attested to it:

> I, a man of the Caribbean have found that it is in the study of Western Literature, Western Philosophy and Western History that I have found out the things that I have found out, even about the under-developed countries.[21]

Can we ever reconcile between the two identities of Europe and Africa without one being negated and de-legitimized by the other?

Indigenization, Acculturation and Epistemic Ambivalence

Replacing the completely eliminated labour force of Tainos in Jamaica, the Africans captured en masse from their homes to become slaves in a strange land were faced with the daunting task of maintaining their dignity. Since they were seen as *sub-human* by their overlords, they had to, in essence, hold on to their humanity by holding on to remnants of their culture, their Word. Their concept of their own humanity, since it could not fit into the European mould had to depend on this retention. And so began in the initial stages of African settlement here, according to Wynter, the process of *indigenization*, whereby Africa was replicated on Jamaican soil.

Wynter uses indigenization in preference to *acculturation;* the latter referring to the adoption of another culture. Acculturation came later. Through the process of indigenization, the Africans brought with them their belief systems, their language, their religions, and their art forms — their culture, and through acculturation, this culture did not die but became fused with the European one. Features of African spirituality, which included the veneration of the ancestors, the existence of a Creator God along with lesser but still powerful deities, as well as certain forms of syntax, grammar and language survived in practice.

One of the most influential historical periods in Jamaican history, which was to go on to affect the culture, is the period of Christianization. During this period, a number of missionaries came to the island to 'claim souls for the Kingdom of God'. This started in the late eighteenth to early nineteenth centuries. Maureen Warner-Lewis, however, writes that there had been Christian penetration in the Kongo[22] region, (one of the regions from which Africans came to the West Indies), with the introduction of Catholicism to the king's court from the fifteenth century. Thus some Africans who came as slaves or indentured labourers to the West Indies had probably already been exposed to this religion and also adopted some of its elements. Though Warner-Lewis does not give any Jamaican examples of such, it is possible that some of the Africans who came to Jamaica would have already known about Christianity.

Psalm 68 verse 31, *'Ethiopia shall soon stretch forth her hands unto God'*, was pivotal in the adoption of Christianity by the blacks. Brodber notes that this psalm was a primary tool used by the eighteenth-century missionaries to justify their mission.[23] The conversion of black people to Christianity was not only important to their own well-being as humans it was also divinely ordained. This psalm became a mantra, so to speak, and the view of black people as the 'chosen' was used largely along with the already indigenized African spiritual retentions to fight against slavery and to give spiritual support to Pan-Africanism through the accompanying tenets of Ethiopianism and Black Liberation Theology.

There were different reactions to Christian indoctrination or more accurately different levels of blending: one reaction resulted in the intermixture of African and European spirituality. To the chagrin of the missionaries, many blended Christianity with African religions, the overarching spiritual practice being that of Mayaal, (more commonly spelt 'Myal') to produce Revivalism. A second reaction was the nearly wholesale adoption of orthodox Christianity with a conscious rejection of African belief systems, seeing them as evil. A third reaction was the adoption of a black variant of Christianity and with this the transformation of the 'white' God, saints, and prophets into black while paradoxically rejecting African spiritual belief systems. This reaction was very prevalent in the thinking of early Pan-Africanists and black missionaries. Yet there was to a small but still significant extent the powerful conscious retention of African religion among a number of blacks who, while not wholly free from the Christian hegemony,[24] adhere in large part to African-based religious practices. These practices may be more appropriately defined as 'African' and not 'Afro-Christian' religious practices. Most noted is Kumina.[25] Other religious practices such as Ettu, Naggo and Gumbeh (also spelt 'Gumbay') exist to a smaller extent and are more regionally confined. In this respect, I think Wynter's definition of *indigenization* and not *creolization* applies to this category. Finally, there has been in the last seven decades, the most modern indigenous religion encapsulating elements of all of the above — Rastafari. Displaying Judaeo-Christian influence, it also is based on Black Liberation Theology and influenced by African belief systems, while not actively displaying certain elements such as ancestral veneration and spirit possession.

The process referred to by writers such as Edward Kamau Brathwaite[26] as *creolization* was to form the base of what can now be seen in Jamaican culture, whether in religion, the arts, language and so on. A major problem stemming from this creolization is *epistemic ambivalence*, where the orders of knowledge though contending, have no choice but to exist together. Within this epistemic ambivalence is the contention between the universal and the *other*, the *alter* and the *same*, still operating long after the political support for it in slavery and colonialism has been removed.

Black Liberation Discourse

This epistemic retention of European orders of knowledge has manifested itself in black liberation discourse. Marcus Garvey was widely read, though not formally educated beyond the primary level. Coming out of the colonial, early post-slavery period in Jamaica, using a blend of the Pan-Africanist worldview, Ethiopianism, Black Liberation Theology, and democratic ideals, he advanced racial equality and fought for the redemption of Africa and Africans. Garvey's ideology, however, was so entrenched in European epistemology that it advanced the primacy of the European episteme while at the same time challenging its manifestation in racist ideology. Among the initial aims of the Universal Negro Improvement Association and African Communities League (UNIA-ACL) was: '*To assist in civilizing the backward tribes of Africa*'.[27]

The aims of Dr J. Albert Thorne's 'African Colonial Enterprise' based in Jamaica in the 1890s can be compared with the initial aims of the UNIA. Along with '*the improvement of the status of the Black Race*', one of the goals was to: '*Extend the Kingdom of God in those vast regions by leading such as are in darkness and error or superstition to Jesus Christ*'.[28]

A slightly similar mould can be found in an excerpt from Dr Theophilus Scholes's *Glimpses of the Ages,* published in the early 1900s. Scholes was a medical doctor/missionary who advanced powerful Pan-Africanist views, fiercely critiquing colonialism and white theories that advanced black inferiority. In his reference to the secular element of what was considered civilized, he asserted that there should be a distinction between educated and civilized blacks and uncivilized ones:

> the entire division (of Black people) is to be considered as consisting of two distinct classes — civilized and uncivilized. Hence the practice of referring to and of treating Ethiopian communities — British, American and others as though they belong to the uncivilized class is arbitrary and unjust.[29]

These men changed the colour of God and the colour of culture, but not the *identity* of God and the *episteme* of that culture. Of course this over-reliance on European thought systems was characteristic of black intellectuals particularly during the period in which Garvey operated, by those schooled informally and/or formally in the European word. These perspectives were not inspired by the point of view that blacks were innately inferior, but rather, that European culture was not necessarily distinct from African culture. It is a perspective that originates in the view that history is a process of replication. The culture of Europe was seen as a universal cultural model, some elements of which had been copied from African civilization centuries before. Thus, the adoption of European culture by modern day Africans was not *mimicry* but simply, *reclamation*. This of course is a flawed conclusion that does not account for cultural 'difference', and which also chooses to embrace one aspect of African history while rejecting another.

Of course the period in which these early Pan-Africanists operated was a critical factor. The intellectual genre in which they operated also had a determinant bearing on their thinking. Other persons who purported black liberation, such as Alexander Bedward, the Revivalist preacher, and the early Rastafarians operating within the same time period but within the Afro-Christian, non-intellectual genre, did not display this European enmeshment so much. Pan-Africanists such as Walter Rodney would in later years display accommodation for African culture and African systems of thought while using elements of European thought systems.

A primary characteristic of cultural alterity is the use of different discursive descriptions for similar features of the two cultures. Africa is demoted to the status of the emotive and irrational whereas Europe is promoted to the status of the rational and the official. This is one of the reasons why Jamaican language, which is informed so much by African syntax and vocabulary, has not been seen to this day as an official language. Rather, it is considered a 'corrupted form of English', much like Revivalism and other Afro-Christian religions are considered corrupted forms of Christianity. Thus, where Europe and Africa blended in the same way in Jamaican culture, the widely held view is that Europe simply creolized Africa, whereas Africa corrupted Europe. It is unfathomable, if not audacious, to suggest that Europe corrupted African culture.

It is not only in traditional African belief systems that this 'inferior otherness' is created it extends to any order of knowledge which seeks to create a black space within the diaspora. Barry Chevannes in his article, 'Garvey Myths Among the Jamaican People',[30] elucidates a number of ways in which Jamaicans have ascribed supernatural qualities to Marcus Garvey. This is an example of the operation of the 'alter' culture in Jamaica. Chevannes use of the word 'myth' is of course writing from a rational perspective on anthropology where all stories of supernatural occurrences, whether Christian or non-Christian, are considered 'mythology'. However, the contention is that even outside of the realm of intellectual rationalism, these belief systems are seen as 'myths'.

In the realm of religion for example, we have a situation where rationalism is used to critique any 'other' religion but Christianity, especially where the religion is African-derived. Thus, where it is acceptable to believe in the Christian Immaculate Conception and the resurrection of Christ, it is considered ludicrous to believe in the divinity of the ancestors and in the immortality of black prophets such as Marcus Garvey. However, whenever the Christian myths are challenged such as they are by a wide cross section of Rastafarians, it is seen as heretic and evil. So powerful is the Euro-Christian hegemony that it exists even among those people who would claim that they are not Christian and do not attend church. This is of course the result of both primary and secondary socialization into Christianity, which penetrates the media, the education system and the state. In the secular area, European myths, legends and bedtime stories such as those involving 'dragons, fairies, leprechauns, witches and wizards' have been adopted and while they are not looked upon as factual are relatively acceptable and normal. Conversely, retained African myths, legends and stories involving 'Ananse, duppies, river mummas' and others, while they have been retained, seem to be treated with a certain amount of shame.

Wynter, drawing on the work of Robert Redfield,[31] defines the difference between what is seen as 'folk' culture as opposed to 'official' culture. According to Redfield's theory, each religion or culture has a 'high' or 'learned' tradition and a 'folk' or 'little' tradition. The high tradition, existing in the work of philosophers and intellectuals, is carried on through oral and/or written documentation. The 'folk' or 'little' tradition exists mainly in the creative arts through song, dance, rituals and stories among other means of expression. The 'folk' tradition is legitimized when it is taken up by the 'high' tradition, studied, re-fashioned and given back to the people.

Personally, I do not like the terms 'high' tradition and 'little' tradition. They connote a type of superior and inferior binary. Redfield's theory, however, can be used to explain a significant prerequisite for cultural legitimacy. Every culture needs some type of intellectual backing, meaning there needs to be the acknowledgement from those set of people who are considered wise and learned (by that society's standards) that the culture is worthwhile and valuable. Of course, within our society we have to contend with the fact that the criteria as to who is considered learned and intelligent are highly influenced by European signals, though in recent years we see the erosion of this to an extent. This group is included in, but distinct from, members of the wider society who actually practise these traditions informally in their day-to-day lives. Thus, the learned tradition would be comprised of philosophers, griots, medical practitioners, religious leaders, teachers and others. Those in the folk tradition are really the population within the wider society who might not know the philosophical and cultural bases of their traditions but who practise them nonetheless.

Wynter points out that the African population that came to the Caribbean consisted of both those who were in the learned tradition and those who were in the 'folk' tradition. The learned tradition consisted of the religious leaders, medicine men and philosophers, who had undergone years of initiation and training in the philosophy and culture of their people. The result of slavery was that these people were unable to properly serve the function of being leaders, of legitimizing their traditions, given the restrictions and de-humanizing conditions of the plantation. Thus what happened were retentions but discontinuities. In addition, the 'learned' tradition within African culture was to be overthrown by the more hegemonic 'learned' tradition within the European culture. The African philosopher, teacher, and religious leader became the slave of the European philosopher, teacher and priest. Wynter also points out that the Africans adopted elements of the European learned tradition, such as the use of the Bible. The 'folk' tradition might have survived because it had more indirect manifestations in artistry. Indeed, the principal area in which one can see African culture manifested is artistry — dance, storytelling, singing. However, a number of distortions occurred. For instance, while stories of Ananse prevailed, he is now considered just a skilful trickster instead of the divine being which is his manifestation in a number of African spiritual belief systems.[32] Likewise, the hip gyrations, which are originally a part of African fertility rituals, were to become simply a sensual way of dancing.

What needs to be done is the reclamation of a learned tradition within African culture in the diaspora in order for its manifestations in the folk culture to be legitimized — one which focuses on the philosophical inspiration behind our cultural practices and makes conscious efforts to maintain it. This learned tradition has to entail a conscious study of what we know as the folk culture. It cannot however, be forged from the perspective of rational anthropology. It has to be formed within the group of people who actually practise these belief systems.

Major ways in which African retentions in the diaspora have been recognized are through their study by intellectuals, and by the dissemination of information about them. We may categorize intellectuals within the learned tradition. However, simply incorporating the study of African retentions into black studies will not suffice. Studying African culture does not, by itself, legitimize it. Further, if the people who are studying it limit it to being a 'specimen to be studied', which does not at all influence their own personal perspective and culture, then it remains simply an 'object of study'. Acknowledging the value of something does not completely legitimize it.

Some intellectuals have been making inroads in respect of legitimizing African retentions. Of particular note is Carolyn Cooper's drive to legitimize Jamaican language, which has been greatly influenced by African grammar and syntax. Cooper not only speaks about its worth but actually advances its use in 'serious' literature by utilizing it in newspaper articles,[33] and aims to standardize the vocabulary and syntax.

We do have people who are from the learned tradition in some of our African-derived religions. Kumina adherents, for instance, have appointed 'kings' and 'queens' and other people who form the leadership base, all of whom have been schooled in the philosophy and the cultural influences behind the religion. The same may be said of Revivalists, and Ettu and Naggo adherents. However, in large part these leaders along with the traditions that they represent still operate within the sphere of sub-culture, hardly penetrating or actively challenging the mainstream.

Rastafari and Africa in Jamaica

I propose that Rastafari, as a belief structure, a religion, a culture and a political movement has been highly successful at not only deconstructing the hegemonic Euro-Christian knowledge order but also at legitimizing Africa. Rastafari has been able to achieve a level of primacy within society by actively challenging the status quo. Thus it is not just a matter of retention but also active acknowledgement of a connection with Africa through subversion using elements of the 'alter' culture. While a number of the African-inspired spiritual traditions are confined in large part to sections of Jamaica, or different groups that enter the mainstream through avenues such as the creative arts, [34] Rastafarians have in fact entered the mainstream in many areas including academia.

Of course one has to contend with the fact that Rastafari itself, existing within the context of Babylon, has consciously disassociated itself from some African traditions. For instance, ancestral veneration and spirit possession are not central features of Rastafari. Generally, these practices are seemingly frowned upon by them. Chevannes in *Rastafari: Roots and Ideology* makes efforts to grapple with this anomaly. Even while this element might be rejected, he illustrates areas in which the rituals originating from the spiritism characteristic of Afro-Christian and African religions may be seen covertly in Rastafarian rituals. One person, King Baucho Bennett, admits to being both a Rastafarian as well as a Kumina devotee and also speaks about other Rastafarians who are involved in this religious practice.[35] The approach taken to studying Rastafari in this regard has to be dialectical.

Rastafari has deconstructed Europe in two main ways; firstly, through its use of African orders of knowledge as they exist in the Diaspora and secondly, through its efforts to create a black space within a world dominated by the hegemonic white space. For the purpose of this engagement it is important that we not use Rastafari's geographical origin in the West to detract from its African influences. Rastafari, from its very origin within African-derived religious practices and worldviews, is culturally and spiritually, if not geographically, partly African. Three main influences behind the Rastafarian movement have been identified in the studies on the movement. These are Judaeo-Christianity, the body of writings in religious books such as *The Holy Piby, Royal Parchment Scroll of Black Supremacy, the Kebra Negast* and the Bible; the political and religious ideologies of Marcus Garvey; and lastly, African and Afro-Christian religions. These influences are highly intertwined and explain a very fascinating nature of Rastafari: it is a religion emerging in the diaspora, which at the same time glorifies Africa. It is very important that the African influence not be downplayed.

Some writers have focused too much on the Judaeo-Christian influences. Laurence Breiner for example writes that 'Rastafari has no core of preserved African religion, and has not even adopted African elements from the surrounding culture to any considerable extent'.[36] He cites, for example, the lack of possession rituals in Rastafari that can be seen in African and Afro-Christian religions.

Other writers, however, have called attention to the deep influences of African theology and rituals in the Rastafari Movement. Warner-Lewis cites among other things, salt avoidance, the wearing of matted hair, the centrality of the drumbeat, the spiritual and meditational use of intoxicants (in this case marijuana) as African influences. For example, the wearing of matted hair which is largely, though not exclusively a central feature of Rastafari, is a common practice of Central African medicine men. It is believed that this feature was added to Rastafari after members of the movement saw pictures of the dreadlocked Kikuyu Freedom Fighters of the Mau Mau rebellion in Kenya in the 1950s.[37] This is of course an influence with a distortion, since the matted hairstyle is usually the domain of spiritual leaders, persons considered exceptional, and noble recluses.[38] Rastafari emerged among people who were also coming out of a strong Revivalist influence and these influences can be seen even if some are rejected. Robert Hinds, one of the more well-known founders of Rastafari, was a Bedwardite prior to his Rastafarian conversion.

In their efforts to create a black space within Jamaica and ultimately the Western world, Rastafarians have challenged the very foundations of European epistemology. Not only did they change the colour of God like earlier Pan-Africanists, they also changed His personal and geographic identity by locating Him physically on the continent of Africa. Not only were the prophets and deities black, they could be found in Africa and the Diaspora in the persons of Prince Emmanuel (in the case of the Bobo Shanti), Marcus Garvey and others. It was not just a matter of changing the colour of the biblical heroes whose liberation struggles, though they could be symbolically related to the black struggle, were very distant in scope and time period. In addition, the rules of aesthetics, language, even entertainment were deconstructed, not just challenged. It is the African influence that can be credited for this deconstruction not just simply the Pan-Africanist influence. Were we to eliminate the African epistemological influence then Rastafari could only be seen as modernized Garveyism (its primary ideological influence). The Rastas however, using Africa as a knowledge source, reworked the Pan-Africanism of Garvey and earlier Pan-Africanists in theory and praxis.

It is very important to recognize however, that Rastafari cannot be understood simply, or even most importantly, as 'philosophical discourse' in the European usage of the term. Rasta did not begin with the word, the word instead was induced from lived realities and grounded expectations. In this sense there is a pragmatism to the philosophy that belies what some may see as its grandiose eschatological and theological pronouncements and prophecies. It is one thing to talk or write about philosophy, it is another thing to try to live what one preaches day by day, more or less, open for all to see. This is not an easy task, which the praxis of their calling demanded more as necessity than of sacrifice especially given the hostile 'outcast' circumstances in which this task has to be carried out.[39]

Conclusion

It has been my attempt to grapple with an issue that is increasingly the focus of debate in both the intellectual and public spheres. It is one that has penetrated all arenas of Jamaican life: religion, society, creative arts, academia, and racial as well as formal politics. At the physical level we may picture a situation of relative racial harmony with little or no racial conflict partly because there is not a lot of racial diversity to begin with. However, looking beyond the physical view of harmony into the arena of culture we see something much different. There is a continued internal battle within the black culture to reconcile between Europe and Africa. It is analogous to a custody battle between two parents, in which the court awards full custody of the child to the more financially well-off and respectable parent, regardless of that parent's mistreatment of the child, while the other looks on helplessly even though that parent has played an equally seminal role in shaping the child's development. My view is that there cannot be a legitimate Jamaican identity without the *legitimization* — not just *recognition*, of the value of Africa. If not, then Jamaicans partly negate themselves.

Notes

1. Sylvia Wynter, 'Jonkunnu in Jamaica: Towards the Interpretation of Folk Dance as a Cultural Process', *Jamaica Journal* 4, no. 2 (June 1970): 35, 44.
2. Race has been so dominant in human relations that we often cannot separate race from ordinary facets of being human. A very good example of this is Denzel Washington and Halle Berry's breakthrough Oscar wins in 2002. Both won in the Best Actor and Best Actress categories. It was the second time that a black man was winning in that category and the first time for a black woman. The Academy of Motion Picture Arts and Sciences is notorious for its 'white bias'. There were two critiques coming out of general societal discussions. One critique was that Washinton and Berry won simply because they played stereotypically negative black characters. Another perspective saw the wins as a subtle type of 'affirmative action', where the Academy voters awarded Washington and Berry out of guilt. Is it possible though that the wins were based solely on 'performance' and not 'race'?
3. Sylvia Wynter, 'St. Simon's Reflections', *Topic /Quotes for Discussion: Commission on Research in Black Education.* http://www.coribe.or~ages/1 Sylvia Wynter.html.
4. See Rex Nettleford, *Caribbean Cultural Identity: The Case of Jamaica: An Essay in Cultural Dynamics* (Kingston: Institute of Jamaica, 1978).
5. There are levels of heterogeneity and homogeneity in every society. The definition of a society as homogeneous or heterogeneous does not necessarily mean that this society is 100 per cent either. It is simply a matter of degree. The Jamaican population even at the time when the motto was being devised has always been overwhelmingly black. The 2001 Census recorded that over 90 per cent of Jamaicans consider themselves black. The motto does not recognize this. In addition, there is not enough racial diversity to define Jamaica as culturally diverse. It is for this reason that I think the motto is inaccurate. If Jamaica's motto is 'out of many, one people' then the motto of every country should be the same.
6. See Maureen Warner-Lewis, 'African Continuities in the Rastafari Belief System', *Caribbean Quarterly* 39, nos. 3 & 4 (September– December 1993).
7. David Scott, 'The Re-Enchantment of Humanism: An Interview with Sylvia Wynter', *Small Axe: A Journal of Criticism* 8 (September 2000).
8. See Erna Brodber, 'Re-Engineering Black Space', *Caribbean Quarterly* 43, nos. 1&2 (March–June 1997).
9. Sylvia Wynter, 'On the Relativity, Nature-Culture Hybridity and Auto-Institutedness of Our Genres of Being Human: Towards the Transculturality of a Caribbean/New World Matrix'. (Distinguished Lecture – Caribbean Cultural Studies Institute, Faculty of Humanities, The University of the West Indies, Mona, November 10–26, 2002), 7.
10. Sylvia Wynter, 'New Seville and the Conversion Experience of Bartolomé de Las Casas' Pts, I&2, *Jamaica Journal* 17, no. 2 (May 1984) and vol. 17, no. 3 (August–October, 1984).
11. Juan Ginés de Sepúlveda, *Democrates Alter, Or, On the Just Causes for Wars Against the Indians*, 1545. From Boletín de la Real Academia de la Historia vol. XXI, October 1892, Originally translated for *Introduction to Contemporary Civilizations in the West* (New York: Columbia University Press, 1946,1954,1961).
http://www.hotelcapitolgrado.it/Moderna/Materiali/SEPULVEDA_DEMOCRATES.DOC
12. Bartolomé de Las Casas, A *Short Account of the Destruction of the Indies*, Trans. Nigel Griffin (London: Penguin Classics, 1992).

13. Bartolomé de Las Casas, *Apologetic History of the Indies*, 1566. From *Apologetica Historia de las Indias* (Madrid, 1909), originally translated for *Introduction to Contemporary Civilizations in the West* (New York: Columbia University Press, 1946, 1954, 1961). www.columbia.edu/acis/ets/CCREAD/lascasas.htm
14. H.R. Wagner and H. Parish, *The Life and Writings of Bartolomé de Las Casas* (Albuquerque: The University of New Mexico, 1967) quoted in Wynter, 'New Seville and the Conversion Experience of Bartolomé de Las Casas', *Jamaica Journal* 17, no. 3 (August–October 1984): 48.
15. Sylvia Wynter, 'New Seville and the Conversion Experience of Bartolomé de Las Casas' Pt. 2: 54.
16. Las Casas, *A Short Account of the Destruction of the Indies*, 10.
17. See Martin Bernal, *Black Athena: the Afro-Asiatic Roots of Classical Civilization, Volume I: The Fabrication of Ancient Greece, 1785–1985* (London: Vintage Books, Random House, 1991).
18. See John Henrik Clarke, *African People in World History* (Baltimore: Black Classic Press, 1999).
19. Amy Jacques Garvey (Comp.) *The Philosophy and Opinions of Marcus Garvey or Africa for the Africans* vols. 1 & 2 (Dover, Mass: The Majority Press, 1986), 7.
20. David Scott, 'The Re-Enchantment of Humanism: An Interview with Sylvia Wynter': 153.
21. C.L.R. James, 'Discovering Literature in Trinidad: The 1930s' in *Spheres of Existence* (Westport, Connecticut: Lawrence Hill, 1980), 238. Quoted in Paget Henry, *Caliban's Reason: Introducing Afro-Caribbean Philosophy* (New York: Routledge, 2000), 50.
22. Maureen Warner-Lewis points out that 'Congo' was an omnibus term used for Africans taken from Central Africa. These included Koongo-speaking as well as non-Kongo speaking groups. See Maureen Warner-Lewis, *Central Africa in the Caribbean: Transcending Time, Transforming Cultures* (Kingston, Jamaica: The University of the West Indies Press, 2003), 15.
23. Erna Brodber, 'Re-engineering Black Space', 1997.
24. Existing within the Diaspora, these religious practices have to contend with this influence so while there is an overwhelming presence of Africa within the traditions there is some Christian penetration. For instance, I have heard a recording of Imogene 'Queenie' Kennedy, the famous Kumina leader (now deceased) reciting the Christian 'Lord's Prayer' in Kikongo. Lewin, 2000 also notes that the Christ spirit is recognized among Kumina devotees. See Olive Lewin, *Rock it Come Over: The Folk Music of Jamaica* (Kingston: The University of the West Indies Press, 2000).
25. Bakongo who were brought during the post-slavery period as indentured labour are largely credited for the introduction of Kumina into Jamaican society. However, Patterson notes that there is evidence that the religion also came to a small extent during the period of slavery. See Orlando Patterson, *The Sociology of Slavery: An Analysis of the Origins, Development and Structure of Negro Slave Society in Jamaica* (Kingston: Sangster's Book Store in association with Granada Publishing, 1973).
26. See Edward Kamau Braithwaite, *The Development of Creole Society in Jamaica 1770–1820* (New York: Oxford University Press, 1971; Kingston: Ian Randle Publishers, 2005).
27. 'The Initial Aims of the UNIA-ACL'. Quoted in Rupert Lewis, *Marcus Garvey: Anti-Colonial Champion* (Trenton: Africa World Press, 1988), 50.
28. 'Aims of the African Colonial Enterprise'. Quoted in Patrick Bryan, 'Black Perspectives in Late Nineteenth-Century Jamaica: The Case of Dr. Theophilus Scholes' in *Garvey: His Work and Impact* (Trenton: Africa World Press, 1991), 54.

29. Theophilus Scholes, *Glimpses of the Ages: or the 'Superior' and 'Inferior' Races So-Called Discussed in the Light of Science and History*, vol. 1 (London: John Long, 1905), 355. Quoted in Bryan, ' Black Perspectives in Late Nineteenth-Century Jamaica, 52.
30. Barry Chevannes, 'Garvey Myths Among the Jamaican People' in *Garvey: His Work and Impact* (Trenton: Africa World Press, 1991), 123-131.
31. Robert Redfield, *Peasant Society and Culture: An Anthropological Approach to Civilization* (Chicago: Chicago University Press, 1956). Quoted in Wynter, 'Jonkunnu in Jamaica', 45.
32. Trickster deities are common in a number of African belief systems. *Ananse* is the name of the spider deity who was also a co-creator of the World in the Akan religious tradition. Trickster deities create a kind of balance between the mortal and immortal worlds. They remind human beings of their immortality and stupidity by playing tricks on them. The Yoruba deity *Eshu* holds the same significance as Ananse.
33. For decades, while patois has not been excluded from Literature or the Creative Arts, it has usually been used in comedy, or in dialogue (as regards literature).
34. The annual Jamaica Cultural Development Commission (JCDC) Festival for the Performing Arts, the National Dance Theatre Company (NDTC) and other groups have showcased the artistic element of these religious practices.
35. This finding is based on a conversation I had with King Baucho in March, 2003.
36. Laurence A. Breiner, 'The English Bible in Jamaican Rastafari', *Journal of Religious Thought* 42, no.2 (Fall–Winter, 1985–1986): 30-43. Quoted in Warner-Lewis, 'African Continuities in the Rastafari Belief System', 108.
37. The wearing of matted hair is not confined to African spiritual leaders however. It is believed by the Rastafarians and others that it was worn by the Biblical Samson and other ancient Jews. Dreadlocks were also worn by the Saddhus, nomadic holy men who adhere to the Hindu religion. In fact, Alice Walker, 1999 speculates that some Saddhus who came to Jamaica during the period of Indian indentureship might have also contributed to the exposure to dreadlocks in Jamaican society. See Alice Walker, 'Introduction', *Dreads* (New York: Workman Publishing Company, 1999).
38. In a conversation on this subject one academian from Kenya actually spoke to me about the disdain that older members of the society express towards the wearing of matted hair by people who practise the Rastafarian faith or simply embrace the aesthetic appeal of dreadlocks. They continue to view the hairstyle as the domain of healers and other people not considered a part of the general public.
39. Nicosia Shakes and Louis Lindsay, 'Rastafari and Africa in the Diaspora' (paper presented at the conference, 'Uncovering Connections: Cultural Endurance between the Americas and Africa, Medgar Evers College, City University of New York, March 2003).

13 | The Human, Knowledge and the Word: Reflecting on Sylvia Wynter

Anthony Bogues

For the last 25 years [I have been] asking literally the same question: How do systems of knowledge, secular knowledge, protect themselves.[1]
— Sylvia Wynter

I should constantly remind myself that the real leap consists in introducing invention into existence.[2]
—Frantz Fanon

Introduction

Radical anti-colonial thinkers often live on the cusp of dynamic searches that plumb depths, break moulds and construct creative synthesis. If they break the thralldom of the various colonial knowledge regimes, and use the colonial moment both as a starting point and bridge to grapple with the complexities of various forms of human life, then oftentimes they arrive at a similar set of conclusions about modernity. Aimé Césaire and Frantz Fanon are exemplars of this. For Fanon, these conclusions can be summed up in the following passages from *Black Skin White Masks* and *The Wretched of the Earth*.

In the former, Fanon pleas: 'That the tool never possess the man. That the enslavement of man by man cease forever'. He ends the text with a fervent prayer, 'O my body, make of me always a man who questions'.[3] This prayer is not a Pascalian meditation. Instead it is illustrative of Fanon's recognition that the body of the colonial native was a site, a location in which colonial knowledge regimes made strenuous efforts to trap human life in attempts to create new subjects while constructing a bio-political power of death and life.[4] Fanon's prayer was therefore a call for the native to resist, never to rest and succumb to the power that trained and then classified the 'native' and the black into ontological zones of non–being. To conduct this resistance required an openness to shaking the foundations of the West, for breaking new ground. Fanon eloquently notes this form of resistance in the final sections of *The Wretched of the Earth* when he implores his fellow African comrades-in-arms to intellectually leave Europe behind, 'for Europe, for ourselves, and for humanity, comrade, we must turn over a new leaf, we must work out new concepts, and try to set afoot a new man'.[5] For Fanon, the setting afoot of 'a new man' was not the creation of an impossible utopia, but rather the reorganization of modern life along more humane lines. His call was 'for a kind of thing that might happen' and consequently for a practice yet to be written. Such a reorganization of modern life was not possible without the deployment of new concepts about the very meaning and existence of human life.

Aimé Césaire was also very preoccupied with the ways in which the colonial regimes (of ruling and knowledge) created what he called in his *Discourse on Colonialism* the process of 'Thingification' of the human being.[6] His arguments about the failures of colonial European civilization and the ways in which radical change had to establish new categories of thinking are outlined in his essay, 'Poetry and Knowledge', an essay which Sylvia Wynter consistently invokes. In this essay Césaire argues against an Enlightenment view that science and certain forms of scientific knowledge were the final and all embracing frontiers of human knowledge. He observes that: 'In the beginning was the word … and it is on the word, a shaving of the world, a secret unassuming slice of the world, that … gambles all our possibilities.'[7] Here of course Césaire is thinking about both speech and language. Speech as an act that functions to create the human world and language as a process of mediation and creation or in the words of Giorgio Agamben, 'Language, which for human beings mediates all things and all knowledge.'[8] In general it is important to note that the Word was a central category for many radical anti-colonial thinkers. George Lamming puts it well when he notes that, 'For it is one of the mischievous powers of language, and particularly that aspect of language which relates to names that it enables us to rob things of their power to embarrass us.… A name is an infinite source of control'.[9] How to rupture this power of naming by destabilizing the Word, reformulating language and its relationship to human behaviour and the history of thought became the project of one of the most formidable radical Caribbean thinkers, Sylvia Wynter.[10]

Wynter's radical intellectual roots reside in the anti-colonial post-1945 moment. She herself states in an interview:

> My liminality comes from the fact that in my lifetime I was born a colonial subject and I think that in many ways I'll always be grateful for that because the knowledge it gives you is something you have to arrive at existentially.... You know what it is to have gone to school in a curriculum whose function was to *induce* you to be a colonial subject ... in the world I am still liminal because I'm black and a woman — but I'll be very honest with you, far more because I'm black. I'm part of a group that has been constituted as the ontological other of man ... I am therefore part of that liminal group continually questioning.[11]

In working through this 'questioning' Wynter has been preoccupied with many things. However in this essay I want to focus on three nodal points of her thought which knit themselves as a spine and then become the platform from which she launches her probes. These nodal points are: symbolic codes and epistemic ruptures, the liminal and how those who live in a liminal position create 'alternative life-activity in its own right', and her consistent concern about the role of the critical intellectual. In exploring these points I want to argue that Wynter draws her central preoccupation from a radical Caribbean intellectual tradition in which the central figures are Aimé Césaire, Frantz Fanon and C.L.R. James. This tradition has as one of its central concerns an explicit engagement with humanism as a foundational project of Western thought.

Codes and Epistemic Breaks

Sylvia Wynter operates with a concept of history that focuses on historical discursive flows rather than a theory of history. Drawing on Michel Foucault's definitions of discourse, as 'practices that systematically form the objects of which we speak', one of Wynter's objectives is to plot a genealogy of discursive formations around the human, as object of both study and subjectivity. Her genealogy has two phases. In its earlier incarnation Wynter focuses on western humanism and its origins in Europe. She argues that the European concept of man was tightly linked to Christianity. Thus God as the extra-human agent created the concept of the dichotomous spirit/flesh and an order of rule that was religious, with the ideal self being the clergy or life forms which could only be realized in St Augustine's heavenly 'City of God'. For Wynter the period of the European Renaissance opens the pathways for what she calls the 'degodding' of discourse and the rise of secularism that created *man*. However there was a wrinkle in this process. The colonial frame of the 'degodding' made the ideal man the white settler. In Wynter's thought this ideal type remains constant even when the work of Charles Darwin breaks European mental frames, consolidating *man* as a biological creature. Invoking Foucault, Wynter points out that, '*Man* was invented in the terms of a specific culture, that of sixteenth-century Europe [this has meant that we now see] *Man* as a ostensible pre-given and biologically determined human nature'.[12] Of course Wynter is disturbed by this and wants to displace these concepts and their assumptions. In Wynter's genealogy the conception of man within Western humanism leads first to the appearance of 'political man'. By the late nineteenth century, Wynter suggests that the concept of man consolidates itself as primarily that of *man* as a bio-economic being. In this framework, redemption is only possible through the overcoming of natural material scarcity.

However in a more recent genealogical version of humanism, Wynter makes an effort to escape the enchantment of western knowledge by working through a different narrative of origins. Instead, she locates the emergence of the human in Africa and notes how this emergence was accompanied by self-representations that are outside 'the terms of our present epistemological locus and its cultural universe'.[11] Using cave drawings from the Southern Africa region, Wynter argues that these drawings converge with a human phase that she calls, 'auto-hominisation'. For Wynter these drawings not only demonstrated the humanness of African people but illuminated human essence as one that was 'uniquely hybrid'. The importance of this shift in Wynter's thought is that it allows her to deploy a concept of the human in which human life is not purely organic and biological but one in which the word/logos becomes she says the 'directive signs of a specifically human code that — in my own — terms, of the governing code of symbolic life and death specific to each culture'.[14]

This is of course a huge claim and directly linked to Wynter's concepts and deployment of two things: episteme and auto-poiesis. It is to the relationship between the two that we now turn our attention. The concept of auto-poiesis was developed by two Latin American scientists, Humberto Maturana and Franciscio Varela.[15] The term was their answer to a series of questions about the processes of self-organization, of biological life and human cognition. Maturana's neuroscience research led him to argue that the nervous system is not only self-organizing but also self-referring. This meant that perception should not only be viewed as representational of an external reality but rather should be understood 'as the continual creation of new relationships within the neural network'.[16] Put another way it meant that human cognition did not '*represent* an external reality, but rather *specify* one'.[17] Furthermore, they argued it also meant that living systems were also cognitive ones. For Maturana and Verela, language was the primary distinction between multicellular living systems and human society. We of course know that the German social theorist Niklas Luhmann also argued for an auto-poiesis that was social and grounded in language as a medium of communication. We should also recall here the series of debates in Western thought about poiesis, in particular Hannah Arendt's discussion in *The Human Condition* between *poiesis* as the activity of production and *praxis* as the activity of action. In Wynter's hands the term however not only took on a different set of meanings but became central to her thinking about the features that precisely constitute a human person.

Beginning with Peter Winch's assertion that humans live their lives, 'according to the regulatory representations of that which constitutes *symbolic life* and that which constitutes its Lack, its mode of *symbolic death*'.[18] Wynter then argues that, 'culture is for me, primarily, the societal machinery with which a particular society or group symbolically codes its sense of self'.[19] This process of coding represents a double movement since it is both behaviour and knowledge. What Wynter wants to work through is how this double movement becomes auto-poiesis. The symbolic codes operating as self-making moments guide behaviour not through communication but in Wynter's words, through, 'self instituting modes of being'.[20] In Wynter's thought therefore auto-poiesis becomes a term for describing how human beings create the ways of living, of labour, language and material production that combine to make the self and then society. It is both word and deed. The question that we can now pose is: to what extent is there a relationship between symbolic codes and episteme in Wynter's thought?

In the work of Foucault, episteme is a structure that defines the structures of knowledge. Although in his later work Foucault oftentimes replaces this usage with the word, *dispositif* — meaning the network that binds and governs the different ways in which discourses interact. Wynter's initial use of episteme is very Foucauldian, for instance when she describes the 'discursive processes of which our present model of being ... was instituted ... at the same time as the disciplinary discourses ... displace those earlier classical episteme'.[21] However I want to suggest that over time there is slippage in Wynter's usage and that in her latest work, episteme is *partly* replaced by symbolic codes and the process of auto-poiesis. The major reason for this is that Wynter centres the subject and this centring drives her into the direction of thinking about discourses as acts of self-making human processes. In Wynter's thought therefore auto-poiesis becomes an active generator of fields of meanings in which symbolic codes are inscribed. What this means is that Wynter is able to leave spaces that can then be opened for the generation of alternative symbolic codes.

Perhaps at this point it might be useful to further explore Wynter's relationship to the work of Foucault, since some commentators in a mistaken series of analysis about the relationship of post-structuralism to Wynter's thought have signalled that this is one of her most recent important influences.[22]

In the first place it is a simplification to say that Wynter is Foucauldian. For sure she appropriates from Foucault elements of both his genealogical method as well as his preoccupation with the life of discursive formations. However Foucault in both *The Archaeology of Knowledge* and *The Order of Things: An Archaeology of the Human Sciences* is concerned about conducting historical analysis of systems of thought and discourse while following George Canguilhem's method of reversing the subordination of concept to theory. Wynter is not so preoccupied with this kind of study. Rather, she wants in the first instance to pluck out from the human sciences not *how* we study but *what* we study. So while Foucault often has to fight to return to questions of subjectivity and therefore the human, Wynter always remains on the ground of the human. This means that even her stated interest in knowledge is not really about its ruses, nor its relationship to power but rather she wants to grapple with a series of relationships between knowledge, culture and human behaviour. Also, she is not concerned with the nature of power per se but with the conditions that would facilitate epistemic ruptures. As a consequence, when Wynter turns to the use of codes and the neural firings of the brain she is not just wrestling with historical or genealogical matters but instead is engaging in an intellectual practice that combines a knowledge of the human gained from biological and complexity theories to organize new meanings of human life and of the human itself.

There is another difference with Foucault. Gilles Deleuze in an essay on Foucault observes that in the latter's work:

> A statement always represents a transmission of particular elements distributed in a corresponding space. As we shall see, the formations and transformations of these spaces themselves pose topological problems that cannot adequately be described in terms of creation, beginning or foundation.[23]

Conversely, Wynter's focus is on the foundational, on tracing origins in order to understand the human and then to mark out the possible conditions for the emergence of the 'human' as a major event in historical terms. In other words for Wynter the study of the object of *man* is to emancipate that object in a series of moves that I would call *critical negativity*. In Wynter's thought, Foucault's notion of the invention of *man* as an object of study is limited since it does not take into account that 'as the West was inventing Man, the slave–plantation was a central logic of the entire mechanism by which that logic was being worked out'.[24] Her direction is therefore different from that of Foucault. What her reading of Foucault allows her to do is to consolidate a break with reductionist readings of Marxism.

In what other ways does she break with such readings of Marx? In what is now considered a classic interview with David Scott, Wynter recounts her Guyana sojourn and reflects on the anguish of the racial divisions between Afro- and Indo-Guyanese. This division partly lead to a historic external intervention and to the collapse of the first People

Progressive Party government then led by Cheddi Jagan. In an extraordinary segment of the interview Wynter recounts how she watched Cheddi Jagan move about and recalled his gentleness and kindness. However in the midst of this evocative moment Wynter says,

> what was traumatic for me was the stark nature of the division between black and Indian. . . . I tried to speak to Cheddi ... [about this and suggest] that [the] greatest emphasis was to see if we could begin to build a common history ... but Cheddi at that time was a very orthodox Marxist, and to suggest that the superstructure was not automatically determined by the mode of production ... would have been heresy for him ... from that moment I said no, there is something important that this paradigm cannot deal with. A lot of my thinking came out of that experience. It was not a matter of negating the Marxism paradigm but of realizing that it was one aspect of something that was larger.[25]

From this experience Wynter sets out not to negate Marxist theory but instead to theorize society in ways where the orthodox Marxist 'base and superstructure' paradigm became more complicated and operated in other ways that in a one-directional, binary fashion. In this, her intellectual trajectory was not dissimilar to many radical anti-colonial thinkers whose concern about race pushed them into opening other spaces in social theory. From her concern with the so-called 'superstructural' Wynter then quickly moves to think about questions of culture. In the end she would argue that 'our behaviours are ... primarily motivated by the Word'.[26] However it is important to note that Wynter continues to take from Marxist theory a concern about the role of laws in governing human action. So even when she shifts her focus from economy to the Word, she continues to search for how:

> in the case of humans, does the mediation by the verbal governing codes and their clusters of meaning, their recoding of the behaviour-motivational bio-chemical reward and punishment system specific to purely organic forms of life take place? What are the *laws* that govern their mediating and recoding function?[27] (emphasis added)

There is another feature of Marx's thinking which infuses Wynter's critical intellectual practice: the work of critical negation. We know of course that it is the Hegelian dialectic which opens the doors for the work of negativity in Western thought and that Marx made this negativity a material rendering of the conflict between social and class forces. One way to examine negativity is to understand it as binary, as the work of negation creating a new thesis which is wracked by its own contradictions. In Hegel's and Marx's hands the work of the negative is a dialectical rhythm in which the 'negation of the negation' is an unstable resolution that eventually leads to a telos. [28] At first blush Wynter's thought seems to follow this pattern. Christian man gives way to political man, then gives way to economic man and then finally to the human. However by posing the question *After Man,* Wynter reaches for a different perspective on the work of negation. This is the work of negation as criticism. In Wynter's hands negation is intrinsic both to the dialectical rhythm and active engaged criticism. [29]

Diana Coole opines that it is Nietzsche's work which sets free the negative 'from the logical, synthetic march of the dialectic'.[30] She also points out that negativity freed from the stricture of the dialectic suggests an 'ontological process since it indicates *becoming*, a productivity that engenders and ruins.... Being, thinking, politics and perception ... are all modulations of becoming'.[31] For Wynter this process of restless becoming is located in a series of *epistemic breaks*. These breaks interrupt the episteme of governing orders and construct new codes of human becoming. In Wynter's thought these breaks are not reversible because they then become 'the very condition of the collective behaviours through which each system realizes itself as such a system'.[32] Therefore these breaks create new codes in a process of auto-poiesis. This means that the work of the negative as criticism requires intellectual labour that is foundational. For Wynter it is not enough to critique the 'laws' of capitalist production. Instead she would argue that it is more important to grasp how the contemporary dominant concept of the human reinscribes an economic system generating systems of classification that create different categories of humans.

We now turn to Wynter's rendering of how one such epistemic break historically occurred.

Humanism, the First Break

The debate about humanism and its role in Western thought has been the site of much contention. Of course, one dimension of this contention has been in the area of definition. There are several definitions of humanism and these need not detain us, for Wynter is not concerned with suggesting new definitions nor any theory of humanism. Her two-fold project is in another direction. In the first instance she wants to demonstrate how humanism was brought into being as an example of epistemic break. In the second place, she wants to show how critical intellectuals should function in order to facilitate an epistemic break in the present. There are two reasons, I think, for Wynter's preoccupation with humanism. Firstly, following the tradition of radical anti-colonial thinkers, Wynter is concerned with the human. Of course, this is also one central thread in Western radical thought. Marx himself argued that communism was the 'positive suppression of private property as human self-estrangement, and hence the true appropriation of the human essence ... it is the complete restoration of man to himself as a social, i.e. human being'.[33] Anti-colonial thinkers challenged this concept of the emergence of the human rooted only in forms of private-property alienation, pointing out that the question of the human was a concrete historical object profoundly shaped in modernity by European coloniality and empire. Therefore the ways in which these forms of rule created and made material classification systems of difference were additional human practices that had to be taken into consideration in the question of human emancipation. Obviously Wynter's training in Spanish literature also partly accounts for her focus on the human, particularly during the period of the European Renaissance.

These two factors coalesce to create in Wynter's thought the ground for making the human an object for the elucidation of a social theory as well as one foundational plank in her thinking. From this ground she would draw profound conclusions about the nature of Western thought, and the all-important relationship between thought and human activity that creates polity, culture and economic systems. In conducting this exercise Wynter seeks to strip bare all our previous concepts of the human and humanism. She does not wish to rescue humanism but rather wants to bring about new concepts of ourselves. In this she is engaging in the Fanonian exercise of bringing 'invention into existence'. In this way Wynter seems to suggest that there is a hidden human that needs to be brought to the fore out of bondage. Hers is therefore an emancipatory project in which the emergence of the human would transform the contemporary condition of man. In her model of the emergence of the human, alienation and therefore subsequent self-reconciliation are replaced by critical intellectual labour bringing forth the human — *after man*. This perspective allows Wynter to develop a series of arguments about modernity.

Other social theorists of modernity, Marx and Weber in particular, wrestled with the origins of modernity either as the way in which merchant capital and the emergence of class forces placed their stamp on European societies, or in Weber's case located it in the domestic economy and values of the Calvinist middle classes in Europe. But, Wynter locates European modernity in the flowering of a series of discursive formations in the period of European history called the 'Renaissance'. However, if she stopped there then there would be nothing original about her thinking. The leap that Wynter makes is one of connections, of trying to see the whole. For Wynter, the Renaissance becomes the break and the start of modernity because it created the material and discursive conditions for the voyages of Christopher Columbus. As she noted in her interview with David Scott, 'it was the 1492 event that would set in motion the bringing together of the hitherto separated branches of our human species within the framework of the single history which we now live'.[34] Of course this event had two faces, since it was conducted with the genocide of the indigenous populations of the Americas, racial slavery and colonialism. However Wynter maintains that the event represented an event of possibilities, one in which humanity could move 'from an ecumenically human perspective and *to* an ecumenically human interest'.[35] If for other thinkers, modernity and its secularism represented the emergence of man, for Wynter it was the emergence of a specific *type* of man, political man. In this regard therefore Wynter changes the conventional meanings of the political to argue that political man was bourgeois man.

Deploying the work of J.G.A. Pocock, she makes the point that the epochal shift in the West was based on the 'transfer of the central behaviour-regulating "redemptive process"'. Pocock's work argues that the form of humanism which emerged in the political domain during early modernity was 'civic humanism'.[36] This form of humanism was a way of thinking, organized around the conception that 'the development of the individual towards self-fulfilment is possible only when the individual acts as a citizen, that is a conscious and autonomous participant in an autonomous decision-taking political community, the polis or republic'.[37] What Pocock does not do, Wynter achieves by arguing that this political man had a social goal of rational redemption, an ideal self-representation codified as the white settler, and an episteme in which reason, science and rationality were conflated.

Wynter does not think about modernity in terms of systems, rather she works through a figuration of man. This figuration is not singular but instead represents man as collective species, one that constitutes itself 'through modes of symbolical self-representation ... the mode of self-representation through which the first form of secular man autospeciated it/himself, as well as the real world'.[38] For Wynter this self-representation has the quality of the 'aesthetic',[39] while being political. One is not speaking here of the aesthetic as a literary form, the ways in which the word becomes literature or poetry. Nor is one thinking of an Aristotelian poetics. I say this because we know there is a politics of literature, not one in which we become engaged in debates about the committed writer or the modes of representation of political events, but rather one in which as Jacques Rancière puts it, 'there is a specific link between politics as a definite way of doing and literature as definite practice of writing'.[40] Rancière continues that, 'Politics is first of all a way of framing ... it is a specific intertwining of ways of being, ways of doing and ways of speaking'.[41] An aesthetic view of politics and human practice allows us to understand that self-representation is also about the ways in which the human labours upon him/herself and therefore creates the human and the social world. This creation requires 'ways of being, doing and speaking'. And since words even when they become flesh sometimes do not resemble what they say, then an aesthetic is needed. For it is thought that does the resemblance. However, at the same time 'ways of being, doing and speaking' are forms of creation which are profoundly political because they involve the central question of polity — how shall we live together?

It is in writing and therefore in the acts of language that Wynter's epistemic breaks occur. In relationship to humanism this break occurs when the rewriting of knowledge takes place. She notes, 'the rewriting of knowledge of the *Studia* was therefore a counter-writing to the order of knowledge of the clergy, the new knowledge in whose context a new template of Identity, that of Natural Man, was being brought into existence in the new narrative representations of Renaissance Europe'.[42] For Wynter therefore epistemic breaks are political moments, ones in which human beings cast off in acts of writing and speaking the old and construct a new meaning of self-representation. She notes:

> We can therefore put forward the following hypotheses: that ruling groups in all human culture, including our own, are ruling groups to the extent that they embody their culture's optimal criterion of being, or code of symbolic life; that therefore the great transformations in history are always transformations of the code, of what it means to be human, and, therefore, of the poesies of being and mode of symbolic co-specificity.[43]

This does not mean that Wynter ignores political economy but rather that she sees political economy as another instance of human labour and self-representation which works alongside the normative knowledge order of society. So for her the emergence of a political economy of industrial capitalism is only possible because of the Darwinian story of the evolutionary anthropology of the human, and the creation of a bio-economic man whose social goal is material redemption. In this paradigm those who are poor and jobless become in Wynter's thought a certain category of man. They are not just materially poor or exploited but are fixed within a normative order of the human that allows for their constant reproduction as poor. In the end therefore the transformation of the capitalist order requires not only economic and political changes but normative epistemic breaks about the nature of man. Thus for Wynter the real revolutionary transformation requires a new mode of thinking that is *After Man*. The question we must now turn to is who are the agents for this transformation? Our answers will lead us into two other areas of Wynter's thought, that of the liminal and the role of intellectuals.

Liminality and the Epistemic Break

Reflecting on the political ideas of one of C.L.R. James's classical text, *Beyond A Boundary,* Wynter notes that the pattern of the text was the working out and therefore uncovering of 'large areas of human existence' which James's work on politics, history and economics left out.[44] For Wynter these lacunae which James addresses in the text revealed 'a separation, a gap ... between the mode of popular desire i.e. what the masses wanted to live by and what the ruling elements wanted them to live by'.[45] This situation of conflict, Wynter argued, established amongst the 'masses' an 'alternative life-activity in its own right'.[46] Over time in Wynter's thought the figure of the masses was replaced by the category *liminal.* This category, she argued, would allow for a general classification of people who were outside of official society, groups that were excluded and oppressed and who were not captured in the formal categories of western radical political theory. Oftentimes in deploying the category of the liminal Wynter seems to want to work through the original meaning of Fanon's, 'wretched of the earth' — *les damnés* — as a substitute for the liminal. Perhaps there has been an unfortunate historic translation error of Fanon's ... *Les damnés,* in its translation as wretched.[47] In English, wretched means to be in an unhappy or to be in an unfortunate state, a state which can be of one's own self-making. In such a state there is no description of or any trace of power nor of oppression. However if we read damné as accursed or as C.L.R. James recommends, as condemned, then the meanings shift and there is the possibility of power becoming central. But more importantly from Wynter's perspective, a new translation allows a form of naming, a classification of a group which has the capacity to confront power and reformulate their social location. From this stance it is easy to see how Wynter's can move from masses to liminal to *damnés.*

When Wynter's usage of liminal first appears, it seems to be influenced by her reading of the Ethiopian anthropologist Asmarom Legesse. She underscores Legesse's point that while human beings are trapped in the 'ordering categories and prescriptions of our epistemic orders ... that liminal groups of any order are the ones most able to free us from these prescriptions, since it is they who existentially experience the injustice inherent in structure'.[48] Wynter further notes that 'liminal categories ... experience a structural contradiction between their lived experience and the grammar of representations which generate the mode of reality ... the liminal frame of reference, therefore unlike the normative, can provide ... the outer view'.[49] In her deployment of the category, liminal Wynter extends both Legesse's and Victor Turner's meanings. In his seminal study, *The Forest of Symbols*, Victor Turner draws from the Ndembu language the description of healing and knowledge practices in which a group of people were set aside in spaces apart from the rest of the society in order to train for and practice specialized or secret knowledges, for example healing and certain forms of initiation. This exclusion was a process of deliberate setting aside, not one of marginalization.[50] In a profound sense Wynter's use of liminal takes into account the notion of being excluded and setting aside. However she adds to the setting aside, the notion of marginalization plus the idea that this location produces special knowledge. Where I think Wynter sometimes conflates the *damnés* with the liminal is that she is moved to think of structural reasons for poverty and oppression and in doing so her sense of marginalization takes on greater force. One intriguing feature of Wynter's thought is that her preoccupation with the category of those who are excluded and marginalized by official society is not a recent one. Perhaps the clearest explorations of this feature in her thought can be found in two of her early essays: the seminal, 'Jonkonnu in Jamaica'; and the unpublished but remarkable essay on the cultural politics of the Caribbean, 'We know where we are From: The Politics of Black Culture from Myal to Marley'.

The literary critic Norval Edwards notes that many of Wynter's early essays were 'characterized by sophisticated theoretical acumen, referential and allusive density, and a blistering polemical style'.[51] I would add that they were also characterized by a deep attachment to thinking about the Caribbean both within its own terms and its history and culture. In addition Wynter's gaze was firmly fixed on the various subaltern groups of the region. We should add here one final point about Wynter's work in the Caribbean. If within the immediate post-independence period there were intense debates that raged around a Caribbean social theory (the story of the plantation, creolization or cultural pluralism debates) then Wynter's intervention in this period was an unusual one. Her move to establish culture and various dimensions of artistic performances as possible optics to understand Caribbean society was not only a way to broaden the debate but was one that desired to refocus the debate on Caribbean subjectivities. It was also integral to her search for a relationship between the aesthetic and the political . Thus in her article 'Jonkonnu in Jamaica' Wynter uses the performance of dance as a mode to enter the two major existing debates within the Caribbean intellectual tradition. The first was the debate about creolization and the second was about the relationship of so-called folk culture to the history and nature of Caribbean society.

Beginning with a discussion of R. Coulthard's book, *Race and Colour in Caribbean Literature*, Wynter takes up many of the arguments of J. Price Mars about the relationship of African culture to the cultural history of Haiti. She observes how Price Mars following the lead of Césaire, 'represented more clearly with his study of folklore, a *negritude* which was *indigenist*'. She continues,

> the history of the Caribbean islands is in large part the *indigenization* of the black man. And this history is a cultural history — not in "writing" but of those "*homunculi*" who humanize the landscape by peopling it with gods and spirits, with demons and duppies, with all the rich panoply of man's imagination.[52]

From this view Wynter then argues that:

History has mainly been about the European super structure of civilization. Yet, in the interstices of history, we see, in glimpses, evidences of a powerful and pervasive cultural process which has largely determined the unconscious springs of our beings; a process which we shall identify and explore as the process of "*indigenization*" a process whose agent and product was Jamaican folklore, folksong, folk-tales, folk-dance.[53]

In this piece Wynter is preoccupied with the ordinary person. She notes that the social location and history of this group creates an entire cultural world which is ignored and denigrated by official society. Thus she hopes not only to restore the so-called folk to its proper place but also wants to posit that this culture offers valid alternative ways of thinking, living and being. She notes,

> Folklore represents the attempt to prolong and recreate a system in which community and society and the social order is primary; folklore is not only the relation of Man to nature but of Man to himself. Folklore was the cultural guerrilla resistance to the Market economy. [54]

For Wynter, there is no domination without resistance and those who are liminal construct new spaces in the process of that resistance. In thinking about the cultural history of the region this way, Wynter argued for a social theory that would not just describe Caribbean social formation but would bring to the fore what Kamau Brathwaite has called the 'inner plantation'.[55] Brathwaite has suggested in his essay 'Contradictionary Omens' that Wynter's essay argues against a theory of creolization. He notes that she makes the point that creolization is about a process of 'false assimilation' in which dominated people adopt elements from those dominant ... in order to obtain prestige ... indigenization process represents the more secretive process by which the dominated culture survives and resists'.[56] I would suggest that Wynter's theory of Caribbean society posits that the yoking of two cultures created a cultural process of creolization which then becomes the template upon which Caribbean discursive practices occur. Recognizing that forms of cultural encounters existed, Wynter wants to argue that the relationship is neither static nor one devoid of power. Instead, precisely because of power she observes that the subaltern engaged in forms of symbolic coding which challenged the normative order. In other words, Wynter is arguing for a more dynamic approach to the encounter between European culture and various forms of African cultures in the Caribbean and suggesting that typologies which ignored alternative symbolic codings were inadequate. This point can be richly discerned when we examine her unpublished essay, 'We Know Where we are From: The Politics of Black Culture from Myal to Marley'.

Written in 1977, this essay alongside Wynter's novel, *The Hills of Hebron,* represents her clearest statements about the ways in which subaltern knowledge practices create a 'powerful symbolic counterworld' as part of a 'popular cultural signifying system'.[57] Wynter notes that when radical ideas are organized in this mode they are able to spread out in 'secret subterranean currents'. In this she is working through a Lacanian understanding of the symbolic in which she observes that there is a 'symbolic function' which operates as a 'double movement ... man makes an object of his actions, but only to restore to this action in due time its place as grounding'.[58] Using the initial activities of Leonard Howell, the central founder of Rastafari, Wynter observes that when he refused to recognize King George as his ruler he was,

> rejecting the political identity coded for him in the cosmos of the British Empire as imperial subject. To the actual and symbolic elements that articulated the "British Subject" he counter-posed a counter signifying system in which our King and Africa, the Motherland are legitimated as the symbolic home.[59]

Wynter then argues that this rejection was of central significance in a process of self-transformation and therefore became a counter-world which invented and structured 'its own symbolic order'. The critical element for this process is a form of knowledge since she suggests that the order created 'goes beyond a simple inversion of terms. Rather there is a displacement, a change of signs'.[60] The politics of this 'change of signs' reside in the historical cultural practices of Myalism and a 'radicality of desire which refuses all limits'.[61] This desire then becomes the foundation of the 'revolution in the structures of power' and is the politics of a 'black counter culture of the Americas ... engaged in ... cultural revolution'.[62] At this point Wynter calls our attention to the 'counter-invention of the self ... as the central strategy of the "politics" of black culture'.[63]

In this essay Wynter is also concerned to settle some accounts with orthodox Marxism. She notes the history of George Padmore's relationship to the international communist movement in the early twentieth century and opines that while 'commonalty is one side of the dialectic, differentiation is the other'. This differentiation is grounded in racial oppression and racial hierarchies of labour. Such a system rooted in the history of modern racial slavery and modernity meant that the slaves were sold as what Wynter calls '*piezas* — pieces in a rational quantified system which took the norm of labour power'. From this position she enunciates one of her most important statements in the essay. She writes:

> *I want to note here ... that the Pieza /Negro was the first and total example of the reduction of the creative possibilities of man to a single possibility — man as producer. It is this reduction of man from the totality of his possibilities that defines capitalist rationality.* And capitalist rationality is itself defined within the paradigm of production.[64]

Here Wynter is operating well within the radical tradition of James, Fanon, and Du Bois. This is a tradition in which the figure of the black slave becomes the site where modernity exposes its entrails while at the same time the black slave retains the capacity to write a new history of the human. For Wynter one difference between orthodox Marxist theory and what I would call her own *social cognitive theory of the human*[65] is that while, on one hand, the former operates from a productionist perspective that enunciates 'labour power as the fundamental human potential', she on the other hand proclaims a 'radical desire for happiness' as the driving force for radical transformation.[66] In this she is not dissimilar to James who in his 1947 essay 'Dialectical Materialism and the Fate of Humanity' observes that both Hegel and Marx 'arrived at a theory of knowledge from their examination of men in society'.[67] James then states that this theory of the knowledge of man posits that the purpose of man's life is 'freedom and happiness'. In using the word *purpose* James distinguishes its religious flavour from that of its historical sense. He notes: 'Purpose, not in the religious sense, but in the sense that if we examine man's history through the centuries he has sought these aims'.[68] From Wynter's perspective in her 1977 essay a similar understanding of purpose serves as the wellspring for a politics of symbolic displacement and changes in the dominant sign system, creating a radical politics of the Word.

The Intellectual

If in the 1970s Wynter was preoccupied with subalterns and their attempts to construct new symbolic orders in the last two decades of the twentieth century, she has developed her social theory of the human. In doing this, she has come to place a greater reliance upon the critical role of the intellectual in the academy. She herself has paid scant attention to the conventional protocols of the academy flying as she puts it 'low under the radar screen' to be able to continue her intellectual work. Wynter is an intellectual/writer, one for whom writing is a supreme political act not carried out for the purposes of tenure or promotion. She writes because for her it is one mode of political practice. Hence there is a vast body of unpublished Wynter essays and book-length manuscripts.[69] Wynter sees the role of the radical intellectual as one in which intellectual labour is about creating the foundations for epistemic ruptures. Her central example of this is the way in which European lay intellectuals 'degodded' European religious thought. She writes in a recent essay, 'Unsettling the Coloniality of Being/ Power/ Truth/ Freedom', the following:

> The challenge to be confronted at this juncture is this: While from the Renaissance onwards, Western intellectuals have, by mean of the natural sciences enabled us to obtain nonadaptive knowledge ... we have hitherto had no such parallel knowledge with respect to ourselves.[70]

In Wynter's view this new knowledge must go beyond the 'ethnoclass limits of our contemporary ones'. This means that even though subaltern thought is important for the expression of radical desire, Wynter wants to leave to intellectuals the fuller arguments that would create the platform for epistemic break. There is no full discussion of the nature of intellectuals in Wynter's work and I would argue that there is a serious tension between her present writings and thought and the earlier essays from "Jonkonnu" to her 1980s essay on the figure of Matthew Bondsman in the writings of C.L.R. James. In these and other essays, Wynter is driven to understand the 'means ... whereby the natural environment was the dominant challenge, now the conceptual and aesthetic in a situation where man's greatest obstacle to the realization of his powers, to the free play and development of his faculties is now the socio-cultural environment'.[71] It should be noted that C.L.R. James consistently locates the ground for the creation of a new society upon the actions (intellectually and politically) of the ordinary person. In 1968, he presented a ten-point programme at a conference in Cuba which argued that 'the function of this Congress is that intellectuals should prepare the way for the abolition of the intellectuals as an embodiment of culture'.[72] Conversely, Wynter in her more recent work over-represents the role of the intellectual. This over-representation is also present in her social theory of the human.

While it is historically accurate to point out the creative work of radical intellectuals in history, such a perspective becomes one-sided when it ignores the historical movements of people in their radical quest for 'freedom now'. Moments of historical rupture require both. This means that radical intellectuals should not only keep their eyes on the code domination of the various discursive formations but also on the strivings of the oppressed. In her recent essay on African Cinema, Wynter makes attempts to do this, however her emphasis is only on the power of the episteme. As a consequence her moves to think about the central figures of her essay that make attempts to rupture the hold of the episteme are not successful because of her sole reliance upon the critical intellectual as *the* agent of transformation. Perhaps this reliance is a result of Wynter's sidestepping of how power works as a material set of networks that function and morphs into social systems of domination. Perhaps also it might be that Wynter's almost exclusive reliance upon the Word / Logos limits her grasp of the tension between poiesis and praxis . If in the former there can be production which reifies the fluidity of human experience then in the latter action is not necessarily telos-orientated. But more importantly praxis involves the combination of all forms of reason. Radical politics is therefore not only about the Word. In such a context the removal of domination and its guises requires concrete actions of the liminal and the construction of a radical politics of speech, word and action.

By Way of Reflection

Sylvia Wynter remains one of the most important radical intellectuals of the contemporary period. Her social theory of the human provokes us to rethink not only how we live but *how* and *what* we think. It also provides for us an alternative theory and narrative of modernity. What Wynter's intellectual work continues is the quest which Fanon, Céasire and James began in the early twentieth century — a quest generated by radical anti-coloniality — what is the nature of the human? However Wynter has placed on this quest her own stamp by developing a distinctive understanding of culture, consciousness and the symbolic codes which govern human behaviour. In other words starting from her concerns about so-called 'superstructural' questions she has made an extraordinary attempt not only to locate the human historically, but to strip bare the trappings which presently cover the human's emergence. In this regard she is a singular figure summing up in a theory of the human the strivings and impulses of some of the central questions asked by emancipatory thought in the twentieth century and plotting a possible way for us to ask the new ones.

Notes

1. Van Piercy, 'Sylvia Wynter interview' in *Berkley Graduate* (April 1988): 13.
2. Frantz Fanon, *Black Skin White Masks* (New York: Grove Press, 1967), 229.
3. Ibid., 232.
4. See Anthony Bogues, *Empire of Liberty: Power and Desire* (forthcoming) for a discussion on how biopolitics as a form of political power operates through coloniality and empires.
5. Frantz Fanon, *The Wretched of the Earth* (New York: Grove Press, 1963), 316.
6. Aimé Césaire, *Discourse on Colonialism* (New York: Monthly Review Press, 2000), 42.
7. Aimé Césaire, 'Poetry and Knowledge' in *Refusal of the Shadow: Surrealism and the Caribbean*, ed. Michael Richardson (London: Verso, 1996), 140.
8. Giorgio Agamben, *potentialities: Collected Essays in Philosophy* Trans. Daniel Heller-Roazen(Stanford: Stanford University Press, 1999), 47.
9. Richard Drayton and Andaiye, eds., *Conversations : George Lamming, Essays, Addresses and Interviews 1953–1990*. (London: Karia Press, 1992), 38.
10. There has been a growing amount of secondary literature on the thought and critical intellectual practices of Wynter. See in particular, Paget Henry, *Caliban's Reason* (2000); essays in Demetrius Eudell & Carolyn Allen, eds., *Journal of West Indian Literature* 10, nos. 1&2 (November 2001); and the interview by David Scott, 'The Re-Enchantment of Humanism: An Interview with Sylvia Wynter' in *Small Axe* no. 8 (September 2000): 119-207.
11. Van Piercy, 'Sylvia Wynter interview' in *Berkley Graduate* (April 1988):13-14.
12. Sylvia Wynter, 'Africa, The West and the Analogy of Culture: The Cinematic Text After Man', 30.
13. Ibid., 45.
14. Ibid.
15. It should be noted here that Wynter's intellectual interest are wide-ranging not just cutting across the social sciences and humanities and that any profound understanding of her work requires a familiarity with new developments in the life sciences, particularly biology, as well as in the areas of cognitive science.
16. Cited in Fritjpo Capra, *A New Scientific Understanding of Living Systems: The Web of Life* (New York: Anchor Books, 1997), 96.
17. Ibid.
18. Sylvia Wynter, 'Beyond the Word of Man: Glissant and the New Discourse of the Antilles', *World Literature Today* (Autumn 1989): 641.

19. Sylvia Wynter, 'We know where we are coming from: The Politics of Black Culture from Myal to Marley', 1977. This is an unpublished mss which I found in the C.L.R. James archives at the library of the Oilfield Workers Trade Union in San Fernando, Trinidad. I want to thank the union executive for inviting me to give the annual C.L.R. James lecture in 2000 which then allowed me to work in the library.
20. David Scott, 'The Re-Enchantment of Humanism: An Interview with Sylvia Wynter', *Small Axe*, no. 8 (September 2000): 90.
21. 'Beyond the Word of Man: Glissant and the New Discourse of the Antilles', 642.
22. See in particular Paget Henry's *Caliban's Reason* (New York: Routledge, 2000), Chapter 5. What is missing in this chapter is an analysis of how Wynter's thought is shaped by her extensive readings and grasp of modern evolutionary theory and theories of complexity and human cognition. I also want to suggest that Wynter's preoccupation with issues of language and culture are concerns which she has maintained from her early intellectual activity as a critic in the Caribbean and is not a result of any so called linguistic turn in Western philosophical thought.
23. Gilles Deleuze, *Foucault* (Minnesota: University of Minnesota Press, 1988), 3.
24. David Scott, 'The Re-Enchantment of Humanism: An Interview with Sylvia Wynter', *Small Axe*, no. 8 (September 2000): 165.
25. Ibid., 141-142.
26. 'Africa, The West and the Analogy of Culture: The Cinematic Text After Man', 27.
27. Ibid.
28. For a good study of the role of the negative in Marxist thought and politics in general see, Diana Coole, *Negativity and politics: Dionysus and dialectics from Kant to Poststructuralism* (London: Routledge, 2000).
29. For a fine discussion of negation as criticism, see Paul Bove, *Intellectuals in Power: A Genealogy of Critical Humanism* (New York: Columbia University Press, 1986), Chapter 6.
30. Diane Coole, *Negativity and Politics*, 87.
31. Ibid., 230.
32. Sylvia Wynter, 'The Ceremony Must be Found: After Humanism', *Boundary 2*. Volume X11, no 3. (Spring/Fall 1984).
33. Karl Marx, *Early Writings*, 348.
34. *Small Axe*, no. 8 (September 2000): 193.
35. Ibid., 194.
36. The major work of Pocock on these issues is J.G.A. Pocock, *The Machiavellian Moment: Florentine Political Thought and the Atlantic Republican Tradition* (New Jersey: Princeton University Press, 1975).
37. J.G.A. Pocock, 'Civic Humanism and its role in Anglo-American Thought', in his *Politics, Language and Time: Essays on Political Thought and History* (Chicago: University of Chicago Press, 1989), 85.
38. Sylvia Wynter, 'The Ceremony Must be Found: After Humanism', 51.
39. Ibid.
40. Jacques Rancière, 'The Politics of Literature', *SubStance* No. 103. vol . 33, no. 1 (2004):10.
41. Ibid.
42. Sylvia Wynter, 'The Ceremony Must be Found: After Humanism', 29.
43. Sylvia Wynter, 'Africa, The West and the Analogy of Culture: The Cinematic Text After Man', 53.

44. Sylvia Wynter, 'In the Quest of Matthew Bondman: Some Cultural Notes on the Jamesian Journey', in *C.L.R. James: His Life and Work*, ed. Paul Buhle (London: Allison and Busby, 1986), 131.
45. Ibid.
46. Ibid.
47. The original title of Fanon's book is *Les damnés de la terre*.
48. Sylvia Wynter, 'The Ceremony Must be Found: After Humanism', 38.
49. Ibid., 39.
50. I want to thank Geri Augusto for spirited debates on this point and other parts of this essay.
51. See Norval Edwards's essay in *Journal of West Indian Literature* 10, nos. 1&2 (November 2001): 12.
52. Sylvia Wynter, 'Jonkonnu in Jamaica: Towards the Interpretation of Folk Dance as a Cultural Process', *Jamaica Journal* 4, no. 2 (June 1970): 34-48.
53. Ibid., 35.
54. Ibid., 36.
55. See, for a discussion of this, Kamau Brathwaite, 'Caribbean Man in Space and Time,' *Savacou* 11/12 (1973): 1-11.
56. Kamau Brathwaite, *Contradictionary Omens* (Kingston: Savacou Publications, 1974): 15-16.
57. Sylvia Wynter, 'We know where we are from: the politics of Black culture from Myal to Marley', unpublished paper, 1977, 3.
58. Ibid., 4.
59. Ibid., 14-15.
60. Ibid., 19.
61. Ibid., 28.
62. Ibid., 34.
63. Ibid., 36.
64. Ibid., 22.
65. At the Wynter conference in June 2002, Wynter in a conversation with Geri Augusto confirmed that one of the things she was trying to do was to develop a theory of social cognition. In thinking about this statement I have concluded that perhaps this was a short hand for a theory of the human which was based both on cognitive processes as well as the workings of culture and power. Hence my description of her theory as one of social cognitive theory of the human.
66. 'We know where we are from', 39.
67. C.L.R. James, 'Dialectical Materialism and the Fate of Humanity' in *Spheres of Existence*, ed. C.L.R. James (London: Allison and Busby, 1980), 80.
68. Ibid., 83.
69. One example illustrates this. Amongst her vast quantity of unpublished mss is a 500-page plus mss. on the native intellectual. The mss. was written as part of a dialogue/debate in which Wynter was engaged with the Institute of the Black World in the 1970s about the intellectual in the colonial and ex-colonial nations. I want to thank Demetrius Eudell for bringing this remarkable piece to my attention.
70. Sylvia Wynter, 'Unsettling the Coloniality of Being /Power/ Truth/ Freedom', 317.
71. Sylvia Wynter, 'In Quest of Matthew Bondsman: Some Cultural Notes on the Jamesian Journey', *Urgent Tasks: Journal of the Revolutionary left. C.L.R. James: His Life and Work. No 12.* (Summer 1981).
72. The report is published in Andrew Salkey, *Havana Journal* (London: Pelican books, 1971).

Contributors

Jason R. Ambroise is an Assistant Professor of History at William Paterson University in New Jersey. His most recent essay is '*Biocenterism* and the Origins of Our Time' in *Cross Routes – The Meanings of Race for the 21st Century*, edited by Sabine Broeck and Paula Boi (2003).

Anthony Bogues is Professor of Africana Studies and Political Science, Royce Professor of Teaching Excellence, and current Chair of the Africana Studies Department at Brown University. His latest book is *Empire of Liberty: Power and Desire* (forthcoming). He is an Associate Editor of the journal *Small Axe* an Advisory Editor for the journal, *Boundary 2*, and an Associate Director and Visiting Professor at the Centre for Caribbean Thought.

Demetrius L. Eudell is an Associate Professor of History and African American Studies at Wesleyan University in Middletown, Connecticut. He is the author of *The Political Languages of Emancipation in the British Caribbean and the U.S. South* as well as the co-editor with Carolyn Allen of 'Sylvia Wynter: A Transculturalist Rethinking Modernity', a special issue of the *Journal of West Indian Literature* (2001).

Patricia D. Fox is an Independent Scholar, who studied with Professor Wynter and has taught at Indiana University, University of Missouri, Columbia and as a Visiting Professor at the University of Ghana, Leblon. Her work focuses on the representation and the full range of cultural production of peoples of African descent in Spanish and Portuguese- speaking Latin America and the Caribbean.

Lewis R. Gordon is the Laura H. Carnell University Professor of Philosophy, Director of the Institute for the Study of Race and Social Thought, and Director of the Center for Afro-Jewish Studies at Temple

University. He is author of several books, including *Existentia Africana* (2000). He is currently completing a book on Frantz Fanon in the Caribbean context and is the President of the Caribbean Philosophical Association.

Clevis Headley is an Associate Professor of Philosophy and Director of Ethnic Studies at Florida Atlantic University. He has published on Frege, Critical Race theory, and Africana philosophy. He is currently working in the areas of Afro-Caribbean philosophy and Africana philosophy concentrating on the question of black subjectivity and the role of trauma in Africana philosophy. Professor Headley is currently serving as Vice-President of the Caribbean Philosophical Association and co-editor of the *Journal of the Caribbean Philosophical Association*.

Paget Henry is Professor of Sociology and Africana Studies, Brown University. His books include *Peripheral Capitalism and Underdevelopment in Antigua*, *CLR James's Caribbean* and *Caliban's Reasons: Introducing Afro-Caribbean Philosophy*. He is also the editor of the *C.L.R. James Journal*.

Aaron Kamugisha is a Doctoral Candidate in Social and Political Thought at York University, Toronto. He has previously studied at the University of the West Indies, Cave Hill Campus and the University of California, Berkeley, and published articles in the *Journal of Caribbean History*, *Race & Class*, and *Proud flesh: New Afrikan Journal of Culture, Politics and Consciousness*.

Joyce E. King holds the Benjamin E. Mays Endowed Chair of Urban Teaching, Learning and Leadership at Georgia State University, where she is also Professor of Educational Policy Studies in the College of Education. The former Provost at Spelman College, King is widely recognized for her contributions to the field of education. Her publications include three books, as well as many articles that address the role of cultural knowledge in effective Teaching and Teacher Preparation, Black Teachers' Emancipatory Pedagogy, Research Methods, and Black Studies Epistemology and Curriculum Change.

CONTRIBUTORS

Neil Roberts is currently a Doctoral Graduate Student in Political Theory at the University of Chicago in the Department of Political Science. A high school teacher prior to graduate school, he is the recipient of fellowships from the Andrew W. Mellon Foundation and the Social Science Research Council. Roberts is the author of published and forthcoming articles in *The C.L.R. James Journal*, *Sartre Studies International*, and *Philosophia Africana*.

Nicosia Shakes is currently a Researcher on staff at Liberty Hall, Kingston. She is also a tutor in Political Theory in the Department of Government, University of the West Indies, Mona.

Greg Thomas is an Assistant Professor of English at Syracuse University. He is the editor of the journal *Proud Flesh: New Afrikan Journal of Culture, Politics and Consciousness*. His articles have appeared in the *Journal of West Indian Literature*, *The Centennial Review* and *Presénce Africaine*.

Nelson Maldonado-Torres is an Assistant Professor of Comparative Ethnic Studies at the University of California, Berkeley. He specializes in Modern and Contemporary Philosophy, Critical Theory, Postcolonial Studies and Modern Religious Thought. He has published several articles and is working on two book-length projects: *Against War: Views from the Underside of Modernity* and *Fanonian Meditations*.

Index

Afro-Caribbean, 72, 73,169,269
Afro-centrism, 16,28, 42, 213.
Africa, 305-308, 316,318,330,325.
African Diaspora, 292, 310
Africana humanism, 139
Africana philosophy, 64,66, 147
Alterity, 27-31, 44, 48, 52, 69, 70, 71, 145, 271, 321.
American: man, 202, 204; way of life,199; historiography, 20, 46.
Anglo-American intellectual tradition, 174.
Anti-black racism, 240.
Auto-poiesis, 319, 320, 323.
Arendt Hannah, 165, 319.

Bernal, Martin, 15-19.
Berlin, Isaiah, 157.
Blackness, 46, 101, 165, 169, 242-243.
Black Studies, xiv, 5, 27,28,31, 48; and alterity, 29.
Black Jacobins, 40
Black Reconstruction, 14
Black Thought, 50
Biological, 13, 20, 27, 30, 80, 86, 125, 209, 211.
Biko, Steve, 139, 140.
Bogues, Anthony, xiii, 158, 159 .
Bourdieu, Pierre, 191, 192, 194.
Brathwaite, Kamau, xiv, 72, 135, 237, 284, 303, 331.

Cabral, Amlicar, 136.
Capitalism, 136, 164, 172, 198, 268.
Caribbean Intellectual Tradition, xiii, xiii, xv, 259, 330
Catholic Church, 46, 302.
Cesaire, Aime, xv, 136, 157, 166, 237, 315-317 .

Cognition, 116, 141, 262, 319 .
Coloniality, 203-204.
Collins, Patricia Hill, 139.
Consilience, 209, 216, 218, 223.
Copernican Revolution, 185, 232, 167
Creolization, 73, 138, 300, 329-331.
Culture, 72, 82, 131, 143, 146, 219, 220, 223, 224, 321, 324, 327.

Darwin, Charles, 161, 318.
Davis, Angela, 9, 49, 85.
Davis, Carol Boyce, 85.
Diop, Cheikh Anta, 28, 85.
Disciplines, 13, 26, 40, 51, 87, 118, 146, 185, 210, 219, 236, 252, 253, 259, 280.
DuBois, W. E. B, 240-243, 246, 285, 333.
Dussel, Enrique 160.

Economics, 14, 179, 191, 230.
Epigenetic, 220, 223.
Episteme, 13, 28, 29, 61, 69, 162, 166, 260, 263, 268, 271, 320, 323, 335.
Epistemology, 4, 47, 72, 287, 304.
Eurocentric, 15, 16, 27, 60, 69, 89, 137, 194, 197.
Evolution, 219, 224, 225.

Fanon, Frantz, xv, 2, 19, 21, 28, 49, 81, 136, 142, 162, 166, 168, 191, 197, 211, 219, 237, 242, 261, 315, 316.
Feminist, 78, 87, 101, 105, 112, 108, 115, 281.
Foucault, Michel, 13, 78, 86, 132, 160, 166, 260, 318, 320, 321.
Freedom, 29, 66-68, 108, 157-159, 161, 196, 310, 335.

INDEX

Garvey, Marcus, 167, 299, 303, 309.
Genetic, 21, 30, 161, 166.
Godelier, Maurice, 2, 62, 209, 211, 219, 225, 226, 260-261.
Gordon, Lewis, xv, 138, 185.
Gould, Stephen J, 185, 226.
Goveia, Elsa, 116, 140, 165, 237.
Grassi, Ernesto, 221.

Haitian Revolution, 159, 196.
Harris, Wilson, 57, 72.
Heidegger, Martin, 11, 195.
Henry, Paget, xv, 140, 292.
History, 157, 168, 218, 226, 243, 267.
Humanism, xiv, xv, 12, 30, 77, 116, 132, 138, 141, 142, 177, 178, 182, 197, 245, 293, 317, 324, 326.
Humanities, 21, 29, 185, 210, 218, 219, 259, 274, 280.
Husserl, Edmund, 159.

Identity, 26, 31, 59, 78, 89, 118, 177, 276, 277, 327.
Imperialism, 88, 131, 134, 142.
Intellectuals 157, 321, 322, 334 ; Black, 49, 89 ; Africana, 66, 145.

James, C.L.R. 40, 134, 136, 148, 157, 159, 166, 169, 170, 178, 258, 301, 317, 328, 334.
Jameson, Fredric, 158, 171.
Jamaica Journal, xiv.
Jaspers, Karl, 238.

Kant, Immanuel, 161, 262, 264.
Kierkegaard, Soren, 244, 253.

Lamming, George, xiv, 142, 171, 237, 268, 316.
Las Casas, Bartholome de, xiv, 46, 294, 296.
Legesse, Asmaron, 28, 62, 103, 166, 190, 224, 329.
Lewis, Rupert, xiii, 185.
Liminal, 27, 62, 65, 140, 158, 161, 168, 182, 190, 202, 243, 268, 277, 317, 327, 329, 335.
Logos, 19, 141, 146, 318, 335.
L'Overture, Toussaint, 159.

Marley, Bob, 185, 329, 331.
Marx, Karl, 158, 166, 197.
Mills, Charles, 161, 283.
Meeks, Brian, xiii, 185, 274.
Morrison, Toni, 89.

Natural Sciences, 210, 218, 259, 280, 334.
Negation, 143, 323.
Neo-liberalism, 191, 201, 204.
Nettleford, Rex, xiv, 291.

Ontology, 66, 78
Ontogeny, 30, 143, 248.

Padmore, George, 285, 332.
Pan-African, 299, 302, 311.
Parry, Benita, 136.
Pocock, J.G.A., 325-326.
Phenomenology, 177, 270, 273, 284.
Poetics, 136, 146, 266, 270, 272, 274, 286, 326.
Poeisis, 275, 281.
Postcolonial, 106, 138.

Racism, 15, 26, 36, 139, 142, 146, 165, 198, 204, 251, 300.
Ranciere, Jacques, 326.
Rastafari, 134, 292, 395, 308, 309, 332.
Renaissance, 12, 116, 140, 141, 160, 318, 324-325.
Rodney, Walter, 136, 146, 169, 305.
Rojo, Antonio Benitz, 73, 138.

Said, Edward, 131, 135-136, 145.
Sartre, Jean Paul, 173, 176, 237, 283.
Secular, 103, 118, 141, 158, 160, 245, 268, 304, 326.
Sembene, Ousmane, 105, 106.
Scott, David, 140, 164, 293, 301, 325.
Small Axe, 77, 93.
Sociogeny, 19, 30, 143, 162, 248, 261, 163, 269.
Social Sciences, 21, 37, 47, 212, 219, 259, 274, 280.
Subaltern, 104, 119, 138, 203, 329, 331, 333.

Taylor, Clyde, 160.
Taylor, Patrick, 66, 68.
Theology, 11, 216, 304, 310.
Truth, Sojourner, 101-102, 114-115.

University of the West Indies, 161, 171.
Utopia, 172, 191, 193, 204, 316.

Wallace, Michelle, 38, 107.
West, Cornell, 31, 139, 199.
White, Hayden, 3, 6.
Winch, Peter, 319.
Wilson, E. O., 211, 223, 226, 229.
Woodson, Carter G., 13, 44, 47.
Wynter, Sylvia; on after man, 61, 71, 245; on black studies, 28, 38; and the Caribbean Intellectual Tradition, 227, 264, 280; contributions, 60, 144; and freedom 138, 178; on the human, 19, 220, 229, 261; periodization of, xiv; and Marxism 280, 321.

X, Malcolm, 91, 48, 137, 139.

www.ingramcontent.com/pod-product-compliance
Lightning Source LLC
Chambersburg PA
CBHW032031150426
43194CB00006B/234